JIMI HENDRIX

THE DAY I WAS THERE

Richard Houghton

www.thisdayinmusic.com

This edition © This Day In Music Books 2018
Text © This Day In Music Books 2018

ISBN: 9781999592738

Cover photo by Gered Markowitz
Front and back cover concept by Liz Sanchez
Cover design by Oliver Keen
Book design by Robot Mascot
Printed in the UK by CPI

THIS DAY IN MUSIC BOOKS

This Day In Music Books
2B Vantage Park
Washingley Road
Huntingdon
PE29 6SR

www.thisdayinmusic.com
Email: editor@thisdayinmusic.com

Exclusive Distributors:
Music Sales Limited
14/15 Berners St
London
W1T 3JL

Contents

SOUL CITY
15

JANUARY & FEBRUARY
1965, DALLAS, TEXAS

**STARLIGHT
BALLROOM**
16

1965, WILDWOOD, NEW
JERSEY

CAFÉ WHA?
18

1966, NEW YORK CITY,
NEW YORK

CHEETAH CLUB
22

26 JUNE 1966, NEW
YORK, NEW YORK

CAFÉ WHA?
22

5 JULY 1966, NEW YORK
CITY, NEW YORK

**HYDE PARK TOWERS
HOTEL**
23

22 SEPTEMBER 1966,
LONDON, UK

SCOTCH OF ST JAMES
26

26 SEPTEMBER 1966,
LONDON, UK

BIRDLAND
30

26 SEPTEMBER 1966,
LONDON, UK

Marble Arch
31

OCTOBER 1966, LONDON,
UK

**LONDON
POLYTECHNIC**
32

1 OCTOBER 1966,
LONDON, UK

OLYMPIA
32

18 OCTOBER 1966, PARIS,
FRANCE

BAG O'NAILS
34

25 NOVEMBER 1966,
LONDON, UK

1967

TOP OF THE POPS
37

5 JANUARY 1967,
LONDON, UK

**KIRKLEVINGTON
COUNTRY CLUB**
38

15 JANUARY 1967,
KIRKLEVINGTON, UK

REFECTORY
40

21 JANUARY 1967,
GOLDERS GREEN,
LONDON, UK

MARQUEE CLUB
41

24 JANUARY 1967,
LONDON, UK

ORFORD CELLAR
42

25 JANUARY 1967,
NORWICH, UK

THE UPPER CUT
45

28 JANUARY 1967,
LONDON, UK

**SAVILLE
THEATRE**
46

29 JANUARY 1967,
LONDON, UK

IMPERIAL HOTEL
48

2 FEBRUARY 1967,
DARLINGTON, UK

RAM JAM CLUB
54

4 FEBUARY 1967,
BRIXTON, LONDON, UK

FLAMINGO CLUB
55

4 FEBRUARY 1967,
LONDON UK

LOCARNO
55

9 FEBRUARY 1967,
BRISTOL, UK

BLUE MOON CLUB
56

11 FEBRUARY 1967,
CHELTENHAM, UK

CIVIC HALL
59

14 FEBRUARY 1967,
GRAYS, UK

DOROTHY BALLROOM
69

15 FEBRUARY 1967,
CAMBRIDGE, UK

**RICKY TICK CLUB,
THAMES HOTEL**
72

17 FEBRUARY 1967,
WINDSOR, UK

PAVILION
77

20 FEBRUARY 1967,
BATH, UK

ROUNDHOUSE
78

22 FEBRUARY 1967,
LONDON, UK

PAVILION
81

23 FEBRUARY 1967,
WORTHING, UK

PAVILION
82

23 FEBRUARY 1967,
WORTHING, UK

**LEICESTER COLLEGES
OF ART &
TECHNOLOGY**
83

24 FEBRUARY 1967,
LEICESTER, UK

CORN EXCHANGE
84

25 FEBRUARY 1967,
CHELMSFORD, UK

THE SPEAKEASY
85
8 MARCH 1967, LONDON, UK

SKYLINE BALLROOM
85
9 MARCH 1967, HULL, UK

CLUB A GO GO
86
10 MARCH 1967, NEWCASTLE UPON TYNE, UK

SELMER'S MUSIC STORE
89
23 MARCH 1967, LONDON, UK

GUILDHALL
90
23 MARCH 1967, SOUTHAMPTON, UK

STARLIGHT ROOM
91
25 MARCH 1967, GLIDERDOME, BOSTON, UK

ODEON
93
5 APRIL 1967, LEEDS, UK

ABC THEATRE
95
7 APRIL 1967, CARLISLE, UK

ABC THEATRE
95
8 APRIL 1967, CHESTERFIELD, UK

GRANADA THEATRE
99
11 APRIL 1967, BEDFORD, UK

GAUMONT
100
12 APRIL 1967, SOUTHAMPTON, UK

KINGFISHER COUNTRY CLUB
101
13 APRIL 1967, WOLVERHAMPTON, UK

DE MONTFORT HALL
101
16 APRIL 1967, LEICESTER, UK

CITY HALL
103
21 APRIL 1967, NEWCASTLE UPON TYNE, UK

THE ODEON
104
22 APRIL 1967, MANCHESTER, UK

COLSTON HALL
105
25 APRIL 1967, BRISTOL, UK

SOPHIA GARDENS
105
26 APRIL 1967, CARDIFF, UK

ADELPHI THEATRE
107
28 APRIL 1967, SLOUGH, UK

WINTER GARDENS
108
29 APRIL 1967, BOURNEMOUTH, UK

TULIP BULB AUCTION HALL
110
29 MAY 1967, SPALDING, UK

SAVILLE THEATRE
113
4 JUNE 1967, LONDON, UK

MONTEREY POP FESTIVAL
116
17 JUNE 1967, MONTEREY COUNTY FAIRGROUNDS, CALIFORNIA

PANHANDLE
124
25 JUNE 1967, GOLDEN GATE PARK, SAN FRANCISCO, CALIFORNIA

FILLMORE AUDITORIUM
125
25 JUNE 1967, SAN FRANCISCO, CALIFORNIA

EARL WARREN SHOWGROUNDS
126
1 JULY 1967, SANTA BARBARA, CALIFORNIA

CENTRAL PARK
128
5 JULY 1967, SCHAEFER MUSIC FESTIVAL, NEW YORK, NEW YORK

MEMORIAL COLISEUM
130
8 JULY 1967, JACKSONVILLE, FLORIDA

FOREST HILLS STADIUM
134
13-16 JULY 1967, QUEENS, NEW YORK, NEW YORK

FOREST HILLS STADIUM
134
16 JULY 1967, QUEENS, NEW YORK, NEW YORK

CLUB SALVATION
136
8 AUGUST 1967, NEW YORK, NEW YORK

AMBASSADOR THEATER
138
9-13 AUGUST 1967, WASHINGTON DC

FIFTH DIMENSION
144
15 AUGUST 1967, ANN ARBOR, MICHIGAN

HOLLYWOOD BOWL
153
18 AUGUST 1967, LOS ANGELES, CALIFORNIA

SAVILLE THEATRE
154
27 AUGUST 1967, LONDON, UK

KLOOK'S KLEEK
154
17 OCTOBER 1967,
LONDON, UK

THE UNION, OXFORD ROAD
155
8 NOVEMBER 1967,
MANCHESTER, UK

HIPPY HAPPY FAIR
155
10 NOVEMBER 1967,
AHOY HALLEN,
ROTTERDAM,
NETHERLANDS

ROYAL ALBERT HALL
158
14 NOVEMBER 1967,
LONDON, UK

WINTER GARDENS
160
15 NOVEMBER 1967,
BOURNEMOUTH, UK

COVENTRY THEATRE
161
19 NOVEMBER 1967,
COVENTRY, UK

COLSTON HALL
161
24 NOVEMBER 1967,
BRISTOL, UK

OPERA HOUSE
162
25 NOVEMBER 1967,
BLACKPOOL

PALACE THEATRE
163
26 NOVEMBER 1967,
MANCHESTER, UK

BLUE BOAR SERVICES
163
WATFORD GAP,
NORTHAMPTONSHIRE,
UK

THE DOME
164
2 DECEMBER 1967,
BRIGHTON, UK

THEATRE ROYAL
165
3 DECEMBER 1967,
NOTTINGHAM, UK

GREEN'S PLAYHOUSE
166
5 DECEMBER 1967,
GLASGOW, UK

OLYMPIA
169
22 DECEMBER 1967,
LONDON, UK

1968

FILLMORE AUDITORIUM
170
1 FEBRUARY 1968, SAN FRANCISCO, CALIFORNIA

WINTERLAND
171
4 FEBRUARY 1968, SAN FRANCISCO, CALIFORNIA

WINTERLAND
172
5 FEBRUARY 1968, SAN FRANCISCO, CALIFORNIA

STATE COLLEGE MEN'S GYM
173
8 FEBRUARY 1968,
SACRAMENTO,
CALIFORNIA

ANAHEIM CONVENTION CENTER
173
9 FEBRUARY 1968,
ANAHEIM, CALIFORNIA

SHRINE AUDITORIUM
177
10 FEBRUARY 1968, LOS ANGELES, CALIFORNIA

ROBERTSON GYMNASIUM
183
11 FEBRUARY 1968, SANTA BARBARA, CALIFORNIA

SEATTLE CENTER ARENA
183
12 FEBRUARY 1968,
SEATTLE, WASHINGTON

REGIS COLLEGE FIELDHOUSE
184
14 FEBRUARY 1968,
DENVER, COLORADO

STATE FAIR MUSIC HALL
186
16 FEBRUARY 1968,
DALLAS, TEXAS

WILL ROGERS AUDITORIUM
188
17 FEBRUARY 1968, FORT WORTH, TEXAS

ELECTRIC FACTORY
191
21 FEBRUARY 1968,
PHILADELPHIA,
PENNSYLVANIA

ELECTRIC FACTORY
192
22 FEBRUARY 1968,
PHILADELPHIA,
PENNSYLVANIA

MASONIC TEMPLE
196
23 FEBRUARY 1968,
DETROIT, MICHIGAN

OPERA HOUSE
198
25 FEBRUARY 1968,
CHICAGO, ILLINOIS

THE FACTORY
199
27 FEBRUARY 1968,
MADISON, WISCONSIN

THE SCENE
206
28/29 FEBRUARY 1968,
MILWAUKEE, WISCONSIN

HUNTER COLLEGE
207
2 MARCH 1968, NEW YORK, NEW YORK

MANHATTAN
209
MARCH 1968, NEW YORK, NEW YORK

VETERANS MEMORIAL AUDITORIUM
211
3 MARCH 1968,
COLUMBUS, OHIO

MARVEL GYM, BROWN UNIVERSITY
213

8 MARCH 1968,
PROVIDENCE, RHODE
ISLAND

INTERNATIONAL BALLROOM
221

10 MARCH 1968, HILTON
HOTEL, WASHINGTON DC

ATWOOD HALL, CLARK UNIVERSITY
222

15 MARCH 1968,
WORCESTER,
MASSACHUSETTS

LEWISTON ARMORY
223

16 MARCH 1968,
LEWISTON, MAINE

CAPITAL THEATRE
238

19 MARCH 1968, OTTOWA,
CANADA

BUSHNELL THEATER
238

22 MARCH 1968,
HARTFORD,
CONNECTICUT

BUFFALO MEMORIAL AUDITORIUM
242

23 MARCH 1968,
BUFFALO, NEW YORK

INDUSTRIAL MUTUAL ASSOCIATION AUDITORIUM
244

24 MARCH 1968, FLINT,
MICHIGAN

TEEN AMERICA BUILDING
245

27 MARCH 1968, MUNCIE,
INDIANA

XAVIER UNIVERSITY FIELDHOUSE
249

28 MARCH 1968,
CINCINATTI, OHIO

FIELD HOUSE
250

30 MARCH 1968,
UNIVERSITY OF TOLEDO,
OHIO

THE ARENA
251

31 MARCH 1968,
PHILADELPHIA,
PENNSYLVANIA

CENTRE PAUL-SAUVE
253

2 APRIL 1968, MONTREAL,
CANADA

VIRGINIA BEACH DOME
254

4 APRIL 1968, VIRGINIA
BEACH, VIRGINIA

TROY ARMORY
258

19 APRIL 1968, TROY, NEW
YORK

MIAMI POP FESTIVAL
261

18 MAY 1968,
GULFSTREAM PARK,
HALLANDALE, FLORIDA

WOBURN ABBEY
266

6 JULY 1968, WOBURN,
UK

SGT.PEPPERS
266

15 JULY 1968, PALMA,
MAJORCA, SPAIN

INDEPENDENCE HALL, LAKESHORE AUDITORIUM
268

30 JULY 1968, BATON
ROUGE, LOUISIANA

MUNICIPAL AUDITORIUM
270

31 JULY 1968,
SHREVEPORT,
LOUISIANA

MOODY COLISEUM
279

3 AUGUST 1968, DALLAS,
TEXAS

SAM HOUSTON COLISEUM
280

4 AUGUST 1968,
HOUSTON, TEXAS

AUDITORIUM THEATRE
280

10 AUGUST 1968,
CHICAGO, ILLINOIS

COL BALLROOM
281

11 AUGUST 1968,
DAVENPORT, IOWA

MERRIWEATHER POST PAVILION
282

16 AUGUST 1968,
COLUMBIA, MARYLAND

CURTIS HIXON HALL
283

18 AUGUST 1968, TAMPA,
FLORIDA

THE MOSQUE
284

20 AUGUST 1968,
RICHMOND, VIRGINIA

VIRGINIA BEACH DOME
285

21 AUGUST 1968, VIRGINIA
BEACH, VIRGINIA

SINGER BOWL
287

23 AUGUST 1968, NEW
YORK ROCK FESTIVAL,
NEW YORK

CAROUSEL THEATER
288

25 AUGUST 1968,
FRAMINGHAM,
MASSACHUSETTS

KENNEDY STADIUM
293

26 AUGUST 1968,
BRIDGEPORT,
CONNECTICUT

LAGOON OPERA HOUSE
295

30 AUGUST 1968, SALT
LAKE CITY, UTAH

CONTENTS

RED ROCKS AMPHITEATRE
297
1 SEPTEMBER 1968, DENVER, COLORADO

BALBOA STADIUM
300
3 SEPTEMBER 1968, SAN DIEGO, CALIFORNIA

SWING AUDITORIUM
301
5 SEPTEMBER 1968, SAN BERNARDINO, CALIFORNIA

PACIFIC COLISEUM
303
7 SEPTEMBER 1968, VANCOUVER, CANADA

SPOKANE COLISEUM
303
8 SEPTEMBER, 1968, SPOKANE, WASHINGTON

MEMORIAL COLISEUM
307
9 SEPTEMBER 1968, PORTLAND, OREGON

HOLLYWOOD BOWL
308
14 SEPTEMBER 1968, LOS ANGELES, CALIFORNIA

MEMORIAL AUDITORIUM
309
15 SEPTEMBER 1978, SACRAMENTO, CALIFORNIA

WINTERLAND BALLROOM
313
10- 12 OCTOBER 1968, SAN FRANCISCO, CALIFORNIA

CIVIC AUDITORIUM
315
26 OCTOBER 1968, BAKERSFIELD, CALIFORNIA

MUNICIPAL AUDITORIUM ARENA
318
1 NOVEMBER 1968, KANSAS CITY, MISSOURI

MINNEAPOLIS AUDITORIUM
319
2 NOVEMBER 1968, MINNEAPOLIS, MINNESOTA

KIEL AUDITORIUM
320
3 NOVEMBER 1968, ST LOUIS, MICHIGAN

CINCINNATI GARDENS
320
15 NOVEMBER 1968, CINCINNATI, OHIO

BOSTON GARDEN
324
16 NOVEMBER 1968, BOSTON, MASSACHUSETTS

WOOLSEY HALL
325
17 NOVEMBER 1968, NEW HAVEN, CONNECTICUT

CURTIS HIXON HALL
329
23 NOVEMBER 1968, TAMPA, FLORIDA

MIAMI CONVENTION CENTER
331
24 NOVEMBER 1968, MIAMI, FLORIDA

RHODE ISLAND AUDITORIUM
331
27 NOVEMBER 1968, PROVIDENCE, RHODE ISLAND

COBO ARENA
333
30 NOVEMBER 1968, DETROIT, MICHIGAN

1969

REVOLUTION
337
SPRING 1969, LONDON, UK

ROYAL ALBERT HALL
338
24 FEBRUARY 1969, LONDON, UK

DORTON ARENA
341
11 APRIL 1969, RALEIGH, NORTH CAROLINA

THE SPECTRUM
343
12 APRIL 1969, PHILADELPHIA, PENNSYLVANIA

ELLIS AUDITORIUM
346
FRIDAY APRIL 18, 1969, MEMPHIS, TENNESSEE

SAM HOUSTON COLISEUM
346
19 APRIL 1969, HOUSTON, TEXAS

MEMORIAL AUDITORIUM
347
20 APRIL 1969, DALLAS, TEXAS

THE FORUM
349
26 APRIL 1969, LOS ANGELES, CALIFORNIA

COLISEUM
354
27 APRIL 1969, OAKLAND, CALIFORNIA

COBO ARENA
355
2 MAY 1969, DETROIT, MICHIGAN

MAPLE LEAF GARDENS
356
3 MAY 1969, TORONTO, CANADA

SYRACUSE WAR MEMORIAL AUDITORIUM
357
4 MAY 1969, SYRACUSE, NEW YORK

MEMORIAL COLISEUM
359
7 MAY 1969, TUSCALOOSA, ALABAMA

CHARLOTTE COLISEUM
359
9 MAY 1969, CHARLOTTE, NORTH CAROLINA

FAIRGROUNDS COLISEUM
361
11 MAY 1969, INDIANAPOLIS, INDIANA

CIVIC CENTER
363
16 MAY 1969, BALTIMORE, MARYLAND

RHODE ISLAND AUDITORIUM
364
17 MAY 1969, PROVIDENCE, RHODE ISLAND

SEATTLE CENTER COLISEUM
365
23 MAY 1969, SEATTLE, WASHINGTON

SPORTS ARENA
367
24 MAY 1969, SAN DIEGO, CALIFORNIA

SANTA CLARA COUNTY FAIRGROUNDS POP FESTIVAL
367
25 MAY 1969, SAN JOSE, CALIFORNIA

NEWPORT POP FESTIVAL
369
20- 22 JUNE 1969, DEVONSHIRE DOWNS, CALIFORNIA

MILE HIGH STADIUM
370
29 JUNE 1969, DENVER, COLORADO

WOODSTOCK
373
18 AUGUST 1969, WOODSTOCK, NEW YORK

MIDTOWN MANHATTAN
383
SEPTEMBER 1969, NEW YORK, NEW YORK

RECORD PLANT
385
7 NOVEMBER 1969, NEW YORK, NEW YORK

FILLMORE EAST
385
31 DECEMBER 1969, NEW YORK, NEW YORK

1970

FELT FORUM
387
28 JANUARY 1970, NEW YORK, NEW YORK

THE FORUM
388
25 APRIL 1970, LOS ANGELES, CALIFORNIA

STATE FAIRGROUNDS
392
26 APRIL 1970, SACRAMENTO, CALIFORNIA

MILWAUKEE AUDITORIUM
392
1 MAY 1970, MILWAUKEE, WISCONSIN

DANE COUNTY COLISEUM
394
2 MAY 1970, MADISON, WISCONSIN

OU FIELD HOUSE
404
8 MAY 1970, NORMAN, OKLAHOMA

WILL ROGERS AUDITORIUM
406
9 MAY 1970, FORT WORTH, TEXAS

TEMPLE UNIVERSITY
407
16 MAY 1970, PHILADELPHIA, PENNSYLVANIA

WAIKIKI SHELL
408
31 MAY 1970, HONOLULU, HAWAII

ROBERTS MUNICIPAL STADIUM
408
10 JUNE 1970, EVANSVILLE, INDIANA

CIVIC CENTER
414
13 JUNE 1970, BALTIMORE, MARYLAND

BOSTON GARDEN
415
27 JUNE 1970, BOSTON, MASSACHUSETTS

ATLANTA INTERNATIONAL POP FESTIVAL
417
4 JULY 1970, BYRON, GEORGIA

MIAMI JAI ALAI FRONTON
425
5 JULY 1970, MIAMI, FLORIDA

RANDALL'S ISLAND
425
17 JULY 1970, NEW YORK, NEW YORK

SPORTS ARENA
426
25 JULY 1970, SAN DIEGO, CALIFORNIA

EAST AFTON FARM
429
26 – 31 AUGUST 1970, ISLE OF WIGHT FESTIVAL, ISLE OF WIGHT, UK

STORA SCENEN, GRÖNA LUN
456
31 AUGUST 1970, STOCKHOLM, SWEDEN

DEUTSCHLANDHALLE
456
4 SEPTEMBER 1970, BERLIN, WEST GERMANY

**OPEN AIR LOVE AND
PEACE FESTIVAL
458**
6 SEPTEMBER 1970,
FEHMARN, GERMANY

**CENTRAL LONDON
461**
18 SEPTEMBER 1970,
LONDON, UK

INTRODUCTION

It was barely four years from coming into the spotlight at the Scotch of St James in London to his dying in a west London hotel room. But in that time Jimi Hendrix lit up music and perhaps did more than any other musician apart from The Beatles to open people's eyes, ears and minds to what was possible. Certainly, no one did as much with a guitar, whether it was getting sounds out of it, setting it on fire or using it as a manifestation of his sexual desire.

If you were going to explode onto the world's pop scene, you could hardly choose a better time than 1967. Musical barriers were coming down, the Swinging Sixties were getting underway and the Summer of Love was about to bloom. And you could hardly alight upon a better manager to steer you through this maelstrom than Chas Chandler, with his stellar music business connections, a result of being in The Animals.

That you just happen to be the greatest guitarist the world had yet to see, and has seen since, is perhaps a bonus.

Between September 1966 and September 1970, Jimi Hendrix played over 600 shows. This book tries to capture, through first-hand accounts, what it was like to be there. Ultimately, this is a sad tale of a great talent wasted, with the man worked like a pit pony for three years on the American concert circuit by a management eager to milk the cash cow. That Jimi died so young is ultimately a tragedy. That he brightened up so many lives with his unforgettable performances on stage is something to be savoured. Hopefully this book gives the reader a flavour of that.

I missed out on seeing Jimi. I was just 10 years old when he died, and I doubt my father would have let me go even if Jimi had played my hometown in an unremarkable part of East Northamptonshire. Which he nearly did. Before Monterey and the lure of the American market, Jimi played club venues of varying sizes around the UK, and the West End nightclub in Rushden was nearly one of them.

My cousin Nick's father-in-law, a man by the name of Don Planner, was a partner in the West End Club just off the High Street in Rushden - now a DIY shop, West End Wallpapers. Every Friday they had a band on. The club used a London booking agent and Don rang to ask what acts they had available for an upcoming gig. The agent offered them Paul and Barry Ryan, who had recently had a top-40 hit, or some bloke called Hendrix. As he'd never heard of Hendrix, Don booked Paul and Barry Ryan.

Hendrix plays Rushden. I would have loved to be there.

Richard Houghton

The Jimi Hendrix Experience Ann Arbor, Michigan. August 1967. (Photo Wilson Lindsey)

JIMI HENDRIX

Jimi Hendrix was born Johnny Allen Hendrix on 27 November 1942, at Seattle's King County Hospital. Jimi took an interest in music at an early age, drawing influence from B.B. King, Buddy

Holly, Muddy Waters, Howlin' Wolf and Robert Johnson. He was
also particularly fond of Elvis Presley. The 15-year-old went to see
the King of Rock'n'Roll perform when he played a show in Jimi's
hometown of Seattle in 1957.

By the summer of 1958, his father had purchased him a
five-dollar, second-hand acoustic guitar from one of his friends.
Shortly thereafter, Jimi joined his first band, The Velvetones.
After a three-month stint, he left to pursue his own interests.
The following summer Jimi became the proud owner of his first
electric guitar, a Supro Ozark 1560S, and used it when he joined
The Rocking Kings.

After a run-in with the law, facing two years in jail for riding
in stolen cars, he opted to enlist in the US Army in 1961 and
was assigned to the 101st Airborne Division stationed at Fort
Campbell, Kentucky. He was discharged in 1962 due to an ankle
injury. But the medical discharge didn't tell the full story. Jimi's
platoon sergeant, James C. Spears, filed a report in which he
stated, 'He has no interest whatsoever in the Army … It is my
opinion that Private Hendrix will never come up to the standards
required of a soldier. I feel that the military service will benefit if
he is discharged as soon as possible.' On 31 May 1962, Captain
Gilbert Batchman signed a report which alleged, among other
things, 'Little regard for regulations, apprehended masturbating
in platoon area while supposed to be on detail.' Jimi later claimed
he had received a medical discharge after breaking his ankle
during his 26th parachute jump. The military's loss was the music
world's gain.

In 1962 he was living initially in Clarksville, Tennessee before
moving with ex-army buddy Billy Cox to Nashville, playing a club
called the Del Morocco in a group called The Kasuals, with Cox
on bass. In December, Jimi moved to Vancouver to live with his
grandmother. He then returned to Nashville via Biloxi before, in
1963, being invited to New York. He spent most of 1964 playing
with The Isley Brothers, but quit when the tour reached Nashville.
Jimi said, 'You get very tired playing behind other people all the

time, you know. So I quit them in Nashville somewhere.'

He joined Sam Cooke's package tour in November 1964 but, after missing the tour bus in Kansas City, made his way to Atlanta, Georgia, where he joined Little Richard's band. Jimi's younger brother Leon recalled to Mojo magazine how the pair had already met Little Richard in 1959: 'His mom and sister lived in Seattle. I took a bunch of greens over to a neighbour's house, Mrs Penniman, saw this black limo and Little Richard. I ran home to get Jimi, we rode bikes up there and sat in awe at him preaching at the Goodwill Baptist Church.'

He briefly joined Ike and Tina Turner before returning to Richard's fold, but was thrown out in the summer of 1965.

Richard's brother, Robert Penniman, later claimed Hendrix was fired because, 'He was always late for the bus and flirting with all the girls and stuff like that'.

Prior to his rise to fame, Jimi recorded 24 singles as a backing guitarist with American R&B artists, such as The Isley Brothers and Little Richard. Other studio work included that with Don Covay and The Goodtimers (1964, 'Mercy, Mercy'), Frank Howard and The Commanders (1965, 'I'm So Glad'), Rosa Lee Brooks (1965 'My Diary'), and in 1966 he appeared on singles by Curtis Knight ('How Would You Feel'), Lonnie Youngblood ('Go Go Shoes'), The Icemen '(My Girl) She's a Fox'), and Jimmy Norman ('You're Only Hurting Yourself').

SOUL CITY

JANUARY & FEBRUARY 1965, DALLAS, TEXAS

I WAS THERE: ANGUS WYNNE

I saw him several times. I had seen him before he went out on his own as The Experience. I had a club in Dallas called Soul City and a lot of R&B acts performed there. He apparently played there with Little Richard's band at one point, shortly after which he was sacked for being too pretty, according to Richard. He was not a stand-out. He was a little guy standing in the back of the band. He was just playing rhythm. He didn't do any leads at all. I never heard any of that. I never got to see him with Hank Ballard, Curtis Knight, Wilson Pickett, or The Isley Brothers, but he played with them all.

I remember an afternoon in late '67 or early '68, I had two dressing rooms in the backstage area, one for the star and the other for the band. Little Richard was watching a little portable black and white TV that he had in there. I just happened to be walking down the hall and I heard Little Richard scream, 'Band, come here quick!' Which he did often to try and get them to get up and run. They all ran into the room and he says, 'Look, look,' pointing at the television. 'Who is that? Who is that?' And they all shrugged. And he said, 'It's Maurice, look it's Maurice!' And sure enough it was Jimi playing upside down and backwards guitar. He had a bandana around his head that Richard had recognised. And they were all marvelling at his success.*

But I saw him before this when I was in New York. Amongst the Café Wha? and all the other places he worked, I saw him at Steve Paul's Scene. Some friends and I used to go by there and see what was up. He was in there in a jam with Johnny Winter. Eric Burdon was too. He wasn't playing or singing but he was loaded to the gills and we made friends with him. After a while, Johnny Winter came in and that one turned out to be a blistering set, and we were all shaking our heads.

(* Jimi had used the name Maurice James when he was playing with Little Richard).

STARLIGHT BALLROOM

1965, WILDWOOD, NEW JERSEY

I WAS THERE: RICK VITO, AGE 15

I didn't know it was him. He wasn't famous yet. But we realised later that the guy we saw with Little Richard in Wildwood, New Jersey was in fact Jimi Hendrix. My brother and I, me being a guitar player and him being a drummer, I latched onto the guitar player and my brother was right there with me and I go, 'Whoa, he's left-handed'. I'd never seen a left-handed guitar player, but he just flipped the guitar over. To my mind it seemed like he was playing a Fender Duosonic. I've seen footage of him from the same kind of time period playing a Jazzmaster. But I was pretty sure he was playing this little sunburst Duosonic. We remembered that he was a tall, thin guy. He played kinda loud. He wasn't playing freaky stuff. It was cool sounding. You really heard the tone off the instrument, which is what really impressed us about him. He was probably getting some solos. Richard might have tossed him a bone, but Richard's presence was so overwhelming at the time.

Another thing I remember about the gig was that Richard had two big guys who were bodyguards standing either side of the stage, kinda dressed in Middle Eastern garb with big scimitar swords hanging from their waists and just standing there with their arms folded. But it was amazing.

I later confirmed for sure that it was Jimi Hendrix with the deejay from Philadelphia, Jerry Blavat. He was the one who promoted that show. It was put on in a converted old building that used to be called the Acme food market. Jerry said it was his birthday that day and it definitely was Jimi.

I played in Little Richard's band for two weeks myself and,

knowing the way Richard is, I don't think he would have given any billing to Jimi. It was an amazing band. People were going nuts. It was a dance show. All the black kids were up in front going crazy and dancing and all the white kids were behind them. It was just one of those things you never forget. Even if it wasn't Jimi Hendrix I'd never have forgotten the show. But it was such cool rock'n'roll.

I live in Nashville and he got a lot of those gigs with Billy Cox because they used to live right downtown in Nashville, on Jefferson Street, and at that point in time Nashville had a real strong R&B scene with a bunch of clubs. The acts would come through there, and that's where those guys picked up their sidemen gigs when they got out of the army.

Calling himself Jimmy James, Hendrix joined Curtis Knight and The Squires in October 1965 and played at various New York venues over the following year, including the Purple Onion on 4th Street, the Club Cheetah on Broadway at Times Square, Ondine's at 59th and 3rd, the Queen's Inn on Queens Boulevard, and The Lighthouse. He also picked up work with Joey Dee and The Starlighters and King Curtis and The Kingpins in this period. Unhappy that he wasn't being paid enough or paid at all, he was asked, 'Why are you with Curtis, you don't need him?' He replied, 'Because it's his guitar.' Two days later someone bought Jimi his own white Fender Stratocaster. In May 1966, Jimi quit Curtis Knight and got a fresh gig with Carl Holmes and The Commanders. This lasted less than a month before Jimi was at a loose end again. Out of work, Jimmy wrote to his father in August 1965, 'I still have my guitar and amp and as long as I have that, no fool can keep me from living.'

Jimi got his break in New York at the Café Wha? Previously a garage that used to be a horse stable on MacDougal, between Bleecker and West 3rd Streets, accessible via steep stairs to reach the dark, dank basement, it was bisected by a trough once used as a gutter for horse dung. The new owner, Mr. Roth, immediately recognised it as an excellent site for a coffee house. Roth spent his last $100 on a truckload of broken marble to make the floor, which he personally laid, and sprayed the walls with black paint to create the feeling of a cave. Roth hired Hendrix, on the recommendation of folk singer Richie Havens, as the frontman for a group called the Blue Flames. The Flames played five sets a night, sometimes six nights a week, at Cafe Wha? for little more than tips.

CAFÉ WHA?

1966, NEW YORK CITY, NEW YORK

I WAS THERE: DONALD SZTABNIK

Back in the mid-Sixties while in high school on Long Island, I often went into NYC and we would wander around Greenwich Village looking 'for music and Bob Dylan'. On one of our regular sojourns to Bleecker and MacDougal Streets, we stumbled into the Cafe Wha? We had no idea who was playing but were thrilled that we got our underage butts into our seats near the stage. This was a late afternoon show and loved this great R&B and rock'n'roll band with the fantastic guitar player. We thought we were so cool. And we were 'so cool' when we found out years later that the fantastic guitarist was Jimi Hendrix in a sharkskin suit.

I WAS THERE: ROBERT ROWLAND

I was in a band in 1966 called The Tangerine Puppets. We got our name from a song off the first Donovan album. We lived in Forest Hills in Queens and two of my band, Tommy Erdelyi and John Cummings, ended up several years later forming the Ramones as Tommy and Johnny Ramone. John was my bass player in The Tangerine Puppets and Tommy, a fantastic guitarist, was the first drummer with and co-produced the first four Ramones albums. I was lead singer, Richie Adler played rhythm guitar and a fellow named Scott Roberts was on drums.

In Forest Hills, one of the guys who played with us sometimes was a guy named Randy Wolfe. He was 14, 15 years old. He lived on welfare with his stepfather, Ed Cassidy, and Randy also played in John Hammond's band. John had a group called John Hammond and the Blue Flames, and Randy played in that group too.

Jimi at that time was Jimmy James and was playing the chitlin' circuit with the Harlem beat groups and stuff like that. He wanted to play in the Village, where all the clubs were in those days. The people who knew Jimi told him, 'Listen, if you want to play down in Greenwich Village, you gotta play original stuff, you got to play the blues and stuff like that.'

So Jimi went out and bought a couple of John Hammond albums and learnt note for note and in the same key all those songs. Then he went down to the Village, got John Hammond's band and called it Jimmy James and the Blue Flames. Randy was part of that band and a fucking great guitarist. He's 15, 16 years old and playing lead guitar for Jimi Hendrix.

Jimi would play down at the Cafe Wha? where we, The Tangerine Puppets, would play every weekend. In the afternoons they would call it the Hootenanny and would have seven or eight acts. You would play about 20 minutes apiece. Jimi would play in the afternoons because he wasn't well known enough for them to give him an evening slot. He used to go outside the Cafe Wha? and panhandle in the street.

He played a lot of the clubs in the village too. The club scene was big then. Today the big acts play theatres and arenas and stuff like that, but back in the mid-Sixties, before The Bottom Line came around, which held 400 or 500 people, The Bitter End was probably the number one rock club in New York and only held 150 people. In those days acts would do two shows a night and three on the weekend. When I played in a band we used to play in some places and do five, six sets a night. You'd go 40 on, 20 off. Now you tell a band, 'You got to do two sets a day' and they go, 'What are you, crazy?' It's a lot different now.

I saw him at a club called the Electric Circus, a very famous club back in the mid-Sixties in the East Village. I saw him in a club in the West Village called Salvation. And then he was playing down at the Cafe Wha? At that time Chas Chandler, who had just left The Animals, had started his own management company with Mike Jeffrey, the manager of The Animals. Keith Richards' girlfriend, Linda Keith, said to Chas, 'You gotta come down and see this guy at the Cafe Wha? This guy is incredible, he'd be great for your management company.' They went down and Chas Chandler was really taken aback by him.

It wasn't the loud feedback guitar that you think of with Jimi Hendrix - it was pretty straight blues stuff. But he was so good that Chas Chandler said, 'I'm going back to England. Would you be interested in coming to England and I'll manage you?' Jimi said, 'Let me think about it,' and Chas said, 'You've got to let me know really quick.' Randy could have gone with him, but his family wouldn't allow it. He was too young. So Randy could have been part of The Jimi Hendrix Experience. After that Randy and his stepdad moved to California. Jimi had another guy in his band called Randy, so to differentiate the two he called Randy 'Randy California', as I think he was originally from California. He and his father formed a band called Spirit.

Another time I saw Hendrix just jamming. There used to be a club on 46th Street called Steve Paul's The Scene. Steve Paul also owned a record company. They had incredible jamming sessions there. The biggest acts in the world would go there, like 1am or 2am in the morning. I saw him jamming there with Leslie West from Mountain on bass.

I WAS THERE: KEN WILCZAK

I saw Jimi several times. The most memorable was at a club on McDougal Street, Greenwich Village, NYC. I sat at a table not far from Les Paul and his sons. Jimi was called up to jam with Danny Kalb. He goes up and picks up a right-handed Les Paul, flips it over and plays some of the most incredible blues I ever heard. He blew everyone away, including Les Paul, who stated that Jimi was very special and destined to be a major force in music. It was a night etched in my heart and soul that continues to inspire me when I play. Jimi was a guitar god then and forever!

I WAS THERE: JOSEPH TOMASELLO

I saw him several times at the Cafe Wha?, but not as Jimmy James. He used a different name and the kid from Spirit was there, Randy California, sitting at the same table with me. I was 11 and gallivanting all over the city but already worked in a record store as a gofer. We used to follow my friend's older brother around the city and sneak into shows. At the Wha? it was daytime afternoon shows with dayglo soda. I had no idea who he was but I later saw him open for The Monkees in Forest Hills in 1966. Yeah, we were there to see him, and not The Monkees.

Jimi played the Club Cheetah at 53 Broadway, New York a number of times during 1966, including a two-week booking with Curtis Knight and The Squires in May followed by a one week booking later that same month with Carl Holmes and The Commanders. In June, he appeared as Jimmy James and The Blue Flames. It is this 26 June show that was witnessed by Linda Keith, then girlfriend of Rolling Stone Keith Richards and later to champion Jimi's cause to Chas Chandler. Linda Keith: 'I didn't take any interest in the band at all. And then suddenly I saw the guitar player….'

CURTIS KNIGHT and the SQUIRES

CHEETAH CLUB

26 JUNE 1966, NEW YORK, NEW YORK

I WAS THERE: JAYNE KELL, AGE 15

I actually saw him three times. The first was at the Club Cheetah in NYC. I had not yet turned 16. My mother and my aunt took my cousin Julia, who was 13, and myself for a week to NYC. Our mothers stayed in one suite, Julia and I in another at the Waldorf - their mistake, our great fortune.

My cousin and I snuck out and made our way to the Village and heard there was going to be a great concert that night at the Club Cheetah. I have totally forgotten the band who we went there to see but will never forget who we actually saw. After talking our way in, we edged up to the front and – POW! Like lightning, our lives were forever changed. Talk about being awoken. He was beautiful, dressed like a rock god and sexy. But it was the guitar that spoke to me. It truly rocked my 16-year old world.

Linda Keith persuaded Chas Chandler of The Animals to come and see Jimi perform at Café Wha? Chandler was impressed but headed off on a three-month tour with The Animals the following day.

CAFÉ WHA?

5 JULY 1966, NEW YORK CITY, NEW YORK

I WASN'T THERE: ROD HARROD

Chas was about 6ft 4, a man giant and a heart of gold. He was leaving The Animals at the end of the American tour because he was wanting to understand the business side. He didn't leave because he had found Jimi. And then Linda Keith, Keith Richard's girlfriend, took him to see Jimi at Cafe Wha? An afternoon performance, I think it was. Chas saw the song 'Hey Joe'. Jimi was then Jimmy James and The Famous Flames.

On the morning of 21 September 1966, a Pan Am airliner from New York landed at Heathrow, carrying among its passengers Jimi Hendrix. Barely known in his own country and a complete stranger to England, he had just flown first class for the first time in his life.

HYDE PARK TOWERS HOTEL

22 SEPTEMBER 1966, LONDON, UK

I WAS THERE: ROD HARROD

I knew Chas very well. He was a very, very good friend of mine. I lived in a place called Hyde Park Towers Hotel, a music biz hotel in Bayswater. I lived there, off and on, permanently. The Animals used to stay there, as did many, many acts. Because they lived in Newcastle, if they were down in London that's where they would stay, and we'd all get drunk in the bar. Late one afternoon, Chas was in the reception signing in with this scruffy, moronic-looking male across the reception. Chas came over. He said, 'Hi Rod. I've just brought this guitarist back from America. Can you put him on in the club?'

'The club' was the Scotch of St James. I didn't own it but was the host and booker and ran the place. First of all, I looked across the room and I said, 'Chas, do I have to?' It was a very upmarket club and this guy looked as though he had slept in the gear he was in - which he had, on the plane. He was dressed in the only clothes he had, with purple velvet trousers that were like a second skin.

Coming from the airport, Jimi and Chas stopped off at Zoot Money's place because he was a friend of everybody and - knowing it would impress Jimi because he was concerned as to how British musicians would like him, how he would fit in, was he an interloper - Chas took him there. They borrowed Andy Summers' guitar and jammed at Zoot's place. From there they went to the Hyde Park Towers, which is where I bumped into them in the foyer.

They spent about two hours at the airport to get his seven-day work permit. They were trying to sell him to immigration as a famous American songwriter coming over to try and help other songwriters sort out a songwriting dispute. I would have been breaking the law if I'd given him any money to appear, so he was appearing for nothing. When he performed on the Monday night, that was 48 hours before the visa ran out.

Chas said to me: 'Rod, I really need to get some record companies to see him quick.' I said, 'Chas, I don't know. I'm certainly not putting him on tonight.' It was a Thursday and I refused to put him on. I said, 'Chas, I'll talk to you about it.' And Chas kept on at me over the Friday and Saturday.

The words that have rung in my head for 50 years are, 'Rod, I need this. You owe me.' Chas said, 'You owe me a favour because we brought a load of people here.' I used to be a host at the Cromwellian Club and suddenly they became successful. I took Chas and a couple of other people down in a taxi from the Cromwellian Club and Chas started bringing people over. I said, 'Doesn't introducing you to your soon-to-be wife count?' I can't remember if Lotte was a chambermaid at the hotel or if it was her friend who was a chambermaid, but I introduced Lotte to Chas and she later became his wife. And he said, 'All right, you got me. But I really need it. I still need to get some record company people to see him.'

On the Sunday afternoon I was in the TV lounge and he came in and, before he reached me, I said, 'Chas, you win. I'll put him on tomorrow night if you like.' 'Oh, great man. Who's the band in there this week?' Because we'd have a resident band for the week but then we'd also have star nights. I said, 'They're called The VIPs.' 'Oh,' he said, 'I know all of them. They're a great band. They're from Carlisle, on the same circuit as us. Mike Jeffery booked them when he used to have his club in Newcastle.' Which was the Club A Go Go in Newcastle.

I WAS THERE: GORDON HASKELL

When I was in the band The Fleur de Lys our manager Nicholas Wright was also the Animals' photographer and arranged for us to live at Cranley Gardens, South Kensington, The Animals' main flat. They were away on a long tour of the USA. It was during this time in 1966/67 that Jimi Hendrix was also living there, awaiting Chas Chandler's return. Hendrix only had an acoustic guitar and we showed him the main music shops in Charing Cross Road and Denmark Street.

Most of his time he spent drawing and painting in his bedroom. We were very busy working as a session band for Atlantic - Polydor Records so were out most days at the studio and barely talked to him. When Chas came round eventually, he invited us all to the first gigs of Hendrix, which were sensational and intimate, in small clubs like Blaises, just up the road in Queensway. Hendrix also played with us in the Speakeasy on two occasions. He was remarkable. He used our guitarist's right-handed Stratocaster and simply played upside down, which really means he could play as well backwards as forwards. He also sat in on bass while I (the bassist) watched.

The guitarist for the Animals was Hilton Valentine, who produced one Fleur de Lys session at Kingsway Studios, where we cut four songs and Hendrix overdubbed on them. The tracks were never released as none of us were that happy with the choice of songs. Our last meeting was at the Saville prior to his first USA trip as 'Jimi Hendrix' after 'Hey Joe'. We never saw him again.

SCOTCH OF ST JAMES

26 SEPTEMBER 1966, LONDON, UK

I WAS THERE: RON HARROD

When he appeared at my club, the Scotch of St James, it was the first time he performed as Jimi Hendrix. He had to change from being Jimmy James, which he did on the plane coming over, as there was already Jimmy James and the Vagabonds. If he hadn't, there would have been no Jimi Hendrix, because he only had a seven-day tourist visa. That was all Chas could get him on the way in from the US.

I thought I'd get down there about 11 o'clock to sort something out. It was a Monday night. There wasn't a single record company person there. Chas invited them, but nobody came. Jimi went on and did four or five songs and when he came off stage, a couple of guys were jumping over the tables and chairs to try and get to him. One guy in particular was saying to Chas, 'We want to manage him.'

I've got a picture of the actual amp he plugged into, which belonged to the lead guitarist of the VIP's. He was an electronics buff.

America turned Hendrix down, virtually. He's sold more albums since he's died than he did in his life.

Jimi turned everything way beyond advisable levels. Feedback was coming from everywhere and it was a club that only held 120 in the downstairs room maximum and another 50-odd upstairs, if you squashed them all in.

We only served miniatures, like you get on an airline. A Scotch and coke would be 12/6 (62p). It was empty when I took it over. They weren't doing a thing. But I peppered the industry with free memberships and on our official opening night we had three Beatles, three Rolling Stones, two Who and two Kinks out of 130 people. It's like the whole of the charts was there, and remained while I was there. We would have a house band every week. One week it would be the Graham Bond Organisation with Ginger Baker and Jack Bruce. Another week we'd have Mick Fleetwood and Peter Green, and Rod Stewart would be in another band. Those were our weekly bookings.

The jam sessions were unparalleled. But then every month to six weeks I booked a top American soul or blues or Motown artist, from Gladys Knight and the Pips to Solomon Burke and Fontella Bass. Other than having a sister outfit of the Krays coming and putting pressure on us to pay protection money, everything went well. When Princess Margaret was there I put a bottle of Black Label on the table in front of her and left them to serve themselves rather than serve them miniatures. It was that type of prestige place. We served no beer. The only time we served beer was when we sent for some expensive Swiss beer for Darryl F. Zanuck.

So it was unusual, even on a Monday night, to have virtually nobody there who was famous. Except for one person who claims he was and who has dined out on it for the past 50 years - Mr Paul McCartney. He says it was one of the most important days of his life, but I can't recall him being there.

Kit Lambert and Chris Stamp, The Who's managers, were there, and when Jimi had played they were falling over themselves, tripping over the chairs to get to Chas. They told him, 'He's great. We want to manage him.' Chas said coldly, 'Sorry, boys, I'm going to be managing him with Mike Jeffery.' 'Well, we want to produce him.' 'Sorry, boys, I'm going to produce him.' They were trying desperately to think of a way to get involved. 'Well, we're starting this label. We'd like to put him on our label.' And he said, 'Now you're talking. Let's go upstairs.' They went to the quieter part where the Chesterfield armchairs were and thrashed out the heads of an agreement of a record deal on one of our burgundy paper napkins. And I don't know how you write on one of those.

That was in September, and they were under a legal obligation that they couldn't start the label until the following March. But that agreement was enough to get him his visa. 'Hey Joe' was not on their label, Track Records. It was on Polydor because Chas needed a record out. He was broke. To keep him and Jimi in Hyde Park Towers he'd sold off most of his collection of bass guitars. Jimi wouldn't have had a look in if Chas hadn't been in with the 'in crowd' and known all of us.

Chas leant on everyone in a very nice way to do this and do that and support him. Brian Jones introduced him on stage at Monterey. He was on a record label owned by The Who's management, so The Who were close to him. He was accepted right into the inner circle of the top echelons, but mainly because Chas was.

At the same time Chas went upstairs to talk with Kit Lambert and Chris Stamp, Zoot Money and his wife Ronnie and Kathy Etchingham arrived. Kathy was renting a room in Ronnie Money's house in Fulham.

And Linda Keith arrived from somewhere. Keith Richards lost his virginity to Linda. Jimi was putting a hit on Kathy and Linda was getting very uptight, as if she owned Jimi. Linda introduced him to Chas, she'd got him a gig here, she'd given him a guitar, etc. There wasn't an altercation as such, but Jimi admitted he was virtually living in Linda's hotel room in New York, which is where she was staying because the Stones were out on tour. At one time she gave him a white Stratocaster, which went the same way as about five or six other Strats broken on the back of beds when Jimi got uptight or a woman tried to use it as a hold over him. The one he brought to England was almost cream with smoke-dust. It was far from white, with burns on the head where he stuck his cigarettes while playing.

Kathy had been clubbing it the night before and was asleep upstairs. Ronnie Money went up and said, 'Kathy, you've got to come and meet this guy downstairs - he's phenomenal'. Kathy said, 'Oh God, I'm tired, I'm asleep.' She wouldn't come down. But they brought her down to the club that night and that was the beginning of three years of living with Jimi. That first night she stayed in a single bed in Hyde Park Towers and they stayed there a few weeks. Then they, with Chas and Chas's Lotta, moved into Ringo Starr's flat in Montagu Square, which McCartney used as a demo studio and John Lennon and Yoko Ono used. That's where they took the pictures of the nude album, Two Virgins. Ringo had to throw Jimi out because he got high and threw paint all over the walls. Then they moved to an address in Mayfair.

Kathy had been my deejay at the Cromwellian. She followed me over to the Scotch, but Kathy took the deejay booth and output of music as being her domain. I normally left her to her own devices but had a copy of a Beatles acetate, which was their next single. There were eight of them. The Beatles had one each. George Martin had one. Brian Epstein had one and there were two locked in the safe at EMI. One of the acetates found its way to my club. If you have that and you're running a top club, you play that to death maybe every two, three or four records so everybody who's in there that night can say, 'I heard the Beatles' new record first'. But Kathy played it twice and then said, 'It doesn't fit with my format'. So I said, 'You go and perform your format somewhere else, Kathy.' And I fired here. So an ex-girlfriend took over. I didn't mind Kathy being there socially. She was a good friend of Brian Jones. She was a good friend of Keith Moon. I think she had an affair with both of them.

Are You Experienced was premiered at the Scotch as a thank you to us for putting him on. It was the first time it was ever played.

Bassist Noel Redding was the first to audition for the Experience (he auditioned and accepted Hendrix's offer to join on condition that he advanced him his train fare). Redding had been working in a variety of English groups that were going nowhere fast. Apparently, he was chosen because Jimi liked his attitude towards music and his 'Afro' hairstyle.

Drummer Mitch Mitchell had an acting background and had starred in children's television programme, *Jennings and Derbyshire*, as a teenager. Now a session drummer, he'd worked with The Pretty Things, Bill Knight and The Sceptres, The Riot Squad, Georgie Fame and The Blue Flames, and The Who (as a session drummer while the band was deciding on a replacement for Doug Sandom, their eventual choice being Keith Moon).

BIRDLAND

26 SEPTEMBER 1966, LONDON, UK

I WAS THERE: RON HARROD

Chas asked if he could use my club to audition members of the Experience and we had to say no, because the bars didn't have grilles on them and knowing musicians, they'd have got greedy! But we had another club to the back of us, in the process of being refurbished, a place called Birdland in Duke of York Street, so I said, 'You can use that, Chas. Just lock up and drop the keys in at the Scotch afterwards.' So that's where the Experience were auditioned.

Noel Redding turned up at Michael Jeffery's office in Gerrard Street wanting to audition for Eric Burdon's new band, The New Animals. The guitarist from Brian Auger's band, Trinity, had got the Animals gig but they said to Noel, 'Can you play bass guitar?' and he said 'So-so.' Noel was not a bass guitarist but he fitted the image. So they sent him down to play bass and he got the gig because he looked the part. He doesn't play bass on 'Hey Joe', Chas does. It was recorded in Kingsway Studios, which became De Lane Lea - one of Pink Floyd owns them now. Noel wasn't getting it, and Chas was very money conscious. He wasn't tight, but he didn't want massive studio bills so played bass on 'Hey Joe'.

Hendrix first met Eric Clapton at a Cream gig at the London Polytechnic on Saturday, 1 October, 1966. 'Jimi came on and stole the show,' recalls Clapton. 'He did his whole repertoire. He did a fast Howlin' Wolf song. Very powerful. He played the guitar behind his head, between his legs, with his teeth, slapped it round on the ground a bit. I just went, 'Yeah - this is it! This guy is bound for glory.' Chas Chandler later found Clapton with his head in his hands. Clapton looked up and said, 'You didn't tell me he was that fucking good!'

MARBLE ARCH

OCTOBER 1966, LONDON, UK

I WAS THERE: PHIL SWERN

My first job in the music business was in 1966 when I joined Strike Records as errand boy/tea maker. They operated unofficially out of a flat in the Marble Arch area of London. At the time they were enjoying their one and only hit with 'That's Nice' by Neil Christian but were investing in several other up and coming acts.

In the flat below lived Jimi Hendrix, and one day I got in the lift and there was the man himself. He said, 'Hey man, do you work upstairs? There's a new Roy Harper album I know is coming out soon – any chance you can get me a copy?' I immediately went upstairs and into the cupboard and removed a white label copy of the record, then went back and knocked on Jimi's door. He answered and was very grateful and invited me in for a cup of tea. I thanked him but said I had to get back to work, so he said, 'Well, come back tomorrow at 3.30 and join me for tea.' I agreed and the following day turned up to find he'd made tea with cucumber sandwiches. I was shocked but ended up staying and chatting with Jimi for over half an hour … I was only 18 and concerned he might give me drugs, or whatever, but he was so gentle and quiet.

We chatted about the blues and other styles of music and he played me his demo of 'Hey Joe' before I realised I was going to be late back for work. I got a real telling off for not being around to make tea for all the staff at Strike. but it was worth it!

LONDON POLYTECHNIC

1 OCTOBER 1966, LONDON, UK

I think my fiancé Dave and I paid five shillings (25p) to get into the Regent Polytechnic and got a free beer included. It was an early Cream gig and some of their best-known numbers were getting a first airing. One of the Cream invited Hendrix on stage to jam with them. They said he'd been brought over by Chas Chandler. We all thought, 'Who is this Jimmy Hendricks and why can't we just have Clapton?' Then he started to play, with some of his visual trademarks. Playing behind his head, which I'd only ever seen Joe Brown do four years before on the Billy Fury tour, with his teeth and with loads of feedback and volume. After he left the stage Clapton played like never before, obviously not wanting his thunder stolen. I was amused to read Roger Waters' recollection of the Poly gig. He thought he'd paid 'a pound or so'. He might have been able to afford a pound or so, but we couldn't! Neither could any of the students there.

OLYMPIA

18 OCTOBER 1966, PARIS, FRANCE

I played at the Paris Olympia with Jimi with a band called John Drevar's Expression. We were being promoted by the Harold Davison Agency – he was married to Marion Ryan, Paul and Barry Ryan's mother – and they had a hit with 'Sorrow' around that time.

We flew over and the kit followed on in our van. We supported Jimi with a couple of bands – one was French and I can't remember their name, the other was Eire Apparent, who I think were also with Chas Chandler at the time. One or two members formed Joe Cocker's Grease Band soon after. They did a lot of gigs with Jimi. The gig was amazing. As the drummer, I was set up about six feet above the band on a podium, and it was all going out live on French radio. Part-way through our set a little man climbed the ladder to my kit and cut the lead of my hanging mike – apparently I was hitting it with my drumsticks and ruining the broadcast!

The 'Stars Bar' backstage was also an amazing scene, especially for a young 17-year-old, as I was. Stevie Marriott, P.P. Arnold, the deejay Emperor Rosko and of course Noel, Mitch and Jimi, all chatting and drinking, during and after the sets. Jimi did his burning guitar thing whilst on stage and it was a terrific set. The thing that struck me was that he was just such a nice, down-to-earth guy – he was quite quiet but chatted with us all. In my innocence I didn't realise that Mitch and Noel were really only sidemen – I thought the three were a true band that were mates. It wasn't until they left Jimi or were forced out (I think they wanted more money but that's just hearsay) that I realised Chas had just recruited them because they were good, but only on a wage per gig.

Unfortunately, I haven't got much evidence of all this – just my plane ticket, boarding pass and a postcard of the Olympia as it was then. It has been completely rebuilt since. So I don't tell a lot of people – they just don't believe me when I say I supported Jimi Hendrix!

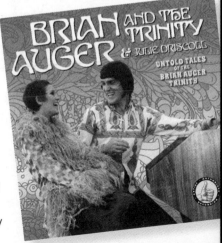

In November 1966 Hendrix jammed at The Cromwellian Club in London with organist Brian Auger. Reputedly the first gig at which Jimi played through Marshall equipment, Brian Auger recalled, 'I have a mental picture of Jimi being introduced to me in the break and he seemed like a very nice guy. He asked me if he could sit in and I said, 'Absolutely, yeah, what would you like to play?' Jimi showed me a chord sequence and said, 'Can you play this?' I said, 'Yeah, it's pretty straight forward. It turned out to be the chord sequence for 'Hey Joe'.'

The Jimi Hendrix Experience officially launched with a showcase gig at The Bag O'Nails, a tiny but influential music biz mecca in London's Soho. As well as key journalists invited by Hendrix's manager Chas Chandler, a Bag O'Nails appearance ensured The Experience would be seen by the venue's regular clientele, including Paul McCartney, The Who, Eric Burdon and others. Chandler sold a number of his guitars to finance the showcase.

BAG O'NAILS

25 NOVEMBER 1966, LONDON, UK

I WAS THERE: JOHN MAYALL

When Jimi first came to England, Chas Chandler put the word out that he'd found this phenomenal guitar player in New York, and he could play the guitar behind his head and with his teeth and everything. The buzz was out before Jimi had even been seen here, so people were anticipating his performance, and he more than lived up to what we were expecting.

I WAS THERE: TERRY REID

We were all hanging out at the Bag O'Nails: Keith, Mick Jagger. Brian Jones comes skipping through, like, all happy about something. Paul McCartney walks in. Jeff Beck walks in. So does Jimmy Page. I thought, 'What's

this? A bloody convention or something?' Here comes Jim, one of his military jackets, hair all over the place, pulls out this left-handed Stratocaster, beat to hell, looks like he's been chopping wood with it. And he gets up, all soft-spoken. All of a sudden, 'WHOOOR-RRAAAWWRR!' He breaks into 'Wild Thing' and it was all over. There were guitar players weeping. They had to mop the floor up. He was piling it on, solo after solo. I could see everyone's fillings falling out. When he finished, it was silence. Nobody knew what to do. Everybody was dumbstruck, completely in shock.

The Jimi Hendrix Experience made their TV debut on ITV's *Ready Steady Go!* (Marc Bolan was also on the show). The group also recorded 'Foxy Lady' at CBS Studios, London that day. The US version of *Are You Experienced* listed the song with a spelling mistake as 'Foxey Lady' and that's how it's still known among many North American fans.

'Hey Joe' was released in the UK on 16 December 1966. It hit the Top 10 in January 1967 and went on to reach No.6 in the charts. Backed by '51st Anniversary', 'Hey Joe' was recorded at De Lane Lea Studios, London, produced by Chas Chandler. Inspired by Tim Rose's slower version recorded earlier in the year, Hendrix had performed the song at the Cafe Wha? in New York when Chandler first saw him play there. Rose was to re-record the song in the 1990s, again claiming it as his arrangement of a traditional song.

'Blues, man. Blues. For me that's the only music there is. 'Hey Joe' is the blues version of a 100-year-old cowboy song. Strictly speaking it isn't such a commercial song and I was amazed the number ended up so high in the charts'

Jimi Hendrix

The same day 'Hey Joe' hit the shops, Jimi played Chislehurst Caves in Kent, where he met Roger Mayer, who was to play a major role in developing his array of guitar effects. Mayer recalled, 'I went there and brought some of my devices, such as the Octavia. I'd shown it to Jimmy Page, but he thought it was too far out. Jimi said, the moment we met, 'Yeah, I'd like to try that stuff'.'

Blaises, named after cartoon character Modesty Blaise, was a sweaty club in the basement of the Imperial Hotel on Queen's Gate, South West London. David Gilmour told *Mojo* magazine he saw Hendrix early in his career there. 'I saw him playing live at this club, Blaises, South Kensington. He jammed with the Brian Auger Trinity, with Julie Driscoll singing. This little place was packed with Beatles and Stones types, so you think, 'Something's going on'. This kid came in and strapped a right-handed guitar on the wrong way. He was an absolute phenomenon from the beginning.' Jeff Beck recalled: 'One night we were out on the town looking around for some girlies and went down to Blaises in Queens Gate. I heard this sound blasting up the road and got out of the cab, then went in, and there was Jimi. I couldn't believe it, He was singing 'Like A Rolling Stone'. He added, 'I just went away from there thinking I'd better think of something else to do. I'll become a postman.'

❝The first time I heard 'Hey Joe' on the radio, I completely freaked and immediately ran out and bought the record. I didn't even have a record player❞

Mark Knopfler

On 29 December 1966, The Experience spent all day at the BBC's Lime Grove Studios in West London, starting with a 9.30am rehearsal, waiting around all day for their appearance on TV show *Top of the Pops*, broadcast that evening across the UK.

1967 The Jimi Hendrix Experience played the first of what would be over 240 gigs in this year when they appeared at the Bromel Club, Bromley, England on 4 January.

TOP OF THE POPS

5 JANUARY 1967, LONDON, UK

I WATCHED IT: DANEK MARCUS PIECHOWIAK
When he first came on the scene I was still an art student in Bideford, North Devon, and the entire arts school assembled in the common room after school to watch him do 'Hey Joe' on *Top of the Pops*. It was the first time he'd been seen in this country on television.

I WAS THERE: KEVIN MOLYNEAUX
I remember the first time I saw 'Hey Joe' on *Top of the Pops*. It was outstanding, just incredible. The first time I saw him was before 'Hey Joe' came out. He wasn't playing. We used to spend a lot of time up Denmark Street and Charing Cross Road, in all the guitar shops. He was standing outside the Palace Theatre with Chas Chandler, on

the corner of Charing Cross Road and Shaftesbury Avenue. Chas
Chandler was about nine foot tall and there's this guy with what
seemed at the time an extreme haircut. I remember thinking, 'Who
the bloody hell's that?' 'Hey Joe' came out fairly soon after.

Known as The Kirk, the Kirklevington Country Club was in the village
of Kirklevington, near Stockton-on-Tees. Originally a filling station, a
local dance band leader converted and extended a large first-floor
room to create an out-of-town dance hall. With a capacity of around
400, many acts that were to go on to bigger and better things were
to pass through its doors, including the Jeff Beck Group, Mott the
Hoople and Dire Straits. Jimi started with 'Wild Thing' and the
volume was apparently so loud that all the glasses in the cocktail
bar shattered. After the gig, one of the bouncers used the N-word in
referring to Jimi and was rewarded with a punch from Chas Chandler.

KIRKLEVINGTON COUNTRY CLUB

15 JANUARY 1967, KIRKLEVINGTON, UK

I WAS THERE: BRIAN SMITH

The Kirklevington Country Club was situated just outside the village
of Yarm in what is now Teesside and was then Cleveland, on the
main arterial road, the A19. The club is no longer in existence. The
'Kirk', as it was known, billed his appearance as 'The current rave of
the London scene, Clapton, Dylan, and James Brown rolled into one.
The most exciting coloured artist from the USA. Have you ever seen
a guitarist play with his teeth? Don't miss this man.'

A party of Redcar Jazz Club committee members received an
invite from John McCoy, singer with The Real McCoy and owner
of the Kirk, to visit his club to see Jimi that night. There was one
problem: we had the Alan Price Set on at our club with a 10.30pm
finish. Fortunately, Hendrix's session was not due to start until

11.30pm, with the Kirk roughly 30 minutes' drive from Redcar.

When Alan Price finished, several of us jumped into our cars and set off for the Kirk, including Alan Price and his group. There was a connection, Chas Chandler was a close friend of Alan from The Animals. We arrived just in time to see the last few numbers of The Real McCoy, who were supporting that night. The place was full and we stood there having a drink and chatting until Jimi and his backing support came on stage.

I WAS THERE: NEVILLE HENDERSON

We found ourselves no further than 12 feet from the band when they started. I can't remember what they opened with, but my attention was drawn immediately to this wild man on guitar. I remember thinking how mobile he and drummer Mitch Mitchell were, whilst Noel Redding seemed a lot more reserved, the quiet man of the band. I gradually became more drawn to Hendrix, with his strange technique and playing a right-handed guitar upside down on his left side. By the end of their set I remember thinking long and hard about what I'd just witnessed, a true guitar genius ably backed by two other great musicians. I couldn't believe it.

Afterwards, when the huge crowd had all gone, we sat together at tables having a drink and a chat. I recall saying to my wife, Marg, 'Just look who we are sitting with!' Next but one to my left was Alan Price, then Chas Chandler and directly opposite me were Jimi, Mitch and Noel. The Real McCoy guys were also there. It was a terrific hour of chat we had. I remember Noel Redding did most of the talking and I was struck by how quiet Jimi was. When I spoke to him he'd quietly answer, but he wasn't a conversation hogger, as I thought he might have been. Some of the detail he did divulge was how when playing Café Wha? in Greenwich Village as Jimmy James, at the time backing Curtis Knight, he was approached by Chas and persuaded to come to

London, where auditions for a suitable backing group were set up, with the Jimi Hendrix Experience born. They very quickly released their first single, 'Hey Joe', to test the water, but it was currently in the charts at No.6, and they were working on another, 'Purple Haze'.

What we were seeing here was Jimi in the early days of his flamboyant career. I was very impressed with this guy. By now it was getting late, the roadies were getting impatient and we had to end the conversation, so we said our goodbyes and headed for home. As I thought about it next morning, my whole conception of Hendrix had changed. Here was a really quiet, modest guy, and a quality musician - totally different to what I'd thought before. We all had a great night in his company.

REFECTORY

21 JANUARY 1967, GOLDERS GREEN, LONDON, UK

I WASN'T THERE: HAMZAH MUNIF

I had a ticket to see Hendrix in Golders Green. That Friday night I pull this chick and tell my mates I'm going to see her the next night and not bother with Jimi but will catch him later. I can't remember the girl's name, where we went or what happened that night, but I can remember missing Jimi and never seeing him. I was also going to see him on the Isle of Wight but broke my leg playing football and couldn't do that gig either. It's the saddest story in the world!

JIMI
HENDRIX
at
SPEAKEASY
Thursday, 19th January
Telephone 580 - 8810
10 p.m. - 4 a.m.
Bistro food at bistro prices

On their first appearance at London's famous Marquee Club on 24 January 1967, The Jimi Hendrix Experience broke the house record. Support band The Syn would later evolve into Yes. Peter Banks, guitarist with The Syn and then Yes, remembered: 'It was a very peculiar gig. All The Beatles were there, and the Rolling Stones. Clapton and Beck and every other guitar player in town came along and we had to play to all these people. They were waiting for Jimi Hendrix, but we had to play once, come off and then play another set. So people were going. 'Well, thank God they've gone.' Then we came back on again.'

I WAS THERE: ERIC CLAPTON

He definitely pulled the rug out from under Cream. I told people like Pete Townshend about him and we'd go and see him.

I WAS THERE: PETE TOWNSHEND

The thing that really stunned Eric and me was the way he took what we did and made it better. And I really started to try to play. I thought I'd never, ever be as great as he is, but there's certainly no reason now why I shouldn't try. In fact, I remember saying to Eric, 'I'm going to play him off the stage one day.' But what Eric did was even more peculiar. He said, 'Well, I'm going to pretend that I am Jimi Hendrix!'

MARQUEE CLUB

24 JANUARY 1967, LONDON, UK

I WAS THERE: TONY SPARSIS

I lived in north Kensington during the Sixties and early Seventies and we'd go up the West End every night. We'd go up on a Friday night and come back Sunday afternoon, visiting places like the Tiles Club, Whisky A Go Go and what was the Flamingo Club.

We saw Georgie Fame loads of times down there and would go to places like Ronnie Scott's upstairs, where we saw Earth, Wind and Fire in the early days, Otis Redding and Zoot Money. It was a fantastic time to be around. We'd go up the Ram Jam Club in Brixton to watch Bob Marley. At the time we didn't know what was happening. We didn't know what a mark these legendary bands were leaving.

Me and my brother were once given two and sixpence, a pork pie and an apple and had to go into this studio in Holland Park and scream. They were recording bits of soundtrack for the film, *A Hard Day's Night*.

We got chatting to Otis Redding at the Tiles Club in London. And one of his roadies asked, 'Do you know where we can go for a quiet time and a smoke?' I thought, 'Yeah, there's the Brigadier Club in Notting Hill Gate.' It was a West Indian club down in the basement and we went there with Otis Redding and smoked dope with him. The Bar-Keys were with him. That was north Kensington.

Hendrix needed a bloody bath most of the time. I saw his first performance at the Marquee in '67 and that was the first time he appeared live on stage in the UK. He ran off a whole stack of stuff. He wasn't with Mitch Mitchell at the time. We sat outside talking to him. Nobody knew who he was. He was just a bloke who played in a band in the Marquee. He went back to the Flamingo a few weeks later. They put a second concert on and you couldn't get in the place.

Jimi was paid £39 for appearing at Norwich's Orford Cellar in January 1967, and apparently told the club management he would happily return for the same fee to play the 300-capacity venue, so grateful was he that they had booked him. He never returned.

ORFORD CELLAR

25 JANUARY 1967, NORWICH, UK

I WAS THERE: PETE GOODRUM

The Orford Cellar was part of the Orford pub. It was where Nando's is now, the entrance to the cellar being next door via an alley off Red Lion Street.

I went to the Orford that night at the last moment. A schoolfriend had tickets and a girl had stood him up so I went with him. I have the

overriding memory of being aware that one was watching a genius.
And there was the speaking voice. So, delicate, I suppose is the word.
It seemed to not fit with his singing voice but prove the 'gentleness'
that those who knew him claimed he had. Playing his stuff now I
think we didn't realise how close he was to jazz and blues. Legend
has it that coloured beer bottle tops were introduced partly because
in the Orford Cellar it got so hot the labels came off.

The press ad from the Eastern Evening News in 1967 promoting
the Hendrix gig referred to 'teeth players' and seemed to indicate
that the rest of the band played with their teeth too!

I WAS THERE: RICHARD PILCH, AGE 20

I was well into my music, especially live bands at the Orford Cellar.
It was a small club, maybe 250 capacity, down some very old wooden
steps which nowadays would be deemed a fire hazard. There was a
small wooden stage and it was always dark in there. In one corner
there were always US servicemen and 'ladies of the night'. There
was a small bar run by Duoro and Jenny Potter, also acting as a
cloakroom. I remember reading in the Eastern Daily Press that the
Jimi Hendrix Experience were due to appear. He had a hit record
out, 'Hey Joe', at the time. It wasn't until March that 'Purple Haze'
was released.

In those days you couldn't buy a ticket in advance and you had to
queue up. You could become a club member for a year for about 10
shillings (50p). The cost to get in was around 7/6 (37p). My friend
and I got there as early as we could and already the queue was
snaking around the block. We slowly got nearer and nearer, and with
about 10 more people to go the bouncer said, 'That's it lads -no more
room'. Fortunately, we knew the bouncer, Charlie, quite well so he
wandered back and said, 'Hang about lads. I'll let you in when the
crowd has gone.'

It was unbelievably crammed and there was no support, just a disco.
It got hotter and hotter. Howard Platt, the promoter, came on about
eight and said Jimi wasn't sure if he was going to do one set or two. We

later found out Jimi wasn't there. The walls were starting to get very wet, condensation running down them. In Noel Redding's autobiography he states that the Norwich gig was the hottest he had ever played. Hendrix eventually came on about 9.45pm and by this time we were soaked in sweat. He was very loud but wonderful. We stood about four metres away from the band. What a brilliant night. He didn't have a huge repertoire and played a lot of blues. He did it all, playing with his teeth, behind his back, between his legs. During the last number, everything was turned up to 11 and the guitar smashing began. Because we were so near the front we could have picked up any piece of that guitar and sold it now on eBay, but hindsight's a wonderful thing. So we went home, our ears ringing, saying how much we'd remember this night in years to come. I was lucky enough to see Hendrix twice more, once in Dereham in Norfolk and on the bill at a concert in Boston, Lincolnshire, which also included Pink Floyd, The Move, Geno Washington, and Cream. All for £1!

The Upper Cut was a nightclub owned by British heavyweight boxer and British & European title challenger Billy Walker. Located in Forest Gate, East London, it was created from a former skating rink and billed by the Stratford Express newspaper as 'a plush big beat palace'. It lasted barely more than 12 months, but hosted a range of top acts during its brief lifespan, including The Who, Small Faces, The Pretty Things, Otis Redding, Sam and Dave, Booker T and the MGs and Nina Simone.

Jimi wrote 'Purple Haze' while waiting to go on stage at boxing champ Billy Walker's nightclub The Upper Cut

The Who performed on the opening night. The Jimi Hendrix

Experience appeared there twice. The first occasion was on Boxing Day 1966 when Jimi was billed as 'Jimmy' and admission was 5/- (25p). Hendrix reputedly wrote 'Purple Haze' whilst waiting to go on stage. A blue plaque, affixed to the railings adjacent to where the club stood, now marks this feat.

Slightly more than a month later, the Experience returned to The Upper Cut, when Jimi was billed as 'American top soul singer and guitarist extraordinary'. Admission had increased to 8/6 (37p) for 'gentlemen' and 7/6 (33p) for ladies.

THE UPPER CUT

28 JANUARY 1967, LONDON, UK

I WAS THERE: KEVIN MOLYNEUX, AGE 16

I played in a band at the time and still do now. Jimi was a massive influence on me. I started off listening to The Shadows, like everyone else, in the really early Sixties, then got into the Bluesbreakers, The Who, The Kinks and everyone else that was around.

The Upper Cut was an old roller-skating rink. We queued right round the corner, past the pub and down Romford Road to see him. It was quite something. I remember he had a 100-watt Marshall stack with an Indian blanket over the 4 x 12 cabs.

> I thought there must be more than one guitarist on stage, because it sounded like 20 people playing

It was just overwhelming. There was no one else playing like that. It made all the others seem quite dull. The Beatles were a major thing, but he just blew everyone out of the water. My band played at The Upper Cut a few times, so I can actually say I played on the same stage as Hendrix. We were called Sounds Like Six. It sounds corny but it was the Sixties.

I bought a Fender Stratocaster when no one else wanted them. They'd gone out of fashion. I paid about 70 guineas for it in Baldwin Burns, just off Charing Cross Road. Hendrix came over and was using Strats and suddenly the price went up again. They'd definitely gone out of fashion. I wish I still had it. It'd be worth a fortune. It was sonic blue, which is the colour for me.

On 29 January 1967, The Jimi Hendrix Experience supported The Who, along with Koobas and Thoughts at the Saville Theatre, London. Eric Clapton and Jack Bruce of Cream, plus Brian May, later of Queen, were all in the audience.

Sunday
29th January 1967

in order of appearance

THE KOOBAS
THE JIMI HENDRIX EXPERIENCE

intermission

THE WHO

Programme compered by Mike Quinn

THANKS

SAVILLE THEATRE

29 JANUARY 1967, LONDON, UK

I WAS THERE: BRIAN MAY

I heard the solo on 'Stone Free' and refused to believe someone could actually play this. It had to be some kind of studio trickery, the way he talks to the guitar and the guitar talks back to him. I was already playing in a band called Smile and thought I was a reasonably good guitarist, so I knew it wasn't possible. I went to the Saville, determined to be a disbeliever, but was swept off my feet. I thought, 'This guy is the most astounding thing I've ever seen.' And he did the 'Stone

Free' solo live, absolutely perfectly. It was back to the drawing board for me.

I WAS THERE: ERIC CLAPTON

I don't think Jack had really taken him in before... and when Jack did see it that night, after the gig he went home and came up with the riff to 'Sunshine of Your Love'. It was strictly a dedication to Jimi. Then we wrote a song on top of it.

On 1 February 1967 The Experience played the New Cellar Club on Thomas Street, South Shields, in the North East of England. Jimi took a train from London, changing at Newcastle. Noel Redding recalled that transport

hassles meant the band arrived late. The club had a revolving stage and the band were set to swing – literally – into action when Jimi's amp blew up. Redding had to rely on an amp from the support act.

Jimi accidentally put his guitar through the low ceiling and, witnessing the crowd's positive reaction, repeated the act. The resultant damage was left untouched for months and was christened by the club as 'Jimi's hole'.

After their set, the crowd tried to grab the band and Redding feared they might be crushed as the revolving stage took them back out of sight. The set included 'Killing Floor', 'Stone Free', 'Rock Me Baby', 'Hey Joe' and 'Wild Thing'. Admission was six shillings (30p).

IMPERIAL HOTEL

2 FEBRUARY 1967, DARLINGTON, UK

I WAS THERE: ANNE SODERMAN

My memories of seeing Jimi Hendrix at the Imperial start from being one of the first people to arrive, along with some of my friends, and going up to the Ballroom where the band were to play. It was called 'The R'n'B Club'. Not long after we arrived and took our places at the front, to the left near the windows, we turned around when we heard someone arriving, and in walked Jimi Hendrix with the other band members in tow. Jimi had such a presence and an incredible aura about him. As far as I recall he was wearing a Sergeant Pepper-style orange jacket or cape.

The ballroom was absolutely packed. I think at the time there should have been a maximum 150/200 people, but there were far more than that. People were standing on tables and chairs, as the ballroom floor was so crowded. We were lucky to have our places at the front, just a couple of feet away from the stage, which was only about two feet high.

The first number the band did was 'Star Spangled Banner', turned into 'God Save the Queen' and then 'Wild Thing'. It was incredible. At one point during the set, between songs, Jimi was talking to the audience, and some spittle flew from his mouth and landed on my right cheek. I remember that vividly.

With so many people at the gig, and it being on the first floor of the hotel, we could feel the floor bouncing, everyone moving to the music and having such a brilliant time. Some friends of mine who I believe ran the club told me at the time the band were booked six months previously, when they weren't that well-known, and agreed a fee of £50.

I WAS THERE: CHRISTINE GARSTIN

We were a large group of new mods who hung out in the Bolivar, the cellar bar in the Imperial Hotel. There were quite a few musicians in our group and they rented the ballroom to run a soul club and play themselves. When they booked Jimi, they thought he was a soul act. He had released 'Hey Joe'. It was only a small stage and by the time they'd set up the sheer size of the speakers took up most of the stage. I

Christine remembers the speakers shaking at the Imperial and the manager thinking they would topple

was right at the front. When he started up the sheer volume meant the speakers were shaking and the manager, Gerry, an ex-river policeman, panicked and was running back and forth, holding the speakers thinking they were going to topple.

The club only held a couple of hundred and a few people actually left, because it certainly wasn't soul music. After he finished, Jimi came into the cocktail bar and had a drink with the owner, Nick Ridley. He was so softly spoken, a gentleman. I saw him again at Kirklevington Country Club, booked by the legendary John McCoy, who had a knack of booking the stars just as they teetered on top-level stardom. Prior to the Kirk, John had a small cellar club in Middlesbrough called the Purple Onion. It held a couple of hundred people. He booked Stevie Wonder after 'Uptight' and I'm proud to say I was there that night too. I stood talking to that beautiful soul.

I loved 'Hey Joe'. It was a very sexy record, but to be honest I always thought Jimi was a musician's musician.

I WAS THERE: ALLENE NORRIS

Before spending 23 years on BBC local radio, I worked on several newspapers. It was when I wrote a pop page on The Northern Despatch, a newspaper that no longer exists, that I was sent to interview Hendrix, who was staying and playing in the Imperial Hotel. As a youngster I would have coffee with my parents on Saturday mornings there and it was all beautifully served, with napkins and a silver salver to take your cake off. It was quite upmarket really. Since then it's become offices and all sorts of other things. I think the main part of the building is an Italian restaurant called Rigatoni's now.

It had a boulevard bar which was in the basement and that was a very popular meeting place for young people in Sixties gear, with short skirts. It was an ideal place for him to play in the town rather than, say, a local theatre.

I interviewed Hendrix in his hotel bedroom and found him quite a shy person. There was a white poodle on his bed. He was just on the verge of becoming a big star, but quite modest about it. When I left and went to hear him play it was sensational and memorable. As soon as he stepped out on the stage all that shyness went. He was a terrific entertainer, no doubt about it. He wasn't totally famous then. He was on the rise and this was probably one of his last gigs before he became a really big star. He was certainly well worth seeing. He was known to play his guitar with his teeth. People thought, 'How stupid!' but then it was, 'Yes, but he plays it well with his teeth. It's not just a gimmick. Actually, he can play.'

But I was amazed at what a quiet sort he was. The Sun or one of the more common newspapers would have had a headline saying, 'Allene Norris went into his bedroom', you know? But it was quite above board, I can assure you.

He was rather quiet, but all that changed when he was in front of an audience. He was obviously in his element on stage. That night he had a favourite guitar stolen, and although I rang the local newspaper about this incident, they didn't seem very interested. Of course, as time went on they became very interested. Then all sorts of tales came up over the years about where it was. It's believed it's still somewhere locally. Rumours abound as to the ultimate fate of Jimi's stolen guitar and whether it still languishes on top of a wardrobe somewhere in Darlington.

MY MUM AND DAD WERE THERE: SALLY ARGYLE

My mum and dad were at the gig, separately at the time. Their paths hadn't quite crossed then. My mum caught the drumstick when it was thrown into the crowd by the drummer at the end of the gig.

I WAS THERE: KENNY BEAGLE

It was a cold wintry night when The Jimi Hendrix Experience played the ballroom of the Imperial Hotel. I use the word 'ballroom' loosely, because I guess the room held 250. 'Hey Joe' was in the charts and featured on *Top of the Pops* that night. I went with my then-girlfriend, Lynn, now my wife of 48 years. Everyone was excited to be seeing this phenomenon dominating the music press.

When Jimi was setting up he was having trouble with his equipment. After much cursing he started. The sound was incredible, far louder than anything we'd heard previously. It wasn't just the virtuoso guitar playing, it was the sheer style - Jimi played differently and looked different. He was electrifying. The equipment broke down again and his language was, let's say, 'industrial'. He played 'Hey Joe', 'Stone Free', Bob Dylan's 'Like a Rolling Stone', and a magnificent version of The Troggs 'Wild Thing'. The gig is still talked about today and has drifted into folklore by the fact he had a guitar stolen. The town still abounds with stories of who took it and who's owned it since. Recently, I went to a local bar to see a band called So What. The singer said he'd heard about Jimi's guitar being stolen and he had it, but potential buyers should hurry as he only had five left!

I still listen to Jimi Hendrix to this day. His three studio albums are essential listening to anybody who loves music. The influence of the man on the electric is unparalleled. A true legend.

I WAS THERE: ROBERT PICKERSGILL

I was the drummer with Jimmy James, aka Terry Scott and the West Coast Promotion. Hendrix was out of his head throughout the gig at the Imperial. He never missed the loss of one of his guitars at the end of the evening. The Fender Stratocaster has been re-sprayed and its current owner is well known among the band members.

The Imperial was the place to go in Darlington

I WAS THERE: BRIAN WALLACE, AGE 18

According to people who say they were there, the Imperial must have held 2,000 people. But there was only about 100 to 150 there. I saw loads of bands there every Thursday night. We went to the Cleaver pub in Skinnergate before we went to the Imp. Hendrix was a bit of a let-down for me and a few others as Thursday night was a soul night, so we expected a black soul band from the USA. Normally the soul bands were good to dance to. Hendrix was completely different.

There's all sorts of rumours going round about Hendrix's stolen guitar, but a few of us know the true story of who nicked it. I've listened to loads of folks saying this or that about it. It was no big deal then, as no one expected Hendrix to leave a legacy like he did. It wasn't until a few years ago that it was even mentioned. Then suddenly everyone knows someone who knows someone who nicked it, but no names have ever been mentioned. The two guys who got it? One was in the army.

I WAS THERE: DAVID DURKIN

I was there with some friends drinking in the upstairs bar. We watched as Hendrix, Chas Chandler and a couple of handlers passed by the bar entrance heading to the ballroom. We didn't have tickets but could hear the music. There was a half-time interval, then we just walked in for the second half. It was a decent show, with the obligatory teeth-playing. I just found out this past December that my sister was in the audience. I never knew! The one thing I remember vividly was that Hendrix was smaller than I imagined. He was bent over a little and wearing a waist- length cloak. He looked out of it.

I WAS THERE: SUE DAVIDSON

My friend and I were sat on a piano to the right of the stage and could see Chas Chandler trying to stop the speaker falling over when Jimi was rubbing his guitar strings on it. It's the best gig I've ever been to. Another friend, Christine, managed to blag her way into the after-gig party, and I've been jealous ever since.

I WAS THERE: DOUG DAVIDSON

I was there, as was my future wife. I was also a mad Animals fan. To my eternal shame, after the brilliant gig I saw the legend Hendrix sat on the stairs with Chas Chandler. I bounced up to the pair and said, 'Great, Jimi'. I then proceeded to target Chas with questions, asking whether The Animals were going to reform!

MY FRIEND WAS THERE: GORDON VALENTINE

The small stage was about table-height and a friend of mine was sitting nearby. He rested his hand on the edge of the stage and Hendrix stood on his fingers accidentally. My friend still boasts, 'Jimi Hendrix stood on my fingers!'

During a session at Olympic studios in London, UK on 3 Febuary 1967, Jimi completed the recording of 'Purple Haze', using Roger Mayer's Octavia pedal for the first time. The track which became one of Hendrix's best-known became the opening track on the Experience's debut American album.

I WAS THERE: ROGER MAYER

The basis was the blues, but the framework of the blues was too tight. We'd talk first about what he wanted the emotion of the song to be. 'What's the vision?' He would talk in colours and my job was to give him the electronic palette which would engineer those colours so he could paint the canvas.

RAM JAM CLUB

4 FEBRUARY 1967, BRIXTON, LONDON, UK

I WAS THERE: CARL MITCH

I remember seeing Jimi at the Ram Jam Club, opposite the police station. I remember the manager telling the band, 'We don't like crap like that here.' Jimi's response was, 'I will never play here again.' He never did. A few weeks later 'Hey Joe' went Top-10. The site of the Ram Jam Club is now a KFC.

FLAMINGO CLUB

4 FEBRUARY 1967, LONDON UK

After the Ram Jam Club in Brixton, Jimi and the Experience head for the West End of London to play the Flamingo Club. One of the earliest bootleg recordings of the Experience captures a covers-heavy set list that includes 'Can You See Me', 'Stone Free', 'Hey Joe', 'Like A Rolling Stone', 'Wild Thing', 'Catfish Blues', 'Killing Floor' and 'Mercy Mercy'.

LOCARNO

9 FEBRUARY 1967, BRISTOL, UK

I WAS THERE: DAVID MORRIS, AGE 19

I knew nothing of Hendrix or his music prior to seeing him on Top of The Pops when 'Hey Joe' entered the charts. I'd never seen anything like it, and it was clear to see the sheer artistry behind the extrovert showmanship, which itself made a huge impression.

I played guitar in Bristol band The Exiles in the mid-Sixties, and we supported many top bands of the time. Sadly, this didn't include Hendrix, but I saw him around that time at the Locarno, within the New Bristol Centre, now the O2. I clearly remember the performance. His appearance lasted only for around 30 minutes, as was common in those days, but its quality remains with me. I will always regard him as the best rock guitarist of all time, possessing the unique ability to translate the sound in his head directly to his Strat with unparalleled clarity and lyricism.

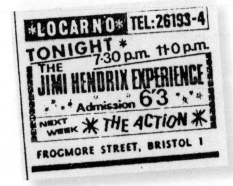

It was Hendrix's appearance on the scene

that convinced me it was time to give up gigging, given the game-changing nature of his ability - that and the fact that I was preparing to get married!

Jimi made the journey down to the Regency spa town of Cheltenham in Gloucestershire. Its biggest claim to rock 'n' roll fame is being the birthplace – and burial place – of Rolling Stone Brian Jones. Jimi was paid £40 to appear at the Blue Moon night club, a small venue previously used as a billiard hall and located over a branch of Burton's the tailor's in Cheltenham High Street.

Despite appearances, David was impressed by Jimi

BLUE MOON CLUB

11 FEBRUARY 1967, CHELTENHAM, UK

I WAS THERE: TONY FISHER, AGE 18

I was stationed at RAF Little Rissington, but my hometown was Winchcombe. I spent most weekends in Cheltenham at the Blue Moon, the Waikiki Club or the Prom Club. I'd heard his music but had no idea of his upcoming appearance. I remember this black guy climbing the steps and thought he was jumping the queue so slightly blocked his progress. Imagine my surprise and amazement when the queue-jumper came on to the stage. I kept a broken guitar string in my wallet for many years but had no proof of it belonging to him. Later that year in July I saw him at The Festival of the

Flower Children at Woburn. I was in the RAF at the time and was the only one there with short hair! I took his albums on my overseas tour and played them non-stop. I was devastated by his untimely death. I'm still in love with his music.

Tony thought Hendrix was queue jumping at Cheltenham's Blue Moon Club

I WAS THERE: MARGARET MAYELL

I'd have been 17 or 18. He was quite a change from other acts I saw there. Lee Dorsey and Cream were memorable evenings too. It's so long ago that I haven't got much of a memory of it apart from being blown away by his performance.

I saw him again at the Colston Hall, Bristol, on the same bill as the Walker Brothers and Englebert Humperdinck. Because it was a larger stage and venue, I remember more of him playing the guitar around his back, him on his knees. I'd never seen anything like it. It's so sad that he died so young.

I WAS THERE: JERILYN PLEDGER, AGE 17

Not really my cup of tea – I was more into Motown. I lived in the Forest of Dean and it was a long way to go to Cheltenham on the back of a rickety old scooter. He was great though and what he did with the guitar was not seen before he made it talk.

I was 17 and only went a few times and can't really remember the other groups. I was more interested in seeing Stevie Wonder at Bristol and the Sam and Dave show at the Regal in Gloucester. Not long after all that The Blue Moon closed.

It was a great time - plenty of discos and great music, one of our favourites was the Bristol Hotel down the road several times a week, catching the bus to Gloucester. If we couldn't get a lift home, we'd hitch back – a bit scary now.

I WAS THERE: DIANA POWELL

Many moons ago we went from Hereford. We were four friends and had to queue up two flights of stairs to get into the Blue Moon Club.

We just got in and there he was - just hair, guitar and the noise, amazing and scary all at the same time. The electricity he gave out was truly mind-blowing. He was the best and was never to be replaced.

I WAS THERE: IAN RODGER

I was the DJ when Jimi Hendrix played the Blue Moon Club. He'd just had his first single, 'Hey Joe', and it was going up the charts. The original DJ was Dave Bennett. He eventually went on to pirate radio. I think I begged the club's owner Eddie Norman to give me a chance.

I introduced him on as Jimi Hendrix and said he was going to feature his hit song 'Hey Joe', rocketing up the charts. It was just an incredible atmosphere the whole night. We signed him for a relatively low fee. The speculation before he came was that he wouldn't turn up - that he'd just break his contract and go somewhere else. But he didn't, he came out and put on a tremendous show. Nobody had ever seen anybody like Hendrix play guitar before. It was just out of this world.

I had worked in the cloakroom at the Blue Moon, hanging up coats. I probably started working in the cloakroom just to avoid paying to get in. I was an apprentice at the time and didn't have a lot of money so had to pick and choose which shows I went to. I remember being inundated with coats. We'd pile coats up everywhere. Before that I used to go up there because I loved the music - Tamla sounds, the blues, the soul. I was 17, 18.

I started DJ-ing in tandem with an American called Frankie. Our booth was right alongside the changing room. It was probably only about 10ft by 10ft.

The press came because they wanted to interview Jimi after the show and take some photographs. He asked me to make sure the door to the changing room was kept closed, which I did, because he had his hair in rollers. He'd come off stage, was sweating, and put his hair in girls' rollers. It was an incredible sight. I just wished I had a camera.

I WAS THERE: TERRY COX

I happened to be on the platform at Lansdown Station, returning to Gloucester after a fantastic show by Jimi with my then-girlfriend Jill. He was with Mitch Mitchell and carried a guitar case, I assumed with his Strat inside. I started to talk to him, complimenting him and asking how he felt the gig had gone. He was very quiet and politely spoken. I remember his eyes were bloodshot red and he seemed understandably tired. Then about half a dozen youths about our age saw him and came over and started to ask him 'stupid' questions like, 'How do you get your hair like that?' and trying to make fun of him. We were rather embarrassed by their attitude and decided to leave him alone.

CIVIC HALL

14 FEBRUARY 1967, GRAYS, UK

I WAS THERE: ALAN GRAVES

He was there twice. The first time we were playing with him. I was playing in a local band. I can't remember the name because I played in so many places. They'd just brought 'Hey Joe' out. They were relatively unknown. What was surprising was that there were so many people there. It was quite full and it was quite a big hall.

Our manager wasn't very up on pop groups. The reason he was our manager was because he had a van. We started off and Jimi Hendrix came and stood at the side of the stage listening to us. And our manager came up and was chatting away to him and I didn't think much more about it until the interval and I said to the manager, 'What were you talking to Jimi about?' And he

Alan's band supported The Experience at Grays Civic Hall

said, 'Who's Jimi?' I said, 'Jimi Hendrix.' He said, 'Oh, that geezer with the funny hair do. I thought he was in a group. I told him I was going to get a drink for my boys and did he want one?' We talked to Jimi about this and he said, 'He was really funny, he said he didn't have a clue who I was', and he was so polite and so nice it was unbelievable'.

When they started the place was quite full and I think he was introduced. It wasn't often bands were, but somebody said, 'And now, ladies and gentlemen, The Jimi Hendrix Experience!' And all the people surged towards the front of the stage. Jimi started with 'Wild Thing.' I've never seen so many frightened young teenagers in my life. They all ran to the back of the hall again because it was so loud. We sounded like a little record player compared to him. It was unbelievable. We were all dumbstruck with it.

They didn't have microphones on the drums in those days and with those two Marshall stacks, Mitch was going absolutely crazy trying to be heard over the top of that in the big hall, really pounding hell out of the drums. But you could still hear him. It was really early days. There were no sound engineers. They just went on and played. Jimi had a lot of problems. He had to keep tuning his guitar.

Some of the arrangements he did at the Civic Hall were great. He did 'Mercy Mercy', which the Stones did on their third LP, an old American R&B number. He did it so well and so

different, and 'Walking the Dog', the old Rufus Thomas number. So many old songs that he brought new life to and made them totally different. Even when you hear bootleg recordings of him and dodgy sound, you can still hear what he's doing coming through, the incredible solos and things. It doesn't matter how bad the recording is, it's worth listening to.

In the break we had a chat with him and he was one of the few that came and spoke to us. We played with so many bands there – The Nashville Teens, The Hollies, most of the pop groups. Status Quo were a nice crowd. Jimi Hendrix was one of the few that didn't treat us as though we were just some tuppenny-ha'penny local band. He was really nice. We couldn't get over that. We were just in awe of it all.

He sat in the dressing room, picked up our guitarist's guitar, which was right-handed and the strings weren't changed round, and he showed our guitarist a few things. He was literally playing an upside-down guitar and could still manage to play a guitar like that, with all the strings round the wrong way. We had a job playing it the right way up!

He was playing some old rhythm and blues stuff and it was still good. He was just so incredible. The guy was so talented and wasn't showing off or anything. We played a lot of rhythm and blues stuff and he said that was unusual. There weren't a lot of bands playing that sort of stuff then. A lot of local bands were pop bands. There was nothing big and fancy about him. He was so quiet. In a way he slunk around. He was very softly spoken. When he died, we couldn't believe it.

For three guys they were an incredible band. He would just do things off the cuff. You could see the excitement and enjoyment they had together. The atmosphere came across to the audience. It was electric.

I had gone professional. I played with Long John Baldry for a while. We did a lot of Radio 1 shows with him. We joined when he had had hits with 'Let The Heartaches Begin', 'Mexico', things like that. We were doing really big places and getting well paid. We bumped into him on a few occasions, but only just for a quick 'hello'.

One time we bumped into him at the BBC. The BBC was still very old-fashioned then. Guys walked around in grey or brown coats. They had all sorts of tape operators and people that positioned microphones, half a dozen people doing the job of one man.

We heard this noise coming from the basement. It was quite a way off, because we were up on the third floor. Somebody said, 'What's that noise?' The other guy said, 'I think they've got the builders in again down in the basement.' It was Jimi. That's where they put them to rehearse, because they were so loud. They wouldn't have them up in the normal studios. We went down and saw them and said, 'Your sound has been recognised as 'we've got the builders in'. He really laughed at that.

I still get a bit of excitement in my voice all these years later, talking about him. There's not many bands you can say that about. He was just so remarkable, and such a nice guy.

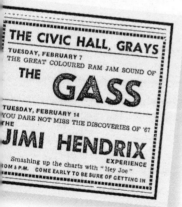

I remember Mitch was using a Premier drum kit, an English drum kit, and I had a set of American Ludwig drums. He said to me, 'I'm saving up for a set like that. I like Ludwigs.' I said, 'You can afford a kit like that,' and he said, 'No, not on my wages.' I think he said he got about £8 a week, which was nothing. When we were playing with Baldry, we were getting £25 a week and hotels and all expenses paid.

I met him years later in a pub where we were playing, hardly recognising him. He said, 'You don't remember me, do you?' I said, 'Your face seems familiar.' And he said, 'Yeah, we played with you a couple of times and I said I was going to get a drum kit like yours.' I said, 'Did you get that raise?' And he said, 'Yeah, it went to £10 or £11.' So they obviously didn't get paid too well. Jimi didn't seem like that. He didn't seem greedy. I think it was management.

I WAS THERE: LINDA BASSETT, AGE 16

I was there. Unfortunately, I only remember the noise of the gig and Jimi playing the guitar with his teeth. Over the years I've told people I saw him playing at the Civic Hall. I don't think people believed me.

I WAS THERE: STUART BRAND, AGE 20

Although it was a big name locally, it wasn't a very big name. Admission must have been affordable for local youngsters. I certainly didn't have much money at the time. As I recall, it was well attended, the Civic Hall stage was massive and the Experience were certainly well spaced apart. The type of music was a change from preppy American imports. Today, most locals still don't believe that Hendrix played the Civic!

I WAS THERE: DAVID LAWSON, AGE 16

I'd seen him on Top of the Pops. We'd go up to the Civic Hall on a Tuesday night. They had all the bands there at the time - Fleetwood Mac, The Marmalade, Zoot Money, everybody. I knew one of the lads in the support band. When the show finished, I remember going round the back. The other lads were packing their gear away and Hendrix was still there, chatting to other people. He had a white Fender Strat. I said, 'Can I have a hold?' as you do. I was in awe of it really, because of the show we'd just seen. Jimi Hendrix gave me the guitar. I held it then handed it back to him and said, 'Thanks very much'. He said, 'No problem.'

I never met Hendrix again. But I ended up with Long John Baldry for about 40 years. I was in a band called Almond Marzipan. You had bands like The Sweet, The Marmalade. That's how we ended up with that sort of name. We took over from a group called Bluesology, with Reg Dwight. So for a little while during the changeover period, Reg was with us. He went on to other things. Changed his name or something.

I WAS THERE: GRACE SHACKLADY

Geno Washington and the Ram Jam Band were the resident group and of course are now iconic in their own right. I also remember seeing The Honeycombs when 'Come Right Back' was in the charts - they had been a late substitution for Unit 4+2, who couldn't make it.

I went along with a few school friends – one was nuts about Jimi, so we were right up against the stage. She spent the whole time crying! There was none of the crush and crowds one sees at gigs these days. I think that there was still room to dance.

I remember how flamboyant he was but not very good looking. However, it was bloody loud and I remember my ears ringing as I walked the mile or so home – it was safe to do that in those days - and I couldn't hear properly for the next

Grace (left) remembers Jimi being 'bloody loud'

couple of days. When I tell people I saw him live, I get quite a few jealous comments. It came in very handy for items such as 'my claim to fame' instances one always had to spout out at training courses, meetings, etc.

I WAS THERE: GERALDINE RIDDLES

I still find it hard to believe. My boyfriend at the time was a big fan. I don't have a good memory for details, although I remember standing there watching him on stage. I'm sure I remember him using the edge of the stage curtain to play his guitar.

I WAS THERE: PAUL BIRCHETT

Mojo magazine ran an article some years ago in which they said, 'He played at a rather small gymnasium with a tiny stage at the end. The atmosphere is totally impersonal, between 500 and 600 people have turned up.' They were right about the number of people there, but Grays Civic Hall was a massive place, more like a ballroom, and I'm sure they could have got a few hundred more people in. In those days, safety and security didn't come into it.

Unfortunately, unless you had your own transport it wasn't the easiest of places to get to. It was about one and a half miles from the town centre. If you lived in and around Grays, public transport or even walking was the only way. Where I lived in Aveley, it was more of an expedition, sometimes involving three buses. Also, gigs like this for some unknown reason were not very well advertised. It was more a case of word of mouth. Come Tuesday, you'd more than likely have spent all your wages over the previous weekend.

In fact, Grays Civic Hall was the last place you would have expected a gig like this, although about that time in 1966 and 1967 you had acts like The Move, John Mayall's Bluesbreakers with Eric Clapton, Chris Farlowe, Georgie Fame with Alan Price, Zoot Money, more or less every month. But in most cases the place would be only half-full. Sometimes no more than 50 people would be there.

When people start talking about who they've seen over the last 50 years or so, my claim to fame that I saw Jimi Hendrix at Grays Civic Hall normally ends the conversation. Unfortunately, for the life of me I can't remember what he played that night. It seemed to go past very quickly. He was on stage for one and a half hours, if that, and I think he played 'Hey Joe', 'Stone Free', tracks off his forthcoming album, including 'Red House' and finished with 'Wild Thing'. Without a doubt, it's still up there as one of the best gigs I've seen and I was right up front, about 15ft from the stage. I think the reaction from the rest of the people was that they'd never seen anything like it and anything after that became insignificant by comparison. Friday nights at Aveley Public Hall were great too – we had The Creation, The Action, The In Crowd, Shotgun Express, Steampacket, The

Birds, Geno Washington, The Artwoods and more. All great gigs, but perhaps we had seen something beyond greatness.

I WAS THERE: BOB KIRBY, AGE 21

I can remember it as though it was yesterday. It's only in retrospect that you realise what a big moment it was. Because it was the 'Hey Joe' tour, he wasn't really huge. He wasn't a superstar as such so for us this was more of an interesting gig. It certainly opened our eyes, believe me. We had a local band. We started doing The Shadows, who were huge at the time, and became an instrumental band. We were schoolfriends and played instrumentals for a few years.

We found that if you're doing covers you can get jobs or work at working men's clubs and places like that - you have to be more formal and we'd got more interested in R&B, so started playing Chuck Berry, 12-bar blues and got into American blues and worked ourselves out of getting gigs at working men's clubs. Then we started getting lots of work in various blues clubs and pubs. We were a competent band. We weren't fantastic. I think we were the first in the area to have a harmonica player, so got into the real rhythm and blues and got quite a following.

We were contacted by a guy who had an agency and he said they were setting up national tours and were using the Civic Hall as one of the main venues. The Civic was quite a large hall with a really large stage. I think it lent itself quite well to that, and because of the sort of material we were playing we lent ourselves towards supporting acts coming through. We got a residency as such. Every couple of weeks there would be a big band and we were always there. I can remember The Zombies, The Nashville Teens, Geno Washington and the Ram Jam Band, John Mayall with Clapton, pretty much all of those. We were all still working. We were never a professional band as such, but ended up playing in quite a few clubs in London and played with Bluesology with Elton John at a club called Tiles.

We knew of Hendrix because 'Hey Joe' had been released and we'd heard about his abilities and things he did, so got to the gig quite early. We were setting up our gear and Noel Redding and Mitch Mitchell walked in. They were proper Jack the lads, laughing and joking. We just kept on setting up.

My girlfriend's father, Ron, who became my father-in-law and used to drive us about and help us with the gear, was talking to somebody in the wings, because it was quite a large stage with the curtains either side. I suddenly realised it was Hendrix. He was wearing a British army uniform. They turned up wearing what they were going to play in, basically, and I didn't see too much of any roadies. He was chatting to my father-in-law and I heard Ron saying, 'Are you in the band?' Hendrix said, 'Yeah' and Ron said, 'What do you do?' and Hendrix said, 'I play guitar a bit'. He was very, very quiet, a reserved sort of guy. I didn't expect him to be like that.

The impression I got was that perhaps it was because they'd only just got together, the three of them. It was Noel and Mitch, then there was Jimi. They weren't exactly thrown in at the deep end, but it was a case of, 'There's your dates – off you go.'

I wouldn't say it was Jekyll and Hyde but it was such a contrast. Off stage he was James Marshall. On stage he was Jimi. It was so noticeable. He was very self-deprecating. He didn't have an ego that I could see. They disappeared and we did the first half and we came off and there was a break while they were setting their gear up. We thought we'd go and watch so went down to the front - the curtains were closed at the time.

There were always lots of people there, a big crowd regardless of who was playing. We were standing there and suddenly you heard the amps being switched on and this 60-cycle humming coming from the Strat's single coil pick-ups and thought, 'Wow, that's going to be good.' He was introduced and everyone rushed down the front, the curtains opened and we were hit by this wall of sound. In those days you never saw Marshall stacks - it was the first time I'd seen them played – and everyone just rushed back again.

We played with a lot of bands and a lot of good guitarists – we played with Clapton and Mayall - and they were all playing Les Pauls and were having high-gain sound. But with him it was a Marshall and the sound from his guitar was interesting. With most guitarists you can watch them and get a rough idea of what they're doing and what scales and box-scales and things they're doing to get that sound, but I couldn't work out what Hendrix was doing. It was upside-down guitar, but it was, 'What is he doing? How is he achieving that?' He was doing things I'd never seen anyone do before.

All the other guitarists I'd seen seemed to be very precious about the instrument, but he wasn't. When he started shoving the Strat across the side of his Marshall stack, my first thought was, 'Holy sacrilege.' There was no way we could afford any Fender Strats or Telecasters, because they were pretty expensive. You had groups like The Zombies and The Nashville Teens and suddenly you've got this complete contrast to anything you've ever seen before, and I think most people watching had that puzzlement.

The quality of sound was excellent. The other thing was, I don't know how much rehearsal they'd had but the other guys seemed to be following him. I wouldn't call them a tight three-piece at that point. It was Hendrix, and the other two were just doing what they needed to do or were finding their way, because a lot of the stuff he was doing had weird timing.

He did all the stuff with his teeth and behind the back but what impressed me most is that technical ability he had. He didn't have, as far as I could see, a huge pair of hands but he had a way of playing that nobody else had. He played 'Hey Joe' and a lot of other familiar stuff but a lot of his set was blues. He'd just developed this technique. I had no idea what he was doing but it was fascinating watching him abuse his Strat.

Then it got to the end of the set, where he threw the Strat on the floor with the volume full up and just walked off the stage. There was this huge feedback and that was it. The roadie came on, switched the amps off and that was the end of the show.

It was a seminal, 'What have I just seen?' moment. In those days, a lot of bands did covers and you were learning other people's music. With his music, it didn't seem to have any sort of format as such. It's only as the years have gone on that that gig has assumed a real big part of our lives.

When he died, it was a bit like Kennedy. You began to hear on the grapevine he was being controlled by – I wouldn't call them Mafia – the big guys in the States. So he tended to do what he was told. It seemed to me he was on the cusp of moving into another type of music. If he'd lived a bit longer I wonder which way he would have taken his music and if it might have been more towards jazz or that side of things. I think he got a little manipulated and controlled. It was such a waste. I wonder if some of the substance abuse was to help him through a lot of these things.

The thing I remember most is how reserved he was off stage. It was really black and white between the on-stage and off-stage Hendrix.

DOROTHY BALLROOM

15 FEBRUARY 1967, CAMBRIDGE, UK

I WAS THERE: MICK POTTER

The Jimi Hendrix Experience was supported by my band, The Breed, from Cambridge. Tickets were 10/6 (53p) and it all took place in the main ballroom. Our meeting or get-together was in the dressing room above the main ballroom stage. 'Hey Joe' had just been released and was climbing the charts. Speaking to Jimi was so natural, he made us feel very much at ease. He wanted to try Ray's guitar, even though it was right-handed. It made no difference, he just made it sing. Apparently, he had a Walsall pedal and Francis our drummer said he had some Swan Lighter Fluid to enable him to burn his guitar on stage! Mitch Mitchell also spoke at length with us and swapped ideas. Apparently, he chatted up Francis's now-wife of many years outside. I hasten to say they were not an item in those early teenage days. We were very young, just normal lads in a successful local band, not realising what Jimi Hendrix was to become today - a true legend loved by all.

I WAS THERE: BARRY GAWTHROP

I was a roadie for a local band agency run by Ken Stevens and Dave Kidd. The Dorothy was a great venue split over many floors, with three or four music rooms. At one end was the Oak Room, a low-ceilinged, panelled room. In the middle was the main ballroom, a big space with a sprung floor - a proper ballroom. At the other end, right at the top of many flights of stairs, was a small room called by the bands the 'sweat-box'. When it got hot, and it did, the water ran down the walls. The band I was with was playing in the Oak Room, Geno Washington and the Ram Jam Band were in the ballroom, and Jimi was in the sweat-box. In Cambridge at the time it was mostly soul dance, and Geno was the main attraction. Jimi was unknown. I popped in to see him and the music was not what I had heard before and very, very loud. At the end of his set he placed his guitar down and left it and it started to feed back. His roadie came running at speed to sort it out.

My local school band was Jokers Wild, who had David Gilmour on guitar, who later joined Pink Floyd. Locals did not understand their music unless you were on the same drugs. At the time the local band that could pack venues was The Soul Committee, a seven piece-brass section. Dick Parry was in the group and went on to work with Pink Floyd. They were fronted by two USAF black guys, Fitz and Dennis from the local air base. They were fantastic - like Sam and Dave.

I WAS THERE: PAUL MORGAN, AGE 17

The Dot (known as 'the Dot' to locals) was a unique venue in as much as you could find all ages (often from the same families but not all out together) enjoying themselves in as many as four different music spaces plus at least two bars within one building. The large ballroom might have had a dance band playing for the older generation, demonstrating their ballroom skills. Stairs from this level would take the younger ones up to the top of the building. At one end there was a small room known as 'The Sweat Box', which I recall was used for local bands and maybe discos. Through a large bar at the other end and up more stairs was what was called The Blue Room, used for jazz and other music and visiting bands.

My recollection of the night Hendrix played there is that I would have gone to the Dot with friends that had purchased tickets earlier in the week. We probably would have met in the Prince of Wales Bar in the basement of the same building. It truly was a great venue and also housed a cake and bread shop and coffee bar and tea rooms. It now houses a very large Waterstones bookshop.

Although Cambridge is a university city, the Dot was frequented mainly by locals. Few from the academic community would have been there, maybe partly because there was a strong 'anti-gown' feeling in the town in those days, especially from the young. At this time myself and most of my friends were into our fashion and were all Mods. We liked the styles of music that were current for our creed, such as soul, R&B, Motown, Stax and more. Jimi Hendrix we would have considered to be more of a

Paul was a Mod but wasn't going to miss Hendrix at The Dot

hippy. I highlight this because you might expect that us Mods might not want to be at this gig. However, as a group of young men and women at that time we would go to many music events, including dances and discos, and would always be right at the front, as close to the stage and the band as we could get. And as by now Hendrix was well known and had songs in the charts, there was no way we were going to miss him. As there would be a pretty large crowd the venue owners decided to use the ballroom, as it was the larger space. Two abiding memories are of Hendrix standing right in front of me, slightly raised on a small stage playing his guitar with his teeth. As I left the venue, a group of four guys were getting a hard time about their appearance from some local lads as they climbed into an MG 1100, a trendy car in its day. One of the four had an Afro hairdo and was putting a guitar case in the boot of the car. The others must have been the Experience and maybe their driver. They drove away.

RICKY TICK CLUB, THAMES HOTEL

17 FEBRUARY 1967, WINDSOR, UK

I WAS THERE: VICKI FIELDING, AGE 16

I was 16 and had to go and see him. Chas Chandler was standing behind me, very near the stage. Fantastic show - he was playing guitar behind his back and with his teeth.

I WAS THERE: JOHN MANSFIELD

I founded the Ricky Tick Club. We hosted Jimi Hendrix and a load of other big names. When I came out of the army in December 1958 I went to a jazz club in Windsor and there were only about 10 people there and nearly all of them male. I said to the bandleader running the club it was like a gay club. I said, 'You want to get some girls in here.' I went to the local Wimpy bar and the International Club, where I persuaded all the foreign girls to go there. When word got around that all the girls were at the Star and Garter in Windsor, all the boys started going there. It became very popular. Then the bandleader said, 'Why don't you run the club? I'll just run the band.' So it started off there.

Somebody mentioned to me in '62 that there were bands playing in Ealing and one of them was called Alexis Korner. I booked Alexis and he went down very well and I said, 'Can you play next week?' He said, 'No', and I said, 'Do you know anybody else I can book?' He said, 'Why don't you book the Rolling Stones? They play at the Ealing Club.' I booked them, I think, 45 times in 15 months. At that time there were only a few groups to book. Brian (Jones) used to come to Windsor a lot. He always spoke to the fans and bought them drinks. Mick Jagger and the rest of the band were so tight, they wouldn't spend a penny.

I put a show on once in Slough at the British Legion and booked five times in Maidenhead and booked maybe 15 times in Reading but booked in three or four different venues. There was the St John's ambulance hall, a big ballroom called the Oxford Ballroom in Chatham Street, and the Olympic Ballroom. The Ricky Tick was a badge I placed on that venue for the evening.

I didn't have an office. I used to sand and repair floors. But it was usually in empty houses, so if I didn't turn up for a few days it didn't matter so much. I used to use the call-box at Windsor railway station to make and receive telephone calls. Quite often I'd get people phoning up the number. I'd be standing and waiting in line and when the phone rang I used to push to the front, push people out of the way, say, 'That's for me'.

You wouldn't do it today. You've got to think about fire regulations, but we'd get 200 to 300 people in. There was a back door with a staircase and when people went out we used to let people in. You used to have to queue to come back in again.

We went from the Star and Garter to a very large country mansion by the river called Clewer Mead. From there we went to the Thames

Hotel, which is where we had Jimi. Then we had him at Hounslow. In America black people were looked down upon and when they came to England they were treated like gods. They liked and respected English people. Jimi Hendrix. Howlin' Wolf. Sonny Boy Williamson - we had them all.

I WAS THERE: MARTIN FUGGLES

The Ricky Tick was an old mansion house. They covered the walls in black paper, then painted negro faces on the wall. The Ricky Tick grew out of a trad jazz club that John Mansfield and Philip Hayward set up. Philip was the brains behind the outfit and John was the doer. That's probably a bit unfair and it is memories of 50 years ago, but it was Philip who recruited me to DJ there rather than John. The way I remember it is that Philip was always in the foreground and John tended to be in the background.

They started as a trad jazz club and John was significant in getting them into what was then labelled the R&B scene, starting with Alexis Korner in late '62. The following week they put on a band called the Rolling Stones right at the beginning of their existence.

That's where they started growing. Through the mid-Sixties they were promoting all over the Home Counties. Windsor was always the headquarters, but they must have promoted at 20, even 30 different venues during that 1963-67 period.

I was DJ-ing in Windsor through the mid Sixties when it was at its peak. Windsor was very much a Mod venue, never as big as places like the Twisted Wheel in Manchester but still big down south.

We worked in conjunction sometimes with some of the London clubs in having artists over from the States that we would put on and then they'd go and perform in London as well.

Philip recognised that the music scene was changing, the Mod scene was certainly changing, and they were moving on from people like Georgie Fame and Geno Washington and the Ram Jam Band, probably the two biggest draws at Windsor.

In late '66, early '67 there were new names on the scene like Cream, Pink Floyd and a certain Mr Hendrix. They were coming in as the Ricky Tick was tailing off. In mid '67 they stopped. Philip went off on his own to take over another place, more of a nightclub-type venue, which is how I think he saw the music scene evolving and where he felt the future was likely to be, and where he was more likely to make money doing that.

John went off and had a junkshop-cum-second-hand furniture shop.

I only DJ-ed on one occasion with Jimi Hendrix. It was a Friday night. I've got my old diary and I wasn't impressed. I wrote, 'Down to work at the Thames Hotel (Jimi Hendrix). Not much cop.' That was probably flavoured by the fact that I was still a soul man really.

He also appeared two or three times at the Hounslow Ricky Tick. That club was opposite the bus station. Jimi appeared there in November and December 1966 and February 1967, when I think they also put him on in Newbury.

It was an amazing place. They'd blocked out the windows. They had a coffee bar with an open fire and had another room with a television in it, so you could go to a gig on a Saturday night and not miss *Match of the Day*. There was no drinks licence. It was just Pepsi. I remember one occasion when there was a bottle of Coke on the organ. Zoot Money was playing, and it was a very pale colour and I reckon it was seven-eighths whisky. It was an amazing place and an amazing atmosphere and featured in the film *Blow Up*. But filming got delayed and they had to give up the lease, so they had to recreate a couple of rooms of the Ricky Tick in Elstree Studios.

Of the bands we had at the Ricky Tick, Geno Washington and the Ram Jam Band were my favourites. At the time they were covering mainly Atlantic and Stax songs – Otis Redding and Wilson Pickett, that sort of thing – and I have to say that was probably my favourite. The new bands - Cream, Hendrix, Pink Floyd – didn't do it for me.

When the Ricky Tick closed, I stopped deejaying. The music scene was changing in a direction I didn't want to go, so I put the records away and only got them out about 45 years later.

I WAS THERE: PETER HATHERLY, AGE 17

I seem to remember it wasn't packed. I went to the Ricky Tick maybe twice a week from mid-1965 to when it finally shut in late 1967. My most memorable night was in July 1966. We were waiting for Solomon Burke to appear. He was to be backed by Bluesology, who had to do an extended set as he didn't arrive until 10.30ish. I remember talking to Elton John, who was then just Reg the keyboard player, about his uncle Roy Dwight, who broke his leg playing for Nottingham Forest in the 1959 FA Cup Final. I was also a big fan of Billy Stewart, who appeared on a Sunday in the Summer of '66 to quite a small gathering. He was excellent, just as the record.

I WAS THERE: ROGER HOUGH

I saw Jimi at the Thames Hotel Ricky Tick when he had only released one single, 'Hey Joe', which he played along with 'Stone Free'. He was absolutely fantastic live. Jaw-dropping. It was love at first sight.

I WAS THERE: PETER CAVANAGH

I was pressed against the window at the back and, not being very tall, had to keep jumping up and down to get a glimpse of him. I remember him playing the guitar with his teeth and at one time someone opened the window where I was, the crowd pushed back, and I tumbled out onto the pavement. I was pulled back inside, and the window was shut again.

I WAS THERE: DAVID MATTHEWS, AGE 15

They produced a very big sound, similar to Cream. However, Jimi was a showman. I'd seen him before in a hall in lsleworth, when he played the blues. Only when 'Hey Joe' was released did I realise who he was. I used to thumb a lift home after the band had finished.

On 20 February 1967 The Jimi Hendrix Experience were drafted in as a last-minute replacement for British teen idol Dave Berry. A poster for the show read: 'Bannister Promotions Present: Mon. Feb 20th. Please note change of programme, instead of Dave Berry we now present The Jimi Hendrix Experience (Hey Joe)'.

PAVILION

20 FEBRUARY 1967, BATH, UK

I WAS THERE: RALPH WHITE, AGE 17

Dave Berry was ill and Jimi stepped in. It was a Mod venue and I think Small Faces were the support act, but my memory isn't what it was. He converted 150 Mods - they couldn't believe what they were seeing and hearing!

I WAS THERE: MARK GREEN, AGE 18

My wife was only 15 and she'd rush out of school, do her homework and we'd go down, virtually every Monday. A lot of us would go when we were teenagers and see the bands. We'd catch the bus down and the late bus home. You didn't have to buy a ticket before, you could buy them on the door. It was a standing venue and women used to dance around their handbags.

He was on *Top of the Pops* the Thursday before. I was quite lucky. He was mingling with the audience before he went up. I was about a yard from him. He was chewing a matchstick.

On stage, he did his usual thing, gyrating over the guitar, but stopped in the middle of one song and said, 'You good people have paid good money to see me. My guitar's out of tune.' So he stopped right in the middle, retuned his guitar then started again, which I thought was very professional of him.

ROUNDHOUSE
Chalk Farm Road, N.W.1
Wednesday, February 22nd, 7.30–11.30
the
JIMI HENDRIX
E X P E R I E N C E
and
THE FLIES
with
SANDY & HILARY
Tickets 5/- in advance or 6/6 at the door

ROUNDHOUSE

22 FEBRUARY 1967, LONDON, UK

I WAS THERE: VALERIE DUNN

I'd just started art school. We had rag week on and thought it would be really good if we could kidnap Jimi Hendrix. When we went to see him at the Roundhouse, we managed to get to the side of the stage before he went on stage and asked him, 'Look, it's our rag week. Would you mind if we just sort of kidnapped you?' He was so sweet. He just turned around and said, 'Guys, I would absolutely love you to, but really don't think it would be possible.' Then he went on stage and that was that. He politely declined.

To see him at the Roundhouse in those days - because it's a small venue - it was absolutely brilliant. Everything was so intimate. And you could talk to them.

I WAS THERE: STASH KLOSSOWSKI DE ROLA

My first impression of Jimi Hendrix was that he was so polite that I thought he was being sarcastic. He was the most softly-spoken person, the most polite human being I'd ever met. He would say things like, 'Would you care to take a seat?' He was utterly delightful, and so we became fast friends there and then and saw quite a bit of each other on various occasions.

When he played the Roundhouse, I had this driver who later on worked for Keith Richards, and we were tooling around in my car and I sent my driver in and said, 'Tell them Prince Stash is here and see what happens', because I didn't have a ticket or anything. I stayed in the car. Much to my amazement, in full stage regalia, Jimi Hendrix came to get me out of the car and take me backstage.

Brian Jones took me round to meet Jimi, who was having a party at his flat in honour of having just received the acetates for the *Are You Experienced* album. We shared an amazing experience. It was as exciting for the band and Jimi as it was for us to listen to it for the first time. It wasn't like the jaded modern age. The whole night we listened to those tracks over and over again, with absolute amazement and great joy.

Jimi was fascinated by all these white girls. They were fascinated with him. There was this very pretty French girl at his flat when we were listening to the acetates and she called out to me plaintively that she was a French girl and she said, 'Oh Stash, you don't remember me?' I looked at her and she was amazingly pretty, and she said, 'I used to be Ronnie Bird's bird.' He had all these girls all around him all the time. And he was fun to be with. One will never see the likes of him again.

Just before Brian and I got busted and they took my passport, there was a plan that we would all be going to Monterey. We would be at the

Speakeasy every night, with Roger Daltrey and Townshend and so on and so forth, and Jimi was there and he was saying it was going to be fabulous. It was a terrible disappointment when I couldn't go. I was forced to stay in England until Lord Londonderry managed through some connection of his to get Roy Jenkins, the Home Secretary, to force the police to give me back my passport. But it took ages. Those trumped- up charges against Brian and myself ruined everything.

To see Jimi play, to watch him operate, was extraordinary. He'd tune his own guitar. Nowadays you have roadies and tuners and the whole deal and a whole row of guitars. But Jimi would sit in front of the audience, retune his Strat and say, 'That's because we care.'

Once we were in a taxi and I looked at him and thought, 'I wonder how old he is?' He looked like an older blues man compared to us. I asked, 'How old are you?' And when he said, I said 'Wow' and he said, 'I know I look much older. That's because I slept outside a great deal.'

To have known people like that is an extraordinary privilege. Those were fabulous times. The world was so hostile to our appearance, everybody was sarcastic, and the straight world was trying to put you down, which made all of us freaks very close to one another. Someone asked me, 'What did Brian think about Jimi's music?' I said, 'Look, you've got it all wrong.' We didn't think about this music. We felt it. The great communion with all of us that were playing that music and loving that music was that when we listened to each other's stuff, we felt very deeply that it was a shared 'wow' feeling. One wasn't some sort of critic that dissected things. It was ridiculous to even talk in those terms. It was all about feeling rather than thinking.

I wasn't in England at the time that he died. I was horrified. But there'd been these terrible shocking deaths of friends, of young people who died suddenly, and Brian was absolutely the most devastating one. Jimi burnt the candles at both ends. We had all been expecting each other to die. Even when I met Brian Jones, I was in Vince Taylor's band and we were saying to people, 'We're the 'Never Reach 25' group'. We were saying that at 23, living really dangerously.

PAVILION

23 FEBRUARY 1967, WORTHING, UK

I WAS THERE: RON RICHARDSON, AGE 18

I was a young and very impressionable 18-year old. What an electric night that was, Jimi playing the guitar with his crotch at times!

All the big acts came to Worthing in those good old days and I'd also seen incredible guitar-playing from Eric Clapton and Pete Townshend that year, but Jimi was something completely different. Dirty guitar-playing! Worthing Pavilion theatre is a very intimate venue, with the crowd in a semi-circle and never far from the stage. Surprisingly (I didn't really like any of their records) one of the best acts musically I ever saw there was Dave Dee, Dozy, Beaky, Mick and Titch.

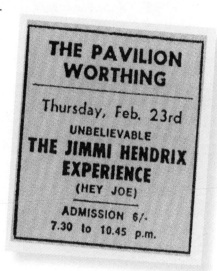

THE PAVILION WORTHING

Thursday, Feb. 23rd

UNBELIEVABLE

THE JIMMI HENDRIX EXPERIENCE

(HEY JOE)

ADMISSION 6/-

7.30 to 10.45 p.m.

I WAS THERE: IAN SCOTT, AGE 19

Promoter Fred Bannister put on gigs every Thursday at the Pier Pavilion (as it was then) or the Assembly Hall. The Pavilion was, and still is, the nicer venue. I remember Jimi wearing red cord Levi jeans and his customary 18th-century military tunic. I remember Noel Redding cracking an off-colour joke about Donald Campbell, who'd lost his life on Coniston Water the previous month, and Jimi remarking, 'Is there a hospital round here, 'cos this guy's sick!' He finished the set with a barnstorming 'Wild Thing'. There were rumours of women fleeing the auditorium in terror at the end. I didn't witness this myself. Having been used to seeing groups like Herman's Hermits and the Applejacks, it certainly was a brain shaker.

I WAS THERE: JOHN FINCH

Jimi broke a string during the first song, which I think was 'Hey Joe'. The one thing that struck me then was his charisma and showmanship. He did a fine rendition of Bob Dylan's 'Like a Rolling Stone' and 'Catfish Blues' by Muddy Waters. He inspired me so much that I've been in a Hendrix tribute band, Dolly Dagger, for the last 32 years.

PAVILION

23 FEBRUARY 1967, WORTHING, UK

I WAS THERE: DENISE TAYLER, AGE 16

I'd go every Thursday and meet my schoolmates there. Then, as I got older, I used to meet the odd boyfriend there. There was no alcohol. They sold Coca Colas out of crates in the bar, which was just a room. I had to run out of there as the bands were finishing at half past 10, run up to the pier and get the quarter to 11 bus home back to Goring, about three miles from town, because it was a school night. A lot of my friends weren't allowed to go.

Sometimes the bands would come into the room where they served the drinks and I'd get an autograph. Most of the time they just wanted to shoot back to London. Once, as I was leaving, Peter Green from Fleetwood Mac stuck his head out of the band's van and said, 'Excuse me love, which way to the A24 to London?' I pointed along the road and went, 'That way!'

Some of the older girls were groupies. I was a bit innocent. I didn't quite know what it meant. But there was a girl in the older years in my school who'd show off she'd been to bed with Dave Dee, Dozy, Beaky, Mitch AND Titch! Whether it was true or not I don't know. I never used to go around the back. Quite often I'd get right down to the front and pull on their trouser legs.

Jimi Hendrix was amazing. He was so beautiful. He had such big eyes. I didn't normally like the butch ones with the moustaches. I liked the pretty ones like Stevie Marriott and didn't ever think I would fancy Hendrix. He was too butch for me. But when I saw him, I was right at the front and he had bright red flared trousers on and a bright red military jacket. And he had such a lovely smile.

He came right down to the front and I pulled on his trouser leg to get his attention and he gave me this amazing smile and had that massive big hair. Then he went a bit spacey. Whether that was, drugs or not, I don't know. But he started playing 'Hey Joe'. He played several tracks with his teeth. There was so much vibration that he played several tracks on his guitar with the vibration on the stage. When I came out of there I was deaf for a couple of hours. It was only six bob (30p) to get in.

I remember getting the bus home and thinking, 'He is so beautiful and the music is so amazing.' He just had this charisma, and the way he looked into my eyes. My Mum said, 'Oh, it's probably just drugs.' When 'Purple Haze' came out, Mum said it was a drug record and I said it was a love track. We had arguments about my putting it on.

LEICESTER COLLEGES OF ART & TECHNOLOGY

24 FEBRUARY 1967, LEICESTER, UK

I WAS THERE: ANDY GOODWIN

I got to see Jimi Hendrix by chance, owing to me working in the kitchens of a large hotel in Leicester where they had young students from various colleges doing part-time work in the evenings. One such chap was flogging tickets to see Jimi Hendrix. I'd never heard of him but took up his offer and went along. Boy, I'm glad I did. He said very little on stage, but his singing and guitar were out of this world. Plucking the strings of his Stratocaster behind his back and also plucking it with his teeth. I was mesmerised and it's a memory that has never left me. Having seen The Beatles and the Stones previously, I still think he was the best live act I've ever seen.

I WAS THERE: MIKE PRUDEN

The gig I went to was held in the hall that was part of the polytechnic, near the Magazine pub. I was quite a purist blues fan and didn't expect him to be as good as he was. But he was excellent and had a great charisma. Mitch Mitchell and Noel Redding were also great and I'm sure they played 'Hey Joe', 'Purple Haze' and 'Red House'.

CORN EXCHANGE

25 FEBRUARY 1967, CHELMSFORD, UK

I WAS THERE: MARION PARKHURST - NEE CLEMENTS

I remember thinking he looked very scruffy, with a scarf tied round his neck. But his playing was amazing. He played the guitar with his teeth and behind his back.

THE SPEAKEASY

8 MARCH 1967, LONDON, UK

I WAS THERE: JEFF BECK

For me, the first shockwave was Jimi Hendrix. That was the major thing that shook everybody up. Even though we'd all established ourselves as fairly safe in the guitar field, he came along and reset all of the rules in one evening.

Hull's Skyline Ballroom was situated on the fourth floor of the Co-op building in Jameson Street. It was used as a restaurant during the day but regularly cleared on evenings to turn the space into a ballroom, with bands using the kitchens as a communal dressing room. When Hendrix appeared there he mingled with the other bands on the bill, including local outfit The Mandrakes, featuring a young Robert Palmer on lead vocals. When The Mandrakes' second guitarist broke a string, Hendrix removed one from his own guitar and restrung it for him.

THURSDAY, MARCH 9th
8 p.m. to 1 a.m. Continuous Dancing to the
JIMI HENDRIX EXPERIENCE
SUPPORTING GROUPS
THE FAMILY   THE SMALL FOUR
THE STROLLERS   THE MANDRAKES
Admission   Tickets from the
12/6   Skyline Box Office
           or the Boutique
           First Floor, Jameson Street
           LATE TRANSPORT
SKYLINE
BALLROOM
JAMESON STREET, HULL

Patricia paid 10/6 to dance to Jimi

SKYLINE BALLROOM

9 MARCH 1967, HULL, UK

I WAS THERE: PATRICIA CHAPMAN, AGE 17

I think tickets were 10 shillings and sixpence (53p). I stood inches away from him, dancing with my friend, in what was a very small room.

I WAS THERE: CHUCK MADSEN

My wife and I were at that gig, but I cannot recall who the supporting acts were. I keep getting mixed up with a gig featuring The Cream with Ginger Baker, Jack Bruce and a poor 'guitar player'. I'm now 75, and some other aspects of an ageing memory is that I can't remember whether the cost of a ticket was 5 or 10 shillings (25p or 50p). Another vivid memory is the breakdown of the sound system for about 30 minutes. Hendrix left the stage, was full of sincere apologies and was so polite. He returned to give a performance unlike anything ever heard. Absolutely superb.

CLUB A GO GO

10 MARCH 1967, NEWCASTLE UPON TYNE, UK

I WAS THERE: COLIN BRANTHWAITE

The thing I can't remember is how I got the ticket. I was a member, but did I get it in advance or did I queue? I can't remember what the weather was like either, but it was probably cool. As I travelled by train from Sunderland regularly to go to the club, I got to know the doorman, so maybe he let me queue-jump. I only know that I got in with my two mates.

Colin was underage but went for a pre-gig pint all the same

Beforehand we went for a couple of pints in The Haymarket pub as we knew they served underage drinkers. Often bands playing at the Go Go would be in there before and we were hoping the Hendrix entourage would be. No such luck, so we headed to the club to make sure we got a good standing place. The room was packed but navigable.

We stood for what seemed an age and could see quite well as I'm 6ft 2 and one of my friends was 6ft 4. We muscled forward and eventually were told Jimi would be on soon. I seem to remember the back of the stage had a Hendrix cartoon that someone had drawn. A similar one had been done for The Who.

I don't remember a support band. The lights went down and Jimi and The Experience came on. The place lifted and people piled forward. It was really uncomfortable and really hot. There was no air con or health and safety then. As usual he had bright, vivid clothes on and I think a bandana. He may even have been smoking a cigarette. It was just awesome, seeing him standing in front of us and playing live. I felt so lucky.

I can't remember the first number, but it was loud. As we were slowly being crushed to oblivion we noticed a huge gap at the back had emerged. At that point we decided to move back and found an excellent viewpoint on a raised seating area facing the stage. From then on it was perfect. An excellent vista and the sound less distorted.

The band played for I don't know how long but included 'Hey Joe' and a few blues numbers and quite a bit of ad lib and guitar theatrics and solos. He famously slid his guitar up and down on his Marshall and as he did so the neck went through the ceiling and smoke billowed from the speaker. No one moved! I had never seen anything or heard anything like it before, although The Who and Cream came pretty close.

The place was lifting and the atmosphere electric. We were all just staring and applauding and almost in a state of euphoria when it ended.

I wish I could remember exactly what he played and in what order, but it doesn't really matter now. Suddenly it was all over after an hour or so. We ran to try and get in the Jazz Lounge to see him where he was to appear later, but had no chance of getting in. So it was the last train home from a night I've never forgotten.

I WAS THERE: IAN DALGLIESH

I parked my scooter alongside a dozen or so others and joined the queue outside the Go Go. For the sum of six shillings (30p) entrance fee we were in. As it was my regular haunt we were soon inside and took up our regular position at the left of the small stage. The room was packed and, as always when a top band was on, the atmosphere was electric and the walls dripping with condensation. Wow - what a sound! Nothing like that had ever been heard there before. I can't recall the set-list but the highlights for me were 'Foxy Lady' and my favourite, 'Stone Free'. Most people remember when he hit the ceiling with his guitar and then continued to poke more holes in the plaster until his Afro was covered in powdered plaster.

I WAS THERE: ADRIAN HERVEY

I was a member of the club from 1962 to its demise. Prior to that date I worked in London and frequented the Marquee, where the resident band were Alexis Korner's Blues Incorporated. The first group I saw in Newcastle was in a condemned building. The Animals sounded really raw and exciting and went on to become the resident band in the A Go Go. Many great bands played at the club over the years, including guests from the States.

The morning of Jimi Hendrix`s gig, I bought a copy of *Are You Experienced*. The queue outside the club stretched right along the street but as a member I got straight in and paid, I think, six shillings (30p). We stood at one corner of the stage and listened to a sound unlike any before. The club was always big on dancing, but this was music that demanded listening to.

I remember one day my son bringing some friends back to our house and introducing me to them, saying, 'This is my father, he saw Jimi Hendrix!' Great days.

The Jimi Hendrix Experience appeared at the International Club in Leeds, UK on 11 March 1967. Despite 'Hey Joe' being in the charts that week, local promoter Stuart Frais remembers the Lewis Street club being 'virtually empty'. Frais promoted the Leeds show and the following two nights, after paying a total fee of £60 for the Experience for three dates, having booked them before 'Hey Joe' broke.

The following day, The Jimi Hendrix Experience performed at the Gyro Club, located in the Troutbeck Hotel in Ilkey, Yorkshire after spending the afternoon at the town's Essoldo cinema. However, the show was suspended two numbers in when the police arrived and cleared the room due to safety concerns caused by the size of the crowd, estimated at 900. The Troutbeck is now a residential care home.

Later in March 1967 as 'Purple Haze' entered the UK singles chart, Hendrix sold a Fender Stratocaster guitar at Selmer's Music Store in central London, where Paul Kossoff, later to form Free, worked as a sales assistant.

SELMER'S MUSIC STORE

23 MARCH 1967, LONDON, UK

I WAS THERE: PAUL KOSSOFF

He had an odd look about him and smelled strange. He started playing some chord stuff like in 'Little Wing', and the salesman looked at him and couldn't believe it. Just seeing him really freaked me out. I just loved him to death. He was my hero.

GUILDHALL

23 MARCH 1967, SOUTHAMPTON, UK

I WAS THERE: RICHARD HAYES

I ended up in a band called John Drevar's Expression on keyboards and as I recall I went to see The Alan Bown Set with our guitarist Melvin. I believe they didn't show through illness and Jimi replaced them. I seem to remember we were offered a refund at the door. This might have explained the poor turnout, as he was unknown.

But we went in. Melvin was gob-smacked and we easily stood near the stage. We must have heard one of the first live versions of 'Hey Joe' – he announced its release. Melv is no longer with us but he and the band got to play with Jimi at Paris Olympia the week before I joined them.

I WAS THERE: FRANK PEARCE

If my memory serves me correctly, the original concert was for Geno Washington and the Ram Jam Band on that date, but that was cancelled last minute and the Alan Bown Set were headlining. Jimi Hendrix was the support. Most people had come to watch and listen to funky soul music. Hendrix was a complete surprise and many people went to the bar not understanding quite what to make of this extravagant guitarist. The musos in the audience were amazed and slightly baffled by his expertise and showmanship. I was taken aback at this life-force and unsure of this new style of rock/blues music. I later saw Hendrix again at the Isle of Wight Festival, shortly before he died, and appreciated him a lot more. Around that time I saw many bands at the Guildhall, some quite famous as well as up and coming ones, including Rod Stewart with the Soul Agents. My last gig there was a sold-out gig for Joe Bonamassa - Jimi would have liked that as an axe-man.

STARLIGHT ROOM

25 MARCH 1967, GLIDERDOME, BOSTON, UK

I WAS THERE: MICK FRANKS

I've always been a harmony freak – The Beach Boys, The Four Seasons, that kind of thing. And I was in a band called The Sons of Adam and the singer got married and it all fell through. We had a good four years with them. These guys approached me and said they wanted to start a harmony group where everybody can play and sing at the same time. We got together, did a couple of rehearsals and got a good harmony sound. One of the guys was really good on arranging.

We started up in August '66. We did the Gliderdome a few times. We arrived there and there was his name on the bill. Jimi was in the next dressing room to us. He chatted with us and played one of our guitars. Although he was left- handed, he tried to play our 12-string Rickenbacker and it was amazing. He was the most quiet, polite, shy gentleman you could wish to meet.

Mick Franks still has a tone knob from one of Jimi's guitars and a signed card

We were doing a soundcheck at the beginning of the evening and Mitch Mitchell walked in and said, 'That cymbal! That is incredible. Do you want to sell it?' I said, 'No way', because a drummer idolises his cymbals more than he does his drums. Cymbals are so individual, like fingerprints. I said, 'I'm not selling that, no.' When I think about that now, that cymbal could have been on the recordings made by The Jimi Hendrix Experience. It was a Zildjan. You've got two main types of cymbal. You've got a ride, which you actually play your rhythm with, and you have a crash cymbal which you hit on the corner and it reaches its maximum vibration. This was a ride crash. It was in between the two. It's how the alloy is formed, and that cymbal got crashier and crashier as it matured. I sold it in the end.

That particular night, there was a revolving stage. When he went on stage he was a monster. He finished with 'Wild Thing' by The Troggs. He was kneeling on the guitar, which might be when he knocked one of the knobs off, the stage went around, and we started with a Beach Boys number. What a contrast. Everybody went to the bar for a drink. They didn't care tuppence for us after seeing what they'd just seen. It was just amazing.

He was playing the guitar on the mic. stand and one of the knobs caught and it dropped off the tone-knob from the Strat. There's a photograph of Jimi with the guitar taken the following night and it shows the guitar with the knob missing. While we

were packing up at the end of the night, Pete the roadie spoke to him in the dressing room. He picked this knob up off the floor and kept it together with their autographs. He sold it five or six years ago. Three thousand quid he got, for a little bit of plastic.

Jimi, Cat Stevens, Engelbert and Gary Leeds.

On 31 March 1967, The Jimi Hendrix Experience embarked upon their first UK tour along with The Walker Brothers, Cat Stevens, Engelbert Humperdinck, The Californians and The Quotations. Aware that he didn't necessarily appeal to a Humperdinck audience, Jimi told Keith Altham of the New Musical Express, 'We'll play for ourselves – we've done it before, where the audience stands about with their mouths open and you have to wait 10 minutes before they clap.'

ODEON

5 APRIL 1967, LEEDS, UK

I WAS THERE: BEV HENRY, AGE 13

That evening in 1967 was so rare. I often think I must have dreamt it. That night was my 13th birthday. The headline act was The Walker Brothers, who were my passion at the time. My parents bought two tickets and I went with my best friend Helen. Engelbert opened the

Bev barely remembers Jimi's performance at the Odeon

show. Jimi and Cat Stevens were in between, before The Walker Brothers. Sadly, I can't remember much about Jimi's performance. My music preferences were different then. My 14th birthday was very boring by comparison. Looking for excitement I bought a packet of cigarettes from a machine close to home. Not a wise move in retrospect.

I WAS THERE: PAULINE TROUSDALE

My cousin and I sat next to Jimi in The Vine before the gig. We hadn't a clue who he was, but soon found out! We were a bit gob-smacked as he smashed his guitar at the end of his act. We didn't blame him though - everybody was screaming for The Walker Brothers. Oh, those innocent days! We never dreamt he'd become so famous. I'll never forget that night.

I WAS THERE: BILLY WALKER

I went across to The Vine pub, opposite the stage door. Everybody was milling around the theatre, going in to see the show and coming out from the first performance. I stood in the doorway and it was just me and the barman. The door opens and in walks His Royal Highness, Jimi Marshall Hendrix. I just looked at Jimi and could see he had skin problems on his face, which we all had in those days.

A lot of the people who came to see the show would say, 'Oh, we came to see Cat Stevens'. But I'd come to see Jimi. I hadn't come to worship the Walker Brothers or anybody else.

Jimi walked in with Mitch Mitchell. They sat in the corner, about 25 metres away. Mitch went to the bar and ordered two pints. Jimi was wearing the Sgt. Pepper's Heart Club attire, a la John Lennon, and had worn-down boots. His stage boots were his off-stage boots.

I didn't go up and say, 'Can I have your autograph?' That was the wrong moment. I finished my drink and left quietly. I'd come within a metre of him.

I went to see the show and he did 'Like a Rolling Stone'. He must have made it about eight minutes long, maybe more. He also did 'Wild Thing' and 'Hey Joe' and when he finished he set fire to his guitar. He played the guitar with his teeth. It was him hitting the guitar on full volume, then he would make out he was playing with his teeth - a pure theatrical occasion.

Meeting him in the pub was a dream moment for me. My dream came true without me even wishing it.

ABC THEATRE

7 APRIL 1967, CARLISLE, UK

I WAS THERE: HOWARD GOODALL, AGE 9

My family stayed the night in a hotel in Carlisle, the first and only time as a child that I stayed in a hotel, as we misjudged the drive and the traffic to get to our campsite in Oba, Scotland. I saw Hendrix at breakfast the next morning. My mother heard the gig from the bathroom whilst she was having a bath.

ABC THEATRE

8 APRIL 1967, CHESTERFIELD, UK

I WAS THERE: MURRAY CLAYTON, AGE 15

I went to see Hendrix at the ABC on one of the many package tours of that era. Although I can't remember what he played, I remember him doing the thing with the pyrotechnics and seemingly setting fire to his guitar.

I WAS THERE: MICHAEL RANDALL

My late mother-in-law was at a nightclub, The New Carlton Club, near Chesterfield. Late in the evening, after the ABC concerts, Hendrix, The Experience and other members of the tour arrived at the nightclub to relax. Hendrix, The Experience, Humperdinck and others autographed menus and beermats.

I WAS THERE: MARIA TRACEY

My Mum, Valerie Tracey, always tells me I went to see him before I was even born. I was born in July 1967. For a tiny town like Chesterfield I never really believed it and always thought she had mixed the venue up with somewhere bigger, maybe Sheffield. Hendrix wasn't actually supporting Cat Stevens and Engelbert Humperdinck. They were supporting the Walker Brothers. The reason she went is that she was 'in love' with Scott Walker.

Her abiding memory of Hendrix, rock legend, guitar god and Sixties icon? 'Ooh, he were bloody scruffy!' Also, he 'wasn't very big' and had an unzipped fly held together with a large safety pin, 'But you couldn't see owt though.'

I WAS THERE: RICHARD ELLIS, AGE 18

The Walker Brothers were top of the bill but for me Jimi was the main man. It seemed quite surreal having Humperdinck and Jimi Hendrix on the same bill. I was just coming up for my 19th birthday. In those days, you'd get all these tours that would have probably half a dozen acts on, all half-hour slots. We'd to go to the City Hall in Sheffield and on the same bill see PJ Proby, Cilla Black, The Searchers, The Fourmost. We saw that Jimi Hendrix was on in Chesterfield. Okay, so he's on with Engelbert, The Walker Brothers, Cat Stevens but, 'It's Jimi Hendrix – let's go!' I think half a dozen of us went.

He came on and just took over the stage. He was amazing, playing guitar behind his head and setting his guitar on fire. He sprayed it with lighter fluid or something. I thought he was brilliant. The place was full.

Just before that we'd seen The Beatles at Sheffield City Hall and you couldn't hear a thing. This wasn't anything like that. When Jimi was on it was more like a bit of reverence. A lot of people had gone to see him. It was as if people had actually gone to listen to him and watch him perform rather than women and girls screaming.

We just picked up on him. There were four of us, big mates together. It was Mick, I think, who said, 'Have you heard this Jimi Hendrix?' and we started listening to him. I thought, 'Yeah, this guy's got something different to The Beatles, different to all the others. A couple of us had been to see Bob Dylan not long before at Sheffield City Hall. They thought he was great but walked out halfway through the concert. But the two that had been to see Dylan started listening to Hendrix and thought he was the bee's knees. So I started listening and thought, 'Yeah'.

Then we saw he was on at Chesterfield. I think we got a minivan. There was six of us who stuck together. We got the tickets and he was just superb. He was a class of his own – a different sound, a different performance. You'd got Cat Stevens sitting there singing away and you'd got the Walker Brothers doing, 'The Sun Ain't Gonna Shine (Anymore)' and Engelbert doing 'The Last Waltz'. Then you got Jimi setting fire to his guitar and playing it behind his head and you got Noel Redding and Mitch Mitchell.

We go to Ireland quite a bit and there's a place called Clonakilty, and a pub there called O'Donovan's where Noel Redding played until he died. They've got loads of his stuff in there.

Jimi was like chalk and cheese compared with the other acts. The way Freddie Mercury of Queen held the crowd at Live Aid is how Jimi Hendrix was with an audience. Everybody was enthralled by him. When I heard he had died it was like some part of you had been taken away. Like a lead weight in the bottom of your stomach. To me he was a genius. It was horrendous to think there's going to be no more Jimi, no more exciting guitar work. He was a king, a god, really, the way he played that guitar. He made it talk, he made it sing.

Those were the days...

A RARE pop poster from yesteryear is to go under the hammer at Christies later this month.

The promotional bill was printed to prevent a star-studded show which took place 40 years ago at the Granada Theatre in Bedford.

The line-up on April 11, 1967, included such hitmakers as Jimi Hendrix, Cat Stevens and Engelbert Humperdinck, but, strange as it may now seem, none of these was topping the bill.

That honour fell to the Walker Brothers whose hits included Make It Easy On Yourself, My Ship Is Coming In and The Sun Ain't Gonna Shine Anymore.

The poster is 1 of 47 among 204 that are up for grabs at a specialist auction of rock and pop memorabilia, and are expected to fetch between £400 and £600.

Former fan Lorna Chantrell, who was at the concert, said: "Those were the days. I was a mod, 15 and in love, in love with Jimi Hendrix and Scott Walker.

"And they were going to be playing LIVE at the Granada Cinema! I budgeted my mum to pay for me to go.

"I still remember what I wore. I had a favourite beige crocheted maxi dress with bell-bottomed sleeves and it was alert. The Granada was a fantastic building and the demolition of it a few years ago was a tragedy.

"The noise in there was tremendous. When Jimi Hendrix came on stage I opened my mouth...

GRANADA THEATRE

11 APRIL 1967, BEDFORD, UK

I WAS THERE: JENNY RUSSELL AGE 13

Though I was only 13, I remember it quite well, but as everyone else in the building I would have been screaming! It's what you did.

At the time, I was more a fan of Cat Stevens and the Walker Brothers but was already developing a taste for rock and progressive music which is still with me today. My mum kindly came with me but was more a Humperdinck fan and would definitely not have been screaming. My husband, who went to loads of the early concerts and saw lots of great bands, didn't see Hendrix. He says it's the only thing he is jealous of me for.

I WAS THERE: BOB STOCKWELL

I was a big Walker Brothers fan but was completely blown away by Jimi Hendrix. I'd never seen anyone play a guitar like that before. I remember him playing 'Hey Joe' and 'Purple Haze' and was a big fan after that. When the Walker Brothers came on, Mitch Mitchell came and stood by us, drinking a bottle of beer. It's sad that none of the Experience are longer with us.

I WAS THERE: IRENE DAY, AGE 20

I was there with my then-fiancé. I seem to recall it was the last Walker Brothers tour, but my lasting memory was of Jimi Hendrix playing the guitar with his teeth – I'd never seen or heard anything like it live. I bought the record 'Hey Joe' and just played it non-stop on my friend's Dansette record player. To hear and see Jimi

Irene remembers Jimi playing with his teeth

Hendrix sing and play is something I have never forgotten. A truly memorable experience.

GAUMONT

12 APRIL 1967, SOUTHAMPTON, UK

I WAS THERE: RITA LOCK, AGE 13

I was a huge Walker Brothers fan. My friend and I decided to go to a concert at Southampton Gaumont, now the Mayflower. We were both 13, and rarely left the Isle of Wight. We must have known about the concert from the *NME*. We had to go to the local phonebox and use directory enquiries to find a number to contact the theatre, find ferry times and train times. We then had to convince our parents. The line-up was The Walker Brothers, Cat Stevens, Engelbert Humperdinck and Jimi Hendrix. A bizarre combination! We went to the early evening performance - and yes - they did it all again later that same evening. It must have been so difficult for him - the theatre was full of screaming teenage girls only really wanting to see The Walker Brothers. The set was short - but they all were. I remember 'Purple Haze' and 'Hey Joe'. I also remember a much older man in the audience, clearly only there for Jimi, who walked out when The Walker Brothers came on. We were horrified.

Rita remembers Jimi playing 'Purple Haze' and 'Hey Joe'

I WAS THERE: ANGELA SIMPSON, AGE 11

I was very keen to see Cat Stevens. I didn't really know who Jimi Hendrix was until then and had certainly never heard anything like it. It was amazing, but I'm not sure my parents were that impressed; they were looking forward to Englebert! I think the show had only come to Southampton because one was cancelled at another venue and the contract demanded they do another date. How lucky were we?

KINGFISHER COUNTRY CLUB

13 APRIL 1967, WOLVERHAMPTON, UK

I WAS THERE: LYNDA DIMMOCK

Every Thursday local bands would appear at this club and this particular night The Californians were on the bill at the Gaumont, about six miles away, with Jimi and due to appear at the Kingfisher later. When they arrived, they brought with them The Jimi Hendrix Experience and Cat Stevens and his band. Jimi and his band sat at the next table from us and were really quiet until the guy who organised the evenings asked if he would perform. What followed was brilliant. He played three or four songs. I can honestly say it was an amazing experience to watch him, something I will never forget.

DE MONTFORT HALL

16 APRIL 1967, LEICESTER, UK

I WAS THERE: MARILYN LEADER, AGE 15

The audience was quite varied as Engelbert was from Leicester and appealed to a lot of 'old people'. My friend and I were 15 and found it easy to sneak in without a ticket, pretending we were there with a family group. We didn't even have to flash our bus ticket at the doorman hoping he would think it was a valid ticket. If there were no seats left there was always room to stand around the edge of the hall.

Jimi Hendrix was on first and was the most extraordinary artist I'd ever seen. I think I already had 'Hey Joe' and 'Purple Haze' on single courtesy of my Dad, who worked in the electrical/record department at the Co-Op. But however loud I played them at home when my parents were out, nothing could compare with the excitement of his improvising on stage. Whether or not I already knew he was going to contort himself into such strange positions and play the guitar with his teeth beforehand, I'm not sure, but as I was struggling to play the guitar at all I was overwhelmed.

We would normally rush out of concerts to try and get autographs as soon as the music finished and before the National Anthem started, but as my friend really wanted to see The Walker Brothers we had to sit through the rest of the concert. We couldn't risk not being able to get back in again. So the next month I was eager to take advantage of an offer from strangers to go to a concert in Spalding, which turned out to include many big names, including Pink Floyd and Cream as well as Jimi Hendrix.

I WAS THERE: STEVE TURNER

Jimi had had some success with 'Hey Joe' in the UK and now the plan was to build up his 'wild man of rock' image on a package tour of UK theatres with an Irish boy band called Eire Apparent. I saw them with a mate. We were students at Birmingham and the tour came to the de Montfort Hall in Leicester. Half the audience had come to see the boy band and cleared out at the break before the Experience came on. Jimi was great and was running through his stage tricks, like playing his guitar through his legs and with his teeth. But then he went a stage further and turned his back on the audience, held the neck with one hand and with the other arm in the air played a solo with his dick! You couldn't actually see anything, but it was obvious from his movements that that was what he was doing. We were full of admiration and far as I can remember no one was shocked or outraged. I haven't been able to find anything that confirms this story, but in a later interview Jimi did admit to doing some pretty wild things on stage that he wasn't particularly proud of and soon dropped.

CITY HALL

21 APRIL 1967, NEWCASTLE UPON TYNE, UK

I WAS THERE: RICHARD DIXON

As a fresh-faced public school boy, I boarded a bus in Sunderland
to go to my first concert. It was in Newcastle on one of those
'package' tours, half a dozen groups performing two shows.
The headliners were the Walker Brothers, with Engelbert
Humperdinck and Cat Stevens also on the bill, but I was only
interested in the Jimi Hendrix Experience. It was the early
performance as I had to get the bus back. As I remember it,
the majority of the audience were pre- and pubescent girls
who screamed throughout. I was very shy with members of the
opposite sex, but the young girl next to me was on her own and
we got talking about how ridiculous this screaming was. Sadly, I
did not have the courage to ask her out.

Jimi came on in the first half and did half a dozen songs ('Hey
Joe' and 'Purple Haze' included) and with his signature guitar
playing behind his back and with his teeth was amazing - much
to the delight of the girl and I. We were in the front row of the
second section of the stalls and pretty close to the stage. Some
of the girls started throwing jelly babies onto the stage, some of
which he ate, commenting, 'I dig your candy, keep throwing it'.
Some he threw back.

There was a DJ compering and when the final act came on,
only two came on stage. He announced that Scott Walker was ill
and couldn't appear. Cue much anguish in the audience until a
blonde lock of hair protruded past the curtain - the screaming
reached a new peak and the lock of hair was attached to Scott. I
guess they sang their hits, but I can't remember.

I was at the Isle of Wight in 1970. Jimi was on the last night, by
which time I was completely exhausted. In those days the bands
played all night, so sleep was at a premium. I decided to get a bus
to the port to beat the 600,000 rush on Monday. If only I had

known what was to befall Jimi two months later. I missed Jimi's last UK performance for a night lying on a pavement just so I could get home a few hours earlier. What a fool!

THE ODEON

22 APRIL 1967, MANCHESTER, UK

MY SISTER WAS THERE: DAVE WALLACE

A couple of years ago, in a family gathering, I asked my grandson Joe, 17, how his guitar playing was developing and what he was practising. 'I'm into Jimi Hendrix,' he said. 'I saw Jimi Hendrix,' my sister Kathleen said. Joe was absolutely gobsmacked, and the rest of us somewhat surprised but impressed, to say the least. Why? I was her younger brother by four years, aged 23 at the time, mainly into Frank Sinatra, Micki and Griff type stuff, and her husband Irving would've been 33, with similar tastes.

Whilst I and my future missus Sue were into rock and pop, but had moved on from concerts such as Del Shannon, Roy Orbison, The Beatles and The Searchers to the cabaret clubs, Wishing Well, Swinton, Talk Of The North, and Patricroft, where Lulu, Long John Baldry, Strand and Witnesses Irish showbands were the attractions, my sister and her husband were not really into that scene. Indeed, they met bell-ringing. You get the picture.

It came to pass though that the hotels in Manchester reserved tickets in advance for guests for shows and concerts. This is where they obtained their tickets, being 'in the know', not needing to stay at the hotels but being able to collect tickets without the need to queue up all night. They'd attended theatre shows but this was their first pop concert.

All they can remember is that they attended the 8.30 show, were on the balcony, and everybody around was well behaved though excited through Jimi's set, which was brilliant. Then in the break, the MC, who I believe was Nick Jones ('that idiot', as Irving referred to him) paraded in front of the curtain, prodding it and shouting, 'Are you in there, Scott?' whilst whipping the audience up into a frenzy. Young girls were standing on the seats, screaming, fainting and being carried out.

The noise level was too much for Irving, who thought Jones had ruined the gig, so he and Kathleen left before the second half started as they wouldn't have been able to hear the Walker Brothers or Cat Stevens above the screams. I read somewhere that Jimi went into the wings to observe and admired Engelbert's performance, impressed with his singing and the way he put over his songs.

COLSTON HALL

25 APRIL 1967, BRISTOL, UK

I WAS THERE: GEOFF PIKE, 26

I went with a crowd of mates, plus MY MOTHER! When Jimi rolled on his back whilst playing, Mother screamed - she thought he had collapsed.

Great memories. Next time he was, of course, top of the bill. I was at both gigs but particularly remember the April '67 gig. Jimi was third or fourth on the bill. 'Hey Joe' had just entered the charts.

Yes, she liked all music. She went to a lot of shows. She went with us to a lot of roll'n'roll - Gene Vincent, Little Richard, Jerry Lee Lewis etc.

SOPHIA GARDENS

26 APRIL 1967, CARDIFF, UK

I WAS THERE: DENNIS BLISSETT, AGE 19

I suppose I must have seen an advert in the *South Wales Echo* or *Merthyr Express*. I was living in Dowlais at the time. When I got there it was amazing. There were no seats, and I said to the people next to me, 'Is this really live? It's not televised or anything?' It was something to get to see such a star live and in Cardiff.

I can't remember what happened to my ticket. I remember not seeing any programmes or merchandise.

I heard that Jimi Hendrix, during one Cardiff concert, went into a popular music store called Gamlins and wanted free equipment, the owner refusing.

As a keen musician myself, I often went into that store, and couldn't help asking the owner if the story was true. They say it wasn't, but who knows.

I WAS THERE: TONY PARRY

The day Jimi played the Capitol was dry and sunny. I was driving down Churchill Way towards Queen Street, where the Capitol was located. The car in front was an open top MGB and there were three

people in it, two in the front seats and one sat on the boot with his feet inside. I quickly realised it was Jimi Hendrix, mainly because of his brightly-coloured jacket, long scarf and trademark Fedora-type hat he favoured. This was before his show and he was obviously taking time out to see the delights and sights of Cardiff. The Capitol hosted many

Tony saw Jimi in a MG

pop package shows in the Sixties and I was a bouncer, or 'dance hall attendant' as we were rather grandly called. There were always two performances so I actually saw Jimi play twice that night. My enduring memory is of him rolling head over heels across the stage whilst continuing to play his guitar, a bit of a party piece.

ADELPHI THEATRE

28 APRIL 1967, SLOUGH, UK

I WAS THERE: JUDY MARNES, AGE 14

I remember Cat Stevens, the Walker Brothers and Engelbert
Humperdinck. I believe Jimi played guitar for Engelbert! I remember
being in awe of Jimi Hendrix and a little scared. We were quite near
the front and he was large, with big hair and on another planet. But I
really appreciate the performance we saw now.

I went to a few gigs around that time. We were very lucky as
the groups would do the rounds together and even come on
stage during the interval whilst at the cinema (the Ambassador in
Farnham Road, Slough).

I also saw Gene Pitney, The Paper Dolls, Marmalade, Mud, The
Tremeloes and The Who, whoy were in full equipment-smashing
mode (I couldn't get in as we didn't have tickets so stood outside until
Keith Moon hung out of the dressing room window shining a green
light on his face).

The tour arrived in the coastal resort of Bournemouth. Much
favoured as a place to retire to by the better-off thanks to the
favourable climate, an out-of- season seaside town was hardly the
most rock'n'roll venue for Jimi to be playing. He had apparently
spent the whole of Friday night at the Speakeasy Club in London,
arriving home at 7am that morning, and at 4pm still hadn't left for
the evening's performance. A friend drove him the 110 miles to
Bournemouth in a white MG Midget sports car, and his arrival at the
venue was witnessed by fans. The Midget owner complained that
when he went back to his car after the gig it was covered in 'I love
Jimi' messages scrawled in red lipstick and the windscreen wipers
and petrol cap had been stolen. They drove to a nearby garage and
Jimi helped him wipe the lipstick from the screen.
He is reported to have finished his set by swinging his Stratocaster
over his head and throwing it towards his amplifier.

WINTER GARDENS

29 APRIL 1967, BOURNEMOUTH, UK

I WAS THERE: RICHARD GARRETT, AGE 30

I'm a lover of the Swing Era but there are always people like Hendrix who are quite unique. We lived in Weymouth, 30 miles away from Bournemouth, visiting the Winter Gardens, the only big theatre at the time. We saw Duke Ellington, Count Basie, dozens over the years.

I remember it like it was last night. There was a Beach Boys type group on the bill, then Hendrix, followed by Engelbert, then Cat Stevens, then the Walker Brothers.

We brought my wife's niece and her boyfriend. We were six or eight rows from the front. It was a really big stage. You could get a symphony orchestra on there, with room to spare. Hendrix came on early and that set the tone for the evening. The bouncers were on the edge of the steps, keeping the girls off. I don't think anybody sat down that night. He did three or four numbers. He did all the tricks with his guitar. He was dressed in an admiral's uniform of the Horatio Hornblower period.

Richard and Doreen saw Jimi in his military uniform

Are You Experienced was released in the UK on 12 May 1967. The album was recorded between late October '66 and early April '67 and spent 33 weeks on the charts, peaking at No.2. It was issued in the US on August 23 by Reprise Records, where it reached No.5 on the Billboard chart, remaining on the chart for 106 weeks. The track 'Foxy Lady' included a Jimmy Page riff lifted from October 1966 single 'Happenings Ten Years Time Ago' by The Yardbirds.

Music critics widely regard *Are You Experienced* as one of the greatest debut albums in the history of rock'n'roll. An immediate commercial success, within seven months of its release it had sold more than one million copies.

UK and US versions of 1967 album Are You Experienced

❝I heard Hendrix playing Are You Experienced and I said, 'What the fuck is this?' It blew my mind! The way he used that whammy bar? Forget about it. He'd knock those strings out of tune and then he'd stretch them right back into tune. The guy was unreal ❞

Leslie West (guitarist, Mountain)

TULIP BULB AUCTION HALL

29 MAY 1967, SPALDING, UK

I WAS THERE: SUE BRINDED, AGE 15

I remember having to nag my parents to let me go. My dad had a
van and finally agreed to take Andrea (sadly passed on), another Sue,
Carol, Liz, Jane and myself. Andrea's dad picked us up. Spalding
is about 40 miles from
where we all lived in
Lincolnshire. It was a
boiling hot day and I wore
a green mini- sundress
with trendy suede shoes.
I also had false eyelashes
and the ultra- violet
lighting in the venue
melted the glue! We had
a place right at the front
of the stage. I had to peel
them off and put them in
my purse.

Jimi wore a purple outfit with gold trimmings, his huge Afro hair
and a 'tache. I also remember silver platform boots. We were all
starstruck. 'Purple Haze' is the one song that sticks in my head, after
which he smashed up his guitar. We were moved back from the stage
by bouncers.

I WAS THERE: MARILYN LEADER, AGE 15

I was in my last year at school in Leicestershire. My friends and
I used to do some washing up at the university halls after school
and at the end of each week we used to walk down the main road
to go and collect our wages. We were just walking down the main
road one day when this car pulled up and these two boys started

talking to us. They were from London. I never did work out what
they were doing, going towards Leicester. They said, 'What are
you doing this afternoon?' They asked us if we would like to go
to a pop festival in Lincolnshire. We said, 'We don't know' and
they said Jimi Hendrix was playing, so we agreed to go with them.
They mentioned other groups, but not Pink Floyd. We came
from very respectable homes so had to work out what to tell our
parents. They would never have let us go. We told our parents
we were going into Leicester and then babysitting in the evening
so would be home late. We didn't really have much idea where
we were going or, as I recall, who else was on the bill apart from
Hendrix when we agreed to go.

We arrived at a large barn in Spalding, with a lot of people
trying to get in through a sliding door. We joined them. My friend
got in, but I hadn't when the door closed. I went around the back,
looking for a way to get in, and found the stage door. By then we
knew that, amongst others, Jimi Hendrix, Pink Floyd, Cream and
Zoot Money were due to perform. I chose the least well-known
name, Zoot Money, told the doorman I was his wife, and he let
me in.

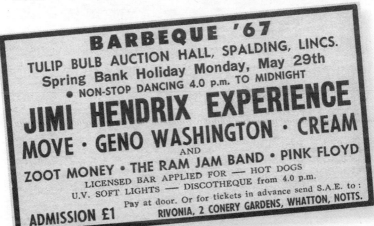

BARBEQUE '67

TULIP BULB AUCTION HALL, SPALDING, LINCS.
Spring Bank Holiday Monday, May 29th
● NON-STOP DANCING 4.0 p.m. TO MIDNIGHT

JIMI HENDRIX EXPERIENCE

MOVE ● GENO WASHINGTON ● CREAM
AND
ZOOT MONEY ● THE RAM JAM BAND ● PINK FLOYD
LICENSED BAR APPLIED FOR — HOT DOGS
U.V. SOFT LIGHTS — DISCOTHEQUE from 4.0 p.m.
Pay at door. Or for tickets in advance send S.A.E. to:
ADMISSION £1   RIVONIA, 2 CONERY GARDENS, WHATTON, NOTTS.

It was already very crowded but I found my friend and we got a place to stand somewhere quite near the front. Although I was quite young I'd already seen a lot of live bands, but Pink Floyd were quite magical. I loved the way they looked, especially Syd Barrett. It was the first light-show I'd ever seen, lots of pink and green.

Afterwards, we found out where Jimi Hendrix was staying and went to try and get his autograph, but he wouldn't come out of the hotel. Mitch Mitchell and Noel Redding did though. The former wrote his name on my arm, using moles as dots for the Is. I kept my arm covered in a plastic bag for weeks.

We had to find a way of getting home so started hitch-hiking. It was usually very easy to get a lift if you were female. Some Mods in a Mini stopped for us. It was quite a squash with six of us in there, and quite a distance back to Leicester on mostly rural roads. My parents were not at all pleased when I arrived home in what must have been the early hours of the morning. They didn't believe my babysitting story.

I WAS THERE: JENNI RAYNER

My overall thought about Barbecue '67 is that we really had no idea we were seeing future icons. It's strange that our little town has gone into history. I remember the excitement and the heat and people climbing the pillars to see the bands.

I was a big Geno Washington fan, so that was my highlight. He used to play regularly at the Boston Gliderdrome, which featured a lot of American artistes. We were incredibly lucky back then. The town I lived in, a few miles from Spalding, had 'dances' every Saturday night with chart-topping artists.

I WAS THERE: SUE WILKINSON

I saw Jimi Hendrix at Spalding Festival. I travelled by coach from Peterborough to Spalding that morning with lots of happy, laughing people. It was a brilliant day. Hendrix came out on stage and it took him around 15 to 20 minutes to tune up, which was agitating, but his guitar caught fire so that livened things up a bit! Once he got going he was absolutely astounding. It was well worth the wait and being packed into a cattleshed.

SAVILLE THEATRE

4 JUNE 1967, LONDON, UK

I WAS THERE: PAUL McCARTNEY

Jimi was a sweetie, a very nice guy. I remember him opening at the Saville on a Sunday night. Brian Epstein used to rent it when it was usually dark on the Sunday. Jimi opened, the curtains flew back and he came walking forward, playing 'Sgt. Pepper'. It had only been released on the Thursday, so that was like the ultimate compliment.

It's still obviously a shining memory for me, because I admired him so much anyway, he was so accomplished. To think that that album had meant so much to him as to actually do it by the Sunday night, three days after the release. He must have been so into it, because normally it might take a day for rehearsal and then you might wonder whether you'd put it in, but he just opened with it. It's a pretty major compliment in anyone's book. I put that down as one of the great honours of my career. I mean, I'm sure he wouldn't have thought of it as an honour. I'm sure he thought it was the other way round. But to me that was like a great boost.

I WAS THERE: TONY DERRINGTON

Two things stand out in my memory of this gig, Denny Laine and Hendrix's opening number. Denny Laine still hadn't released the album he was working on, only two singles, 'Say You Don't Mind' and 'Catherine's Wheel'. This was long before ELO and a stunning performance. When Jimi came on we were not expecting him to open with the opening song of the just-released Beatles album, a song they never performed live themselves.

I WAS THERE: WENDY GREENE

He destroyed a few guitars! It was not uncommon for members of the Stones and Beatles to book a box for the Saville gigs. Imagine the reaction when he played Sgt. Pepper just days after it was released.

Monterey International Pop Music Festival is remembered for the first major American appearances by Jimi Hendrix (he'd become a star in the UK but not yet in his native US) and The Who, as well as the first major public performances of Janis Joplin (Columbia Records signed Big Brother and The Holding Company on the basis of their performance at Monterey). It was also the first major performance by Otis Redding in front of a predominantly white audience, and he performed a sensational set, recorded for posterity in the film of the event, Monterey Pop.

The festival was planned in seven weeks by promoter Lou Adler, John Phillips of The Mamas and The Papas, producer Alan Pariser, and publicist Derek Taylor. The festival board included Mick Jagger, Paul McCartney and Brian Wilson.
Rolling Stone Brian Jones, seen milling around with his German girlfriend, Nico, introduced Jimi Hendrix to the crowd. Few people even knew who he was when he arrived on stage in a ruffled orange shirt and crotch-strangling red trousers. The guitarist played a blinding set, ending with an unpredictable version of 'Wild Thing', which he capped by kneeling over his guitar, pouring lighter fluid over it, setting it aflame, then smashing it.

An estimated 200,000 attended the festival over three days. The festival embodied the themes of San Francisco as a focal point for the counter-culture and is generally regarded as one of the beginnings of the 'Summer of Love', featuring bands that would shape the history of rock and affect popular culture from that day forward.

SET LIST:
01. Killing Floor
02. Foxy Lady
03. Like a Rolling Stone
04. Rock Me Baby
05. Hey Joe
06. Can You See Me
07. The Wind Cries Mary
08. Purple Haze
09. Wild Thing

MONTEREY POP FESTIVAL

17 JUNE 1967, MONTEREY COUNTY FAIRGROUNDS, CALIFORNIA

I WAS THERE: PAUL BODY

If you read UK music paper the *NME* in the early part of '67, you
knew who Jimi Hendrix was. If my memory serves me well, they
compared him to an African Bushman as he was so wild on stage. So
later, when we heard he was playing the Monterey Pop Festival, we
had to see him. We didn't know anything about how to get tickets.
That wasn't going to stop us, and neither was my having a job, which
I quit to go to Monterey. Originally Jimi and The Who were playing
on different days.

As much as we wanted to see Hendrix, we bought tickets for
Sunday. I think we voted on it or something. We saw Otis Redding,
Janis Joplin, the Electric Flag, Buffalo Springfield and The Byrds
with David Crosby and that STP sticker on his guitar. Sunday rolled
around and Jimi had been switched to that day. So after days of
breathing in the same air as Brian Jones and Nico, days of trying
spot The Beatles, who were rumoured to be there, after days of
patchouli oil and hippie girls, it had come down to the last night. Eric

Burdon introduced The Who and they opened with my favourite Who song, 'Substitute'. Then they saluted rock'n'roll's past with a scorching version of 'Summertime Blues' and destroyed the stage during 'My Generation'.

Some people were shocked, but I had seen them do it on TV, so I knew what was coming. As the smoke cleared, I had visions of 'Pictures of Lily' in my mind. Brian Jones, dressed in all sorts of flowing robes with his perfect blond hair, introduced The Jimi Hendrix Experience. They started off with 'Killing

Paul quit his job to go to Monterey

Floor', a Howlin' Wolf song. Jimi was taking the blues out of the juke joints and bringing them to the suburbs. 'Hey Joe' was cool, totally unlike the Love version. Jumping Jimi's version was moody. The introduction to the Dylan song, 'Like a Rolling Stone', was hilarious. At this time, we had only heard of 'Foxy Lady' and 'Purple Haze', so he offered up those two magnificently. Oh, and he looked damn cool. All three of them - Jimi, Mitch and Noel - looked smashing. I felt like the girl in Wizard of Oz, like I wasn't in Kansas anymore, everything had shifted. 'Wild Thing' ended the night with Ronson lighter fluid, feedback and Jimi rolling around on the floor. Robert Christgau hated it, called Jimi a psychedelic Uncle Tom. To paraphrase Walter Brennan in *Red River*, you were wrong, Mr Christgau. Quit my job? Man, I would do it again. Jimi and the fellas were something.

I WAS THERE: MICKY DOLENZ

It's funny; I was in New York a few months before and someone told me, 'You got to go down to the Village and see this guy play guitar with his teeth.' I don't remember his name even being mentioned, but sure enough we went down to the Village and saw this guy play with his teeth. Months later I go to the Monterey Pop Festival and on stage comes this band, and it was the same guitarist. It was Jimi Hendrix.

I WAS THERE: JOHN A GREENWALD

Call it an almost-all-access Pass. In effect that's what I had at the Monterey Pop Festival, allowing me to go almost anywhere I wanted except backstage. The perks of being an usher. An awesome perk at that, all because my history teacher was in charge of the ushers.

So it was that I could remain in the arena after everyone else departed following Ravi Shankar's remarkable Sunday afternoon show, and that placed me in a rare and fascinating place, as the members of a British rock band I'd never heard of, The Jimi Hendrix Experience, were scheduled to do their soundcheck.

I do not exaggerate. In fact, it wasn't until later I even realised he wasn't a Brit at all, but from Seattle. That said, it didn't take many chords screaming out of the amps to draw me to the lip of the stage, where I found myself standing next to renowned rock photographer Jim Marshall as we both gaped in awe.

Jimi Hendrix was something else again. Dressed in a uniform-like black jacket, elaborately decorated and embroidered in gold with a high straight-back collar lined in red, unbuttoned to reveal a bare chest festooned with gold medallions, he looked unlike any pop star I had ever seen.

Then there was the way he played. The effortless command of the instrument. The power. The intensity. The flare for the theatrical that prompted Jim Marshall to turn to me and exclaim, 'This cat is wild.' Wild he was, and we would only learn later that he hadn't revealed all his tricks.

As I left the arena to grab a quick bite before the evening show, I spread the word to all my friends that Jimi Hendrix was a must-see that night.

Now to appreciate the atmosphere in the arena for the final night, it's important to remember this was the culmination of a weekend of exceptional music by an all-star cast of musicians, including career-defining performances by Janis Joplin and Otis Redding.

John didn't know Jimi was an all-American boy

So the audience arrived in a state of high expectation on Sunday evening that was only amped up even more by a rumour that somehow evolved into something approaching fact: John, Paul, George and Ringo - yes, The Beatles- would be making a surprise appearance.

The rumour floated around the arena like wafts of reefer smoke throughout the weekend to the point where someone told me, oh so confidentially, he had talked to someone who'd seen Ringo's drum-kit backstage. More than anything else, what had got us to this point was a lame attempt at humour by Derek Taylor, former publicist for The Beatles, when he told members of the press The Beatles were present at the festival, 'disguised as hippies'.

That did it. Reporters filed stories, which got printed, circulated and repeated, and suddenly the Monterey Pop Festival was confronted with a problem it hadn't anticipated: large numbers of people without tickets converging on the arena. Looking back from where I was standing, I could see people scrambling over the fence as the evening progressed.

By the time The Who stepped on stage, the audience was

throbbing with excitement, helped along by an encore performance by Janis Joplin, and the lads managed to crank up the adrenaline levels even more. When they got to the 'My Generation' finale with Townshend's windmills, Moon's smoke bombs and the big guitar smash up at the end, they had audience members' eyes, mine included, popping out of their sockets. How do you top this?

What I didn't know was that after the soundcheck, Jimi Hendrix had raced around the Monterey Peninsula looking for lighter fluid.

But first the Grateful Dead. Yes, in a stunning bit of bad scheduling, the Grateful Dead came on between The Who and Jimi Hendrix. Some might argue that the Dead's trippy meanderings would settle the crowd down a bit, but that's not what happened. Remember: Beatles.

That particular bubble of expectation was finally popped by Peter Tork of The Monkees, givven the thankless task of coming out mid-set and telling us The Beatles were not in town. Then the Dead completed their long, strange and rather desultory musical trip and disappeared into the night.

Which brings us to one of the most iconic moments in rock history: Hendrix at Monterey Pop. My vantage point for what was about to transpire was off to the left if you were facing the stage, about halfway back standing against a wall, in my area of responsibility as an usher. I wasn't as close as that afternoon, but I was close enough to take it all in.

As the performance began, Jimi was facing an audience that with few exceptions was seeing and hearing him for the first time, and the first impression he made was visual. Since the afternoon he had made some changes. Now he was wearing a bright yellow shirt with puffy sleeves and ruffled collar, a black brocaded vest, probably a match with the jacket he had worn earlier, red trousers, and to top it off a pink feather boa. No shrinking violet, he.

Then the playing began, and the second impression was just as powerful. Every eye in the arena was glued to Jimi. While electric guitar players commonly reveal their feelings and emotions with facial gestures, Jimi expressed himself with his whole body in almost a primal way, adding to the sense of drama.

Then there were the tricks. Playing behind his back. With his teeth. With only one hand. He was like the Harlem Globetrotters of the guitar.

All of this was quite gripping, but then there was the song selection. Strikingly eclectic. Blues one minute with 'Killing Floor' and 'Rock Me Baby.' Bob Dylan the next with 'Like a Rolling Stone.' And in each case, as with 'Hey Joe', he made it his own. 'Like a Rolling Stone' could not be more different than 'Purple Haze', but to Hendrix they were equally valued, which told us as we watched that Jimi was like no one else.

Then there was the finale. It left me as gobsmacked as everyone else, and this comes after just witnessing all The Who's theatrics. There were the torrents of managed feedback: The humping of the amp. And the lighter fluid introduced with much drama and solemnity. As the guitar caught fire we entered the realm of performance art. At this point the destruction of the guitar was almost anticlimactic but seemingly essential. 'Wild Thing' indeed.

The Mamas and Papas would close out the show, giving everyone the opportunity to figuratively lean back on a pillow and smoke a cigarette.

We had all experienced a remarkable moment in history, and that stage in Monterey is now regarded as sacred ground, though the actual wood upon which Jimi trod is no longer there. Still, all these years later, people want to see that place where Jimi burned the guitar. It is now legend, and I was there.

I WAS THERE: SYLVIA HOLCOMB, AGE 21

I saw Jimi Hendrix twice, first time at Monterey. It's hard to remember very much but I remember we hadn't heard much of him, if any. We were waiting to see Janis again and stayed to see a couple more before going home. I don't remember what song he opened with but I do remember 'Foxy Lady'. He was great, we were shocked and just stunned at how he played that guitar.

I WAS THERE: JOAN JAMES

He was awesome. He could make that guitar laugh, cry, talk, whine, whatever. As I'm sure you know, he burned it. Very dramatic. Everyone was high so maybe the effect wasn't as shocking as it might have been. He wasn't that well known (at least I hadn't heard of him) prior to that. It put him on the map.

I WAS THERE: KATY RANKIN, AGE 13

My Dad bought me day and night tickets for all three days. He'd drop me off at 9am for me to roam the fairgrounds all day on my own, then I had to meet up with my older sister (who Dad paid to chaperone me) for the evening shows then drive me home. Dad got great seats just to the left of the stage - a great vantage point for all the music that weekend.

My sister wasn't a real big fan of having to go every night to 'have' to listen to the music, smell the pot, hippies, etc. The one act she enjoyed hearing? The Who, until they started breaking up the equipment and stage. When Jimi lit up the guitar she actually left our seats and left the grandstand, but if someone mentions the festival to her now? OMG, 'It was wonderful!' I was thoroughly in heaven all three days, all the people-watching I did, hearing Janis in the afternoon, knowing in my gut she was going to be a phenomenon, and when they brought her back for the evening show I knew I was seeing history. When Jimi walked out on stage it was electric throughout the grandstand. We all knew we were in the midst of something incredible! Except for my sister, of course.

I WAS THERE: GENOA WOODS

I was in the hippie movement in the Sixties. It only cost four dollars to get in to see all those great artists. They had a 50-year anniversary of the Monterey Pop Festival this last summer and the tickets started at $350 at the same fairgrounds location. The only survivor was Eric Burton. I mean no Mamas and Papas, no Jefferson Airplane, no-one else from the original. Very sad.

Purple Haze, the second single by the Jimi Hendrix Experience was released in the US on 19 June 1967 and became many people's first exposure to Hendrix's psychedelic rock sound. In December 1967, producer Chas Chandler heard Hendrix toying around with a new guitar riff. 'I heard him playing it at the flat and was knocked out. I told him to keep working on that, saying, 'That's the next single!' In concert, he sometimes substituted lyrics for comic effect; 'scuse me while I kiss the sky' was rendered 'scuse me while I kiss this guy' (while gesturing towards drummer Mitch Mitchell).

PANHANDLE

25 JUNE 1967, GOLDEN GATE PARK,
SAN FRANCISCO, CALIFORNIA

I WAS THERE: RUPERT BYERS

I was in a store on Haight Street in San Francisco in 1967 that
only sold posters. It was called The Print Mint. I met a guy from
the same area of Southern California as me. He said he'd been
in Europe and had met a management guy that paid him to go
to San Francisco, rent an apartment and go to all the media and
radio stations to promote a new band. We kept in touch while he
was in San Francisco. No one I knew had heard of Jimi Hendrix
at that time. He said Hendrix was going to be big. I laughed and
scoffed. I said, 'I bet he will really be big, burning his guitar,
playing it behind his back, humping it, etc.' He just kept saying,
'You'll see'. Every time I saw my friend I joked that Hendrix
would fall flat because all the SF bands were what was happening.
Then he left and returned to Europe, giving me the key to his
apartment, paid up for three more months.

FREE CONCERT IN THE PANHANDLE
Golden Gate Park · San Francisco

I had no money to get tickets to see
Hendrix when he finally arrived in
San Francisco, but I was in the park
when he played on the flatbed truck
on the Sunday afternoon and he
was everything my friend said and
more. Nothing would ever be the
same again. All-girl band The Ace
of Cups opened for him. While
they were playing, he was in the
front row taking photos of them.
He'd just bought a fancy new
camera. Then he went on and blew
everyone away.

FILLMORE AUDITORIUM

25 JUNE 1967, SAN FRANCISCO, CALIFORNIA

I WAS THERE: MICHAEL LAZARUS SCOTT

I went to this show with my best friend Michael Lindberg.
Jimi had made his US debut with the Experience at Monterey
three days earlier. Raves about his performance led us to this
spectacularly upside-down bill, Jimi opening for Garbo Szabo and
the Jefferson Airplane.

Way back then the concert experience was a much different
animal. The show cost all of $2.50 and you didn't have to buy
tickets in advance. Each band played two sets. The concert started
at 9pm and was over at 2am. The stage was pretty low and most
folk sat on the floor. When the Experience took the floor, Mike
and I were in the second row, right in front of Jimi. In my 18
years leading up to this moment I'd never seen or heard anything
like this. Black music at this time was mostly Motown, all slick
suits, processed hair and flashy dance moves. Now here was Jimi
with his wild hair and rainbow-coloured glad-rags playing a low-
slung, upside-down Strat. It was mind-boggling.

The Experience was the first power trio I ever heard. Bands
normally had a rhythm instrument to fill in the gaps and keep
the music flowing. Jimi was rhythm, lead and vocalist rolled into
one. This was also the first time I saw or heard Marshall stacks.
Louder than hell, a complete sensory overload. I remember
looking at Mike, both of us shaking our heads in disbelief.

At the top of the stairs in the Fillmore's lobby was a tub of free
apples and suckers. Thank you, Bill Graham - you were absolutely
the best thing ever to happen to rock'n'roll. Sitting between us
and Jimi was a very pretty blonde hippie girl who had a sucker in
her mouth. Jimi was doing his thing right in front of her when she
took the sucker from her mouth and handed it to him. Jimi stuck
it on the headstock of his Strat, gave her a 'watch this' smile and
sashayed over to his Marshall stack and proceeded to hump his

guitar into the speakers. The stack was feeding back like a jaguar on heat. Jimi was bumping and grinding like Tempest Storm as he looked over his shoulder at blondie with the most lecherous grin I'd ever witnessed.

This concert was a definitive milestone in my life of rock'n'roll adventures.

Jimi Hendrix played the Earl Warren Showgrounds twice in 1967. They were originally developed as the permanent location for the Santa Barbara National Horse and Flower Show as well as to attract and support other equestrian and agricultural events in the Santa Barbara area. The 1 July 1967 attracted a crowd of 1,908. The 19 August 1967 attendance was slightly larger, at 2,729.

EARL WARREN SHOWGROUNDS

1 JULY 1967, SANTA BARBARA, CALIFORNIA

I WAS THERE: COLLEEN ISAAC ANDREW, AGE 14

It was a great concert, as you can imagine. Complete with the smashing of his guitar at the end. I saw him twice that year with my best friend. Tickets were $3.50. My favourite songs were 'Purple Haze' and 'Foxy Lady'. I was a bit of a stoner in the day.

I WAS THERE: CLIFFORD H CROSS

Throughout the Sixties, actually since I was nine in 1958, I played drums. I was fortunate to jam with many bands along the West Coast in California. Knowing many in the music industry got me into lots of concerts and often on stage to sit in, playing conga, or with front-row or backstage passes. For the Monterey Pop Festival I had excellent seats given to me by fellow performing musicians. I watched in awe from box-seats as Jimi burned his guitar.

For both Hendrix concerts in Santa Barbara (1 July 1967 and 19 August 1967) I was living on my sailboat in a slip in the harbour. I was with a beautiful red-haired lady named Sandy, with whom I was spending all my spare time. We had dinner at the Harbor Restaurant on Stearns Wharf early evening, then went for a sail to watch the sunset while smoking a joint after taking LSD.

I already had tickets for both concerts so the evenings were planned. We got on my Harley and rode up the 101 Highway about five miles to the Earl Warren Showgrounds. Being summer concerts, the air was warm and made you feel alive and part of nature as it flowed past us.

I WAS THERE: DEBBIE WRIGHT, AGE 16

When I saw Jimi Hendrix I don't think I really knew what I was going to be experiencing. I was there by myself. My Dad answered a country and western question on AM radio station KIST and I won the ticket and a poster. When Dad told me the answer I thought he was kidding, but he was right and the rest changed my love of music forever and history!

I had no idea where I was. I was nervous since I had recently moved to Santa Barbara. He was on the Are You Experienced tour. The stage was in the middle of a big concrete floor surrounded by hundreds of people. It was hard to see him through the pot smoke if you weren't close to the stage. I think I got a second-hand high and became a freaky dancer. He made a lasting impression on me. Even in college in computer science I messed around typing punch-cards that said things like 'Purple Haze is in my brain' or 'Mellow Yellow', printing 50. It was those memories he brought. I loved him and that concert. He was larger than life. When I think back I realise the whole thing was quite innocent.

CENTRAL PARK

5 JULY 1967, SCHAEFER MUSIC FESTIVAL,
NEW YORK, NEW YORK

I WAS THERE: JONATHAN SEGAL

I saw Jimi live three times. The second time was at Hunter College
where the Soft Machine opened, and the third was at the Singer Bowl,
with Janis Joplin and The Chambers Brothers also on the bill. But the
first time was at the Schaefer Music Festival, at what is a skating rink
in winter and, back in the Sixties, was a summer concert venue seating
5,000 people outside. I hadn't heard of Jimi Hendrix and went to the
concert to see The Young Rascals. The scheduled opener was folk
singer Len Chandler, who never showed, but on came Jimi with Mitch
Mitchell and Noel Redding and they proceeded to play material from
the *Are You Experienced* album. As far as I know, none of his songs were
yet on the radio, so I had no prejudicial conceptions, no hype in my
mind. I am a pianist and needless
to say my mind was blown. It was
as if the mothership had landed
with no warning. I remain to this
day a major admirer and still
perform a jazzy version of 'Up
From The Skies'. Okay, it was
jazzy when Hendrix did it. In fact,
it's still one the most genuinely
cool tracks ever recorded.

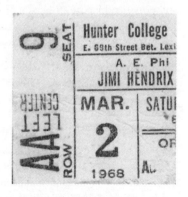

I WAS THERE: LARRY KLEIN

I saw and heard Jimi and the band eight times. First time was in Central
Park, opening for The Young Rascals, who we were there to see. I think
it cost $1.75 to get in. This was before *Are You Experienced* was released
and they were phenomenal. No one, it seemed, knew who they were.
They got a massive standing ovation. Mouths were wide open. There

was nothing one could even put into words. It was stellar! Jimi did somersaults while not missing a beat. At the end he pulled his guitar apart while still plugged in, then threw the whole bloody mess over his shoulder, almost catching a piece of Mitch Mitchell in the process. Aside from the theatrical performance, we were so flabbergasted.

I also saw Jimi twice at the Fillmore East, once at Hunter College, Manhattan and once at the Philharmonic Hall in the Lincoln Center during the *Axis* period, which was maybe the best time. I believe Ravi Shankar opened the show and it was Thanksgiving Day. I also saw him once in Queens at the Singer Bowl with Big Brother and Janis, Soft Machine and I think Ted Nugent and the Amboy Dukes opening. I also saw him at Madison Square Garden, which was the worst, right after the Toronto airport affair.

Jimi was signed up to open for The Monkees, a manufactured US pop band created to cash in Stateside on the popularity of The Beatles. Targeted firmly at the pre-teen market, with zany sub-Beatles antics, comprising three Americans fronted by Mancunian Davy Jones, The Monkees were the prototype boy band, presaging Take That, Westlife and Pop Idol by more than 30 years.

Monkees guitarist Mike Nesmith first heard Jimi Hendrix on a tape at a dinner party with John Lennon, Paul McCartney and Eric Clapton. He and bandmates Peter Tork and Mickey Dolenz witnessed Jimi's Monterey appearance and encouraged their management to sign Jimi up to open for them. Hendrix joined the tour in Jacksonville on 8 July 1967. He did not go down well with their teenybopper audience.

WEST COAST SUCCESS FOR HENDRIX EXPERIENCE

JIMI JOINS MONKEES FOR GIANT U.S. TOUR

THE Jimi Hendrix Experience are meeting with phenomenal success in America. They have now been fixed to join a nationwide tour with the Monkees tomorrow (Friday).

The tour travels around the States and will not fin-

Hendrix group are expected back in Britain on August 23.

Manager Chas Chandler reports that since the group's astounding successes at the Monterey Pop Festival and the Fillmore Ballroom, San Francisco they have steadily built up enormous interest and demand on the West Coast.

SPENCER IN STATES

SPENCER DAVIS made a

holiday visit to New York last week, prior to his group's American tour which starts on July 28.

Davis and his manager John Martin, met United Artists Records chiefs regarding forthcoming record plans.

COMEBACK FOR JET

JET HARRIS, who won the MM's pop poll as best instrumentalist before giving

MEMORIAL COLISEUM

8 JULY 1967, JACKSONVILLE, FLORIDA

I WAS THERE: P KEVIN DYKES

As a young kid I saw Jimi Hendrix at the Jacksonville Memorial
Coliseum when he opened for The Monkees. My father took me.
It was one of my favourite TV shows and I don't think I'd heard
of him. If I recall correctly, Jimi opened with 'The Star Spangled
Banner'. Most everyone was in shock at his playing for two reasons.
One, it wasn't typical for any black musician to play anything close to
what Jimi was playing. Two, most of the kids were teenyboppers that
came to see The Monkees, so playing like this was a total shock to
them. I loved all types of music and really loved seeing Jimi Hendrix
and thought he killed it. He blew The Monkees away on stage. I
think the biggest thing that shocked me was the stage show. Lighting
the guitar on fire had never been seen. I couldn't believe he was
doing that to his guitar. They were so expensive.'

I WAS THERE: SUSAN POST DANIELL, AGE 14

It became a rather infamous concert, the first of eight opening
for The Monkees. I was 14 and the audience was predominantly
girls aged 12-15. I'm sure we didn't fully appreciate what we were
experiencing and hearing that particular night.

I'd flown back to Jacksonville the evening before, met at the
airport by a good friend and my Mom and stepfather. Walking to
the baggage claim area, my friend kept going on about these 'three
weird guys' they'd seen at the airport's front entrance, describing the
hair, clothing, etc. They were gone by the time we left. However, the
next night Hendrix and company walked out onto the stage, and my
friend starting elbowing me, saying, 'That's the three dudes from the
airport yesterday!'

I WAS THERE: LARRY MCKENZIE AKA WYATT HURTS

It's hot, very hot, and I'm pedalling my bike to Regency Square Mall as the sun beats down, urging me to turn back and head to the community pool instead. But I have a mission. In my pocket is my weekly allowance and every Saturday I make this pilgrimage to purchase one of the newest hit singles. The Beatles and the Rolling Stones are at the top of the charts, but my taste lies more in bubblegum rock. I pay the 65 cents for my new 45rpm record and spend the rest of my dollar on ice cream. Then I pedal home, past the

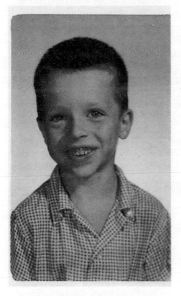

Larry was a Monkees fan until....

pool, head to my bedroom and crank up my record player. I'm just learning to play the guitar, and with each stanza of lyrics I pick the needle up out of the track and write them down then drop the needle back into the track to catch the next verse. I do this maybe two or three dozen times until I get it all down. Then I do it all again to learn the chord progression.

My hometown of Jacksonville is flat and divided by the St John's River, where many famous musicians have started out; Pat Boone, Mae Axton, Ray Charles, The Allman Brothers Band and Lynyrd Skynyrd all have roots here. I live in the suburbs, where all the new homes and schools are. I'm living on the cusp of a revolutionary time but I'm unaware of any of it in the comfort of my upper middle-class home. My neighbourhood is all white, my school is all white, my television with only three stations is pretty much all white, and the radio is segregated into country, rock and soul stations.

The only black people I ever see are mostly downtown, where we lock the doors as we drive through, so they won't 'jump in and get us'. On the very rare occasion when a black person is seen walking through my neighbourhood you can be sure that each neighbour is watching and calling ahead, monitoring their every move.

My father works as an insurance agent during the day and a musician at night. But his crooning days are numbered. The British Invasion has brought The Beatles to our shores and dominates the radio. Then The Beatles play the Gator Bowl on 11 September 1964 and someone gets the idea to revolutionise TV the same way The Beatles have conquered the radio, and The Monkees are born.

My two most favourite TV shows were *The Monkees* and *Batman*, and soon The Monkees were coming to do a show in my hometown. Batman was staying put in Hollywood. My grandparents buy tickets for me, my siblings and my Uncle Jim to see The Monkees live in concert. And on 8 July 1967 we file into the Jacksonville Coliseum. I think every white kid in town from eight to 16 is there. Somehow we missed that Jimi Hendrix was the opening act. Our brains are saturated by Monkees' mania, so when a tall black man with an Afro appears on stage we're confused and my grandparents are shocked, to say the least.

The music he made was as loud as a jet engine but still couldn't penetrate the screams of thousands of adolescences screaming, 'We want the Monkees! We want the Monkees! We want the Monkees!' I can hear the echo to this day. My grandparents' shock slowly turns to amazement as they watch the pure joy and excitement unfold all around them. Papa screams into my ear, 'That man can really play that guitar!' I'm guessing Hendrix may have only been on stage half an hour, but each song he played only amped up the anticipation of wanting to see and hear The Monkees.

Now this could be a false memory, but I recall Hendrix smashing his guitar to pieces as he left the stage, and I thought to myself, 'That guy's crazy, now he's gonna have to go and buy a new guitar.' But just like 99% of everyone there, I was counting the minutes waiting for The Monkees to take the stage and did not realise I was witnessing musical history.

2018 update: I currently perform every day of the week in Key West, Florida. I play a few Hendrix songs, but nothing by The Monkees.

I WAS THERE: TARA ARDIS, AGE 17

I saw him in Jacksonville, Florida when he opened for The Monkees. I went with my younger brother and three high school friends. We lived in South Carolina. My mother drove us down and dropped us at the venue. At first, I was a bit startled by Jimi but then I decided he was pretty good and he could do a whole lot better than opening for screaming teenyboppers.

JIMI HENDRIX QUITS MONKEE TOUR

'Think Mickey Mouse has replaced me'.

JIMI HENDRIX phoned the NME on Saturday with the sensational news that he had quit the Monkees' American tour after only seven shows. The Hendrix Experience will remain in the U.S. for at least two more weeks to complete their new single and undertake some further bookings on the West Coast.

"Firstly they gave us the 'death' spot on the show—right before the Monkees were due on," Jimi declared. "The audience just screamed and yelled for the Monkees! Finally, they agreed to let us go on first and things were much better. We got screams and good reaction, and some kids even rushed the stage.

"But we were not getting any billing—all the posters for the show just screamed out—MONKEES!

"Then some parents who brought their young kids complained that our act was vulgar. We decided it was just the wrong audiences. I think they're replacing me with Mickey Mouse!

"There was no tension between us and the Monkees whatever. And all the rumours about being segregated on the plane were just nonsense. I got on well with both Micky and Peter and we fooled around a lot together.

"There was a fantastic girl singer on the tour—an Australian girl called Lynne Randell. She's got a record out in Britain, so you may be hearing more of her.

"In New York we all went out to see the Electric Circus club in the Village, which just completely blew my mind. There was a group called the Seeds playing there but they had all these funny little acts going on between things. One guy walked up on to the stage and stood

JIMI HENDRIX wears the expression he might put on if you mention Monkee audiences to America to him!

there and growled for about five minutes, then he said 'Thank you,' and walked off! There was another guy who came on in a strait-jacket and then rolled around on the floor for half-an-hour. Then some funny little guys came swinging down on ropes from the ceiling. We couldn't believe it!

"I've been reading those reports about my new single being 'The Burning Of The Midnight Lamp.' Well it's true that I have recorded a track with those words in the song but I'm not sure that that is going

to be either the title or the single. "We had a great time in LA, where Dave Crosby and a group called the Electric Flag came round to see us at the Whisky A Go Go. I love the West Coast, all those beautiful people.

"Chas (Chandler) and Mike (Jeffries) are making arrangements for an autumn tour of Britain for us when we get back—it would be great if we get some of these really groovy American groups from the West Coast on the show with us," Jimi concluded.

FOREST HILLS STADIUM

13–16 JULY 1967, QUEENS, NEW YORK, NEW YORK

I WAS THERE: DEBRA D'ARCO

We went to see The Monkees at Forest Hills and Jimi Hendrix opened for them. I was very young at the time. I remember wearing a baby blue mini-dress with white polka dots, white Gogo boots and a poor-boy peak hat. I went with my dear cousin Denise and aunt Florence, who was a trooper to take us at the age of 12 and 14. Jimi wasn't really accepted by that crowd. I wasn't into him and didn't even know who he was. But I became a big fan, and still am today. Now, at 62, I still follow select guitarists like Clapton and Gary Clark Jr.

Jimi didn't get to play long. He was taken off the stage. We were a bunch of kids waiting for Davy Jones and Mickey Dolenz and he was just in the wrong place with the wrong crowd. But he was phenomenal, attacking that guitar.

FOREST HILLS STADIUM

16 JULY 1967, QUEENS, NEW YORK, NEW YORK

I WAS THERE: BARRY KIPNIS

I saw Jimi Hendrix at Forest Hills. My brother took me there to see The Monkees when Jimi Hendrix opened for them. I'd never heard of him and thought it was bizarre when he smashed his guitar at the end of his set. His playing was awesome.

I WAS THERE: BELINDA BECHTEL

I saw Jimi as an opening act for The Monkees in Forest Hills Stadium. We didn't know how special the occasion was but were very impressed with the music and the shape of their hair, going up and down with the sway of their bodies. They were extremely wonderful as far as I could tell whilst screaming my head off: 'We want Davy!'

I WAS THERE: BOB GUERRIN

I remember hearing 'Purple Haze', thinking how cool it was. It was 1967 and the music scene was exploding. I went to the record store and bought four LPs: *Are You Experienced* by the Jimi Hendrix Experience, *Surrealistic Pillow* by Jefferson Airplane, *Disraeli Gears* by Cream, and *Freak Out* by Zappa. I was hooked. In the meantime, I'd already purchased tickets to see The Monkees at Forest Hills. I had no idea Hendrix was opening for them. Bizarre was an understatement. I watched in awe and, to be honest, confusion as he played. The vast majority of the audience was essentially saying, 'What the fuck?' I went the first night. My musician repertoire expanded after that night. The following summer I saw The Who open for The Doors at The Singer Bowl in Queens, New York. It struck me the same way Hendrix originally did. It wasn't just his music. I was an early fan of Pink Floyd, The Grateful Dead, Cream. It was the times, the music, the drugs. There was so much going on, like an assault on the senses. A very pleasurable assault.

I WAS THERE: ROBERT ROWLAND

When he came back to the US as The Jimi Hendrix Experience he was given the worst booking of all time, the opening act for The Monkees tour. My friend Richie Adler and I went and saw the show and I think they were booing him. The audience was all pre-teen girls. They couldn't really fathom The Jimi Hendrix Experience. Either right after that, or a few shows later, Hendrix was fired from the tour. It was a horrible combination.

The Experience played eight shows on that tour, including four nights at Forest Hills. After the 16 July show, it was announced that the Daughters of the American Revolution were protesting that Jimi's act was too obscene for such a young audience. Chas Chandler cooked up the story with tour promoter Dick Clark but had to convince co-manager Mike Jefferey. Chas remembered, 'It took us all that day and night to convince Jeffery we had to get off the tour and I said, 'Just remember one fucking thing. Jimi is signed to me, and you don't have a fucking contract with him'.'

CLUB SALVATION

8 AUGUST 1967, NEW YORK, NEW YORK

I WAS THERE: ANTHONY PALAZZO, AGE 15

I was a freshman at Cardinal Hayes High School in the Bronx. My brother had a friend whose brother wanted him to 'house-sit' his apartment on W 8th Street in Greenwich Village. I was an aspiring drummer, so jumped at the opportunity to go and 'watch' the place while he was at work. It was the summer of 1967, I was naive, no drugs or drinking other than a little Mr. Boston's lemon-flavoured gin before school dances at Good Shepherd in Inwood. As I strolled along 8th Street, I saw the *Are You Experienced* LP in the window of a store, maybe Village Records, down a few steps from street level. I was immediately drawn to the colours, the psychedelic lettering, the fisheye lens photo. I went in and bought it, rushed back to Mr. Levitas' apartment and slapped it on the turntable. I had heard Scott Muni play 'The Wind Cries Mary' on WNEW FM but had no idea what to expect from the rest. I was blown away and completely transformed. I, like most everyone else, was a huge Beatles fan and saw them at Shea Stadium in '65, my first major concert when The Cyrcle who did 'Red Rubber Ball' opened for them. But EXP? That was a whole different ballgame. I loved 'Fire', and 'Foxy Lady' and its feedback opening and 'Third Stone from the Sun' were my other faves. My brother's friend thought it and I 'weird', but to his credit he did accommodate me as I played it over and over. He challenged me to play Mitch Mitchell's 'Fire' drum-breaks on a pillow.

I implored him to take me to Club Salvation and he did. As we sat at a table I drank Coca-Cola and watched the trio in awe. Jimi's Afro seemed to touch the ceiling. His presence was overwhelming yet so friendly. 'I see we meet again' was his favourite opening line. 'Purple Haze' and 'Foxy Lady' stood out. The set was short and to the point, with not much improvisation. He hung around a bit, but I was too intimidated to approach him. Then he was gone and I was forever 'experienced'.

The day Jimi died was my high school girlfriend's birthday. I was again a freshman, this time at Lehmann College in the Bronx. A group of us were sitting on the lawn between classes listening to someone play guitar, hippie style. A classmate came over and asked if I'd heard the news - Jimi Hendrix was dead. 'What?' I said. I was devastated. When it sunk in I cried like a baby. I felt I had lost a close friend, having seen him seven times by then. I thought he would last forever, he made everyone at his shows feel that way and you knew it was gonna be a special event. He will always be The Man with the Guitar. Some say he was a shooting star that fell to earth. To me he was a supernova that exploded into the universe from which he came.

I met Mitch Mitchell in Colony Records in NYC in 1967 when I was a 15-year-old drummer. I met him again many years later at the jazz club, Michael's, on the Upper West Side at a David Sanborn gig. We shook hands and spoke briefly. He was drunk and it saddened me greatly. He was never the same after Jimi passed. It was like he died with him.

When the Jimi Hendrix Experience
play at The Ambassador Theater,
Washington DC, Nils Lofgren
was in the audience. 'When I
saw Jimi Hendrix, I just was
possessed. I realised, 'Oh my
God, this is what I want to do.
It's going to be my career.' And
there was no turning back.'

NILS LOFGREN

AMBASSADOR THEATER

9-13 AUGUST 1967, WASHINGTON DC

I WAS THERE: PAUL DALEY, AGE 19

In the summer of '67, I saw Jimi at a free afternoon show for
schoolchildren. Early in the summer of '67 I had moved from
DC to NYC but missed my old friends. We were all extremely hip
and knowledgeable about folk, rock and jazz. I hitched back for
a short visit and, luckily, a friend had heard of a free afternoon
performance. It was this guy who used to be called Jimmy James,
who had a good rep from playing at the Cafe Wha? in the Village.
Now he was Jimi Hendrix and there was some buzz about him.
And it was free.

I remember going to an unfamiliar part of town and squeezing
into an old movie theatre with lots of little black kids in the
middle of a sunny afternoon. My friend probably got the word
from someone she met while student teaching, or from some
musician. But we had no idea what we were about to see and
hear. Lots of little kids, now in their late 50s, got 'experienced'
that day. Me too. Jimi did the show just to give something to
the kids. His flamboyant look was fully justified by his smashing
sound. Within a few weeks, I owned the album.

I WAS THERE: BILL HAVU

I played with Hendrix. I was in a band called the Natty Bumpo. I had a place in DC with my friend Cam Bruce. We were living there, the two of us, but prior to that the whole band lived together in this big house up in Chevy Chase. So I was in DC and had been going to American University. This was during the Vietnam protest era and it was pretty impossible to get an education because if the students weren't out protesting at the Pentagon, the teachers were, and vice versa. I went to probably all the various marches and 'be ins' and what have you during that period.

Cam and I had an apartment on Corcoran Street in the heart of DC, right up on Dupont Circle, the epicentre at the time, about a 15-minute walk from the Ambassador Theater, just up and around the corner from Columbia and 18th and just south of the Adams Morgan community.

Natty Bumpo was kind of crossover. It had folk roots to it, and then we got pretty heavy into rock the more we stayed together. The more we played the more we heard. The Byrds were an influence and, later, Cream. We had a lead guitarist but he had nothing anywhere near the chops Hendrix had. Not that that changed us, because we wrote our own songs. We had about 60. We were unique. We were well known in the area and were tapped to be house band for two long runs in a row. One was with Hendrix. It was just luck that we played with him. We were just there. He came in off that Monkees tour, which he quit, and the Ambassador said, 'Yes, we'll take him'. I don't think they knew at the time what they were getting.

The Ambassador was an old movie house built back in the teens, having a renovation in 1922 after the ceiling collapsed from a snowstorm. When the movie house went under, Joel Mednick and his partners leased it, took out the seats and used it as a dance club. It had a big stage as it had been a theatre at first, and a sloping set-up meant you had a big floor in front of the stage but also an area where people could stand and see over each other's heads. It could hold over a thousand.

It only lasted six months, because they had no age limit so kids were hanging out. They didn't serve alcohol but there was a curfew in '67, and under-18s would be picked up by the police routinely in front of the place. The city council and other notables thought it was a menace and wanted rid of the hippies and rock'n'roll music in those pretty puritanical times. We were lucky it existed as long as it did. It was a kind of flashpoint in DC in terms of music history for the area. Prior to that there had been lots of jazz across the street at the Showboat. That was Charlie Byrd's place, now called the Songbyrd Lounge. That's where we had our 50th anniversary party as the Ambassador was torn down. It's now the SunTrust Bank Plaza.

There was a Thursday afternoon concert for the Adams Morgan community, then part of the African-American community. It was pretty much the ghetto, so it was a freebie. Kids, adults and whoever could come and there was Les McCann and other black musicians, mostly jazz and blues, and then Hendrix.

We were more familiar with Jimi than most people were, because Cam Bruce and Tom Wright knew The Who, and The Who were aware of Hendrix and were playing that very week, opening for Herman's Hermits at the Daughters of the American Revolution Hall. We knew who Hendrix was, although I don't know we knew much of the music.

I played that Thursday afternoon because Mitch feigned having appendicitis. In fact he wasn't ill. He played that evening. He just didn't want to do it because it was free. They were paid sidemen. Noel did it, but Mitch wouldn't. I was the nearest union drummer. We played one night – Wednesday's opening night. So we were a little familiar with him.

He said, 'Do you want to play a set?' I said, 'Yeah, sure.' Lucky me. I was in the right place at the right time. I sat on that stool and didn't know what the first song was going to be. I had no clue. He just said something to the effect of, 'Oh, my drummer's not here today so we have the drummer for the Bumpo. It'll be okay,' then he hit a chord. I just launched right into it. I don't remember the song, although it was probably 'Foxy Lady'. It was something that was very much part of his repertoire at that point. It was all three-chord blues and pretty easy to play along. Mitch's playing was phenomenal though. I wish I played as well as he did. He was a great drummer. Years later I talked to a couple of guys that were there and they said, 'It sounded good to us'. There's no recording. There's only a few pictures that Virginia Vertiz took. One shows Hendrix and Noel down the side of the stage and Mitch behind him - you can't see his head - and you can see my drumkit off in the corner, where they just had to move it off the stage. You can see the face of the bass drum where it says 'Natty Bumpo' on it. That's my only physical photographic evidence that it actually happened.

Cam invited Jimi over to our shabby little apartment for dinner after we played with him, and he said, 'Sure'. It was a three-storey apartment building with two apartments per floor and a basement. We had the front apartment on the third floor. It was impromptu. Mitch and Noel didn't come. We intuited from that they kind of had their own thing. They kept their own counsel, and Jimi did his thing. This was early on. This was right after they split from the Monkees tour. This was the very first time he'd been back to the States with them as the Experience. And while I think they were bonded musically as a group I don't think they were totally bonded socially.

Hendrix showed up and had a whole bunch of hangers-on from our band. There were probably 20 people in our little one-bedroom apartment at 1823 Corcoran. We didn't have any money. We were so broke back then we had no food. But we had plenty of beer, so we went downstairs to the kitchen. There was a group of Korean guys studying with the FBI and they shared the big refrigerator with us. And in there was one of these five-gallon commercial aluminium-cooking pots you see in restaurants, full of a Korean rice mixture that these guys ate, enough to serve us all. It was just a huge pot of food. We liberated it and not knowing Korean cuisine, dished it out to everybody. Then we realised it was full of chilli peppers. It lit your mouth on fire. Hendrix went ahead and ate it. But I remember most of the people who tried it were aghast at how hot it was. It was hysterical. There was a lot more drinking and I lost track of what happened for the rest of the evening, but I do remember that Jimi sat quietly in the corner on the floor - we didn't have much furniture - and just observed us interacting with each other. He was a very considered, quiet, contemplative person.

We had just bought a new Ovation, a round-back acoustic guitar, and it was our pride and joy. Somebody stepped on it and broke it and we were incensed. I remember Chuck Smith getting in their face, saying, 'Look man, you're going to have to replace this guitar. We need this guitar.' And one of them said, 'We can give you one of Jimi's, we can give you a Stratocaster.' And we said, 'What are we going to do with that? It's left-handed. We can't play that.' I can't remember how we got compensated. I don't even know that we did. But things were crazy back then.

I WAS THERE: PHIL HERZOG, AGE 14

Our high school band played there a few times. We opened for a few notables. It was such a happening place with great musical artists. I was a young hippie type caught up in the movement. With no age restrictions our band went regardless of whether we were playing there or not. One

day we were driving down there. I asked our drummer Dean, 'Who's playing tonight?' He told me, 'Some guy named Jimi Hendrix. I just heard him on the radio and he sounds good.' Needless to say we were amazed at what we saw. Our jaws dropped, along with those of everyone else there. That was the first night of five he played there. Admission was a couple bucks. We returned for a few more shows. Since our band played there too we had the run of the place.

One night, we went upstairs where the dressing room was to smoke 'something' and ran into Jimi. Briefly chatting, we invited him to join us. Sadly he declined. Too bad selfies didn't exist then.

On his last night we'd attended another concert in town at DAR Constitution Hall. The Blues Magoos and The Who opening for Herman's Hermits. Imagine that! Knowing we would miss Jimi's last show we skipped The Hermits and headed over to see Jimi. So did The Who and Magoos as I recall. That night, as we watched from backstage, Jimi made love to his Strat, climaxed on it with lighter fluid, set it on fire, smashed it and threw it to the audience. A thrilled girl in the audience caught it.

Then an employee or bouncer took it from her, much to her dismay. Could you imagine that memory? The following weekend it was displayed in the lobby, autographed. I recall hearing more recently that years later it was stolen from the person who possessed it. I wonder who has it now? I like to think it's the girl that originally caught it.

I was a very lucky young kid to have experienced all the bands that summer and years later, including Woodstock. We didn't see Jimi there, unfortunately. Too much rain, mud and acid, plus we had a long road trip ahead of us.

I WAS THERE: CHARLES SMITH

I remember walking into the lobby, and there he was standing like he was in outer space. He was just staring. He never saw me. I knew he was really stoned. I thought, 'Boy, that doesn't look good'. He wasn't just playing music; he was invoking dark spirits.

Jimi and Noel on stage at the Fifth Dimension, Ann Arbor, 15 August 1967 (photo by Wilson Lindsey)

FIFTH DIMENSION

15 AUGUST 1967, ANN ARBOR, MICHIGAN

I WAS THERE: DANNY BLACKBURN, AGE 16

I saw both shows. The first was 18 and under and the second 18 and over. In 1967 all the new live shows were at teen clubs, none of which sold liquor. I was a roadie for a band, and we practiced there during the week so I got in early. The first show was kids. There were maybe 25 to 50 people and nobody knew who he was. After the first show, we got on the phone, called the band and told them to call friends and stop whatever they were doing and get down here. 'Real history is taking place!' The second show was better attended, with perhaps 50 to 100 people. He did the thing with lighter fluid, lighting his guitar, and playing with his teeth. The songs were from his first album. I had heard it but not memorised it yet. The second show was all the music community in Ann Arbor. Several knew in advance, I saw Scott Richardson of the SRC on TV and he announced it. I think it was a Tuesday night.

I WAS THERE: ROGER WHITE, AGE 17

I saw Jimi Hendrix play before I knew who he was. I was working at a swimming pool in Dearborn, Michigan and waiting to start my senior year of high school. 1967 was called the Summer of Love but with the Detroit riots I saw tanks rolling down the streets and John Lee Hooker singing, 'The Motor City's burning.' But as suburban teens we were listening to the music coming out that summer, 'I Was Made To Love Her' by Stevie Wonder, 'For What it's Worth' by Buffalo Springfield, 'Higher and Higher' by Jackie Wilson, 'Happy Together' by The Turtles, 'Cold Sweat' by James Brown, 'Gimme Some Loving' by The Spencer Davis Group, 'Pleasant Valley Sunday' by The Monkees and 'Brown Eyed Girl' by Van Morrison.

We'd hang out at the record store, Dearborn Music, still open today, looking for new arrivals. A friend, Frank Lamar, would go dumpster-diving at the radio station, WKNR, to see what singles they were throwing out. He played me a 45 he'd found, 'Hey Joe'/'51st Anniversary' by The Jimi Hendrix Experience. Sitting in my room, listening to that single for the first time on a small portable record player, the one that struck me was '51st Anniversary'. It had a drive and sound that took me past the plodding rhythm of 'Hey Joe'. But that one lone single and the mention that he played

Roger's first exposure to Hendrix was a single his friend found in the radio station dumpster (photo: Margaret White)

at Monterey Pop Festival was all we knew about Jimi Hendrix.

Shortly after I saw an ad for the Ann Arbor teen club, the 5th

Dimension, where I'd see local bands like The Rationals, Bob Seger
and the MC5. It announced The Jimi Hendrix Experience was
going to play two shows, at 7pm and 10pm, on Tuesday 15 August.
I asked a girl from school, Peggie Benmore, to go but her family was
leaving on vacation and her father told her there would be lots of
other shows. I talked to Ken Everets, the drummer in my brother's
band the Family Medicine Chest, into going so he could drive.

We went to the 7 o'clock show. It was still a bright sunny day as
we went into the building, a former bowling alley, and we wound
our way through a dark maze that included a boutique into the
club. It held maybe 100 people. You could buy a coke at the front
'bar' and it had big carpeted boxes you could stack up to sit on
around the small stage in the back, which was only a foot off the
ground. It wasn't crowded but I noticed a tall, slim black guy
walking through the club. He had a huge Afro and was wearing a
wild jacket with large eyes on his chest. I'd later recognise that coat
on the cover of Are You Experienced. At the time we didn't even
know Jimi was black.

The opening band for the first show was The Thyme, regulars at
the Grande Ballroom in Detroit, but when the Experience came on
everything changed. The stage was filled with a wall of Marshall
amps, the band all had big Afros, Mitch Mitchell sneering from
behind a huge kit like a kid looking for trouble and on the right Noel
Redding, standing thin and delicate with his bass. I was standing to
the left. There was one person in front of me. As Jimi stepped to
the mic, I was close enough to have reached out and touched him
as he roared to life like nothing I'd ever heard before. The only song
I recognised was 'Wild Thing' but, as Are You Experienced and
Axis: Bold As Love came out, I seemed to remember hearing most
of those songs. Working himself into a frenzy with an astounding
set, Jimi finally threw his guitar onto the stage. Kneeling over it,
he ripped the strings loose, then leaping to his feet he battered the
guitar on the stage till the body broke off. Hanging from one string,
he pulled the neck loose and rushed to the front of the stage and
handed it to someone in the frantic crowd. Then Jimi turned ran to

the back of the stage, vaulted over that huge Marshall stack and was gone. The crowd was a mix of emotions, but everyone knew we'd experienced something as we walked out past people waiting for the next show.

The next day, telling people about the show at the pool, one of the jocks jokingly asked, 'Was he as good as The Beach Boys?' I just shook my head, he had no idea. I later learned Hendrix had been on tour with The Monkees but had been kicked off after a few shows and picked up some gigs on his way back to New York. The 5th Dimension was one of them.

I haven't run into many other people who were at that show, but one was Ron Ashton, guitarist, bassist and songwriter with The Stooges. He'd gone to the 10pm show and told me hundreds of people have claimed to him they were at that show, far more than could ever have fitted into that small room. Hendrix played Detroit three times and I was at two of them, the Masonic Temple Auditorium in February 1968 and Cobo Arena in May 1969, but they were nothing like that first up-close Experience.

I visited the Rock & Roll Hall of Fame in 2005 to find they had a Jimi Hendrix exhibit. The earliest American promotional material they had was a handbill for that Ann Arbor show. But they had the wrong date on it. They listed it as 1968. I let the front desk know it was inaccurate and I knew this because I was there.

The hardest part after this show was waiting for the record to come out. They say Are You Experienced was released in mid-August, but it seemed to take months before copies were shipped to my local record store, and the first shipment only came in mono. After repeated playing, my copy got scratched and Peggie Benmore bought me a stereo copy to replace it for Christmas. I married that girl on 18 September 1970, the day Jimi died. Peggie found out Hendrix had passed at our wedding reception and was crying as her father took her to the dance floor. She let him believe it was the dance.

I WAS THERE: HARVEY ROBIN

The Fifth Dimension opened the previous year with Mitch Ryder and the Detroit Wheels. I was playing with The Inmates (Joel Schkloven, Jack Tann and Steve Rice) and we had a Bar Mitzvah to play in Detroit on Friday, so I planned to take Debbie to the show. She was only 16, but the Fifth Dimension advertised itself as a Coffee Den and Boutique Shop with rotating bands, catering to the 16-to-21 age group. She bought a pair of bell-bottoms. I couldn't bring myself to do that. She spent the whole night trying to teach me the Boogaloo. You had to flip your wrist around while side-stepping in one direction and flip the other wrist around as you made a 180. I didn't get it. She laughed a lot.

My band, The Inmates, had sort of dissolved with the end of the school year. I went back to Detroit to try and see Debbie more often and hook up with the scores of musicians I knew there. However, Pete the Witch, Terry Kelly, Bob Hodge and I all spent too much time summering at our parents' trailers in Lexington to get much of a band together. We were all guitar players. So where do we get a rhythm section? I went back to East Lansing to see if anyone was around. The only musicians I found were Dave 'Lurch' Killion and Otho 'Buck' Otte, both piano players. We hung out for a few days until we heard Hendrix was going to play at the Fifth Dimension on Saturday. We just had to go. Buck and I sat on the mattress in the back of Dave's VW van, while Dave sat astride the milk crate he used for a driver's seat. Good thing Ann Arbor is only 60 miles from East Lansing. Turning up E Huron Street, we saw a fire truck parked out front of the Fifth Dimension. Everyone had heard of Hendrix's fiery performance at Monterey exactly two months before, so I thought it was just a publicity stunt. There was no line out front and I didn't expect there to be one. We had gone to so many gigs and seen so many famous musicians for so little money at nearly empty clubs for so long that it would have surprised me if there was. However, we were stopped at the door because the joint was full.

Then Buck went into action. I don't remember the gist of his convoluted argument, but somehow he convinced them to let us in.

The place was packed. We had to slither in along the back wall to get any kind of view of the stage and wound up with a pretty good spot to the left. The Thyme, a local group from Kalamazoo, had opened before we got there. There was also another group on the bill called The Hideaways, but we didn't see them either. Our timing was perfect because Mitch Mitchell was busy setting up his drums. Hendrix walked out onstage to an excited but relatively quiet crowd. His hair was a frumpy mess. Like me, he had evidently been trying to get his hair to frizz out like Dylan's on the cover of the Blonde on Blonde album. I never quite got that down either. In fact, when I got back to Detroit earlier that summer, I thought it best to get myself a proper 'men's haircut' to keep my dad off my back. And I hadn't bought my wire-rim glasses yet. There's a photo of me looking off in the distance (for some reason) through Buddy Holly glasses, while Hendrix was singing 'Hey Joe'. He had a pencil-thin moustache, almost like my dad's Clark Gable imitation, but more of a turned-down Fu Manchu type. His red, white and blue floral smoking lounge jacket, over a blue and gold brocade vest, with a string of yellow beads, or shells around his neck, didn't look comfortable. By the end of the set, he was sweating profusely. I jotted all this down in my notebook, hoping to write a poem about it later.

The white pants made him look a bit like the Good Humor man, who drove his white ice cream truck down our street on Saturday afternoons in the summer time. Noel and Mitch also sported far-out interpretations of the Dylan hairdo. Noel had a striped shirt with polka dots and Mitchell had some kind of silky thing on and a big scarf around his neck. I thought, 'I don't care how much I like these guys, I'm not going to dress like that! I'll stick to my blue jean jacket, blue jean shirt, and blue jean pants.'

Of all the tunes in all the gin-joints in the world, they opened with a somewhat sloppy version of The Beatles 'Sgt. Pepper's Lonely Hearts Club Band'. I was a little disappointed, but Hendrix's solo was very cool. It led straight into 'Foxy Lady'. Hendrix only had one Marshall stack and it started to make crackly noises. He was playing a Gibson Flying V with hand-

painted floral designs and a floral guitar strap, which he deftly
unhitched and swatted his amp with. The sound was thunderous,
but it worked. The crowd started to get a little more excited.
Maybe they were going to need that fire truck outside. Jimi then
grabbed his all-white Fender Stratocaster and played the first
three chords of 'The Wind Cries Mary'. I hadn't heard the song
before. Hendrix's first album had been released in the UK a few
months earlier but wasn't released in the US until a week after
the Fifth Dimension gig. Thwack! The opening three chords were
repeated and followed by a dreamy floating style of guitar playing
and equally fifth dimensional lyrics. I loved it. He followed
with 'Purple Haze', which I had heard over the radio but was
completely unprepared to hear in person. My jaw was not the
only jaw that went slack during the execution of that song. During
the solo, Jimi laid the white Strat on the floor and knelt down over
it as he had done at Monterey back in June. The crowd pushed
in harder to the stage and I couldn't see if he had a lighter in his
hand, but if he did, he either changed his mind or it wouldn't
light, because he just sort of tapped and banged out a frenetic
lead on it for a minute or two and finished the song, the Strat still
in one piece.

The Experience also played 'Hey Joe' and a number of other
tunes we'd come to recognise as some of the greatest guitar
playing ever. But I stopped taking notes at this point. The little
spiral notebook I kept in my top pocket everywhere I went got
put back. I just stood there agape like everyone else. There was
so little talk in the audience. Everyone simply stared at the stage
for the rest of the performance. There were occasional cries of
'Groovy' and 'Far out', but mostly silence. Hendrix talked a little
to the crowd. I don't remember leaving the club or driving home.

We saw Seger there, then The Woolies, just before Christmas,
and The Yardbirds just before New Year's. I was about danced
out. The Fifth Dimension continued to host local groups, mostly
managed by Jeep Holland and his A-Square Productions. But with
The Yardbirds and The Who, just one month before Hendrix, the

fare started to get more international. How times had changed. For me, forever.

My group, Wilson Mower Pursuit, had been together about six months, when our second guitar, George Korinek, read in a jazz magazine that Hendrix was a sensation at the Monterey Pop Festival. We found out he was playing the Fifth Dimension, a small club fashioned from an eight-lane bowling alley.

We went down in time for the second set, and on our way in, passed by Gary Quackenbush, lead guitar for SRC. I knew Gary from college, and asked how was Jimi Hendrix. Gary said, 'Wow, I just saw the greatest guitar player in the world!'

The stage was about six to eight inches high, and we stood just a few feet away. Jimi played 'Sgt. Pepper's Lonely Hearts Club Band', 'The Wind Cries Mary', 'Fire', 'Hey Joe'. He introduced one bandmate as 'Bob Dylan's mother'. We left the club flabbergasted. I never saw him again live, but at that same venue saw The Jeff Beck Group and The Mothers of Invention and eventually we played on that exact same stage.

Wilson Mower Pursuit Performing 'Lights' on the Robin Seymour Show 1968

Robert with his band, the delightfully-named Wilson Mower Pursuit

I WAS THERE: WILSON LINDSEY

I was working part time as a photographer and music writer for a number of newspapers and publications.

The *Detroit Free Press* was a publication I did a lot of work for over a few years. They asked if I wanted to cover that show and I jumped for it as just a few days before that Eric Burdon was in town with The Animals and I photographed that show for the *Free Press* and he was raving about Hendrix when I happened to mention to him that I was going to see his show at a little club in Ann Arbor.

He said, 'You won't believe it.' So I was really looking forward to it. I hadn't heard any of his music. His album hadn't been released in the US. It didn't come out until the end of August. It was about a week or two after I saw him before I heard the album. But I heard him at a club, photographed him and had a chance to chat off and on during the entire day. It was much better than any album.

The writer that called me about doing the job, Loraine Alterman, was the lead entertainment writer for the *Detroit Free Press*. She went on to work for *Rolling Stone* and *The New York Times*. She was my boss back then and was really revved up to see him, and so was I. It definitely lived up to the hype.

He was very nice, very softly spoken and very open to virtually any questions. That was a stark contrast to the other two times I had a chance to meet with him and chat with him. He was a different person then.

He did two sets. The club held about 250 people. One of the things I took away from this show was some of the best pictures I remember taking back in those days. I jumped on the stage when they were performing and got some very good close-ups, as well a chance to see up close and personal what his guitar technique was. As a guitarist I found that fascinating. It was just extraordinary the power the group had. They tore that club down. I'd seen numerous real good acts up to that point. Detroit always turned out top-notch musicians and major acts – it's the home of Motown and number of R&B and pop acts and I knew a lot of those guys. Hendrix was obviously something special. His effect reverberates to this day.

HOLLYWOOD BOWL

18 AUGUST 1967, LOS ANGELES, CALIFORNIA

I WAS THERE: HAROLD SHERRICK, AGE 13

I saw Jimi Hendrix open for The Mamas and Papas two months after Monterey Pop. Ticket prices were up to $5.50 and the cheapest seats I had, were $2.50. I went with a friend from school. Scott McKenzie was also on the bill. When Jimi hit the stage, I'd never heard anything so mind-blowing. He opened with 'Sgt. Pepper' and closed his set by setting fire to his guitar and throwing it in the pool in front of the stage. The next day we went out and bought *Are You Experienced*. This was truly one of the highlights of my life in music from that wonderful Summer of Love.

The group's fourth single in the UK, 'Burning of the Midnight Lamp' was released on August 19, 1967. American R&B girl group The Sweet Inspirations provided backing vocals (founded by Emily 'Cissy' Houston, mother of Whitney). The single peaked at No.18 on the charts and was backed with specially-recorded B-side 'The Stars That Play with Laughing Sam's Dice.'

SAVILLE THEATRE

27 AUGUST 1967, LONDON, UK

I WAS THERE: TONY DERRINGTON

The Crazy World of Arthur Brown was the main support and Arthur with his head on fire made a memorable entrance, then he played a fantastic set.

I was at the first show and don't remember 'Summertime Blues' so perhaps he opened with something different. My main memory of Jimi was the wall of sound. Just incredible.

Klook's Kleek was a jazz and rhythm n' blues club at the Railway Hotel, West Hampstead, North West London, named after a 1956 album by jazz drummer Kenny Clarke, *Klook's Clique*. There were over 1,200 sessions at the venue, around 300 featuring jazz and the remainder rhythm 'n' blues. Zoot Money, John Mayall, Ten Years After, and Graham Bond recorded live albums at the club. The UK Blues boom of the early Sixties brought to the club many living legends. In October 1967 Jimi Hendrix jammed with John Mayall's Bluesbreakers, standing in briefly for guitarist Mick Taylor.

KLOOK'S KLEEK

17 OCTOBER 1967, LONDON, UK

I WAS THERE: JOHN MAYALL

When he sat in with you, he would just fall right into whatever you were doing. He was a natural musician and I don't think upstaging was any part of his persona. He loved to play, he dug music and loved the attention he was getting.

I WAS THERE: MICK TAYLOR

I just thought he was amazing. For a guitarist to have that energy in his playing, and also the control and the rhythm. You know, for most guitarists it's incredibly difficult to play like that, or even play anywhere near that standard in a three-piece group. I mean, Eric Clapton did it with Cream. And Hendrix was great, the way he switched from rhythm to leads. His guitar and his voice were almost like the same thing.

Cream released their second studio album Disraeli Gears on 2 November 1967, going on to reach No. 5 on the UK Albums Chart. 'We went off to America to record Disraeli Gears, which I thought was an incredibly good album. And when we got back, no one was interested because Are You Experienced had come out and wiped everybody else out, including us. Jimi had it sewn up. He'd taken the blues and made it incredibly cutting-edge. I was in awe of him.' Eric Clapton

THE UNION, OXFORD ROAD

8 NOVEMBER 1967, MANCHESTER, UK

I WAS THERE: BERNARD GALLAGHER

I remember seeing Jimi Hendrix play Manchester Uni. I made the mistake of standing in front of one of his speakers!

HIPPY HAPPY FAIR

10 NOVEMBER 1967, AHOY HALLEN, ROTTERDAM, NETHERLANDS

I WAS THERE: HANS VROON, AGE 16

My friend and I got on our Puch moped after football training to go from Schiedam. When we arrived in the centre of Rotterdam we saw placards advertising the performance, just two hours before the concert. To our great surprise we found the venue was still selling tickets at the box office. My favourite Dutch band, Q65, were supporting.

The hall was far from full and could have accommodated hundreds more people. After a fantastic performance by Q65, we had to wait a while for Jimi to start, but the atmosphere was great and the wait was a bit more fun. When Jimi, Mitch and Noel arrived the fans became a bit noisier. With the first notes from Jimi's guitar, a huge sound broke into the room to welcome him and his band members. The sound was fantastic and especially hard.

The highlights were the famous hits, especially 'Hey Joe', which sounded fantastic. The guitar solos Jimi played with his teeth were unforgettable and received with loud cheers.

The nice thing was that there was enough space to dance, which was made use of. Also a bit of narcotics were used (not by me) as we saw a bunch of people 'dancing' - jumping up and letting themselves land on their knees on the concrete floor, not once but 20 times in a row. The 'stuff' probably did its work. I thought it was a bit frightening.

It was sensational when Mitch Mitchell broke his drum-set and threw parts of it into the hall. Unfortunately, I was not at the front. It would have been a nice souvenir. Jimi then smashed his guitar into 45 pieces and the concert ended. Richer in Experience, we returned to Schiedam to tell everyone what we had witnessed. It was an experience I never wanted to miss and I'm still proud to be one of the few Dutch people who saw Jimi live. And his music lives on!

Beginning on 14 November 1967, The Jimi Hendrix Experience embarked on their second UK tour, this time as headliners, supported by The Move, Pink Floyd and The Nice, playing 31 shows in 16 cities.

At each gig, the headliner was allotted exactly 40 minutes. The Move, who preceded him, had just half an hour, and Pink Floyd were allowed 15/20 minutes.

Hendrix was on his way to becoming a major star; his first three singles, 'Hey Joe', 'Purple Haze', and 'The Wind Cries Mary', had all been top-10 hits. His debut album, released in May, sat in the top-20, staying there for 33 weeks. Pink Floyd had also seen chart action, with 'Arnold Layne' and 'See Emily Play' reaching the top-20. The Move also had three top-10 hits, including 'Flowers In The Rain', and Amen Corner were about to score what would become their biggest hit thus far, 'Bend Me, Shape Me'.

During the tour Hendrix commonly wore a glimmering, pale-blue, crushed velvet suit with flared trousers. His set was packed with dynamic numbers, enabling the guitarist and his band to show off not only their amazing playing skills but deliver a show full of great showmanship. The set included 'Hey Joe' and 'Purple Haze' as well as a version of the Beatles' 'Sergeant Pepper's Lonely Hearts Club Band' and The Troggs' 'Wild Thing'.

At his performance at the City Hall, Newcastle-Upon-Tyne, Hendrix was having equipment problems and in frustration rammed his Gibson Flying V into his speaker cabinets. Like an enormous arrow, the guitar became stuck in the amplifier, which the audience greeted as if it all was part of the act.

ROYAL ALBERT HALL

14 NOVEMBER 1967, LONDON, UK

I WAS THERE: BARRY KEANE

I was fortunate enough to see Jimi Hendrix play live seven times between January 1967 and August 1970. I watched him perform in a variety of venues, from a club in the heart of London to a field on the Isle of Wight with 500,000 others. I even saw him play in a cave. That was at Chislehurst, where we were jammed in so tight I actually lifted my feet off the floor and stayed upright. To hell with health and safety! I watched him play three times at the Saville Theatre in Shaftsbury Avenue, London. This venue was owned by Beatles manager Brian Epstein. My fiancée and I were at the first show on Sunday 27 August 1967, when Epstein was found dead in his London flat. They announced at the end of Jim's show that the second performance was cancelled. I remember leaving the gig and passing people queuing for the second show, thinking they haven't heard the news yet. This was over 50 years ago. No smart phones then.

Every Hendrix concert I saw was memorable for different reasons. The first was at the Marquee Club in Wardour Street on 24 January 1967. I was 16 the previous June and had recently seen the Cream play live at the Bromel Club in Bromley. After watching Jimi, I said to a friend that Eric Clapton had a real rival now.

Perhaps the most memorable occasion was at the Royal Albert

Hall. Our seats were where the orchestra sits at a classical concert, so we watched the gig from behind the bands (also including The Move, Amen Corner and Pink Floyd). Just before the Experience came on the roadies piled huge speakers in front of us, obliterating our view. Sod this, I thought, so got up and sat down on the side of the stage. When Jimi came on I was a few yards from him as he played. Bliss! At the end I rushed forward to pat him on the back, thinking, 'He feels just like a normal person'. I don't know what I was expecting? Sparks to fly perhaps! I suppose what I mean is he was just a man who happened to be blessed with this incredible ability to play guitar like no one else.

Jimi's short time in the limelight was akin to a huge firework exploding in the sky, with an incredible display of sound and light. Then the spectacle disappears. And, just like the firework, Jimi was gone....

I WAS THERE: NIGEL MOLDEN

I was present at the first appearance by Hendrix at the Royal Albert Hall. I had only been living in London for two months, studying for a degree in sociology. It was unusual for a package show to appear at the RAH, although this show was obviously something different, with Pink Floyd, The Nice, The Move and Amen Corner also on the bill. Whether such a large auditorium was suited to such a presentation remains debatable. I was seated in the balcony, quite some distance from the stage. In addition, the acoustics have always left a great deal to be desired.

Each band was allowed about 20 minutes, clearly inadequate for them to present their normal performances. Syd Barrett went on the record with his dissatisfaction. The psychedelic appearance and flamboyant demeanour of The Jimi Hendrix Experience was strikingly different and confrontational. The audience reacted with a great deal of screaming and shouting throughout, and it was certainly not an opportunity to watch or listen intently. But it was a particular moment in time and I was lucky to have experienced an example of musical and social history.

WINTER GARDENS

15 NOVEMBER 1967, BOURNEMOUTH, UK

I WAS THERE: ALAN WOLSEY

Wednesday 15 November 1967 should go down in the annals of rock history in Dorset, as it's the day 'The Big Guns Came to Town'. Five (yes, five) top-selling groups – Pink Floyd, The Move, Amen Corner and The Nice as well as The Jimi Hendrix Experience, all for 15 shillings (75p). Try getting that today.

Four of us set off early from Weymouth in my Ford 'Stand Up' 1953 Popular for a 40-mile journey – Jed Stone, Boney Hall and girlfriend Carole (a Jane Fonda lookalike), and me. Quite a squeeze.

We arrived at the Winter Gardens, went around the side to where the groups' vans were, put our ears to the entry and exit doors and listened to the first performance at 6.30pm. Two for one, we thought. Nobody else thought of it.

When it was our turn, we could go in at our leisure as we had pre-booked seats. The entire set went on for around 20 minutes longer than the two hours specified.

John Allen Hendrix (as I have always called him) headlined. A metal barrier was erected across the stage to stop would-be fanatics encroaching. I had an end seat in the centre aisle, Row B. A great view. Nobody stood up during the performance, everybody was transfixed by what they witnessed. He played everything from 'Hey Joe' to 'Bold as Love', which was as he said, from his forthcoming LP, Axis: Bold as Love.

He did use his teeth. It was loud and a really-polished set. One young lad crept down the aisle and sat alongside me on his backside. The heavies soon removed him.

Noel Redding was 19, Mitch Mitchell was 21 and 'The Man with the Guitar', as the Isle of Wight Festival compere introduced him, was approaching his 25th birthday. It's sad to think they're all now gone.

Looking back, I'd have loved him to have played 'All Along the Watchtower', to me the greatest track ever laid down on vinyl. But that was to come into his brilliant musical mind a few years later.

COVENTRY THEATRE

19 NOVEMBER 1967, COVENTRY, UK

I WAS THERE: PATRICK TIERNAN

The first number he did was 'Fire'. I seem to remember 'The Wind Cries Mary', 'Hey Joe' and 'Purple Haze'. He wore a wide brimmed hat with a feather in it and crushed red flares. I asked my mates if they would come with me. Nobody would, so I saw him alone. I don't think I've seen anyone that good since. I always remind my mates what they missed.

COLSTON HALL

24 NOVEMBER 1967, BRISTOL, UK

I WAS THERE: MARTYN COLE

I was probably 15 or 16. I was a Mod, into The Who, the Stones and The Beatles. Pink Floyd were definitely something different. What made me go to that concert was the fact that we could see four or five current names there that were in the charts or thereabouts, all on the same bill. So a schoolfriend and myself got tickets to see this 'roadshow' at the Colston Hall. The artists played an afternoon matinee and an evening show. We went to the matinee, the bands playing including Jimi Hendrix, Pink Floyd, The Nice with Keith Emerson in the line-up, The Move, and Eire Apparent. One of the other bands there was the original Amen Corner, with Andy Fairweather-Low. Hendrix had a couple of hits, including 'Purple Haze'. I think The Move were second-billed, the up and coming group at the time.

I recall Hendrix setting fire to the amps and his guitar with lighter fuel and The Nice playing 'America' whilst throwing Bowie knives across the stage into wooden targets.

OPERA HOUSE

25 NOVEMBER 1967, BLACKPOOL

I WAS THERE: SIMON PHILLIPS, AGE 15

The tour was coming to Blackpool, 15 miles from where I lived. Tickets were 4s/6d (23p). My parents were okay with me going so long as it was the early show - thankfully, as it turned out, from the Hendrix point of view. We got to the Opera House early evening. The stage was a mess of all sorts of amplifiers, loads of them in two rows. We were in the centre stalls, about 12 to 18 rows back from the stage. When the show started, the place was about half-full and the compere invited those in the circle to come down into the stalls for warmth and to make the place look fuller. Imagine - this was Hendrix and the Floyd playing for pennies!

Floyd had a strobe low down at the front, projecting silhouettes high up onto the backdrop of the stage and the stage curtains. The sound was loud but clear and each instrument could be distinguished. The combination of light and sound was exactly what I hoped it would be from reviews I'd read of their London shows. I was mesmerised, but all too soon it was over. Afterwards, The Move did about 20 minutes at deafening volume, and then Hendrix did about 50 minutes. Just before he came on, they closed the stage curtains, blocking out all the other amplifiers on stage. We saw his set was being filmed from the right-hand side circle. Two songs are now on Youtube. I read in the local paper that, about 10 minutes into the late show, playing to a half-full house, Jimi said, 'This ain't my scene, man' and walked off stage.

I WAS THERE: PAUL ARCHER, AGE 15

I'd seen Jimi on TV shows and got the records. he certainly wasn't a disappointment to me. He was so exciting and new. His showmanship and guitar playing were so different. Jimi topped the bill, playing for about 30 minutes. Highlights were 'Purple Haze' and 'Wild Thing'. The atmosphere was a bit quiet as the theatre wasn't full, but overall it was very exciting. The second time I saw him was at the Isle of Wight Festival. Jimi came on in the early hours. He seemed quiet at first, like it was an effort he didn't want to make, but about 30 minutes in things started to click. Although not his best it was great to see him back on stage again, for what would be the last time sadly.

PALACE THEATRE

26 NOVEMBER 1967, MANCHESTER, UK

I WAS THERE: JAMES HARRINGTON

My old man saw Hendrix three times and sold some pot to Mike Jeffreys for Jimi. I also have a mate, Spider Mike King, who used to play guitar for Nico in Manchester, and he saw Hendrix a few times. Once he got him to sign a Dylan LP, sadly stolen in the Seventies. Another time Spider had bought a Fuzz Face effects pedal, Jimi and the boys were coming out of the BBC and Spider ran over and was like, 'Hi Jimi, I saw you play last night and I've just been out and bought one of those fuzzboxes you use. How do they work?' And Hendrix showed him how he had his set.

BLUE BOAR SERVICES

WATFORD GAP, NORTHAMPTONSHIRE, UK

I WAS THERE: GISELA OAKES

We were at Teacher Training College in Newbold Revel, between Rugby and Coventry. We'd been on a History trip to the British Museum and stopped at the services for refreshments on the way back, when Jimi Hendrix and his entourage came in. There must have been about 10 of them. I remember him carrying his tray to the table, looking shy. He seemed rather embarrassed because people recognised him. We'd all like to have gone over and spoken to him, but just sat there staring, not quite believing he was actually there in such an ordinary place.

Axis: Bold as Love was released in the UK on 1 December 1967 as the follow-up to the band's successful debut, Are You Experienced. The original UK issue came in a gatefold sleeve with a large black and white portrait photo of the group by Donald Silverstein spread over the inside and an orange sheet insert with overprinted lyrics in red.

Reprise Records chose not to release it in the United States until 1968, fearing it might interfere with sales of the first album. Axis: Bold as Love charted at No.5 in the UK and No.3 in the US. Many of the songs on Axis: Bold as Love were rarely performed live. Only 'Little Wing' and 'Spanish Castle Magic' were performed regularly.

THE DOME

2 DECEMBER 1967, BRIGHTON, UK

I WAS THERE: MIKE ROBSON

A whole crowd of us went there by train. The Move were sensational – it was during their *Something Else* period. Floyd took too long to set up but played a great show. I don't remember what Amen Corner or Eire Apparent were like. Hendrix blew them all away. He was very charismatic, and kept giggling and pointing at Noel Redding, saying, 'Look at his hair!' It was the only time I ever saw him. It was earsplittingly loud, and I was near the front.

I WAS THERE: JOHN FINCH

I remember Pink Floyd playing two songs supporting Jimi Hendrix at Brighton Dome. One was 'Set the Controls for the Heart of the Sun'. It was a great evening and Hendrix had to pull out all the stops to headline such great bands.

I WAS THERE: JUNE BASHFORD

My husband (my then fiancé) and I went to see Jimi at Brighton Dome. He was fantastic and we were in the first couple of rows. Also on the bill were The Nice, featuring the late, great Keith Emerson, who I worked with for a few years at Lloyds Bank Registrars before he left to pursue his musical career. He was then saving up for his first Hammond organ. He is sadly missed, as of course is Jimi.

THEATRE ROYAL

3 DECEMBER 1967, NOTTINGHAM, UK

I WAS THERE: PAUL MAYFIELD

It was the first Hendrix tour. I think I paid ten shillings (50p) and went with four friends. The sound was so incredible. There was no health and safety restriction over the level. In the old Theatre Royal the big old amplifiers and speakers were wrapped right around the whole stage and the ceiling and the sound was such that you almost felt yourself pinned back in the seat. Hendrix came on last and when he started to play, he was zapping so much power that the lamps at the side of the theatre were flickering. A report in the Nottingham Evening Post the next day said there was a power surge because he used so much juice. When you came out you were deaf. I remember trying to speak and you couldn't hear the traffic passing by. It was very difficult to have a conversation.

I WAS THERE: EILEEN MARY

I was still at school (I was born in 1952). There had been a 'different' (for the times) kind of gig planned for Spalding Bulb Halls and I really wanted to go, but wasn't allowed, so as a consolation prize my elder, staid sister arranged a different trip, a seated concert in Nottingham I think, with a relative, not my mates. All I remember is feeling he didn't suit the venue, and the audience didn't seem to really appreciate it! The stage was an explosion of colour and sound, yet the audience didn't seem to be feeling it!

GREEN'S PLAYHOUSE

5 DECEMBER 1967, GLASGOW, UK

I WAS THERE: GORDON PHINN

For those of us who lived through it, already glued to our transistor radios and Dansette record players, 1967 was an endless explosion of revelations. Every month, and sometimes every week, amazing music charged our imaginations. Spring's double-a side of 'Penny Lane'/'Strawberry Fields Forever' might be regarded as an opening salvo. We'd been primed with *Revolver* and many ace singles in '66 - The Yardbirds, The Spencer Davis Group, The Animals, The Kinks, The Byrds, Dylan, the Stones, Simon and Garfunkel. The pop song was advancing leaps and bounds, continually breaking down barriers the industry thought permanent. The summer brought *Sgt. Pepper's, Piper At The Gates Of Dawn*, and *Are You Experienced*, a triumvirate of glorious catastrophe for the conventional.

My good friend Angus McRuary and I owned all three between us and our mutual listening sessions were exercises in awe, punctured by the usual teenage gossip. And it was Angus who insisted, much to my and my mother's reluctance, we buy tickets for the December visit to Greens Playhouse of the now infamous Hendrix Package Tour.

Topping the bill, Hendrix and the Experience, all great players. Mitch was a standout in his bright red jumpsuit, drumming above and beyond the call of time-keeping. And Jimi, a firestorm of guitar gymnastics and other worldly sounds that could never have been imagined from his *Top of the Pops* appearances. With such a line-up and such virgin ears trying to absorb and understand, it's probably no surprise to hear we were overwhelmed by the sonic overload ragged glory on display, not to mention the mini-skirted young ladies along our row rubbing their crotches against hard-back theatre seats then common throughout the land. Jimi certainly got them going that night.

I WAS THERE: KATHY DUFFY

I saw Jimi with my brother Gérard. He was a Hendrix fan and I was a Rolling Stones fan, but he had no one to go with so asked me and my friend Jean. Jean and I had seen lots of bands, including the Stones a few times. I liked some of Jimi's music. Jean didn't. The Stones were her heroes too.

It was a mad rush when the doors opened. When he came on, the crowd went wild. He had an orange silk Sixties-style shirt and looked amazing. I've honestly never seen a band so different. It was amazing. His performance was outstanding, playing the guitar behind his back, between his legs and with his teeth. This was unheard of and not been seen before. He was gyrating with the guitar provocatively and Jean decided to leave and wait for us outside. She thought it was disgusting, but Gerard and I were totally entranced.

Unfortunately, Gerard was killed in a motorbike accident just months after the concert. I was heartbroken. He was my best friend as well as a brother. He was only 17. However, the years pass

and life goes on. I'm so glad I went to that concert. Not many folk can say they saw Jimi Hendrix. It's so sad that he passed so young. And I still have Gerard's copy of *Are You Experienced*.

On 20 December 1967 The Jimi Hendrix Experience spent the first of two days at Olympic Studios, London recording 'Crosstown Traffic'. The song refers to Manhattan's traffic between the East and West sides, infamously known for thick congestion. Hendrix played a makeshift kazoo made with a comb and tissue paper in tandem at points with his lead guitar and vocals. The track became the second single from the album *Electric Ladyland*.

Remembered as the last major show Syd Barrett played with Pink Floyd, ending the set dazed and motionless onstage with arms hanging limply at his sides, December 1967's Christmas on Earth Continued was a 'super-concert' trailed as an 'all night Christmas dream party'. Its bill featured The Pink Floyd, The Who, Eric Burdon and The Animals, The Move, Soft Machine, the Graham Bond Organisation and it was topped by The Jimi Hendrix Experience. The Who didn't make it, but the unbilled Traffic did. Poor pre-gig publicity and freezing cold temperatures meant the show was a financial flop and poorly attended. Hendrix played a Gibson Flying Arrow guitar, with Noel Redding reportedly niggling Jimi by playing bass behind his head as Jimi performed tricks with his guitar.

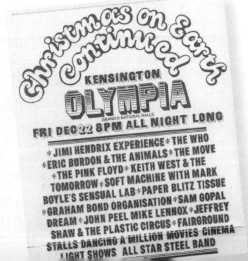

Christmas on Earth Continued

KENSINGTON

OLYMPIA
GRAND & NATIONAL HALLS

FRI DEC 22 8PM ALL NIGHT LONG

* JIMI HENDRIX EXPERIENCE * THE WHO
* ERIC BURDON & THE ANIMALS * THE MOVE
* THE PINK FLOYD * KEITH WEST & THE
TOMORROW * SOFT MACHINE WITH MARK
BOYLE'S SENSUAL LAB * PAPER BLITZ TISSUE
* GRAHAM BOND ORGANISATION * SAM GOPAL
DREAM * JOHN PEEL MIKE LENNOX * JEFFREY
SHAW & THE PLASTIC CIRCUS * FAIRGROUND
STALLS DANCING A MILLION MOVIES CINEMA
LIGHT SHOWS ALL STAR STEEL BAND

OLYMPIA

22 DECEMBER 1967, LONDON, UK

I WAS THERE: KEVIN MOLYNEUX

I saw him again at Olympia. It was a massive place. I was an engineering apprentice and a big crowd of us went up there. It was an all-night thing and they had a fairground in there, with a stage either side. They had light shows going on and bits of film and stuff in rooms off the main arena. It was one of these 'happenings'. To be honest, the place wasn't rammed with people. I don't know why.

The fairground was plonked right in the middle in between the two stages. There was still plenty of room to move about, but as soon as one band finished on one stage the other band came onto the other stage. When Hendrix came on, we were all up the helter-skelter, and about to ride down. You know when everyone tries to come down at the same time? We were all up there and you could see the stage and Hendrix came on and there was a big shemozzle, trying to get down quick to get over to the stage. Incredible.

He was just out of this world. It was unbelievable. The Upper Cut, where I'd seen him before, was a fair size, but it was nothing like Olympia.

They had Traffic play that night. Keith West and Tomorrow played as well. They were unbelievable. Steve Howe, the guitarist out of Yes, was with them. I thought they were going to be absolute crap but were incredible that night. It was a good gig. Pink Floyd were playing as well. It was just before Christmas 1967. We came out about nine o'clock in the morning.

When Jimi died, I didn't like the direction he was going, musically. It left me a bit cold. It was going a bit towards jazz. That's not my thing. I like the old rock stuff. I remember getting that first album. It was just unbelievable. I've given so many records away for some stupid reason but still have *Electric Ladyland* on vinyl. 'All Along the Watchtower' is back on an advert on TV. That music's never going to die.

1968

On 3 January 1968 The Jimi Hendrix Experience landed.in Gothenburg for a four-date tour of Sweden and Denmark. The musicians checked into the Hotel Opalen, then decided to visit Klubb Karl before returning to their hotel to party in the room of drummer Mitch Mitchell. A guest complained to the night receptionist about a disturbance in the room above and the receptionist found Jimi lying on his bed in a pool of blood, the room devastated by an apparent violent rampage. Hendrix had broken the window and injured his hand while wrecking the room. He was arrested and transported to hospital for treatment after police were called to the scene.

After a relatively quiet January (arrest notwithstanding), Jimi flew to the US for more live dates.

FILLMORE AUDITORIUM

1 FEBRUARY 1968, SAN FRANCISCO, CALIFORNIA

I WAS THERE: JUNE YOKELL, AGE 18

I saw him live at the Fillmore West in February 1968 with Albert King. It was so packed I could hardly stand up, so spent some of my time making sure I was close to an exit. I went with my friend from college. We were on a work/study semester from Goddard College, living in the Haight on Ashbury Street. She worked in a crafts store in the Fillmore and I worked for the SF Children's Center and American Friends Society. We used to go to the Fillmore, the Avalon Ballroom or the Straight Theater about three times a week. Jimi was pretty amazing.

June was an avid gig goer

WINTERLAND

4 FEBRUARY 1968, SAN FRANCISCO, CALIFORNIA

I WAS THERE: KRISTINE ALLES, AGE 16

My high school boyfriend was in a rock band and took me to this concert at Winterland. I believe it was a Saturday night. It was packed – wall-to-wall people. It was so hot in there that the sweat was rolling down my back. It was an amazing concert. I wish I'd been just a couple of years older to appreciate it as much as I would now. I saw Jimi play his guitar with his teeth. How I wish I could go back in time. These venues were the best. I'm so fortunate to have grown up in the San Francisco Bay area, 17 miles south of the city. That's where the action was!

Despite its name, Kristine remembers Winterland was very hot the night Hendrix played

I WAS THERE: STEPHAN MIRAMON

I saw Jimi with The Soft Machine at Winterland. I came into the venue as dozens of multi-coloured balloons came down from the ceiling. I kicked one of them to the stage and Jimi kicked it back at the crowd. It was a special moment, as was the show that night. Everyone's jaw dropped. It was standing room only and I worked my way to the front. I was captivated by his presence and showmanship. It's a night I'll never forget, fuelled by some of the best LSD around. I couldn't go home that night, since I still lived with

Stephan dropped acid, saw Jimi, slept on the beach. As you did, living in California in the Sixties

my parents and was too high to deal with the re-entry. I opted to sleep on the beach. It was cold but magical, as was the show.

WINTERLAND

5 FEBRUARY 1968, SAN FRANCISCO, CALIFORNIA

Dorothy remembers the dope, the concert and the boyfriend's car getting broken into

I WAS THERE: DOROTHY DUDER, AGE 15

I grew up in the San Francisco Bay area in the Fifties and Sixties. My aunt lived there, so I spent a good deal of time visiting with my cousins. My aunt was tres chic, Bohemian and very hip. I loved 'the city' and all its colourful people, Haight Ashbury, free concerts in the park, vintage clothing stores, coffee shops and bookstores.

In February '68, my boyfriend asked if I was interested in seeing Hendrix live in concert at Winterland. Naturally I said yes. I had to concoct a fake ID in case anyone asked how old I was. I still remember what I wore: Levi's jeans, a turquoise/white/ lime green striped sweater and squaw boots - suede ankle boots with fringe and leather ties.

We arrived, parked the car in a rather sketchy neighbourhood, and got in line. There were no reserved seats. We all sat on the floor, very communal. A generous fellow sat next to us rolled joints all night long and the place was thick with smoke and the smell of patchouli oil.

If I remember correctly, Albert King opened the show with some classic blues sets. Next was John Mayall and the Bluesbreakers, a personal favourite. Then the headliner. I remember jumping to my feet and dancing until Hendrix finished. He did not disappoint.

We left the show with our heads spinning, our throats hoarse from shouting and our ears ringing. It was a joyous experience. We got back to the car to find it had been broken into, and my boyfriend's suede jacket had been stolen, which scarcely mattered. We had been transformed.

I currently work in Hollywood as a television production finance executive. A poster from that show hangs in my office. Everyone, young and old, wants to hear the story. It was epic, I tell them. Indeed it was. Oh, how I long for a time machine - it would be grand to revisit that night!

STATE COLLEGE MEN'S GYM

8 FEBRUARY 1968, SACRAMENTO, CALIFORNIA

I WAS THERE: ROBERT BUNBURY

I saw him three times. For the first, tickets were $2.75 in advance and $3.00 at the door. The group that opened was The Soft Machine. The concert was in the gym at Sacramento State College and I was able to go in the back dressing room and meet Hendrix. I didn't have a pass. I was a young kid, pretty high at the time, and just wandered backstage. Things were a lot different then. I really don't remember what he said to me. Unfortunately, I got rid of my poster signed by Hendrix and a signed photo of The Soft Machine.

ANAHEIM CONVENTION CENTER

9 FEBRUARY 1968, ANAHEIM, CALIFORNIA

I WAS THERE: DAVID RANDLE, AGE 19

In the months before I went to see Jimi my band performed live in concert with the likes of Cream, The Who, Jefferson Airplane and Steppenwolf.

I come from the perspective of being a recording artist and

fellow guitarist. I had a band called The Brain Police, one tick away from being a major artist signed to Decca Records, London. Our manager messed up our record deal and then there were some economic issues and a couple of guys needed to leave because the money hadn't come through. It was a bad situation but an awesome run. We played with Eric Burdon and The Animals, The Byrds, and Buffalo Springfield. Lots of luminary people. I really enjoyed it.

Bands sometimes don't last that long, especially when they don't get that major break. That's where the revenue comes from. I was 18, 19. Everybody was older – Eric Clapton, Neil Young – but we were right on the precipice. It just didn't happen for us.

Based in San Diego, we did major shows and as we weren't that far removed from the high schools, a lot of kids wanted us to play school dances, so we played about four times a week all over the county, from dance clubs to schools to concerts to listening rooms.

But on the days when we were free, especially when the band broke up, I went out to see people. I saw Hendrix. I saw Led Zeppelin. I saw Jethro Tull. I saw a bunch of people I admired. Hendrix was one of the first after we dismantled.

We played our own music in an acid rock style but had two singers that were really good at harmonising, like The Beatles, so played that and blues-tinged things like The Yardbirds. Maybe we did too many styles.

As a guitar player you're scouring the environment to listen to the next thing. At the beginning, my idol was Clapton, and we were very fortunate to do a couple of shows with Cream in '68. We went up to the Whiskey in Los Angeles in '67 and heard them there. There's a big movement from The Beatles to Cream and the idea of a guitar-centric band and not a vocal-centric band. Strong vocals but built around virtuoso guitar. That was different from anything The Beatles did. George Harrison was a good guitar player, but it wasn't guitar-centric. Even on 'While My Guitar Gently Weeps', they asked Clapton to come in and play the solo.

Music was starting to evolve and things were changing. I remember reading interviews with Clapton about what it was like when Jimi first came to England and wanted to sit in on a show. All these guys who were friends like Jeff Beck, Jimmy Page and Eric Clapton were being wowed by how differently he approached the instrument, how opened up it was, how differently he played from the way they played.

He still had a blues foundation - the harmonic progressions weren't that different, the chords underneath the music, and he was still playing the same scales and modes - atonic and dorian, that sort of thing. But he had a different way of feeling, a different characterisation in the music, a different essence in the way he played.

I can't remember who I went with. That night there were only two people in the world - Hendrix and me. I was there and fully absorbed by what he was doing. I was blown away by Mitch Mitchell as well. I'd never seen a drummer play like that.

We had non-concert shows when playing dances and stuff where we played 'Fire' and 'Purple Haze'. *Are You Experienced* had been released. I wanted to get a really good view. It was floor seating and I was in a good spot. They were very loud. He had plenty of gain on his amplifier.

It was no trouble hearing everything. It was interesting to see the way he approached the instrument. He did a lot of stuff where he picked the strings and started the strings working, the strings would continue to vibrate and he would tremolo the strings, amble off and keep that vibe going.

As he moved his arms around, walked the stage and looked over at Mitch and Noel Redding, he was in his own world, just expecting them to follow. Noel was a guitar player so didn't play bass like a bass player. I remember a slight disappointment that the band could have been tighter and sounded better with a bass player like Jack Bruce. But Mitch was profoundly great and Jimi was just mind-blowing.

He went back and forth between playing straight-ahead blues

things like 'Red House' to psychedelic distorted guitar things on very flowy pieces like 'Little Wing' and 'The Wind Cries Mary'. And nobody was using double stops on the guitar with moveable chord shapes while they were singing. That was really innovative at the time.

I WAS THERE: SYLVIA HOLCOMB, AGE 22

My (now deceased) husband and I saw him at Anaheim Convention Center. We knew exactly who he was. When we got seated it took a while for the first act, The Animals, to appear. Then Jimi walked out, smiling, and started talking to us all. A guy sat just across the aisle from us stood

Sylvia saw Jimi play 'The Star Spangled Banner'

up and yelled, 'Fuck you, Jimi'. Jimi put his hand over his ear, said, 'I can't hear you man'. He yelled it again and Jimi laughed and said, 'You aren't my type, man'. The guy was also black. Security took him out. Everyone laughed. Then he played.

He was so good, he talked a lot also. He seemed very kind. The best part of the show in my opinion was when he got the stool, sat and put that guitar up to his mouth and played 'The 'Star Spangled Banner'. It was so amazing. It was truly something to see. He put on quite a show. He lit up a guitar and did his thing. He was absolutely the greatest. I loved living in Southern Cal in the Sixties.

The Jimi Hendrix Experience headline at the Shrine Auditorium, Los Angeles. Support is from The Electric Flag, featuring guitarist Mike Bloomfield.

❛For years, all the Negroes who'd make it into the white market made it through servility, like Fats Domino – a lovable, jolly, fat image – or they had been spades who had been picked up by the white market. Now here's this cat, you know: 'I am a super spade, man. I am, like, black and tough❜

Mike Bloomfield

SHRINE AUDITORIUM

10 FEBRUARY 1968, LOS ANGELES, CALIFORNIA

I WAS THERE: PAUL BODY

After seeing Jimi at Monterey, I'd been bragging to my friends that they had to check him out. Anyway, he was coming to LA, touring behind *Axis: Bold As Love*. The show sold out in a hurry. I didn't get a ticket so decided to go over to where he was playing that afternoon to see if I could score some tickets. My buddy Mark and I jumped in my car. We parked in a deserted parking lot and started walking towards where we were hearing sounds. We walked through one door and another door and next thing we know, we're on stage with Jimi Hendrix, Mike Bloomfield, Harvey Brooks, David Crosby, and I think Buddy Miles was playing drums, although Mitch Mitchell was there and they were jamming. There·we were, inches away from Hendrix as he jammed. We hung around for what seemed like hours, which it wasn't, but it felt like it. Jimi looked cool and was playing a Flying V instead of his usual Strat.

I tried to say a few words with him after he was done. He was in his own world but he did acknowledge me. They tried to kick us out before the show but we were having none of it. By 'we', I mean Mickey Dolenz and Samantha and a bunch of other people, so we got to hang in the orchestra pit. Jimi the Fox was on fire that night. I looked back at the audience and their mouths were open in wonderment.

Jimi was funny, really digging the moment. He ran down the alphabet and when he got to R, he said, 'R is for 'Red House'' and did a scorching version. Some woman I was standing beside kept calling out for 'You Got Me Floating', but he didn't do it. Peter Tork was sitting on Jimi's Marshall and at the end of that last song Jimi for some reason threw his guitar towards him. Jimi was at the height off powers that night. He was still doing the tongue, the playing with his teeth things, but was also playing some earth-shattering music. That night I thought he was going to be around for 100 years. Well, in a way he has.

I WAS THERE: MARK EDWARD

This was the first time I saw Jimi and I sat in the 12th row, just left of centre-stage. I will never forget it. My memories are crystal clear and fogged with crazy paisleys at the same time. I was a stoned, innocent beach boy. This was the fabled Electric Circus Tour, featuring Jimi, Soft Machine, Blue Cheer and The Electric Flag. Soft Machine also blew me away, but that's another story. I can see why Jimi chose them to open for him. It took me about 10 years to recover fully from that night and realise just how influential it had been on my brain cells. I would never be the same.

Watching Jimi play was like watching fire burn. He was a magician in full control of his magic. Funny, laid-back and with a go-with-the-flow attitude that made you feel there was no ego running his show. Like the best in jazz, it seemed The Jimi Hendrix Experience just blew and grooved on the improvisation of each other's vibes. The sound was other-worldly. There is no way to describe what he wrung out of that guitar, just the purest sweetest colours of a new form of - well, now that I think about it - surf music! I grew up in a beach town in California and Jimi just took his Fender Strat and surfed my mind with it. Unless you 'experienced' it, it's like trying to describe Zen or a spiritual enlightenment. Hence the name.

It was loud. It was raucous. It was fun. As he stood there in the spotlight, I intuitively knew I was witnessing history happening. I think that was part of the magic of Jimi Hendrix. It was almost as if, like a magician, he was doing this *just for you*. He seemed like he was connecting with you and this was a more personal vibe than any other rock group or rock god I ever saw. He was relating to you on a supremely sonic level and it cut right through me.

One particular 'stop' he did for one of his songs - of which I can't remember the title, only the ending chord of whatever it was - really freaked everybody out. It might have been that slide crunch at the end of 'Foxy Lady'. Remember, this was the high hippest of the hip hippie Hollywood crowd, so Jimi totally pulled out all the stops to show them all what he could do. Feedback was relatively unknown.

He ended with such a rumbling blast of massive sound that when it was over, it had sounded like a 20-ton truck screaming to a gravelly halt. This was way more than just a power-chord – this was a call to arms! Directly afterward there wasn't a sound. You could've heard a pin drop. I'm sure there still exist other minds-blown individuals who remember that moment of sheer power. The audience was stunned, as if by a shaman who has stopped all their silly bells and tripping dead in their tracks. Just boom! After a second or two, stunned applause and cheers slowly started circulating around the shocked room. I don't think anybody had been ready for that. I certainly wasn't, and this moment set the trend for what was to follow as my quest for electronic listening pleasure all the way up until today. I have never heard anything like that moment since.

The only other Jimi story I can vaguely remember was at the Hollywood Bowl in September 1968. To be honest, I can't be absolutely sure this actually happened or is a false psychedelically-induced memory I somehow constructed from those stoned-out times. Again, perhaps another Hollywood denizen of those golden daze might be able to back me up here. It's in my brain as clear as day nonetheless. At that time, The Bowl had a shallow lake and fountain between the front row box seats and the stage. For more philharmonic events they did the old 'dancing waters' show. This night however, while Mitch and Noel jammed their frizzy brains out, Jimi unhooked his guitar, doused it with lighter fluid, then walked out into the water of the pool. Etched into my brain is the ultimate visage of Jimi Hendrix standing there, nearly knee-deep in the water, with the reflecting image of colours and costume flowing as he held his guitar horizontally high above his head. Literally letting his freak flag fly. Wow. Just fucking wow! Nothing has ever touched Jimi. Period.

I WAS THERE: TOSH BERMAN, AGE 13

I was lucky enough to go to various music clubs on the Sunset Strip with my dad Wallace Berman, and occasionally my mom Shirley as well. It's hard for me to recall my first show with my parents, but I remember seeing the band Them (with Van Morrison) and the group The Doors (another Morrison) opening up the show for them at the Whiskey-a-Go-Go. It was unusual because the Whiskey decided to have matinee shows for teenagers under 18 and to see obviously night-time acts such as Them and The Doors performing around 3pm must have been an odd choice for these two bands. Nevertheless, I was thrilled to drink my Coca-Cola in a tall glass full of ice, while my Dad nursed a glass of beer. I also recall seeing Ian Whitcomb and The Lovin' Spoonful. But it was on 10 February 1968 that I saw my first proper concert.

I discovered The Jimi Hendrix Experience when I went to London with my parents in 1967, and we stayed in art dealer Robert Fraser's flat in Mayfair. He was going to prison to serve a sentence for having heroin in his coat pocket when he got arrested with Keith Richards

and Mick Jagger. Due to his reputation, and his status in London
society, the justice system decided he must go to jail as an example,
so he was the only member of that party that had to serve time. I
remember being star-struck as people like The Beatles would hang
out in Fraser's apartment. Therefore, I was fascinated with his
records in the living room. One of the albums was *Are You Experienced*.
Before that moment, I'd never heard of Hendrix or the Experience,
so to answer the title's question, the answer is no. Still, I was struck by
the cover of Hendrix being in the centre and Noel and Mitch behind
the leader, looking toward the camera. Their clothing and how
they positioned themselves on the album cover made an impression
on me. Hearing that album in the middle of the Summer of Love,
and in London, made such a fantastic aural presentation. It was the
combination of noise, power and the beautiful melodies that struck
me as being in the present, and music would be entirely different
from now on.

Eight months later, in Los Angeles, my parents took me to see
The Jimi Hendrix Experience at the Shrine Auditorium, near USC
campus. I'm pretty sure that this was the first time I'd been to a
formal concert, and there was a sense of drama before the music
started. The opening acts for Hendrix and the Experience were The
Soft Machine, The Electric Flag, and Blue Cheer.

Blue Cheer made a significant impression, not due to their music,
but just seeing the curtain opening, exposing towers of Marshall amps
on the stage and three small guys (compared to the size of the amps)
behind their instruments. I remember their brief set was a roar of
noise and the spectacle was pure magic. They all had the same length
of long hair and looked very much alike and I remember they bopped
their head in unison to the music they were making. I was familiar with
their hit, 'Summertime Blues', but it was the visuals that impressed me
the most. Seeing that many amps on one stage made a huge statement
to me, like a kid seeing a massive jet or rocket ship for the first time.

The Soft Machine was a total head-scratcher. A trio - a blond
drummer who dressed like Tarzan and sang, an organist who I have
no visual memory of, and a blond bassist who sometimes sang. Of

all the bands that night, they struck me as the most hippie-looking.
Beyond that, they made no lasting impression. The irony is that
in my young adult years I became and remain a huge fan of the
drummer, Robert Wyatt. Around the same time, I followed the career
and music of their bass player Kevin Ayers. In 1968 they meant
nothing to me, but when I first heard their first album in my early
20s, I recognised it as a masterpiece.

The Electric Flag I did know of, often hearing their music on
KMET. Incredible musicians, and very gritty. Hardcore blues done
in the proper manner. They looked beat and in my imagination
I thought for sure they shared a bottle of cheap red wine. In all
honesty, I never liked The Electric Flag. Mike Bloomfield, their
guitarist, was always a guitar god, but compared to Hendrix? Did
Bloomfield ever play the guitar with his teeth? Behind his back? No,
and therefore they were a bore.

Which brings me to The Jimi Hendrix Experience. My
expectations were very high, and I remember being incredibly
excited before they went on. I'd seen numerous photographs of
Hendrix before, and was genuinely impressed with his clothing and
the images of him burning his guitar. Rock 'n' roll has always had a
strong visual element for me. I often think of the band's appearance
as just as much as their music. One of the reasons why I didn't
like The Electric Flag is that their visual sense didn't appeal to my
13-year-old aesthetic. Jimi on the other hand, didn't disappoint. To
be honest, I don't recall the music that much, just the visual aspect
of him being in front of me. We had excellent seats - something
like the fifth row and in the centre. Having such a visible and iconic
figure in front of me was amazing. I felt I was watching a series of
photographs, moving in front of me. I never forget the images. I
imagine he played songs from his first two albums. Did he burn his
guitar? In my memory he did but, again, the image is so strong that I
could have willed it in my brain. I suspect other people at this concert
may have seen things differently. For me, it made a radical change in
how I processed music. Before I heard Hendrix, it was a black and
white world. After hearing that album in London, the world became

technicolor. In a nutshell, Hendrix is my first fully-coloured movie (reality) of the world in front of me.

ROBERTSON GYMNASIUM

11 FEBRUARY 1968, SANTA BARBARA, CALIFORNIA

I WAS THERE: JEFF SEATON

My friend Jock and I pretended to be official recorders for Hendrix at UCSB. We walked in the side door with the band and started setting up with a couple of microphones and a reel-to-reel recorder. One of the managers came out and questioned us. Then Hendrix came out and said, 'It's cool, man.' We got to hear the soundcheck, which was 'Purple Haze', to gauge the back-wall bounce-back, then we sat in the green room smoking weed.

SEATTLE CENTER ARENA

12 FEBRUARY 1968, SEATTLE, WASHINGTON

I WAS THERE: JERRY EVANSON, AGE 17

It was a Monday night in Seattle. A high school buddy convinced me to buy a ticket to this concert by a black rock guitarist I'd barely heard of. We rode his chopper down to the Seattle Center Arena. It was a rather small venue and the place was only about half-full. The dark stage was stacked with Marshall amps. Three dudes strolled out and took their places. When the lights went up, the opening riffs of 'Purple Haze' blasted out from those amps. The hairs on the back of my neck stood up as I experienced the Experience for the first time. It was an absolutely stunning performance.

I was a fresh faced 17-year old. My favourite track was 'Red House', a terrific blues number that showed he was able to break out from the pigeonhole of hard rock. His death in 1970 was a shock on a couple of levels. I saw him again in Seattle just a couple of months before he died. His performance seemed rather lacklustre and at the time I chalked it up to being a rock star hitting the end of a tour. Then I recall thinking about his meteoric rise to fame. By all accounts he was a very shy person. I thought that international fame, his shyness trait and a drug-laced career put him at high risk of a fall. His untimely end must have had his legions of fans wondering what might have been.

I WAS THERE: RICH MACK, AGE 20

Soft Machine opened for him. It was his homecoming show. I really don't remember much about it except it was a good show. People enjoyed it. No one knew what to make of Soft Machine. I thought the concert and the experience was important enough to go in a non-altered state. And I'm glad for doing it that way because he was gone in a few years. I have no idea who I went with, probably a girlfriend.

REGIS COLLEGE FIELDHOUSE

14 FEBRUARY 1968, DENVER, COLORADO

I WAS THERE: THOMAS NEFF JR.

I first heard Jimi around June '67. A good friend returned from his freshman year at the University of Colorado in Boulder and had purchased a copy of *Are You Experienced*. He told me, 'You've got to hear this'. From the opening strains of 'Purple Haze' to '3rd Stone from the Sun', I was left a bit speechless. I had never heard anything like it and wasn't sure if I'd ever be able to understand where he was coming from regarding his guitar style.

It honestly took three or four listens before I decided I needed to get my own copy. Denver radio station KLZ-FM was playing several tracks and it's safe to say everyone was on board. And that record would have to do until the release of *Axis: Bold as Love* sometime in early '68. It was sometime around February '68 that we heard he was coming to the Field House. It was a 'can't miss' show for me and my cronies. I remember thinking, 'Why are they bringing him there? That arena is where they play basketball!' But praise to the student body who, with permission from the priests who ran the college (a Catholic institution), Denver would experience The Jimi Hendrix Experience for the very first time.

It was Valentine's Day, but as 19 and 20-year-old kids, we couldn't have cared less and had three girls in our group of eight. It was about seeing this unique artist who, by that time, had us all dripping with anticipation.

The opening act was The Soft Machine. I don't remember much about their set. Everyone simply wanted Jimi - and now! I did feel sorry for them. At that time nobody could have expected to hold the attention of a crowd who simply wanted Jimi. I would later learn, around 1971, that The Soft Machine was a superb group of musicians. I would go on to purchase two of their albums.

I can't honestly say I remember what song Jimi opened with, but I do remember he would take a song like 'Fire' or 'The Wind Cries Mary', tracks that were probably three to five minutes on the record, and turn them into eight to 10-minute extended versions, with a lot of extended guitar work.

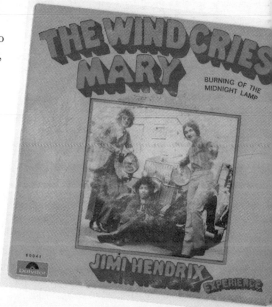

After a little over an hour he closed with a song that came as a surprise to me. Around two years earlier, I bought a single by The Troggs, 'Wild Thing', so knew the song and loved it, but had no idea he'd close with that. And just as it was coming to its conclusion, with Noel and Mitch in the darkness at the back of the stage, he dropped to his knees, took out what we now know was lighter fluid, squirted it over the body of the guitar and proceeded to set it on fire.

No one, I can assure you, had ever seen any American artist ever do anything like that. I'll admit I was stunned and rocked to stony silence. And that was it. No encore, no calls for more, nothing. I can't ever begin to explain what I felt walking out of that venue. It was as if we were allowed to peek, albeit briefly, into the work of a genius. He was a shooting star whose light would disappear. Once was not enough. I knew if he returned, I would need to see him again. There was more to absorb. And that would happen on Labor Day weekend 1968, at Red Rocks.

Appearing at the Municipal Auditorium, San Antonio, Texas, on 15 February 1968, Hendrix apologised to the audience for having to retune between each song. 'We tune so much because we care about your ears'. But after a couple of numbers he stepped up to the microphone to say, 'Well, I guess the rest of the show won't sound too good. You're looking at eight blown amplifiers'. And after three more songs a reviewer at the time described as sounding like 'garbage', the band put down their instruments and left the stage.

STATE FAIR MUSIC HALL

16 FEBRUARY 1968, DALLAS, TEXAS

I WAS THERE: ANGUS WYNNE

When he went out on tour with The Experience, one of the first dates he played was here in Dallas.

He had a date in San Antonio and he was flying from there to here one morning about midday. I was in my office and a girl I knew, a Braniff Airways stewardess, called me and said, 'Jimi's on our flight and we're gonna land in Dallas pretty soon. Why don't you come out?' I drove out to the airport, which wasn't far away, and in those days there was no security. I just walked out the gate and onto the tarmac, they put the stairway down and I met him at the bottom of the stairway, and shook hands with him. He was very friendly, like he was tripping. He told me he'd had some acid. He was jumping around a little but he was just a delightful guy to talk to, and invited us to come over to his

Angus with Jimi at Dallas's Love Field

show that night. Which we did, and we went backstage and in his dressing room and watched the first show he performed, after Soft Machine. And it was incendiary. It was about a 4,000-seat theatre and the place was all ready for him and the local radio stations had been beating the date to death. A guy named Jimmy Rabbit was the main instigator, the guy who cut all the spots for him.

I WAS THERE: JACKIE LASURE DICKSON, AGE 16

I was there! Six days shy of my 17th birthday and so excited to see Jimi. He came on stage decked out in true Texas fashion, boots, vest and cowboy hat – all black. He started talking, saying what a groovy city Dallas was, kicked his boot out and said, 'I've got on pointed toe shoooes!' and laughed. He played everything I wanted to hear and became my all-time favourite guitarist that night.

I was with my high school sweetheart, Mike Caudle, but a whole group of kids

For Jackie there was a music revolution, revelation and evolution

from Grand Prairie were there too. Debra Prather made my purple velvet mini-dress and I wore pink patent Capizio pumps. Mike doesn't remember what he wore, and neither do I. There was a music revolution, revelation and evolution going on at that time and I was lucky enough to see and hear it as it happened. Jimi was truly unique. He was born with all that passion, fire and music in his soul. What would the evolution of his music be like today? Mind- blowing, I'm sure! We didn't get to stand next to his fire for very long at all, but I can listen to 'The Wind Cries Mary' and be back there in 1968.

I WAS THERE: BOB WINGATE, AGE 16

I was at the State Fair Music Hall. I went down the left aisle to see him up close, sensing the concert would be over soon. Some other kids were sitting calmly in the aisle. Soon, Jimi banged his guitar against one of his Marshalls and a guitar knob flew over to our right, about 20 feet into the audience. The next thing I knew my stomach was planted into the orchestra pit railing. Now I was only 10 to 15 feet away from Jimi. I watched him do several interesting things on stage and then he destroyed his guitar right in front of me, as if he was doing it just for me. He started ripping off his strings with his bare hands and throwing them at us. I grabbed one and at the same time a young man next to me grabbed it as well. We fought over it. The string then fell into the orchestra pit. I always wondered why I didn't go back and get it later. He was one of my guitar heroes of all time, an amazing musician and recording artist.

WILL ROGERS AUDITORIUM

17 FEBRUARY 1968, FORT WORTH, TEXAS

I WAS THERE: MARK CAYWOOD, AGE 15

The venue was a pretty old proscenium theatre type place. It was pretty small and low tech but packed, and there was a real excited crowd. Soft Machine opened for him, had an immersive light show and did their Volume 1 album and parts of Volume 2 non-stop, with no break and no chit-chat. Needless to say, my mind was blown, a life-changing experience, and I barely remember Hendrix. Ironic, yes, but such is the chaotic life of rock'n'roll.

He was in a shitty mood for some reason. Rumour had it his dressing room was less than comfortable. He didn't speak much and played with his back to the audience most of the time. I remember he played most of the first album and closed with a pretty crazy, rousing 'Wild Thing'.

I wasn't too young to have smoked a joint on the way to the concert. Thus, the foggy memory! I saw him again in '69 in Dallas at a huge venue and witnessed a much slicker, more professional show. I don't remember many details of that either, but he played a long time, improvised long solos, and seemed to enjoy the gig.

One additional point: searching a 50-year-old memory, the narrative details become foggy or lost, but the sense impressions remain: Hendrix's clothes, the hat, the excitement and adrenaline in the crowd. Things that are rather ethereal when attempting to describe.

I WAS THERE: ELAINE BENDER

The first time I saw Jimi he played a Flying V guitar and Soft Machine opened the show. There were six Sunn amps in a row on the stage behind him. What I remember most was how loud he was. How in the world could he play guitar with his teeth? At some point, he began to destroy one of the amps with his guitar. Pieces of the amp netting began to fall all around us like shrapnel. One of my friends claims he still has pieces of that amp put away as souvenirs.

I WAS THERE: DEMERICE LASSETER, AGE 17

I'll never forget this. The Moving Sidewalks were support and they later became ZZ Top. It was great. The venue was average size, built in the Thirties. It's where the stock show is every year in February. I went with my boyfriend at the time. He is now a record store owner and musician in Austin, Texas.

I WAS THERE: WAYNE PRICE, AGE 21

My wife was pregnant with our first child so couldn't go. I took my baby sister instead. She was only 15 but liked his music. We had pretty good seats, about 20 rows back left of centre. What a great show. Very loud, but that was Hendrix. He did all his showy stuff, including playing behind his back (surprisingly well) and with his teeth. Yep, he turned that cream-coloured Fender Stratocaster toward his face and bit into the strings! Crazy stuff. He had a wall of amplifiers behind him, as did his bass player. I think they were Fender Dual Showman amps, three or four sets of them, with two cabinets each holding what looked like two JBL speakers each (they have a shiny aluminium cone in the middle and are distinctive to gear-heads like myself).

I wish I could remember the last song, when at the end he walked back to this huge bank of speakers and faced his guitar toward them, which initiated this screechingly-loud and warbling feedback, for what seemed like two to three minutes. Then, using his guitar as a sort of jousting spear, he began jabbing into each of these fabulous speakers, causing them to fall
over backward in howling protest. It was stunning to our young brains.

He stepped back towards the front of the stage, still holding his guitar, knelt down and sat back, then put what looked like lighter fluid all over his guitar and lit it, creating
a brilliant fiery end to the concert. As I remember, stage-hands came out to extinguish the fire and the crowd burst into applause. It was the most exciting concert I've ever been to and I wish I could've seen him again before his untimely death.

Michael Hart took this photo of Jimi live on stage in Houston, Texas on 18 February 1968

ELECTRIC FACTORY

21 FEBRUARY 1968, PHILADELPHIA, PENNSYLVANIA

I WAS THERE: TOM SHEEHY

Over 14 months, I came to see the Experience three times in a live setting. I first heard *Are You Experienced* on 25 August 1967. I recall the date succinctly because I saw The Who make their Philadelphia debut the evening before. I was enthralled by what I was hearing and in the context of what I witnessed the night before, began to ponder what this trio would be like on stage. Little did I know I would be able to make my first observation in six months' time. Between February 1968 and April 1969, The Jimi Hendrix Experience executed three performances in Philadelphia which remain in this city's memory as an equipoise of music, culture and politics 50 years on.

I went to a very overcrowded high school where going up and down the stairs between classes was somewhat lemming-like. One January day in 1968, a classmate named Tim was coming down the stairs as I was going up. Tim called out my name then stuck his hand out over the heads of a swarm of students, extending an orange-coloured handbill. I looked at this piece of paper and couldn't believe my eyes. Next to the name of Jimi Hendrix was the name of a place I'd never heard of called Electric Factory, along with the dates February 21 and 22. I was ecstatic.

The Electric Factory opened on 2 February 1968 with The Chambers Brothers. Three weeks later, I went to this revamped tyre warehouse for the first time to see the Experience. It was a general admission room for about 1,500 patrons, decorated in all forms of psychedelia apropos the era of hippies, love, and peace. Jimi took the stage to a rousing ovation, and quickly launched into 'Fire'. The stage was somewhat dark except for a spotlight on Jimi and, between songs, he seemed somewhat jovial as he repeatedly talked to the audience and laughed. As there were two performances per evening for this two-night engagement, the set was not concert-length, but with stellar performances of 'Hey Joe', 'Are You Experienced?' and 'Purple Haze',

I was captivated by what I had witnessed.

This 17-year-old had never seen a band that looked as distinct. I had never witnessed hands and fingers move so rapidly up and down the fretboard of a guitar. I had never heard a sound as colossal and gigantic. Musically, I knew I encountered something never seen before. I had never heard a sound so immense produced by just three musicians. As I walked out of the Electric Factory that evening, I had a big grin on my face, because I knew I would get to come upon this magic again in just 48 days.

ELECTRIC FACTORY

22 FEBRUARY 1968, PHILADELPHIA, PENNSYLVANIA

I WAS THERE: CLYDE CROASDALE

The first time I saw Jimi was at the Electric Factory in Philadelphia. We had tickets to the second show. As we waited in line we could hear some of the first show. Everybody was excited. The Factory wasn't that big. Maybe 500 seats, but there weren't really seats, just benches. We had a bench up front stage left. I could have touched Noel Redding. The stage was dark and the band appeared in silhouette for some of the show. They may have painted dayglo on their hands and faces. That's what someone said. Being a drummer I was fascinated by Mitch Mitchell. I'd never heard or seen anybody play the drums like that. They all had big Afros, which I thought was odd on the white guys. Jimi played all his first album. I remember 'Fire' quite distinctly.

He did all of his tricks. I don't remember him setting his guitar on fire but he did impale his amp with his guitar. I came away thinking I had 'experienced' something extraordinary. Not just the show but the music - at times it was other-worldly.

I WAS THERE: ROBIN STILES

I saw him play at the Electric Factory before he was well known. I was watching an unknown group before he came on. When it was time for him to play, I was surprised to see him get up from the seat directly in front of me and walk up to the stage. At the end of the show he smashed his guitar against the wall. What a wild show.

I WAS THERE: ANDY GUTHRIE

At that time the Electric Factory was really the venue for everybody, from Janis Joplin to The Jefferson Airplane. It was pretty exciting. I was just starting going to concerts in Philly. I saw everybody who came to town. Soft Machine opened and chided the audience for not staying more quiet while they were tuning up. The folks were getting restless to see Jimi Hendrix, and the lead singer said, 'Be thankful for what you are about to receive.'

I was just out of high school. There was a lot of turmoil. We were worried about the draft, getting in college, all that kind of stuff. And that's important, because Hendrix's stuff was pretty radical, revolutionary. I wasn't sure I liked it when I first heard the album. My brother brought it to me. I was into playing guitar and still play guitar now, so warmed up to it after listening to the album a few times and we went down to the concert.

It was all folding chairs. The venue had wide open spaces with folding chairs. It was very psychedelic. There was a tower in the middle of the hall and it had projectors that would put up psychedelic images on the wall behind the band. The sound system was terrible, very amateurish, and I couldn't hear him sing. It was a pretty wild performance as far as his guitar playing goes. He played his butt off, but you couldn't hear any of his vocal. During the tour they probably corrected some of it.

One of my friends who was there walked through the crowd to the stage and got whacked in the head by Jimi's guitar. He remembers it fondly.

I followed Hendrix after that. He was playing with Buddy Miles, who had a group called the Express. Hendrix was starting to record some things. He did 'Changes', he did some live things, and I was looking forward to some new Hendrix music, to hearing something different. Then I remember hearing the news.

I was in the navy and serving on board ship, out of north Virginia, when I heard that he had died. The ship had Armed Forces Radio, and if you wanted it you could turn it on. I remember thinking, 'Wow!' It was a time when a lot of them were going up in flames, like Jim Morrison and Janis Joplin.

It was just horrible. You were thinking, 'Who's gonna survive? What rock'n'roll musician of that era was going to be the next one? Who's going to choose to live?'

I WAS THERE: RICK VITO

I was in university, about an hour and a half away. I was a big guitar player. I was into the first album, trying to learn that stuff. It was so ground-breaking. Nobody had heard anything like that. It far outshone everything, as great as Clapton was with John Mayall and Cream and all that. It was just so different from anything else you'd heard from Jeff Beck or whatever. We had to see Hendrix.

We piled into this tiny car, got as many people in as we could, went to the show, stood in line. They would do two shows, and people were coming out from the first, going, 'You're not going to believe this. You're not going to believe it.' Guitar players I knew were coming out with eyes glazed over.

We were blown away because usually to get in to see an act it was a dollar fifty or two dollars. For Hendrix you had to pay three dollars, astounding by today's standards. But it was the best three dollars I ever spent.

We were pretty close, in front of Noel Redding, not far from where Hendrix was. It wasn't a huge place. It was a hall. No tables and chairs, just bench seats. The thing that's amazing about it was that in those days there were no tuners backstage, so they came out and tuned up for what seemed like 10 minutes. But when they started playing I'd never heard anybody play through Marshall amps using that sense of dynamics. He was able to get gorgeous tones out of the guitar for songs like 'Little Wing'. That had just came out and I don't think I even had it.

The way he was able to build not only the individual songs but the set, starting real slow, with a jam which might have been something like a take-off on 'Voodoo Child', and then went through all the tunes we recognised from the first record and his moves on stage. You'd never seen that on stage before.

He had a really cool sense of showmanship. He was flirting with the girls, he was dynamic, very forceful and masculine. There was nothing sissified about this guy. He was totally meaning business up there. And he somehow brought that all through the music and his guitar playing, which I think was part of his allure.

He was able to convey that where I think a lot of white guys weren't able to do that so well. This guy was a full-on soul brother. He really had the feeling and that really came across, even though he was playing this new wild rock music. It was this blend of who he was and his background, all the Curtis Mayfields and Bobby Womacks and all those cool R&B guitar players he knew about that could play. That all came through. There weren't many people with those kind of roots all thrown into one package like him. What white guys ever had the chance to go and tour playing that kind of music? That didn't exist in that period. To me it all became obvious that this guy was the real deal and nobody could even come close. The only white guy I saw playing around that time that I thought had a great feel in his play, and I saw him about a year after, was Peter Green. That influenced me as much as Jimi but in a more restrained way.

By the end of the show, he just built it to such a climax. It was unbelievable. It was like everybody who was coming out of the first show saying: 'You're not gonna believe this'. That's what I was thinking, 'I don't believe what I just saw and heard.'

I WAS THERE: JEROME A WILLIS

I saw Jimi Hendrix 50 years ago at a converted warehouse which became known as the Electric Factory. I remember the show being in the middle of the week and I had to work the next day. About a month prior I was at a friend's house who had a copy of *Are You Experienced*. I'd never heard anything like it. I told myself if he was ever in the area I had to check him out. As luck would have it, a show was announced. James Brown was going to be in town the same night. I was conflicted but decided on Jimi. I did however catch some grief from friends going to see James.

The entrance fee was minimal, five dollars I think. There were two acts. Opening for Jimi was Vanilla Fudge. Not bad for five dollars. I don't remember how the event was advertised, but it wasn't well attended. Maybe 500 people. The venue wasn't that big, and I remember standing.

The opening act did their thing. However, the crowd wanted Jimi. After about 45 minutes we got him, and he didn't disappoint. I believe he played for about two hours. He may or may not have taken a break. I remember him playing the whole *Experienced* album. He was loud, very loud, and unlike anything I had experienced. The show featured him playing the guitar with his teeth while laying on the floor. He sent us home playing 'Foxy Lady', which was so loud I thought my eardrums were going to burst. He then did something that blew my mind. He rammed the guitar into one of his speakers and proceeded to destroy it by smashing it on the floor. I was stunned, as were my fellow concert-goers. The show was over and it was one hell of a show. However, my ears rang for three days.

MASONIC TEMPLE

23 FEBRUARY 1968, DETROIT, MICHIGAN

I WAS THERE: DANA LAWRENCE, AGE 15

When we went to see Hendrix the first time, I wasn't old enough to drive. 'Wild Thing' had recently come out on the radio and we read about Jimi wherever we could; seeing as this was in the Detroit suburbs it was probably through *Creem* magazine or the *Fifth Estate*, and through WABX, our underground radio station. I went with my girlfriend Wendy, who remains a close friend 50 years later, and with two others. There were four bands on the bill: Thyme (a local band I knew nothing about), the MC5, Soft Machine and Hendrix.

I don't remember much of Thyme's set, but they played only 15 minutes. The MC5 were already pretty much legendary in Detroit, and my recollection is that they played a short set - again maybe 15-20 minutes, with a couple of high-intensity songs like 'Rambling Rose' and 'Kick Out the Jams', followed by their traditional ender, 'Black to Comm'. Then came Soft Machine. I was not familiar with them at the time but remember being mesmerised. This was when they were a trio - Mike Ratledge, Robert Wyatt and Kevin Ayers. It was before their first record came out. I clearly remember them playing 'Hope for Happiness' and 'Why are we Sleeping'. Later that year the first record came out with the rotating disc cover. I still have it today and fell in love with them forever after. I met Mike Ratledge after a Soft Machine gig in East Lansing a few years later, shortly after Robert Wyatt had fallen out of the window and become paraplegic.

We'd never seen anything like Hendrix before. From his clothing, and that of Mitchell and Redding, to the volume of sound, which was immense. Nothing ever came close to being that loud until I saw Blue Cheer with the MC5 and the Stooges at the Grande Ballroom the following year. We had never seen anyone play a guitar backward, above his head or behind his back. He played songs like 'Foxy Lady' and much of what was on the first record. At the end, with the crowd going completely nuts, since few people had ever seen that level of aggression during a show, he destroyed his guitar, the drums came down and Noel Redding was just sat there continuing to play as chaos surrounded them. I think we left deaf and dumb. Certainly, we were awestruck. It was transformative in our lives. After that, we all wanted to be rock stars, to play music.

I WAS THERE: WILSON LINDSEY

There was another show where, as soon as he walked in backstage, I could tell something was up. I don't think that show lasted more than

25 minutes. He broke a string and that was it. He just stormed out early. I've talked to some people who saw him when he came back to play Cobo Hall. I didn't see him then, and they said it was a pretty decent set. From talking to people since, it seems that his sets were either great or underwhelming.

OPERA HOUSE

25 FEBRUARY 1968, CHICAGO, ILLINOIS

I WAS THERE: ROY VOMBRACK, AGE 15

I become a rabid Jimi fan after the release of his first album, and was one week shy of my 16th birthday when some high school friends and I attended the Experience concert at the Civic Opera House - their first appearance in Chicago. There were shows that day at 3.30pm and 7.30pm, and I attended the second. I've since read that both were sold out. It was all ticketed seating and I had a nice seat looking down on the stage from the seventh row near the centre of the first balcony. The opening act was the Soft Machine, a little too progressive and avant-garde for my teenage taste. The only thing I remember is they played one song where the refrain kept repeating, 'We did it again' for what seemed like five minutes. Boring!

Then it was the Experience's turn. There was no teenybopper screaming but the audience was enthusiastic and frankly a little awe-struck by the sound, although I didn't feel it was inordinately loud. Also, the crowd was very orderly. There was no rushing of the stage or anything like that. I reviewed the concert for my high school newspaper two weeks later and wrote: 'Jimi Hendrix was fantastic at the Opera House the 25th. He and his Experience put on a great show, not only musically, but performance-wise also. Jimi's subtle humour, combined with Noel Redding's clowning, made for a fine showing. Hendrix smashed his guitar up in the first show (which I didn't attend but heard about), but only threw it around a little in the second show. What a shame.'

THE FACTORY

27 FEBRUARY 1968, MADISON, WISCONSIN

I WAS THERE: JOHN P LOUDERMAN

I was at that show with several friends. In fact, I had tickets for both shows at the Factory and we were able to get a place in the first row, standing right in front of Jimi for both shows. I was looking right at his feet, his guitar right above my head. Easily the best musical experience I ever had. Jimi rocked it out both shows that night.

I WAS THERE: JON LEWIS

There were two shows that night, and I was at both. I was working for Ken Adamany as a light-show operator. Ken opened The Factory in an old car parking garage, all old concrete and brick with thick support columns. He hadn't changed that. He booked Hendrix for what was rumoured to be $65,000 and, as a consequence, had to have two shows. I didn't do the light-show that night, but I did roadie duty, helping schlep Jimi's speaker boxes and other heavy stuff to the stage. Since I worked there I stayed for both shows, sitting on the concrete floor throughout, less than ten feet then about 20 feet from Hendrix.

He seemed confused when setting up. He did his own connection to his effects pedals, amp and all those Sunn speaker cabs. I think he had eight and Noel Redding had a similar number. Jimi spent quite a bit of time hooking up, periodically seeming to have trouble remembering which wire went where and scratching his head. They got all set and did a very brief soundcheck. When the public was allowed in, it was like a cattle stampede. I sat with my feet touching the stage, about one foot high as I remember, but by the time the crowd got in, I was sitting with my knees up to my chin.

Sitting that close and watching Hendrix work was memorable and is indelibly inked on my memory. I don't know whether it was a good show by his standards, but it was by Lewis standards - my jaw was slack through both shows. Most of my memory is of sound, sound, sound, although I remember thinking he seemed entirely someplace else at the time. He never acknowledged us near the stage by winks or pointing. For him it was the music only. Of course, he may have had perception-altering substances in him. He played with his mouth and burned his guitar, which were the cherries on the sundae of his concert. Most excellent, dude!

I WAS THERE: DON DARNUTZER

I was at that Hendrix show and it was so crowded all you could do was stand shoulder to shoulder, you couldn't turn around. I don't remember it being a big place, maybe 400/500. I remember a wall of Marshall amps with a white fabric background for the oil and water show. Hendrix could recreate all the music and sounds on the LPs, and it was an amazing show. The next I saw him he was playing arenas.

I WAS THERE: PAT NOLES

I was at the Factory. Stacks of Marshalls on the floor. They played the complete *Are You Experienced* album. Everyone thought those sounds on the album must have been studio gimmicks. Nope - he did it live! I was awestruck, and deaf for a week. I recall the sound pressure level as being best encountered in a concrete bunker at five miles distance. But I didn't mind a bit. Don Darnutzer took photos, but he said they'd been lost in the mists of time.

I WAS THERE: JONATHAN LITTLE

I met and interviewed Jimi at the Factory, the legendary club operated by long-time manager-promoter Ken Adamany where Otis Redding was headed when his plane crashed into Lake Monona on 10 December 1967. At the time I was a disc jockey at WISM, the local top-40 station. I sat in a dressing room with Jimi, Mitch Mitchell, and Noel Redding for 10 minutes or so. I asked about this new genre he was creating, that people were calling psychedelic music. Jimi replied, 'It's just music, man. That's the way we play it.' Jimi, Mitch, and Noel were more interested in lining up girls for after the show than they were in talking with me.

I WAS THERE: JOE RIPP

I was at that gig on Gorham Street. I had asked out a high school classmate I was interested in, Ann, and had just bought the Experience LP at the mall where she worked. The Factory was a relatively small venue and I remember being a little intimidated by the wall of speakers set up on the stage. I was sure the volume would be deafening. The concert started quite late and there was a lot of grumbling going on, wondering if the concert would be cancelled for some reason. Finally, Jimi came out on stage, looking wasted, like he was either drunk, stoned, high or all of the above. Then he started playing and it was magical. He seemed out of it the whole time he played, but never messed up a single song. It was a great concert.

Unfortunately for me, my date met another guy she was more interested in and we left separately. But I didn't really care, because I got to see Jimi Hendrix live!

I WAS THERE: KATHY SORENSON

The Factory was just that, an old factory. Bands were put on a makeshift riser maybe only two feet off the ground. My friend Darlene, who was also my cousin, and I stood right in front of Jimi the whole show. We could have reached out and touched him but were satisfied with his frequent smiles at us. It was indeed a night we'll never forget. I'm 69 now and can still close my eyes and visualize that night.

Darlene and I had grown up together and enjoyed the same music. We fell in love with 'Purple Haze' the first time we heard it. When we heard he was coming to the Factory we couldn't wait. We attended with my soon-to-be husband and another friend. They weren't sure they liked this 'new kind of music' but said they'd go with us and give it a try. They never got past the opening band and went to a bar, saying to meet them there because 'this kind of music and hippies' were not for them. My husband later became a hippy and an incredible fan of Jimi's and to this day is still upset that he left the show.

I WAS THERE: GARY STEUCK

I saw the 1968 Hendrix gig just off State Street. For whatever reason – I think I read the equipment hadn't turned up - we stood out in the freezing cold for hours in a mob that kept getting more packed together as people arrived. Whatever buzz we had from the ingestion of locally-available smoking products had been pretty much frozen out of us by the long time in the cold. When the gates finally opened a friend of mine, not a small dude, said it scared him to realize he was getting carried into the venue by the crush. His feet weren't even on the ground. The 'hall' was a former machine shop with huge concrete pillars spaced throughout, holding up the upper floors. I ended up a bit behind one of them with a view of Redding and Mitchell but could only see Hendrix when he moved around the stage a bit. Standing for four hours probably didn't help my mood. I don't remember any seats.

We had a friend of a friend who spent the summer in England so he was proselytising The Crazy World of Arthur Brown and Hendrix. We were also heavy into Cream and had an acceptable stereo and played Cream, Hendrix and *Sgt. Pepper* - which I wasn't crazy over - a lot. We also listened to Pink Floyd at about the same time - a heavily-English playlist. When Hendrix was announced, we bought the general admission tickets and waited with great enthusiasm for the show.

I don't know where the guys were standing who thought the sound was great, but I thought it was loud and very poor quality. Concrete walls, floor and ceiling with those intrusive pillars and the sound just bounced around with all sorts of delay echoes off the various surfaces. Granted I was accustomed to a clean stereo sound and this was my first rock concert. I had spent way too much time of my youth in churches with pipe organs, which can get loud, so I had some appreciation for live music. This I found awful because of the sound system and the acoustics. It was a cacophony more than music. Spyro Gyra produced a loud lush wall of music, but it was all differentiated and of course that technology was 20 years advanced. I just got mush from that Hendrix show. He did the usual destructive act, which I thought a bit bizarre. I still don't understand the primal rush that audiences get from this bit.

I still have an original vinyl copy of *Are You Experienced* and a turntable, so guess it's time to listen to that snap, crackle and pop-degraded copy again. My wife has a convertible and 'All Along the Watchtower' has that incredible bass intro that truly sounds great in that car with the top down. I love the song and the neighbours are good and don't complain when I crank that up when I hit the end of the driveway. I still love the artist. I just didn't like that 1968 show.

The Factory became a computer service bureau and interviewed there in 1972 I had a bizarre moment when I realised I'd seen Hendrix there four years earlier. The VP interviewing me said a lot of people come to the realisation that they had seen a show there in its previous incarnation, and he thought it funny when that odd look came over my face.

I WAS THERE: SUE SWENSON, AGE 19

My father received his PhD from the University of Wisconsin and wanted me to go there. I was the oldest of four and went there in the fall of '66. My father taught economics at Michigan State University but loved travel and loved to live overseas and had an opportunity to teach economics at a university in Nigeria. So the family flew to Nigeria and I spent two months there then flew back by myself via London, with several days and nights there.

In June, after my freshman year, I was supposed to return to Nigeria to rejoin my family, but civil war in Nigeria was ramping up, and they weren't allowing non-essential personnel back in by June '67. so I went to Europe by myself. I stayed in Italy and when

Sue Swenson shows off her latest Carnaby Street dress

my sister, two and a half years younger, finished high school that year she flew over and we hung out then reconnected with my parents in London. That's how I ended in London in the Summer of Love.

I turned 19 in July '67 and sensed the magic. My sister and I visited Carnaby Street's shops and the clothes were all psychedelic. I wore a captain's skirt, that East Indian influence. It was in the air, and people were so friendly. Like being pied pipers, we walked down the street and before we knew it gathered a crowd of guys. We were having an experience like something out of a Beatles movie, and met some American kids going to a party The Beatles were rumoured to be attending. There was a sense of magic, and music was a big deal.

The *Sgt. Pepper's* album had broken and was heard across Europe, played in bars and restaurants in Spain, France, Italy and England. It transformed the whole continent. 'All You Need Is Love' was big. There was a sense of joy, of euphoria. You could feel it in the air.

We were with our parents but had our own hotel room. We went to a nightclub and sat at a table near the front. There was a band and their manager came over during a break and introduced himself. We chatted and he said, 'See that man over there? That's Tom Jones.' We didn't believe him, so he went over, told Tom, and we saw him laughing. He was a huge star and we couldn't believe he was three tables away, an audience member like us.

My sister and I hung out with English and American kids and Jimi Hendrix was a big deal there. I'd never heard of him. He hadn't hit big in the US, but had there, and I bought *Are You Experienced*. When I returned to Wisconsin and started my sophomore year, I heard he was going to play Madison, so I got tickets. My boyfriend at the time and I went to the Factory.

He wasn't a big icon or big celebrity. He had a small following, and we all stood around. There was a small stage, and it didn't have much of an elevation. It might have been a foot high. There was no security that I recall, just a velvet rope-type barrier. I couldn't have been more than 15 feet away. I didn't think anything of it. We just hung out and listened to him.

There weren't any huge frenzied crowds. It was just a low-key venue, as if for some garage band from Portland, Oregon. I look back on it now and think it was sort of surreal. Within months he was a superstar. There was momentum building that I didn't know about.

He broke through into the superstar arena, playing big sports arenas and auditoriums for lots of money in front of big crowds, with the security and expense and all the hoopla. But when I saw him it was very humble and low- key. I look back now and think, 'Was that for real?'

I wish I'd kept the ticket stubs or taken pictures. There wasn't anybody to stop me. I wasn't a big groupie who went to loads of concerts. I saw The Doors and they had the big arena show with all the hoopla.

When I heard Jimi had died, I think I was in my apartment in Madison. I felt absolutely stunned. Around that time Jim Morrison died, and so did Janis Joplin. At the University of Wisconsin, I was part of the student protests against the war in Vietnam. My freshman year at Wisconsin was so traditional, the American college dream where girls get rushed and go on dates and all that. I had that traditional university experience and it was idyllic and all very Fifties.

Then I spent the summer of '67 in Europe, came back to Wisconsin that fall and within six weeks of my sophomore year, there were major protests. I got caught in one against Dow Chemical. They were trying to recruit on the campus, and we think they made napalm. The students didn't want companies making money off the war recruiting on the campus. There was a big protest on one of the major streets and I was there.

We had multiple protests. By the fall of '67 shit was hitting the fan. Wisconsin was a very activist kind of university, like Berkeley and Michigan. A lot of demonstrations, protests, tear gas and pepper gas. By 1970, Kent State University had the incident where the National Guard killed four people (the subject of Neil Young's 'Ohio'). You had protests, upheaval and the Summer of Love, then Nixon got into office in '68 and that was a dark time. When he got elected, the front cover of the student newspaper in Madison was printed black.

By 1970 a lot of the magic and beauty was gone. Martin Luther King Jr. and Bobby Kennedy had been assassinated, Nixon had been elected and then Kent State happened and pretty much killed the protests. That was the year Jimi Hendrix died and then Janis died. It was as if the Sixties icons were not going to be able to move into the next decade.

THE SCENE

28/29 FEBRUARY 1968, MILWAUKEE, WISCONSIN

I WAS THERE: BARRY OLLMAN

My dad, who wrote for *Billboard*, got us tickets for the first show on the first night and we went with my brother, Rick. Jimi blew me away but I remember our dad saying he preferred Soft Machine. We were dead centre, about four or five rows back. At one point he was being a little flirty with a young lady walking to her seat. I remember him saying, 'I'll make it up to you in spades'. I had no idea what he meant but it sounded so cool when he said it.

I WAS THERE: STEVE SCHROEDER

I met Jimi Hendrix as a young child in Milwaukee. Jimi was in an all-white neighbourhood looking to use a phone. He knocked on many doors but the neighbours were afraid to open the door to a black man with an Afro. Milwaukee in the Sixties had a bridge called 6th Street Viaduct, with blacks on one side and whites on the other.

For Jimi to be on the wrong side of town was dangerous for him. My mother, a hippie chick, let him in and he used the phone, drank a couple of Pabst Blue Ribbon beers and had popcorn. I sat on his lap eating popcorn and we were feeding each other while he was on the phone. When the car beeped its horn for him to go he thanked everyone. He left a guitar behind as he was in a hurry. Somebody later came and picked it up. He was a very shy, generous person.

I WAS THERE: JON PARIS

Two shows a night, two nights in a row and I went to all four. The Soft Machine opened and were great. I especially loved that the Experience played the blues. People were yelling for hits like 'Purple Haze' and 'Foxy Lady', and at one point Jimi said something like, 'Aw, you want to hear all that garbage? We want to play some real music for you.' And out came 'Red House', 'Hoochie Coochie Man' and 'Two Trains Running'. Truly a life-changing experience.

HUNTER COLLEGE

2 MARCH 1968, NEW YORK, NEW YORK

I WAS THERE: BOBBY NATHAN, AGE 17

I saw Jimi Hendrix at Hunter College and I was never the same after the experience. Jimi had double Marshall stacks. It was very loud and it was hard to hear Jimi's vocals, because I believe he sang through the college sound system plus a column on each side of the stage. But Jimi did all the tricks, playing behind his back and head, with his teeth and between his legs. I went with my girlfriend at the time, Liz Dunkel. I got his second record, the *Axis: Bold as Love* album, a few weeks prior.

I WAS THERE: DAVID WHITE, 17

1968 was the year the wheels were coming off in the States, with the Vietnam War, assassinations, students in the streets, drugs and a host of other issues. The arc hadn't gone full Charles Manson yet, but one could extrapolate. When it was issued, we put *Are You Experienced* on the turntable of a friend's parents and ran it through their MacIntosh tube amp and Kliptsch speakers. No one had heard anything like that before and, without getting it, parents were nervous and we were enticed. Yes, we may never hear surf music again.

I saw one of the Experience's first US gigs at Hunter College, Manhattan. The auditorium was small in my recollection, only a couple of thousand at most. The stage was cramped with two banks of speaker cabinets, each run by a couple of Sunn heads on top. Hendrix and Redding had to stand on footstools to reach the settings. Actually, there wasn't much need to make adjustments since, in *Spinal Tap* terms, everything was turned up to 11. The band live employed more feedback and distortion than on record. At one point, Hendrix announced they had some high number of blown speakers. But what the hell.

Compared to the *Monterey* film, the band was less showy. Nothing was ignited and, curiously, that seemed to disappoint the audience. That was disappointing to me because the musical performance was extraordinary. The trio managed to fill musical spaces that were overdubbed in recording. Hendrix was sharp and articulate, turning blues scales model. Redding was perfunctory (great hair, however) and Mitchell a little too busy. But what excitement.

I was a high school senior, writing for my school paper. I obtained press credentials from Sid Bernstein who, I think, brought The Beatles to the States. What a nice guy, interested in helping a teenage journalist stranger. After the show, I went backstage, where things were getting along on the Manson arc: I wore a Brooks Brothers tweed coat and silk rep tie, while Hendrix, athletic and lizard-like cool, wore scarves, bangles and a rakish black hat. He was sweet, with a soulful expression. His reaction to a high schooler was somewhere between amusement and helpfulness. I tried to pose my interview questions but there was considerable distraction from alternate states of consciousness and hot and cold running groupies, who were all over Hendrix. I had to leave before finding out who his main influences were.

MANHATTAN

MARCH 1968, NEW YORK, NEW YORK

I WAS THERE: ALAN WHITE

When I got to Action Talents in New York in January 1968 I really didn't have an opinion on Jimi Hendrix. It was before he had his only chart hit, 'All Along the Watchtower' (No.20 on the Billboard Hot 100), and it was a year and a half prior to Woodstock. I had heard some of his music while at Paramount Artists in DC and as we managed Roy Buchanan, who Eric Clapton called the greatest guitar player in the world and who I thought could play circles around Hendrix, I sort of wrote him off.

One of the first things I learned when I joined Action Talents was that we previously had Jimi Hendrix under a management contract, probably from his days playing with Joey Dee and The Starlighters, a Betty Sperber managed artist, but he ran off and broke the deal.

As the story went, we had him working as lead guitar player and lead singer for one of our bands, Curtis Knight and The Squires, when he up and left, abandoning them at a Holiday Inn somewhere in Minnesota mid-week, leaving them with no lead singer, no lead guitar player and no money to get home. One of our staff members had to figure out a way to get the band back to New York, so Hendrix wasn't exactly popular in our office. One day not too long after I joined the agency, he came into the office to meet with agency owner, Betty Sperber. He had someone with him but, given the way he was dressed, I figured him for a roadie or friend. He sure didn't look like a business person.

Real estate was very expensive in New York even then and we had a very small waiting area, just a bench really, right outside the two offices, the staff office and Betty Sperber's private office. Our receptionist must have been out to lunch or away from her desk and I must have been in the rest room, because when I came back, although his friend was sitting on the bench in the waiting area, Hendrix was sitting at my desk and in my chair.

The conversation went something like this:

'Hey man, what's up?'

'I'm here to see Betty.'

'Oh, cool. Well, my phone lines are ringing off the hook, so I need to get to my desk. You can wait out in the waiting room with your friend.'

He didn't move an inch. 'I'm here to see Betty.'

'I understand that, but I need to get to my desk to answer these phones.'

'I'm here to see Betty.'

'Are we going to have a problem here?'

'Ah man,' he said sullenly, went out to the waiting area and sat on the bench.

I started answering phones, got really busy, and never even saw him leave. Betty didn't want to talk about it, so I gathered the meeting didn't go well. I never saw him again and his name really came up again at the office. I always thought the best thing he ever did was have a great idea at Woodstock, to shred the national anthem through a distortion amp. To me, even though it wasn't a record, that was his biggest hit. Keith Richards once said Jimi Hendrix was a nice guy but he ruined guitar. Given the way he had abandoned his band in Minnesota, I didn't even think he was a very nice guy.

I WASN'T THERE: CHRISSY BEAN

I took my first acid in 1968 and was told it was White Lightning. The person who gave it to me told me he was standing on a corner at a signal light in NYC and Jimi was stopped at the light in a white Corvette. He motioned my friend over and gave him a handful of the tabs and said it was the smoothest ride one could have, just like his car. I have to believe it because that trip for me was the only one that was flowing, beautiful, spectacular, with no paranoia or bad vibes. It lasted many hours. Every other acid trip I took was hell for me. Jimi had awesome acid - at least during that time.

VETERANS MEMORIAL AUDITORIUM

3 MARCH 1968, COLUMBUS, OHIO

I WAS THERE: NANCY WASEN

I live in Ashland, about 65 miles from Columbus. I don't know who told me Jimi was playing at Vets in Columbus, but someone did. I had been friends with The Dantes, who were on the bill, for about a year, and it might have been Barry who told me. I went with my best friend Nancy and her boyfriend Bill, who drove his VW down. Bill and I were both stoners, but his girlfriend didn't do pot. We didn't have any, went to a friend's apartment in Columbus, but he was out. Bill said if I ate car sick pills I could get high. Being a thrill-seeker, I went to the drugstore around the corner and bought some. I have no memory if Bill did.

We got to the venue and one thing that struck me was that so many of us were dressed up in velvet and cool clothes. Not like now, where everyone wears jeans. When we got there, I saw one of the crew guys for The Dantes. I also ran into others from Columbus that I knew.

Four O'Clock Balloon opened, then The Dantes, and what a thrill to see guys I knew on that big stage. Then Soft Machine took the stage and the car sick pills kicked in. Apparently, I fell asleep on some girl's shoulder and came to as they were finishing. I thought there were six guys in the band and was shocked to see just three. The drummer, I seem to remember, was in shorts.

When the curtain re-opened it was a frigging wall of amps. I think we were all going, 'Wow!' Jimi came out and was messing with his guitar and just then, over his amp wafted Kenny Rogers and the First Edition's 'Just Dropped in to see What Condition my Condition was In' and Jimi chuckled that chuckle of his.

I wish I could say I remember what songs he played. Set-lists have never been my strong suit. I do know he played 'The Wind Cries Mary' and that has never left me. I remember him flinging his guitar over the curtain at some point.

It was over too soon and as we worked our way through the crowd, I again saw the crew guy from The Dantes, who said, 'Come back and party with us!' Well I hadn't driven, and I'm thinking it was a school night, although I could be wrong. All I know is we left and drove home. Experienced for sure! I went to see The Dantes a few weeks later and found out the party we were invited to was at the Four O'Clock Balloon's home and that Jimi was there. I'm still kicking myself 50 years later. And the gal who's shoulder I passed out on? She was there that night and thought I was a heroin user. I didn't have the heart to tell her it was car-sick pills.

But 1968 was the best year of my life and that show is in my top five. And I've seen hundreds.

I WAS THERE: LYNN WEHR

I was a member of The Dantes, one of the bands that opened for Hendrix. The person responsible for bringing the Experience to Columbus was Johnny Garber, local DJ and manager of our band. Johnny asked Barry Hayden, lead singer of The Dantes, 'Who's hot right now?' Without hesitation, Barry said, 'Jimi Hendrix'. Johnny then called Reprise Records, got the name of Jimi's manager and called him in England. The manager told Johnny he was headed to New York in the morning and would call Johnny when he got to the States. True to his word, he called Johnny the next day and offered three dates that could work. They settled on March 3 for a fee of $4,500. There had never been a rock concert at Vets Memorial on a Sunday night, but they agreed to go ahead. The show sold out in about two hours and the stage was set. This was the only time The Jimi Hendrix Experience played in Ohio.

After the show got underway, a police officer escorted the girlfriend of either Noel or Mitch (I'm not sure which) out of the building for stepping over the posted fire line back stage. About 10 minutes before they were to go on, Jimi came to Johnny and said they would not go on until she was brought back inside. The owner of Central Ticket Office offered his help and went outside, put his arm around the girlfriend and walked her back. Johnny told the officer if he cancelled this show he better call the National Guard, as there would be a riot of 4,000 angry fans. The cop didn't say a word and the show went on as scheduled.

I WAS THERE: FRANK MELCHOR, AGE 18

I was a student at Ohio State University. Ticket prices ranged from $3 to $5. There were three acts before Jimi came on. The first was The 4 O'Clock Balloon, second was The Dantes, an English band, and third was The Soft Machine, with a liquid light show.

I remember where I was when I heard Jimi died. I was in Columbus, Ohio, on the corner of Hudson and High Street. The news was on radio station WCOL. Jimi Hendrix blew my mind.

I WAS THERE: MICHAEL ALWOOD

I was at the Hendrix performance at Vets. During that concert, he sang, 'Scuse me while I kiss this guy', an obvious acknowledgement of the mondegreen.

MARVEL GYM, BROWN UNIVERSITY

8 MARCH 1968, PROVIDENCE, RHODE ISLAND

I WAS THERE: BOB BASKER

The Soft Machine opened the show. At the end of Jimi's set, he smashed his Strat after jamming the headstock into the grill cloth of the Marshall stacks behind him. The amps rocked back and forth. He threw the body of the Strat into the audience and the neck behind the wall of amps. My friend David ran behind the stage and found the neck. He

quickly put it under his jacket
and made for the exit before
being stopped by security or
Jimi's people. He had to give up
the neck.

I WAS THERE: DALE GRADEN

Bob's friend David had a very short career in the guitar recycling business

My good friend Mark Allard and
I were there. We were neighbours,
born one day apart in August
1952, and were sophomores at Barrington, Rhode Island High
School in March 1968. Mark was deeply into all sorts of music and
was the one who somehow got the tickets. I was into Jimi for many
reasons: his music, his smile, his many lyrics, including, 'Castles made
of sand fade into the sea, eventually'. We listened to at least one of
the albums on a reel-to-reel tape recorder I owned, so I'd somehow
taped it.

It was a cold night, and the concert was in the old gym of Brown
University. While we were waiting in line outside, some college kids, a
big guy in particular, were smoking some of the good stuff. It was the
first time I'd seen anyone smoking pot. It sure smelled good.

It was a stand-up concert, and we were able to get to the front
row. We listened to a few or perhaps several songs there. Then, as
expected, Jimi smashed his guitar and, lo and behold, I had the front
in my hands. I shoved it under my shirt and stayed right there. Then,
lo and behold, the drummer gave me one of the drum-sticks. I feel
like I had to struggle a bit to hold on, because there were people all
around with arms outstretched.

When it became obvious that the Experience was not going to
return, I went a few feet under the stage, then exited at the side.
What a night. I held on to the guitar for many years, in a drawer in
my room at our house at 14 Pine Avenue. Somehow, it got lost, not
sure how. But, I had a witness in Mark.

I WAS THERE: HARRY SPRING

When we were asked to play at the Hendrix concert to fill in for the opening band, we scrambled to get our gear together and headed for Brown. When I got to the gymnasium I went looking for someone to tell us where to set up and what time we would be playing. There seemed to be no one around. Finally, in a locker room, there was a guy playing guitar by himself. He was left-handed and really into whatever he was doing, playing an electric guitar unamplified. I said, 'Excuse me, do you know when the back-up band will be playing?' He looked up and said, 'No, man.' I later realised it was Jimi.

I WAS THERE: TERENCE HARKIN

My band Stonehenge Circus almost opened for Hendrix. I got a call on my fraternity pay phone. Is that really how I booked work for us back then? It was a little vague, something about being on standby to fill in for one of Hendrix's opening acts. I can't remember who called - probably the head of a campus organisation booking Hendrix. I recall being disappointed we weren't called on. I hazily recall watching him perform from near the front, possibly even at the side of the stage.

Mitch Mitchell was a fabulous drummer and was great that night, as he was again in 1970 when I saw them in San Bernardino, where tickets couldn't have been more than $10. I was only making $110 a month as an Airman First Class but I could afford to take a date. The strange thing about San Berdoo is that Hendrix was doing new material and the crowd just wanted 'Foxy Lady' and 'Fire'. They must have only had their amps on five at Marvel Gym, because the San Berdoo Convention Center was shaking like an earthquake just hit it, with an audience of thousands.

I WAS THERE: PETER WOOD

I probably drove down from Canton. Stonehenge Circus had covered some Hendrix tunes, and I was pretty psyched about this spring weekend performance at Brown. We convened at Marvel Gym and found there was a waist-high-riser set up for the performance at the end of a basketball court. The riser was not for us. We were the 'contingency' band, ready to play if there was some delay, and set up on the floor to the right of the stage. There were a number of large speaker cabinets onstage and they weren't Marshalls but Fender Showman cabinets. Immediately behind the stage, someone had rigged a white sheet from a basketball net.

Having set up, we adjourned to the locker room. I don't recall seeing Jimi there, but Noel Redding spoke to Bruce Bates, having seen he was holding a Hagstrom bass. Noel asked Bruce how he liked it. Later someone said they had seen Hendrix speaking to a cop or security guard. He was apparently annoyed that a kid had gotten in and asked him for a joint.

The Experience went on as scheduled, and we did not open the show, as we had for The Yardbirds. There was a burst of feedback from Jimi's mic and he wryly commented, 'I don't want to hurt your ears'. I watched most of their set from midway back in the audience of about 200 students and their dates. I did note that Jimi got a little sloppy on the solo of 'The Wind Cried Mary' but the playing overall was awe-inspiring. Toward the end, I moved to where our kit was set up to be sure nobody messed with anything when the show concluded. I also thought there was a chance we would be asked to play after the Experience had gone. We weren't. I was standing so all I could see was the back of their speaker cabinets. As they ended, amidst howling guitar feedback, one of the cabinets was rocked back several times. It was being slammed with a guitar, and Jimi's Strat sailed over the cabinets, hit the sheet and slid into the arms of a roadie.

I WAS THERE: JIM CENTRACCHIO

The Stonehenge Circus was Harry Spring, singer; Bruce Bates, bass; Terry (Terence Harkin), drums; Peter (Woody) Wood, lead guitar; Frank Lombardi, keyboards; and Jim Centracchio, guitar. Terry and

Frank were students at Brown. Harry, Bruce and I were students at
University of Rhode Island, and Peter was a graduate of Brown. We
covered a swath of music - Rolling Stones, Beatles, Moby Grape,
The Remains, Hendrix, Cream, Paul Revere and the Raiders,
Motown, and more.

We got paid to hear The Jimi Hendrix Experience. We were due
to play at a dance right after the show, but the show was so great that
when it ended people there figured that was it and filed out together.
We did get paid, but it would have been fun to do a set or two for
anyone who wanted to dance.

It was the Brown Class of 1970 that sponsored the gig and tickets
were just $2.50. A story on the Internet mentions fighting in the
crowd and Hendrix destroying his Strat, but we saw Jimi toss the
guitar into the air towards the back of the stage, where it landed
in a drapery rigging and slid carefully down to a roadie waiting to
grab it. I believe Terry got us the gig as a last-minute thing. I've seen
posters and schedules that list The Soft Machine, touring with the
Experience, as being scheduled to appear at Marvel Gym. Something
must have happened – illness or whatever – to prevent that. If my
memory's correct, Brown was hiring us to play for a dance to be held
right after.

The poster indicates The Soft Machine would be there along with
the Mark Boyle Sensual Laboratory, a psychedelic light show that
travelled with The Soft Machine. But as they weren't there, neither
was the light show.

The makeshift stage was set up on risers under the basketball
hoop at one end of the gym floor. As you walked in from the main
entrance, street-side, you would pass this area, the end of the
basketball court at that end. Everyone coming into the venue walked
beside the stage to get to the open floor. There was no seating.

The Experience put on quite the show, these three musicians
pumping a loud, heavy volume of sound into the crowd. Hendrix
and Redding had a decent backline of amps and cabinets that
filled the cavern of the gymnasium with a saturation of sound. The
bass guitar was cranked up so high that you could feel the notes

resonating in your chest, to the extent that it felt like the bass-lines passed into your body and then out again. You not only heard the notes. You felt them pounding inside you.

Jimi neither set his guitar on fire nor smashed it. It was either on 'Foxy Lady' or 'Purple Haze' that he placed it on the stage and crouched over it, straddling it and moving it back and forth in a sexual manner, getting all sorts of sounds and feedback from it. He even held it by the headstock and jerked it up and down with the body of the guitar, kind of bouncing on and off the stage, all up and down motion measured in a few inches, just enough to cause it to bang around and contribute to the amplified sounds he generated. At least once during the show, he placed the guitar in front of his face and played some licks either with his teeth or his tongue.

At the climax of the show, he walked to the rear of the stage and began pushing his Strat into one of the cabinets, moving the guitar side to side while pushing back. This caused the amp-stack to rock. As Peter was more to the rear of the stage, he saw the roadie hold the amp up so it wouldn't fall back. During the show, I moved around the floor to soak up the sound, see the crowd and hear what it was like out there. Every so often, I'd drift back to where our equipment was set up, to be sure no one messed with it.

Mitch Mitchell amazed me with his drumming. There was a marked difference between Hendrix and his mates Noel and Mitch. Hendrix was much bigger and black. Noel and Mitch were skinny, small white guys; they looked even smaller than we were. Mitch seemed like a wisp of a thing and as I watched him drum he moved around his kit with his drumming, almost cat-like and floating above it. He was so small in comparison that it was surprising he could put out such a solid drum backing to keep up with the guitars. But he had no problem moving around that kit and playing in his style with ease.

After Hendrix did his thing, pushing and rubbing his guitar into an amplifier, he returned to the front of the stage for the last chords. Then, with one quick motion, he heaved his unplugged guitar high over his shoulder into the large white sheet attached to the basketball hoop and net. It was carefully arranged and choreographed, because the guitar was essentially captured by that sheet, which folded in on itself, allowing the guitar to slowly slide down to the roadie stationed below.

I walked over to the side of the stage where the stairs were set up, and as Jimi came down and was about to walk past me I reached out to tap his arm and tell him thanks for the show and that they played a fantastic show for us. He looked at me and said simply, 'Thank you, man.'

I WAS THERE: TOM MULVEY

I was there and met Jimi right at the stage. There was no security and we chatted throughout the evening. I asked if he would be smashing his guitar and at the end he did. He broke his white Stratocaster in two and handed it to me and three friends. I still have the memories and the strap is framed in my office. Coincidentally, it's the same colour and pattern strap as the one he used at Woodstock.

I WAS THERE: JOHN FARLEY

My now-wife and I were there. It was, as I recall, fairly sparsely attended - 1,500 or so. We sat on the floor about 20 yards from centre-stage. The Soft Machine opened. Hendrix had two columns of Sunns, as did Redding. The show was tremendous - loud, long and pretty faithful to the *Are You Experienced* tunes. I don't remember the setlist, but he did most of the album. I remember he couldn't quite get the level of feedback necessary for the opening to 'Foxy Lady'.

The most interesting thing I remember was the end - he holed the grille of one of the speaker cabinets with the neck of the Stratocaster, then threw the guitar over the amps, the backs of which were aligned with the doors to the venue. The guitar still had the curly cord attached. It sailed over the amps and was caught in mid-flight by a kid who started towards the door with it. He was stopped by one of the police doing security, who brought the guitar back.

Sometime in the late Eighties or early Nineties, I was telling this story in the prosecutor's office, where I worked, when one of my employees spoke up. He was an ex-cop who'd worked his way up to chief in a small town after retirement from the Providence Police Department. He had again retired and came to work as an investigator in my unit. He said, 'I was that cop.' This is what's known as a Rhode Island moment, an instance where the small size of the state is belied by unique connections such as this.

I also saw his second Rhode Island Auditorium concert a year or so later.

I WAS THERE: STEPHEN MARTIN

I was at that explosion of volume! A friend gave me the ticket to see some guy I'd never heard of. When I walked into the bathroom to take a leak, he was in there. At first, I thought I was in the ladies' room because of his hair and clothing. About an hour later, in front of what appeared to be a wall of Marshall amps, he tossed his smashed Fender guitar into the crowd, where it landed at my feet. Being young, naive and thinking a stagehand would come retrieve it, I never thought to pick it up. The kid next to me did. Last year I ran into the kid who picked that broken neck up. He has it mounted on his living room wall.

I WAS THERE: ANTONIO SALVATORE

My friends and I were at Old Meehan Auditorium at Brown University for the Hendrix concert in 1968. In fact, one of my friends has the neck and part of the body, including the neck-plate, of the white Fender Strat that Jimi smashed and threw into the audience.

INTERNATIONAL BALLROOM

10 MARCH 1968, HILTON HOTEL, WASHINGTON DC

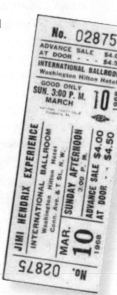

I WAS THERE: GARY MARKWOOD

I missed his first turn in DC at the short-lived Ambassador Theater. I wanted to see both shows of The Who, who were opening for Herman Hermits. But I saw his first show at the Hilton Hotel ballroom. He was amazing. He played great and did all his bits. I was very familiar with the UK scene. I used to read all the magazines like the *NME*, *Melody Maker*, *Disc* and *Rave*. I ordered 45s, etc. from England. So I had lots of stuff that hadn't been released here.

I WAS THERE: MARC CLARK, AGE 18

I was a senior in high school. *Are You Experienced* had been released and was nothing like I had ever heard. I remember hearing 'Hey Joe' as a single, then a bit later 'Purple Haze' and 'The Wind Cries Mary'. I saw them at a Hilton or Hyatt hotel in a ballroom. It was advertised on the radio that the 'not well known' Jimi Hendrix Experience was going to be doing a mini-concert in DC, and the day of the announcement I caught three buses to get there. It was an on-the-spot decision. The ballroom was massive but had only about 70 chairs set up, conference style. There were no seat assignments. It was first-come, first-served. I was front-row centre and little did I know what I was about to 'experience'. Hendrix and the band weren't more than 15 to 20 feet in front of the audience (which turned out to be around 40 people in the chairs).

The triad was mesmerizing, hypnotic, spellbinding, enthralling, riveting and captivating, a far cry from the mainstream entertainers of the time. Jimi was commanding on the guitar, relentless on his guitar riffs and hypnotic in his stage presence. Watching him. you just had to like him. He took you along to another place. Not a bad experience for a $12 ticket and bus fare.

Tickets for the Clark University show in Worcester, MA on 15 March 1968 were priced between $3 and $4 for two sold-out shows in a 600-capacity venue. An un-torn ticket for the show sold at auction for $300 many years later. The first show started three hours late, Hendrix quipping, 'It's not me, it's the equipment. It just got here.'

ATWOOD HALL, CLARK UNIVERSITY

15 MARCH 1968, WORCESTER, MASSACHUSETTS

I WAS THERE: JOHN WITTI

I was at the Clark performance. It was absolutely incredible, and from what I've seen of videos of performances elsewhere, Atwood Hall was probably his best performance, even better than Woodstock. There was absolutely no sloppiness. I got to talk with him the following late morning, outside the old Holiday Inn on Southbridge Street, Worcester. I've stolen one of his lines from that morning. I asked him where he was headed, after he said he was waiting for his ride, and he said to someplace in 'bumfuck Maine'.

He was a really nice, regular, down-to-earth guy just talking to me in what was 'another guy' type conversation. He asked how we enjoyed the show and what we did. I told him we had a band and he asked where we played and stuff like that, back and forth.

I was outside the hall listening.

LEWISTON ARMORY

16 MARCH 1968, LEWISTON, MAINE

I remember I was skating in the rink out back and always came in
the back door. I walked through with my hockey stick and my skates
on my shoulder. All I remember is this guy playing guitar with his
teeth and behind his head. It was so cool. I stayed later than I should
have and, when I came out of the Armory, my Dad was waiting for
me on the corner.

My husband Donnie Duplissis was 17 when he attended his very
first concert. He'd been taking guitar lessons for a few years and
had heard about Jimi. He and three of his friends attended. He
remembers the Armory being so packed that if you wanted to fall
down, you wouldn't be able to. Friends in a local band opened -
Terry and the Telstars. My husband expected a good show but was
blown away by Hendrix. Jimi played a couple of tunes, then the PA
system was fried because of the loudness. Jimi had to borrow the
opening act's Fender Dual Showman amps to continue. After they
got the PA running, Jimi burnt through at least two or three fuzz
pedals. My husband recalls the roadie came out from the back of his
Marshall stack, busy replacing them.

Jimi did not destroy any guitars that evening, but Noel Redding,
after playing the last note, threw his bass guitar up in the air, still
hooked to the amp. He caught it by the neck and drove it into the
stage, splitting it in half! After the concert was over, there was still
a notable sound-wave circling the Armory. Their ears rang for a
couple of days after.

I WAS THERE: ROBERT MURCH

It was my wife and I's second date. We're still happily married today. I was a Hendrix fan from college, Doris had never heard of him. A week earlier, on our way back to her house from our first date, we passed the Armory and I asked if she'd like to go to a concert next weekend. She always dressed very lady-like and dressy and dressed up very pretty for the event. I also knew how the others would be dressed. She meant a lot to me and I wanted to be comfortable so wore a sport coat with dress shirt and tie, and she was beautiful in a pretty dress with a nice fluffy skirt. We stood out like sore thumbs. But we had a blast.

We were on the floor between centre-court and the stage. The problem was that everyone stood on their folding chairs, as did we. Doris is only 5' 2". I'm 6 feet tall. I could see, she couldn't. A little more than two years later, in 1970, we married. I was in the Navy and we were stationed in Maryland. When I came home from work, she told me of the tragic news of Jimi's death and said, 'Did you know he was black?' I said, 'Of course, we saw him in concert.' To which she replied, 'You saw him, I didn't.'

On what I think was the 20th anniversary of his appearance in Lewiston, we were listening to radio station WBLM and they were taking calls from people who attended. One guy called and said one thing he remembered was this young couple dressed in fancy clothes, way out of place. Our boys cracked up, said, 'Hey, they're talking about you guys!' Yep, that was us.

I WAS THERE: DON BOUCHER

I was a junior at Edward Little High School in Auburn, Maine. I was in a little-known rock band and just couldn't miss seeing Jimi in our sister city, Lewiston. We got there real early and sat in balcony seating that surrounds the Armory. We could see a great wall of speakers on stage and knew it was going to be a memorable experience. As the crowd began to enter, the noise level in that space got louder and louder. When the hall was about half-full, a few of us went down on the floor to get a closer look at the stage set-up. We were amazed that the speakers were piled one atop the other, possibly 10 to 12 feet high. During the concert, there were several men standing behind the speaker wall, holding their arms up against them in an attempt to prevent that wall of speakers from toppling back. The whole room shook!

When Jimi finally appeared, the crowd went absolutely bonkers! Each song he played seemed to increase in volume, to the point of near pain on our eardrums. But we couldn't believe we were actually there, watching that great talent before us. As the show wore on, the crowd got so loud and boisterous as to challenge the fever pitch on stage. When it was all over, my friends and I just sat there and watched the crowd attempting to file out the many doors on the street side of the building. It was absolute mayhem.

Eventually, we could see the crowd thinning out some, so made our way down to the floor to head out. That floor was covered with food wrappers, empty pot bags, joint remnants, soda and beer cans. How they got by the cops I don't know. There was also a lot of spilled water and soda, and we could hear our sneakers squeaking as we sauntered to the exits.

My ears rang for around three days after. Everyone was talking about it. We were so young that we never really imagined what a truly magical time we were treated to.

I WAS THERE: DENNIS GERVAIS

Tickets were $4 in advance. He wore black pants, a dark green shirt, black vest and a large black hat with feathers. He ended the show by destroying every piece of equipment on stage. Local group, Terry and the Telstars, opened. We sat in the left balcony, about 75 feet from the stage. It was nearly 50 years ago and seems like yesterday.

I remember standing at the top of the Armory steps, on the left side, by the door. When the doors were opened, the crowd surge literally picked me up in the air and dragged me into the lobby. What a crazy sensation. The scene was wild. All these hippies were arriving in vans, old painted school buses, etc. Bates College sponsored the show. The Armory had no floor seating, only the balconies. Workers assembled bleachers from the football field, on both sides of the floor, under the balconies, and set up metal folding chairs on the floor. It was a cavernous shell of a building and the acoustics sucked.

Word had it that Hendrix leased all the equipment from Maurice Music Mart, and then utterly destroyed every bit of it on stage. Rumour was that they hadn't paid the bill and he died before the store could sue him.

I WAS THERE: TERRY MCCARTHY, AGE 16

I was in one of the bands that opened that show, Terry and the Telstars, a five-piece rock band playing contemporary pop. We'd been together about three years and were kind of nervous about the show. We got pulled in because the band backing Jimi at the time, Soft Machine, got stopped at the Canadian border coming back into the States. They were concealing something they shouldn't have.

We were working with a studio around town in Lewiston and Mr Jeffery, one of Hendrix's managers, contacted the studio and said he needed some equipment and if there was a band available they could open the show. So our manager, the guy who owned the studio, contacted us, we accepted the job and rushed down there to set up equipment for Jimi. He had a lot of his own gear but the PA system and such he did not have so he used ours. We ended up opening the show with another band, the Hanseatic League from Bates College, a Lewiston-located college.

We were nervous but had enough nerve to say when we were performing, 'We're gonna give you a little taste of what you're gonna get in another half hour and we're gonna play a song called 'Fire'.' Boy, did we have a lot of nerve to play that. And we pulled it off pretty well. Some of the comments were that we were young and not quite together enough to be a concert band, but we had a blast doing it.

It was a real thrill watching Hendrix's crew and everybody set up. Jimi and the drummer, once they got a little bit of the equipment into the Armory, wanted a bit of a soundcheck. Danny Caron, our drummer, and I walked around with Noel Redding, talking to him, getting information.

Jimi and Mitch Mitchell were on stage just banging away and I'd never seen anybody play guitar like that. It was such magic. A real thrill. Noel said, 'We're just trying to get the feel for the room, how it sounds, try to get the setting for tonight.'

I was right up front for the show – front-row seats. Both opening bands got a row. The acoustics of the room weren't very good, and Jimi played very loud. I was watching Mitch hit the drums and couldn't hear half of what he was playing, including the cymbal crashes. Jimi played so loud he wiped out everybody else. He did a great show and played the guitar behind his head. He pulled off a Chuck Berry stunt where he did the splits onstage and then grabbed the head of his guitar and pushed himself back up, swung it around and kept right on playing. That was one little trick I hadn't heard about or ever seen before. Quite a show. He pulled out all the stops. He did not burn his guitar. He did not smash his guitar. But he played wild guitar.

I pulled the band together and we'd probably been together about three years. We played through high school, then broke up - everybody was going their different ways. The singer went out west to try and capture a record deal. I went off to school for a bit and the drummer went to school but ended in a band that opened on the road for Bob Seger.

Jimi set a path for the way I wanted to play guitar after I saw him play. He changed my whole idea of guitar playing. It's still a work in progress.

Terry and the Telstars had the honour of opening for Hendrix in March 1968

I WAS THERE: DANNY CARON, AGE 15

Not only was I at the show, but my band Terry and the Telstars had the honour of opening. I was the drummer and at the end of the night after everyone was gone, Hendrix came over, shook my hand and spoke.

I started playing drums when I was six and I'm 65 now and still play once in a while. We were a very young band, 14 and 15 years old, with a lot of talent. Word got out that Jimi was going to play the Armory and he was probably one of the first major acts ever to come to Lewiston. It was the first time we got a taste of hippiedom and marijuana and the whole deal. People from New York and Boston and you can't imagine where all came up to little Lewiston, Maine to see Hendrix play.

A band called Soft Machine were supposed to open and the story goes that they got stopped at the border with some kind of problem and weren't allowed to enter the country. Our manager heard about the incident, jumped on his stick and said, 'I have a young band that's very talented. If you want to use them, they're available'.

It was before all the technology and the massive PA systems were developed. We had Hi Tech horns and a Bogen PA and Dual Showman Fender amplifiers.

We opened up and the crowd was kind. We weren't an original act – we were playing The Doors and Stones and stuff like that – and then at the end they converted our amplifiers along with our hi-tech horns for the PA for Jimi and it was no match for the Marshall amplifiers. I think Noel Redding had maybe 12 Sunn cabinets. It was just a massive wall of amplifiers. They were so loud that you could hardly hear Jimi sing through a little amplifier. The only words you could really hear clearly were when they broke and said, 'Foxy Lady'.

It was the most incredible show I've ever seen and to this day I don't think I've ever seen another artist top the aura of seeing Jimi Hendrix live and in person. They just played one set. We did maybe a 45-minute show and then he came on and played maybe an hour, certainly no more than 90 minutes. It was astonishing. The crowd was very pleased. It was such an experience, all these hippies swarming in on a little town. Quite an adventure.

It was overwhelming for the audience and that was his first tour in America. He came on and just blew everybody off. He played his guitar with his teeth and lit it on fire with lighter fluid and then at the end of the show smashed it on the floor and up against the Marshall amplifiers. Totally amazing.

At the end of the night I went back in to the Armory to make sure we hadn't forgotten any equipment or left anything behind. The place was empty, and here comes Hendrix up out of the dressing room. He walked over and I was like, 'Oh my God'. I'm looking around and there's nobody here that sees him, and he goes, 'Hey kid'. He shakes my hand and goes, 'Not a bad drummer. Keep it up.' I looked around and nobody was in the building but me. No camera or anything to capture the moment. It was a personal moment for me, that's for sure. He was the most soft-spoken, mild-mannered man compared to his stage presence. They were drastically different. He was very kind. He walked out, got into a waiting limousine and off he went with the rest of the band.

When he died, it was a shock. I was devastated. I heard that the authorities found him in a hotel room and he had taken an overdose or vomited and there wasn't any effort to resuscitate him because he was a hippy. It was very sad. He would have turned 75 now and you can only imagine what kind of music he would be creating if he was still alive.

I WAS THERE: GERARD J. CARRIER, AGE 17

Way back in 1968, rock music was ever evolving, becoming more creative with each passing day. Some of the music had started to become 'heavier' sounding in the way of increased volume and distorted guitars. Major artists such as Cream and Jimi Hendrix experimented with this new sound. I was playing in a local rock band. As five young guys with great music aspirations but still in school, we practised weekly and learned top-40 songs like most bands in the area.

I remember seeing a small ad in the Lewiston *Daily Sun* one day that got my attention real quick. Our group was already performing a couple of Experience tunes off their first album, *Are You Experienced*. That's exactly what the ad read – 'Are you experienced?' It was a 'solve the puzzle' type thing the newspaper would run once in a while. I thought it might mean a Hendrix concert was coming to town and mentioned it to my bandmates at rehearsal one evening. They all thought I was nuts. Sure enough, my hunch was right and soon tickets went on sale for the Armory. We bought ours as soon as available, and greatly anticipated the arrival of one of our musical influences to good old Lewiston. We were hoping that would change things in town since the ill-fated Ali-Liston fight a few years earlier that kind of tainted Lewiston a little bit.

That was a first for all of us who had never seen the likes of anyone with international fame. That night, the Tinn Box were all seated in the balcony of the Armory on the right side facing the stage. White Fluff, a great local group, opened with their set, which they'd perfected playing almost every week at the popular PAL Hop dances.

Then here comes the Experience, who instantly hypnotised the huge crowd with their unbelievable sound. Man, I never heard anything so loud in all my life. The bass just shook and Jimi's right-handed Fender Stratocaster (blond finish with rosewood fingerboard) played left-handed, upside down just sounded so radical and gorgeous at the same time. Mitch Mitchell's rapid-fire drumming and Noel Redding's jazz bass runs and octaves melded and fused with Hendrix's guitar wizardry.

It was simply awesome just to be there, seeing the Experience with their wild clothes and Afro hair. I recall that the PA system provided could not match the volume. Apparently, speakers were blown and replacement cabinets had to be brought in. It didn't seem to take that long until everything was taken care of. The concert resumed to its wondrous end. Most of the songs performed were from *Are You Experienced* and the newly-released *Axis: Bold As Love*. It was definitely a unique and musically inspiring and soulful experience.

I WAS THERE: GLENDA LALEMAND CLARK, AGE 15

I was there with my younger brother Wayne. I was so excited to see the great Jimi Hendrix. My parents didn't want me to go because I was so young, but I convinced them to let me go as long as I took my younger brother, who was only 14! I had my licence so we drove to Lewiston from the northern outskirts of Auburn, quite a trip for us. We wanted to be some of the first to arrive so went very early. We got up to the doors and the crowd began to grow behind us. We thought we were going to die because the crowd was growing and pushing so hard we couldn't breathe. We were trapped between the eager crowd and the doors. When they opened the doors, they swung out and it got even worse. Finally inside, we ran to the front of the stage.

I don't remember if there were any seats, because we were standing in front of the stage the whole time. Then we knew it was worth it. We made it in alive and here we were watching Jimi Hendrix perform. The show was fantastic. Jimi played his guitar with his teeth, behind his back, and at the end smashed it to pieces. He was so young and colourful and loud. I remember my ears ringing for a week after. I am so glad we were there. It was the most fantastic thing I had experienced in my young life.

I WAS THERE: LINDA DARLING, AGE 15

It was my first concert. The tickets cost a whopping $3 and I must have held onto my ticket stub for years until it was lost in a move. It was an event I will never forget.

I was living with my parents in a neighbouring town. I can't remember how I got there but went with my brother's girlfriend and her sister. Because it was 1968, my parents still believed a person had to dress up attending concerts. Let me tell you, that was the last time I ever wore a dress to an event. I carried a large purse that held a change of clothes after that day.

There was an opening band and when they finished playing, the curtain closed. For several minutes, the crowd starting stomping feet and yelling, 'Jimi, Jimi'. We were beginning to think he wouldn't

come out. Then we heard him and we all cheered. The curtain
opened and there they were - Jimi, his drummer and stand-up bass
player, with no pyrotechnics, lights or sounds effects. 'Purple Haze'
and 'All Along the Watchtower' will always be my favourites and
nothing can compare to seeing him perform the national anthem
with his teeth as the finale. When people start talking about concerts
they've been to, I still enjoy saying I saw Jimi Hendrix in concert in
Lewiston, Maine. It never ceases to amaze. And although I didn't
know him at the time, my husband was there, too, that night.

I WAS THERE: MICHAEL GUIMOND, AGE 13

My mother had separated from my dad and worked at night. I
snuck out and stood in line at the Armory with Bates College guys
that were a lot older and put us up on their shoulders so we could
see. Real nice guys. It was 4pm when we got there. Doors opened at
8. We went to the balcony and saw the local act opening the show,
Ed Bushy's band, Terry and the Telstars. There might have been
another. They had fold-out chairs on the floor. They wouldn't let
anybody sit on the floor and the front row was away from the stage.

The promoter was from Bates. That's why there were lots of Bates
kids there. His PA system didn't arrive for some reason so Maurice
Music Mart supplied just bull-horns for vocals. I remember before
he came on Marc Biron, Dave's brother, walked across the stage with
a V bird and a Stratocaster to over by Jimi's amp. People thought it
was him and started screaming. Mitch Mitchell had his Champagne
Ludwig set right to the front of the stage. Jimi had 10 Sound City
cabinets with five heads. Beat up, they looked like Marshall stacks.
Noel had eight Sunn 200 cabinets with two 15" speakers in each,
and four heads. When they came on Jimi had green bell-bottoms
for St Patrick's Day and they all had huge Afros. People rushed the
stage and sat on the floor. Security couldn't stop them. The second
album wasn't released but they played 'Spanish Castle Magic' and all
the songs from *Are You Experienced*. He controlled his feed and played
and sang all at the same time. There was nothing like it and still

hasn't been. I was with Dick Landry and Marc Provenchy. Jim had come out with the white Strat. He never played the V but picked up the black Strat only to play it with his teeth then rip the strings off it and throw them in the crowd. While he was doing it, the Strat was hanging off the stage. Someone tried to grab it and one of his big-ass bodyguards came out, tried to kick the guy but didn't connect. Jimi almost stepped on Marc's arm. The crowd was nuts. He only played 35 minutes and said the PA wasn't working good. They took a little break on stage and he was drinking a 16oz Narragansett beer.

When it was over I went home. Nobody was there. Tom Houghton, who lived down the street, had lent me his uncle's 58 Telecaster and Gibson amp four weeks previously. I turned it on and cranked it like never before. The feedback was awesome. I wailed.

I WAS THERE: JOANNE LIBBY

Seeing Jimi Hendrix had been on my mind those last few months. It was so out of character for me to even attend a rock concert. Over the years I found out that my husband had also seen Jimi Hendrix in Baltimore and a friend had seen him in Germany. It always amazed me that the three of us saw him, despite his very short life.

I remember very little of the actual concert. I went with two friends, one of whom must have been the planner. I think there had recently been a snowstorm. We were wearing boots and it was a bit messy on the floors of the Armory. We sat on bleachers on the main floor on the left side of the stage, fairly close to the bottom row. The most striking thing was seeing all the people who were not locals coming in droves. I guess we would later call these people groupies, a term I wasn't yet familiar with. They didn't look like us. They had long stringy hair, long skirts, dark hats and granny glasses. I guess they looked like hippies, which I hadn't seen except on television. It was a culture shock for me. I don't remember the music. My brother recalls that when I got home I told him about the crowd yelling, 'Fire', not because there was a fire in the building but because the audience wanted to hear him sing and play 'Fire'.

I WAS THERE: JAMES LITTLEFIELD

I saw him in Lewiston, Maine along with a bus-load of cohorts from Gould Academy. Thanks to the foresight of our faculty chaperone, our group of say 20 were first in line, thus I looked for the Marshalls and sat front-row stage right. Jimi was set up maybe 10ft away. As close as I was, there was an extra special bit of freakin' before he set his guitar on fire and wondering, if *he* caught fire, what could be done to put him out!

James was worried about Jimi setting himself ablaze

I'd been listening to *Are You Experienced* non-stop since a friend brought it back from Boston on July 4th weekend '67, and I had started getting immersed in *Axis*. So I was surprised he came out alone and soloed into 'Killing Floor', which I had just come across, a day or two earlier, on the Electric Flag album. The rest is a blur until 'Wild Thing' and guitar immolation and destruction.

I WAS THERE: ELLEN PRATT, AGE 13

I went to that concert with my girlfriend Ethyl. I remember being picked up by the rush in the doors, losing my loafers. I can't remember if I ever recovered them. We sat on the last row of the floor bleachers and could see very well. At one time all the lightbulbs busted, one by one around us. It was so intense seeing him go crazy on stage. At least that's what it looked like to us. It was our very first concert. He played the guitar with his teeth and the way I remember he was very into rubbing his guitar elsewhere! Then he started busting up all the speakers and guitars and for us it was kinda scary. A memory for sure.

I WAS THERE: SUSAN SENGSTOCK

A group of us hung out together in high school, including most of the guys in Terry and the Telstars. Somehow, I got to go in with them while they were setting up and was allowed to stay inside till the concert started. Some of us agreed to help set up the chairs on the floor, and because of that got first-pick in seating. Naturally we chose front-row. I wandered up front to the lobby entrance before the doors were open to have a look at the crowds waiting to get in. The long row of glass doors had people literally plastered up against the glass as the crowds kept pushing to the front of the line. Only general admission tickets were sold then. I was glad not to have to stand in line.

When Jimi and his band walked in, they quietly walked to a room to begin tuning up and doing last-minute rehearsing. They didn't make eye contact with anyone as they walked by. We were in awe. Their attire was very colourful and different from what folks in Lewiston were used to seeing, but such were the hippie days.

A wall of Marshall amps lined the back of the stage. I could be wrong, but I recall nine amps on each side with a gap in between. The Telstars came out and played first, and the crowd loved them as they were one of the top bands in the area. They usually finished in the top three, if not first, in any of the Battles of the Bands we had.

When Hendrix came on it was really loud, to say the least. So much so that I got a nose bleed from it. But rock'n'roll was our passion and I loved every moment. Their sound was unique to us. The last song they did was 'Star Spangled Banner', with Jimi's screeching guitar filling the air. I can't say that's one of my favourite songs by them, so it sounded more like noise to me. But his skills making those sounds I know are not easily copied. The crowd went wild.

That memory remains in the minds of many who attended and will remain one of Lewiston's fondest memories of the many bands we were privileged to hear back in the Sixties and Seventies.

I WAS THERE: ANGELA SMITH, AGE 16

I'd never been to a concert. Heck, I didn't know where the Armory was, being from a small milltown, Jay, just north of Lewiston. My friend Marcia and I heard about the concert and don't even remember how. I believe a friend of hers from Lewiston told her, then she told me. This friend drove to Jay in his pick-up to drive us. Duffy, Marcia, myself and Terry: four of us in the front of a small truck. What an adventure.

The concert was awesome and I don't know how we did it but Marcia and I made it to the very front and stood right up near the stage. Amazing. I just remember being in awe of his music. His playing cannot be described, and Hendrix's finish was never to be duplicated. All these years later, when I tell people I saw him live in the very small city of Lewiston, Maine, it makes me smile. For 19 years, I worked in our high school library and the kids thought this was so very cool. And Hendrix's music will live forever.

I WAS THERE: SANDY SPILLER

We were friends with the guys in Terry and The Telstars and went to almost every dance or event they played. We thought it was so exciting and cool that they were opening for Jimi Hendrix. I'm pretty sure if my parents realised who he was they wouldn't have let me go. We were right up front, so close to the stage that I swear we got some of Jimi's sweat on us. It was like being in a mosh-pit, before mosh pits were even thought of. I remember the green shirt, black vest, pants and hat with feathers. And him wrecking all the equipment. I'd never seen anything like that before. It was a trip, for sure.

I WAS THERE: TED ST PIERRE, AGE 16

I was a student in my sophomore year at Gould Academy, a private boarding school in Bethel, Maine, about an hour from Lewiston. I'm not sure where I first heard of Hendrix, probably on the radio. I think we heard an ad for the concert or saw it in a newspaper. As an aspiring musician I read music-related magazines at the time. We approached the school about the concert and they put up a sign-up sheet to attend and provided a bus and driver to take 20 or so people that signed up. On arrival I was amazed at all of the hippies in one place. I had no idea there were so many in Maine.

I think we missed the local opening act. I don't have any memory of them or they were forgettable after seeing Hendrix. The concert was delayed as Jimi had crashed his Jaguar en route. Being a gear-head, this was my first time hearing multiple 100w stacks live. I was also surprised to see Sound City amps as well as Marshall stacks. I'd never heard or seen that brand before. Very exotic.

The acoustics in the Armory were horrible to begin with and the sound system totally inadequate, consisting of a couple of Fender guitar amp cabinets on either side of the stage and no stage monitors. Hendrix sure made an impression in spite of that. He played many of the songs on *Are You Experienced* as well as more obscure tunes I hadn't heard. I remember thinking Noel Redding looked as if he had pyjamas and slippers on.

MY SISTER WAS THERE: LOUISE THEBERGE

My 17-year old sister asked my Dad to buy her a ticket to see Jimi Hendrix at Lewiston Armory. He initially said no, but later gave in and let my sister buy one. At the time, I wasn't interested in seeing Jimi, so I didn't go with her. She said she went alone but I think not. Anyway, she remembered Jimi playing the 'Star Spangled Banner' and breaking his guitar on stage right after. She still thinks about it now and then.

CAPITAL THEATRE

19 MARCH 1968, OTTOWA, CANADA

I WAS THERE: DAVE RICHARDSON

This was the No.1 concert of my life by far. After Soft Machine finished their opening act, we moved from our assigned seats at the back of the balcony to seats in the front row of the balcony. The curtain opened. I expected to see the usual Fender amp. Instead I saw a wall of Marshall speakers. When he started to play it was just feedback for a bit. I'd never heard this type of sound before. Then he started. There are no words. I've spent the last 50 years playing along with Hendrix songs and backing tracks trying to make that hyper-jump from just playing music to playing like Hendrix.

BUSHNELL THEATER

22 MARCH 1968, HARTFORD, CONNECTICUT

I WAS THERE: RON BURATI

I would have been in the front row at tiny Atwood Hall at Clark University in Worcester, Massachusetts seven days previously, but went down with a fever the day before. My brother and a few friends went and raved to me about how close they were. Instead, I saw him a week later at the larger Bushnell Theater.

Ron saw a very brief Hendrix set at the Bushnell

Equipment problems plagued the show and the set was even shorter than his usually-short sets - maybe 30 minutes. I saw him again that autumn at Boston Garden, but we were far away and could only hear his voice and a little guitar. Drums and bass were indiscernible.

I WAS THERE: DIONISIO CARDONA

I was 17 or 18. Myself and a friend took the train to Hartford. We went to the auditorium to make sure we knew where we were going and walked all around the building and found a side-door open. We entered and expected to get thrown out, but there was no one around. We kept looking, came to a dressing-room door and knocked. We were still waiting to get kicked out, but the door opened and it was Jimi. Believe it or not, he was very polite and asked us to come in. We did, with open mouths, and he sat down at a piano and started doodling around on it while he talked to us. He asked us if we were going to the show. There was a tall blonde woman with him in the room. I don't think she spoke. I figure we were there maybe 15 minutes and we left after thanking him. He was very polite and down to earth. Maybe he was high, but I'll never forget that moment. We waited outside until showtime and saw him light his guitar on stage. He was magical. That was the first time I met him.

We did see some people backstage - his opening act. I asked one guy who was restringing his guitar who they were and he answered in a British accent, 'We are Eire Apparent'. I had never heard of them and didn't like their music when I heard them.

Dionisio (right) bumped into Jimi backstage. Another time it was Felix Cavaliere of The Young Rascals

I WAS THERE: RON CATALDI, AGE 15

I saw him live twice - March '68 and then August '68. The first time I ever heard Hendrix I was vacationing in Hampton Beach, New Hampshire, where we got Boston radio. I heard 'Purple Haze' and I'm like, 'Wow – who's this?' I came home and there was a record shop in my neighbourhood I could walk to, and they had one copy of his album. I picked it up and from there on in that was it - I was hooked.

I remember walking home and stopping in at a convenience store to pick up a soda or something, put the record down on the counter and the cashier said, 'Who the fuck is this guy? Where did you get this?' Nobody had seen anything like it, you know? The American cover was very different from the UK cover. That's how I discovered it. When he came round I got tickets to see him in the Bushnell in Hartford, where I grew up.

When I saw him the first time I was in the third row on his side of the stage, which was just fucking amazing. Those were the days when he was wearing tight jeans, the jacket and the hat. I remember he got kinda pissed off - they were fucking with the power. He threw his guitar down at one point. It was just crazy how I'd never seen since, or ever will, a guitar player that played like Jimi. He had massive hands. He was able to command that instrument like it was mind-blowing.

The auditorium in March was only half-filled as Hartford was a city between New York and Boston. Then when I saw him in August it was standing room only. I'd been away on vacation with my family and came home that day and got an SRO ticket. That's when he was starting to wear the capes with the long sleeves. It was still amazing.

In those days they didn't really mic. any of the instruments. Everything you heard from the stage was what you heard. I'm a drummer and I've been playing all my life, and I've always been a huge Mitch Mitchell fan. In 1970 my band opened for Buddy Miles. I had quite a talk with Buddy, because Jimi had passed away that September. They didn't play real long sets in those days. I'm thinking no more than an hour. He played most of the *Are You Experienced* album and was doing some of the stuff from *Axis: Bold as Love*. Of course, he had all the fuzztones and all that equipment. He was always fucking with his guitar and with his tones. It was just crazy. The Bushnell holds 1600/1800, a beautiful theatre. He had the double stack of Marshall amps.

Maybe Noel had a Sunn stack? I can't remember. I can picture him as if it was yesterday, standing there. Being three rows away from Jimi was pretty amazing. I'd been a huge fan since his album came out in the summer of '67. I was a kid but had already been playing drums several years. When he died, I was in a friend's car and we were driving down the road and had the radio on. I heard, 'Jimi Hendrix has passed away'. I was like, 'What the fuck?' I was devastated.

I was at Woodstock too, but I left early. I was working in the record industry and wound up having lunch with Al Hendrix, Jimi's father. He was a great guy. The thing that was remarkable about him was that Al was a very small man. He was not tall at all. But his hands were massive. It was as if somebody had taken the hands from another person and put them on Al's body. I said, 'Al, now I see where Jimi got his hands from.' I told Al I saw Jimi perform twice and he said, 'Well, well, he got more popular as time went on.' He actually started tearing up. That's how much love he had for Jimi. He was a very quiet, very nice man.

I WAS THERE: BILL NORRIS, AGE 19

As a babe in the woods musically speaking, I owned *Are You Experienced* and liked the way the band played the music and what it projected. Come 22 March 1968 I wasn't going to miss my very first rock concert with Jimi Hendrix. I didn't know exactly what to expect or how I'd react butI knew I just had to see it. Soft Machine opened but I don't remember ever seeing them. All I was focused on was the three musicians playing the songs that I was familiar with, such as 'Fire', 'Purple Haze' and 'Foxy Lady'. That day I witnessed music being performed as I had never experienced until then and haven't since.

I went with three friends, Tom Fitzgerald from Westfield, Massachusetts, James Hundley and Bill Storozuk. I think the tickets were something like $4 or $5 and we had second-row balcony seats about 50ft from the stage. Seats like that today would cost mortgage payment money.

I WAS THERE: ARTHUR ROBERT WALTON

The opening act was The Soft Machine. I was in junior high school and it was the first rock concert I'd been to. I begged my father for a pair of bell- bottom pants and a silk Nehru jacket, which he eventually bought me. Interestingly, I switched from drums to guitar in high school. Many years later I played in a band with once-girlfriend Rosa Lee Brooks. I also played with Ricky Rouse, the best Hendrix impersonator I've heard. Hendrix was a huge influence for me, just like every other guitarist on the planet. Nobody has ever come close. He was one of a kind and so genuine.

BUFFALO MEMORIAL AUDITORIUM

23 MARCH 1968, BUFFALO, NEW YORK

I WAS THERE: RICK BALIN

The original Jimi Hendrix Experience played with opening act, The Soft Machine. Jimi wore an all-black outfit with silver buckles around his hat. People kept yelling, 'Take your hat off'. He just laughed. I guess it was a rare thing having such a huge Afro at the time. His second album, Axis: Bold As Love, had just been released and he played  many songs from that and from the first album, and did 'Wild Thing' as his final song. He humped his guitar and rammed it into the stack of amps behind him. It was a great show for sure, and one I'll never forget. He was an amazing guitar player. Noel Redding strutted the stage, at times playing bass over his shoulders, and Mitch Mitchell played drums like nothing I'd ever seen at the time. I remember Jimi switching a line in 'Purple Haze', singing, 'Scuse me while I kiss this guy', pointing to Noel!

Rick at Woodstock at 19 years during Jefferson Airplane's "3/5 Of A Mile"

Rick saw a memorable show in Buffalo

I WAS THERE: DAVID DIBERNARDINIS SR, AGE 19

I was on the 10th row with a bunch of buddies. One kept yelling repeatedly, 'Jimi, take off your hat'. Finally, Jimi says right to him, 'You drop your drawers and I'll tip my hat'. Which he did! We punched him out as he shot a moon at Jimi, but Jimi tipped his hat.

Later that year I was in NYC at The Scene Club and there he was sat at a big table with an empty seat. I brazenly went and sat there, exclaiming, 'Jimi, I saw you in Buffalo'. He asked how many concerts I'd seen, because I looked so young. I said it was my first. I asked if he remembered the heckler yelling to take off his hat? The table got real quiet, Hendrix put his nose on my nose and said, 'You weren't that motherfucking asshole, were you?' I said, 'No, he was our knucklehead friend, but we punched him out for you!' When he laughed, everyone at the table laughed, including Andy Warhol.

Jimi asked if we wanted to stay for an after-hours jam. Noticing my two buddies at the door, stunned that I was talking with him, I said, 'Oh yeah'. A jam with him and a drunk Jim Morrison and others happened, and no one believed us for many years. Later I lived in San Diego, California, and while in Tijuana in 1985 thumbing through records I found a bootleg of the night I was there, called *Woke Up and Found Myself Dead*, which I still have, finally feeling vindicated as to my amazing story.

I WAS THERE: DENNIS THOMANN

I saw Jimi twice. The first time was at the same place I later saw Led Zeppelin, the Buffalo Auditorium. The second was at the Honolulu International Center in 1970 on the Cry of Love tour. The HIC was sold out but my friends - Abby from Maui and Jack from Boston - and I snuck in. That was a great show!

At Buffalo, my brothers and I were in the sixth row for Hendrix and he was absolutely mind-blowing. He had a beanie cap on because he had burned his hair at a previous concert while burning his guitar. This asshole in the first row kept yelling, 'Take off your hat!' He was relentless. Buffalo was a very rough town back then, and by the stage there were Tactical Patrol Unit cops wearing helmets. Finally, the guy yelling jumps on stage and heads towards Jimi. But he was intercepted by a giant Hell's Angel biker hiding behind the PA. He picked that guy up and threw him down to the cops below, who proceeded to beat him with clubs! Jimi wasn't fazed by that idiot. He just ignored the whole episode.

INDUSTRIAL MUTUAL ASSOCIATION AUDITORIUM

24 MARCH 1968, FLINT, MICHIGAN

I WAS THERE: WILSON LINDSEY

The second time I saw him was in Flint, Michigan. I photographed that show and hung out with him briefly backstage. He came into the show and I could tell he was uptight. He seemed to be on edge and somewhat isolated. He didn't really have anything to say to the other members of the band or anybody else. I don't remember the exact things I tried to initiate as far as conversation with him, but his replies were snappy and a lot different than the Ann Arbor conversations I had with him. That whole experience really stood out in my mind. I worked for various record companies for over 20 years and met all kinds of artists, major acts, and as a musician and someone that's worked with people at the top of the game, I know moodiness is not unusual. It's part of an artistic temperament. You learn to roll with it.

TEEN AMERICA BUILDING

27 MARCH 1968, MUNCIE, INDIANA

I WAS THERE: LARRY MCCABE

Back in early 1968, we didn't know much about Hendrix, except that he'd just released landmark single, 'Purple Haze'. As program director of WERK in Muncie, Indiana, I often got calls from booking agents trying to generate cash for their clients. Jimi's group, the Experience, was due to come through our area in February 1968. All the agent wanted was enough money to help defray expenses (lodging, travelling, eating, etc.) I talked to the owner of WERK, whom I had a good relationship with, and made a deal for cut-rate advertising on the station. I then started to search for partners to help promote this one-nighter. Hendrix's agent wanted $3,000. I found a couple of brothers eager to invest and we were in business. We booked the Teen America Building (or Industrial Building) at the Muncie Delaware County Fairgrounds at a very reasonable cost, even though this corrugated steel building had terrible acoustics and only seated a small crowd. It was the only venue available for our budget.

The show almost didn't come off, mainly as Jimi was discovered smoking several joints just outside the building right before the show was to start by some sheriff's deputies. They informed Hendrix that if he tried to smoke pot inside the arena, the show would be cancelled immediately. The show did go on as scheduled, with a 'purple haze' over the crowd, mostly caused by a marijuana-smoking audience. I interviewed Jimi backstage before he went on with a quality reel-to-reel Wollensak recorder and had my picture taken standing next to a stoned super-star. I've no idea what happened to the taped interview. It was probably recorded over later, simply because we didn't have a clue

Jimi was to become such a legend. I later found I cleared $60.00 on the show after all was said and done.

I WAS THERE: CAROL HETZER SALYERS, AGE 13

I was so young I don't even remember it very well. I was sat on the floor near the back, and was more interested in the fact that a guy I liked was there with someone else. Sad, but true. I was a dumb kid! Muncie was a factory town of about 60,000 people. He came to our County Fairgrounds. In later years, I wondered if I'd dreamed I had seen him. When the internet came about, I was able to search and see he was indeed at the fairgrounds. What a weird place to book someone who was a rising star. I used to think, 'Was that really Jimi Hendrix who came to little old Muncie, Indiana?'

I WAS THERE: ROD MCCLURE, AGE 15

My cousin was the drummer in a band and always had albums and stuff like that, and had this album, *Are You Experienced*. I was a Cream fan and a fan of bands like that, three-piece bands. I just thought they looked wild. He let me play the record and I couldn't play it enough.

It wasn't long after that Jimi had got kicked off The Monkees tour at short notice. A local radio station fellow had a chance to book him, so he did. He put him in a place at the county fairgrounds, a big barn of a place.

I'd been playing guitar a couple of years and was barely getting my feet wet and most of my friends in Muncie were musicians to some degree. My best friend was a guitarist and I remember we sat in a restaurant with others and talked about this Hendrix guy coming. We heard the buzz that this guy was really wild, really good, so got tickets, which were about $3.50 or something.

Randy and I got press passes from Betty Harris, a newspaper reporter. She often gave us press passes if we went to see big bands. We could get backstage and let her know how the concerts went and she'd write a little piece in her column, called *Where The Band Are*. We got back in the area where the bands come in and I briefly met Jimi before they went on stage.

All the guys were pretty nice. He was real nice. I was so green I thought, 'This guy's left-handed, he'll probably want to shake hands left-handed', so I extended my left hand and he extended his and shook my left hand. I've always thought that was kinda cool. He was so accommodating. They were just getting ready to go into the back of the building and go on stage.

I went in there and they had another band, The Soft Machine, who were backing them. Everybody couldn't wait until Soft Machine got done so they could see Hendrix. I remember really vividly when he came on stage, he was wearing a hat and there were some redneck kind of people out in the audience yelling, 'Take off your hat'. Hendrix said, 'Well, if I take off my hat, will you take off your pants?' The guy yelled, 'Yeah', and Jimi flipped him the bird and just said, 'Fuck you' and turned around.

About that time the Delaware county sheriff was right by the stage and it looked like he was going to go up on stage and arrest Jimi. Back then, they were a little stricter on stuff like that in middle America - he could have got arrested for indecent behaviour. But this deputy sheriff started to get on stage and Hendrix just flipped around and started playing.

It was like he was in this other world. It was amazing. I remember hearing this swirl of music and saying, 'My God, I hope he records this on his next album.' Then it just erupted into 'Hey Joe' and my stomach sank at that point because I thought, 'I'll never hear that again'. He was just playing around before he went into 'Hey Joe'. It was his way of segueing into it. He started with that and did a couple of numbers. He talked to the audience a little. He said he was so 'glad to be here in Muncie, Indianapolis' when it was actually Muncie, Indiana.

He played pretty much everything on the *Are You Experienced* album plus a few other numbers, more jam-type 12-bar blues. But I always thought it was my own memory where it struck me as so phenomenal, because this guy was from outer space or something. He sounded like a one-man orchestra, the way he played. It was just cosmic.

It hit me hard and hit my friend hard. I've read other people's memories of that evening and they felt the same way.

The gear back then was so primitive. What we were hearing was so primal. This guy was really playing through loud amps and all he had was a fuzztone, a wah-wah and Marshall heads. He was playing through Sunn cabinets, nothing sophisticated at all. The PA was all Sunn equipment. Sound systems were no good back then, compared to the way they are now. But he was able to cut through all that and just blow everybody away. It was a big buzz afterwards. Everyone was talking about how outrageous this was.

The PAs were about the same as guitar amps. They were pretty distorted. But the musicality of it cut through it. You could hear everything he was playing. That part was cosmic. I saw The Who and other bands at the same place and it was the same problem. You just didn't have the technology that reproduced sound at very high levels and do it well.

I was fortunate enough to see Andrés Segovia there in Muncie and he was like God on guitar. But Hendrix was like the devil on guitar. He was just so good.

We did go back afterwards. They were travelling in a bus, and we talked to the band. I mostly talked to Mitch Mitchell and he gave me a drumstick as a souvenir.

The guy that put it on is Larry McCabe. He was the DJ for WERK and he and a few of his friends dabbled in booking a few regional and a few national bands when they got a chance. Larry told me he cleared $80 on that concert.

It could have held 800 or 900 people. They didn't sell it out by any means, because my friend and I went back to the ticket booth after and there were stacks of tickets left. The guy just gave us handfuls. We each had a stack. Years later, after I moved out, my Dad threw mine away. I had one which I ended up selling a few years back. The guy gave me $800 for the ticket. I wished I had the whole stack.

I WAS THERE: GREGORY GRAHAM, AGE 14

The building's still there, although it's not the 'Teen' building anymore and hasn't been for a long time. It was a terrible building for a concert, acoustically not set up for something like this. It was a pre-engineered metal building. I attended with my friend and classmate Tom. We were both into album rock, not necessarily mainstream music for a typical teen. Muncie is a town that includes a college and I think we purchased our tickets in the area they call the 'village', at the music store and head shop. The building still exists today.

There could not have been more than about 2,000 in attendance. The two of us were standing right in front of the stage, to the left as we faced the stage, close to the amps. We couldn't have been more than 10 to 15ft away from where Jimi was most of the time. He was wearing a hat and somebody in the crowd asked him to remove it. He told them, 'Fuck you.' He went to tune his guitar he was going to destroy but couldn't get it right and dropped it off the back of the stage. He ended up using his Fender. He didn't destroy it but did run it though one of the amp fronts.

Despite being 50 years ago, I probably remember more about this concert than all those I've attended since, and this was the first of many.

XAVIER UNIVERSITY FIELDHOUSE

28 MARCH 1968, CINCINATTI, OHIO

I WAS THERE: BOB GILKER

I saw Jimi in concert three times but it was long ago and, given the various mind-enhancing items I was doing then, my memories are somewhat incomplete. I believe I first discovered Jimi's music after hearing about his performance at Monterey. I was about 16 and a friend of mine and I played with the idea of travelling to California from Cincinnati, Ohio to attend. It was impossible to arrange, but I later heard about Jimi's incredible performance. I

Robert saw Jimi three times

bought *Are You Experienced* and played it a lot. It's still my favourite of his music.

My first opportunity to see him in concert was at Xavier University in spring '68. I was a senior in high school and went with a couple of friends. I remember being blown away by Jimi's guitar playing; he was still doing things like playing behind his back and plucking with his teeth. Besides the 'athletic' style of playing, musically it was great.

FIELD HOUSE

30 MARCH 1968, UNIVERSITY OF TOLEDO, OHIO

I WAS THERE: REED SCHRAMM, AGE 16

I talked with Jimi at the University of Toledo. It wasn't like I was in awe. I thought it was interesting he was using The Who's sound equipment. He did however move me in the sounds he created from his guitar. It's stayed with me all these years. I was fortunate to have a job that allowed me to meet a lot of great musicians. Janis, too, moved me and changed my direction on life.

I WAS THERE: KEN ZUERCHER

I was a junior in high school in Toledo. He was scheduled at the University of Toledo and I, along with a large number of my friends, bought tickets for $2. If we were university students it would have been $1.50! Music was in an unprecedented experimental phase. Jimi was at the forefront for many, especially guitar players. He was touring around the time of the *Axis: Bold As Love* record. When we saw him, I expected him to play his songs that were current, but he didn't. He played portions of songs from

Are You Experienced and improvised the entire set! It was a life-changing experience. After the concert, instead of calling for rides, we all walked the four miles home. We walked in almost silence.

Because of The Beatles I took up guitar. Because of Hendrix I made it a career - playing, teaching music and designing and building amps and pedals for myself and other guitarists.

THE ARENA

31 MARCH 1968, PHILADELPHIA, PENNSYLVANIA

I WAS THERE: RICK VITO

We saw him just a few months later in March, again in Philadelphia, this time at a place they held sports shows in. They had a stage set-up but also did wrestling matches and whatever. This was definitely a bigger concert vibe. Both times I had to suffer through this band, The Soft Machine - the worst crap I ever heard. It went on and on and was such a stark contrast to Hendrix. I was just praying I wouldn't have to listen too much of them. But they went on again, droned on.

Both times I got pictures of Jimi. The second time I got pretty close and got a nice shot. I ran up front. He opened the second show with 'Voodoo Child' and same deal. He did more songs from *Axis: Bold as Love*, and I think he did 'Come On' too. It was the same thing – we were just blown away.

He seemed to be able to conjure up all he did in every show, at least at that point in his career. He may have gone on stage tired, but by the end of the show it was as if he'd really spun some magic on the crowd. Those are some of the best shows I've seen in my life.

I'm so sorry the drugs came into play later. I don't think his music was ever as good as the first three albums he put out. But he didn't have a chance to finish them. You don't know what he would have done with a lot of those tracks. But he definitely was thoroughly inspired and ready to conquer the world in those first couple of years.

His performance didn't suffer from being in a bigger arena. In a sense it was better because the sound was bigger. They had really big speakers for the PA and he had this giant wall of amps behind him. It really reverberated nicely. I remember thinking, with The Soft Machine, I wanted to cover my ears because it was so loud and shitty. But when Hendrix was playing loud it was a good loud. Because he was dynamic. He could bring it down real soft and seemed to know how to turn it on in such a way that was dynamic. You went right with him.

When he died, I was still at school. There was a canteen on campus where you could go and get hamburgers and coffee and I went in there and somebody rushed up and told me. I just thought, 'Oh man – the drugs, the drugs, the drugs.' And it was the drugs. It wasn't an overdose of drugs. It was an accident. It wasn't a pleasure drug. I just thought, 'What a waste.' I remember thinking, 'I'm glad I got to see him.' For me it was a real personal thing, being a guitarist, and someone who was able to take inspiration from that and turn it into my own career.

Seeing that quality and what he was able to do just never leaves you. I feel like I was able to pick up on it on another level than maybe a lot of people could, because they weren't players.

I WAS THERE: TOM SHEEHY

The Arena was a venue in West Philadelphia which staged professional boxing, basketball and occasional concerts. This was my first visit and it held around 4,000 people. The support act was The Soft Machine. I had never heard any of their records, and after a pathetic set, I had no desire to listen to them again; I wanted Hendrix. The first thing I noticed as Jimi walked on stage was him wearing a big black hat. He seemed more serious that night then when I saw him the month before, yet by the end of March that year everything musical and cultural grew more pensive and severe, 1968 progressing to be the most consequential year of the Sixties, with America at war in

Vietnam. Little did we know that four days later, Martin Luther King Jr. would be murdered.

Highlights of the performance were 'Red House', during which Jimi's guitar sounded like it was crying, and 'Spanish Castle Magic', which I was elated to hear as that was my favourite track from *Axis: Bold As Love*.

As the performance concluded, Jimi began to knock over his amps with his guitar and Mitch Mitchell kicked his kit about. This was completely unexpected and created loud explosive sounds as Hendrix left the stage. Just then, some hippy jumped on stage and started yelling into the mic: 'They stopped the bombing! They stopped the bombing!' My friend Bruce asked, 'What does he mean?' I thought it was some poetic response to what the audience just experienced, sonically similar to explosions during warfare. It wasn't until I got home and my father told me President Johnson came on TV that night and announced he had stopped the bombing of Vietnam and would not seek re-election, that I understood the significance of that evening.

CENTRE PAUL-SAUVE

2 APRIL 1968, MONTREAL, CANADA

I WAS THERE: DEAN THOMSON

I saw him twice. In Montreal, The Soft Machine opened. I thought they were great. I think they played in the dark and I became an instant fan. Hendrix was great too. He wasn't on stage very long, not by today's standards. I remember watching Mitch Mitchell closely. He really impressed me. I'm a guitar player, not a drummer, so don't usually get bent out of shape by drummers unless it's Ginger Baker doing rolls with his feet on his double bass-drums. I also saw Jimi at Woodstock.

VIRGINIA BEACH DOME

4 APRIL 1968, VIRGINIA BEACH, VIRGINIA

I WAS THERE: ROBERT PHELPS

The venue has since been torn down, but I have images I shot backstage along with his autograph on the radio station that sponsored the shows' notepad. I also have my front-row ticket. That year in the south of the US was a different time, good and bad in its own way. Some clever lad thought it was funny

to put a watermelon on the stage before the show. I thought it was all in bad taste, because I really enjoyed the music and it was a new way and type of music.

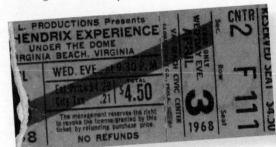

I WAS THERE: SKIP BOYD, AGE 17

I saw him twice at the Civic Center in '68. The venue was a geodesic dome of the Buckminster Fuller type, commemorating Alan B Shepard, the astronaut, who lived in Virginia Beach. The only other concert I'd seen was Gary Puckett and the Union Gap - bubblegum. Hendrix was entirely a new experience. I had no idea such music existed.

I don't remember who else played in April, but the Soft Machine was with him in August. Usually at least one opener, and often two, were included in the ticket price. That April concert was beyond anything I'd experienced. My family was poor and I missed a lot of mainstream pop culture. When I heard a radio ad for the upcoming Hendrix concert, I don't think I even knew who he was. But the music was incredible, loud and very different. I think they kept playing a piece of 'Purple Haze' for a teaser. That concert was a portal into a lot of life-changing events for me.

I WAS THERE: CHANDLER ALBRECHT EDMUNDS, AGE 18

I saw him twice, once at the Virginia Beach Dome and again at the 1970 Atlanta Pop Festival. He was amazing. He played 'The Spangled Banner' amidst a display of fireworks. I can't remember what else he played. The night he played the Dome he demolished his guitar and threw broken pieces to the audience.

I went with my boyfriend and we were in the second row in the second section back from the stage. That show was the night of Martin Luther King's assassination and Jimi announced he was playing at a Martin Luther King tribute in New York the next night.

Chandler saw Jimi the night of MLK's assassination

I WAS THERE: RANDY MELTON

I was a nerdy 10th-grade kid. My joy in life came from playing keyboard in my neighbourhood band, playing soul music with my friends and making a few dollars. From what I recall I'd only recently discovered Jimi Hendrix and it all seemed so new and fresh. It was over my head as a musician, but I couldn't stop listening Jimi was scheduled to play at the Dome in early April but there was some kind of mix-up that changed the date from the 3rd to the 4th. When he did perform I had the good luck of having a ticket land in my lap. My bandmates were all invited, so this group of 16-year-olds scored a car and drove 20 miles from Ocean View. This was the first time I went to a concert without my dad. He took me to see performers like James Brown and Little Richard, who came to Norfolk 's Center Theater.

We arrived at the Dome and found our seats. Just four rows back

THIS SIDE UP AT FRAT. PARTY

Randy's dad took him to see James Brown and Little Richard before he went to see Jimi without him. A fine upbringing (Randy pictured in the middle)

from the stage, stage right. The place was packed and I think every musician in town was there. The vibe in the room was something I never felt before. I was glad I was there. First Soft Machine, a three-piece with organ, bass and drums, played. Maybe it was because I played organ, but I really liked them. I don't remember if there was a curtain rise or if they just walked on but I recall thinking, 'There they are, The Jimi Hendrix Experience!' Jimi was on stage right, just 20ft away. What I saw was way beyond imagination. I could see Jimi's hands and fingers. It didn't seem human. It didn't compute. The sound, the ability to see him play in real time and hear what he was playing took me somewhere I'd never been before or after. It was fun and mystic and right. I saw Jimi grind his guitar into his amp, I saw him set his guitar on fire. It inspired me. I knew I would never be the same again. It still affects me to this day. Have you ever been experienced? Well, I have.

I WAS THERE: STEVE PROESCHER

I think I first heard Jimi on our local underground radio station. Our classical FM station, WNOR FM, played Beethoven during the day but at 11pm changed to 'Roll Over Beethoven' and played all the latest rock. All other radio stations played Top-10. I remember borrowing my grandfather's AM/FM short wave radio and dialling in to listen late at night. I couldn't wait.

At the time, it seemed like every group sounded totally different, and everything we heard was a new discovery. It was either 'Fire' or 'Foxy Lady' that I heard first. I was hooked immediately. My friends and I wore the grooves off our Hendrix recordings.

When we learned that Jimi was coming to the Dome, several of us made plans to skip school and be the first in line for tickets. The venue seated around 1,000 people. We were within the first 10 or so and ended with second or third row seats. Mom dropped us off at the concert (none of us had driver's licenses) and we could hear the band soundchecking from outside. I hadn't quite caught up to the hippie thing and was mesmerised by all the tie-dye, bell-bottoms and long hair, all of which I pursued shortly after. The concert was very exciting. All the hits were played and Jimi broke his guitar into many pieces. Having seen films of the burning guitar at Monterey, we were a bit disappointed he didn't repeat this display. It turns out that the local fire codes prevented him from doing so.

Here's one of the hazy parts. I remember the tickets showing April 3rd as the date. I also remember that Martin Luther King was assassinated the day Jimi played. Of course, that day was April 4th. There are pictures of tickets on line showing the April 3rd date. I don't recall why the date was changed. I seem to recall that the second show was cancelled due to the assassination but may have imagined this after so many years.

Jimi returned to our area on 21 August 1968 and my friends and I were there then as well. The Soft Machine opened both times.

I WAS THERE: JOHN SINGISER, AGE 14

I went with my older sister and we probably got the tickets at a local record shop. It was my first concert. I was very excited to see him. Soft Machine opened. It was right after Jimi's second album came out, so I think he did some songs from that and hits from the first album – 'Fire', 'Foxy Lady' and possibly 'Purple Haze'. I recall seeing photos of him from that show playing a Fender Jaguar rather than the usual Stratocaster.

TROY ARMORY

19 APRIL 1968, TROY, NEW YORK

I WAS THERE: BERT PAGANO, AGE 15

Troy is part of what is considered to be the Tri-City area around New York's capital, Albany. I was a fledgling guitarist. Hendrix had completely turned my world upside down with *Are You Experienced*. The show was initially scheduled for 7 April but due to the assassination of Martin Luther King, it was postponed until the 19th. The venue was an old National Guard Armory building purchased by a local university, later used for entertainment events. At best it was 50% filled, but that didn't matter, I was so psyched to be hearing him live. His opening number was 'Love or Confusion'. The small enthusiastic crowd went crazy. The rest of the show is a blur save for his finale of 'Wild Thing' and his destruction of his guitar and amp. I don't think he set his guitar on fire, probably due to local fire codes. He played nearly all his debut recording plus 'Red House'. It was an amazing evening and left me totally amazed and inspired. It's been 50 years since that night, but it's etched in my memory.

I WAS THERE: DOUG SMITH

Troy Armory was adjacent to the Rensselaer Polytechnic Institute. RPI, as it is known locally, had and still has a very progressive campus radio station at WRPI, 91.5 FM. I remember specifically hearing Led Zeppelin for the first time on their station when I was readying for school one morning. The same was true of when I first heard Jimi Hendrix. I had heard of Hendrix but never heard anything by him until then. I went out and bought *Are You Experienced* and played that record over and over, every day. So, when the show was announced, of course we all got tickets.

It was a general admission show and people showed up the night before to get seats. My father drove us down, leaving from our village of Hoosick Falls, New York to get to Troy. We left about 4.15pm for the 8pm show, unheard of back then. Because we were there so early, when the doors finally opened at 7pm we rushed in and were able to get fifth-row centre seats. The opening band was Soft Machine. They came out at 8pm with a good set and got the crowd prepped for what was to come. We had no idea that what we were in for was a true 'experience'.

The lights went down and the band took the stage. Jimi was still tuning his guitar when they launched into 'I Don't Live Today'. From that point on, everyone was up on their feet and some were on their chairs. They played the entire first album and the place went totally wild. Jimi played between his legs, behind his back, with his teeth and behind his head, all the while undulating like a cat on heat. He dragged his guitar neck along the mic. stand and along the edge of his massive Marshall and Sunn speaker cabinets.

Two of our group managed to get up on stage in the frenzy. Bill made it as far as Noel Redding before being tossed. But Mike made it all the way to Jimi before he was tossed back. After the show, Mike said when he reached Jimi, Hendrix turned to him and said, 'I love you, baby'! It was just frantic in there and I had never seen nor heard anything like it and haven't since. Things settled down a bit. Then, Jimi excused himself while he changed guitars. He put on a beautiful, black Les Paul and proceeded to knock us out with 'Red House'. After that, he sat down with an acoustic 12-string and played some amazing blues.

When he was done with the acoustic guitar, he put his Strat back on and announced their new album *Axis: Bold As Love*. They played 'Spanish Castle Magic' and again the place went totally bat-shit crazy. When the show was over, some of our group ran out to follow the band. There was a limo out back after the show. When they left, they threw some of their things into the trunk then they piled in. A length of the scarf Jimi wore during the show was still hanging out of the trunk after they closed the lid. My friend Charlie grabbed a hold of it as the car was driving away. Finally, the scarf tore and he had managed to get a good piece of it. He still has that piece of scarf.

After we got back home, my father dropped us off in the village. We were so revved up, we ran around climbing on things and just hooting and hollering to burn off some of the energy from the total 'experience' we had witnessed. I read about it in the paper the next day. It was my first concert and one I still remember vividly. It's still my all-time favourite show.

I was home watching the evening news with my parents after returning from a trip to California when the TV announcer told of the death of James Marshall Hendrix. I was totally shocked. That's all I can say. Music lost an incredible artist and the world lost an iconic human being.

I WAS THERE: BRENT GUILBAULT

After seeing the show with the Experience and while walking across a bridge over the Hudson River to get home, my friends and me saw Jimi stopped in traffic so approached and tapped on the window. He rolled it down and was sitting in the back seat between two beautiful young women, smoking a joint. We complimented him on a great show and then my friend asked if he had a pick in his mouth or did he just play with his teeth? He answered, 'With my teeth, man, just with my teeth'. Then the window rolled back up and the limo rolled off.

The Jimi Hendrix Experience recorded 'Voodoo Child (Slight Return)' at the Record Plant, New York City.

'Voodoo Child (Slight Return)' was developed from 'Voodoo Chile', recorded May 2, 1968, during a studio jam with Steve Winwood on organ. The next day, Hendrix returned to the studio with Redding and Mitchell for the filming of a short documentary for ABC Television. Jimi stated; 'We started doing 'Voodoo Child' about three times because they wanted to film us in the studio, to make us look like you're recording, boys, one of them scenes, you know, so, 'OK, let's play this in E, a-one, a-two, a-three', and then we went into 'Voodoo Child'. After his death in 1970, Track Records released the song as a single in the UK, using the title 'Voodoo Chile', which became Hendrix's only No.1 single.

MIAMI POP FESTIVAL

18 MAY 1968, GULFSTREAM PARK, HALLANDALE, FLORIDA

I WAS THERE: DEBBIE NEWTON UMINA, AGE 17

It was $3 to get in for the weekend. It wasn't a big crowd, perhaps 300 people. Back then people didn't stand up and hoot and howl. Everybody just sat there. Jimi and the other guys flew in on a helicopter, landed behind the stage and then did their show. He did all the songs we sing along to now. It was quite the show - John

Lee Hooker, who was great, and Blue Cheer, Frank Zappa and the Mothers of Invention, and of course Jimi. Paul McCartney was backstage while Linda McCartney was in the crowd and photographed the crowd and musicians. There had been much loss that year - Martin Luther King and Bobby Kennedy. A time of great change and lots of peace and love in the air. The wave of mega-concerts had not hit at this time.

Move over, Rover, and let Deb and Tim take over

I remember standing about three feet from the stage knowing I was seeing something new. This was in the days when you could walk right up to the stage, because nobody was standing up or anything. His music resonated. I feel privileged to have been there and still do. It was a super spiritual experience that you have maybe once or twice in life. He had a white shirt on and red pants and had his hat on. He didn't burn any guitars but did play behind his back.

I went with four guys and we travelled down from Titusville, Florida. None of us were high but we all had that experience

while we were there. The concert
was rained out on the second day, so
was a one-day phenomenon.

Frank Zappa's group came
out into the crowd and were just
hanging with everybody and I got
invited to a party but said no - I
had to go home and go to school.
I was trying to be good. Jimi
played, then left in the helicopter.

I don't remember how we
found out. We lived about four
hours above Hallandale.

The weather started to
change and the next day it just
poured rain, as it does in Florida. The stage was out in the open. It
was on the racetrack. The crowd could either sit in front of the stage
on the ground or you could sit in the stand.

I went to other concerts after that like Newport Rhode Island,
where I remember sleeping in the mud because there were so many
people and it was packed, Woodstock-like. This wasn't anything like
that – you could get up and walk around. It was a mellow scene,
everybody getting along. It was really neat to know you were part of
that. It was so tame and mellow. Not everybody was smoking dope.
Not everybody was doing LSD. I wasn't. My group wasn't.

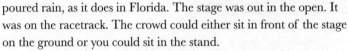

I WAS THERE: JOANNE HAMILTON

The thing that has stayed with me was the sense that the crowd was
all focused on the music and was of one mind. At other big outdoor
concerts, it was hard to focus on the music: everyone milling around,
no one paying attention, sets starting while I was crashing. But this
crowd was alert, alive and paying attention. It was enthused. The
music was a delight for the mind. I always said it was the best set
I'd ever heard, until Trombone Shorty played at Sacramento music

festival maybe three years ago. But Gulfstream was a half century ago and it would be unfair to compare, so I rate the two shows as equally great. Still, I've often wished Jimi had lived so that we could have heard how his music would have evolved.

I WAS THERE: AL HOSPERS, AGE 21

I drove down from Gainesville with a couple of friends. Apparently, some people say there were only about 400 people to see him, but my memory says more, plus there is video of his performance and it looks like more. I saw Blue Cheer, Arthur Brown, Zappa, Jimi and a famous old blues guy whose name I can't remember - maybe John Lee Hooker?

I WAS THERE: ED ROSNER

I saw his first set at the Miami Pop Festival. I didn't see the second set but heard it because I was still on the grounds. My cousin and I watched from the seated area in front of the stage, about 30/40ft away from the stage and directly in front of Jimi. I recall it, visually, fairly vividly. My lasting image was how entertaining he was and what a showman, especially how easily and smoothly he made the move where he ran his sleeve across the strings on the neck of his guitar, never missing a beat. I also recall how he was moving around the stage pushing the buttons with his foot that controlled the various sounds. He did all his standard stage antics - pointing at the crowd with 'kiss this guy/sky', wagging his tongue and the feedback. He just seemed to really enjoy what he was doing, smiling and laughing the whole time. The crowd was mesmerised and he put on a great show. Unfortunately, I missed seeing him burn his guitar during the second set.

I wish I could just turn my visual memory into a photo. I can still see him reasonably clearly in my mind. I don't recall a lot about some of the other acts but can still see Jimi on the stage.

I WAS THERE: LEN TUFFORD, AGE 20

I was probably 25ft away while he played through six Marshall amps and a white Stratocaster. I was blown away by the power of his playing and presence. I went to the concert with my first wife, who was eight months pregnant. It wasn't a pleasant experience at the time for her - it was a hot day and very crowded.

Len took his heavily pregnant wife to see Jimi

In June 1968 Jimi's girlfriend Kathy Etchingham saw an advert in a London evening newspaper for a £30 a week flat on Brook Street, London. Jimi moved in briefly in July before returning to the United States for an extensive tour. Once back in the UK, he gave his girlfriend £1,000 cash (a fortune in 1968) to fill it with soft furnishings from nearby stores John Lewis and Liberty and Portobello Road market. He told Kathy this was his 'first real home of my own'.

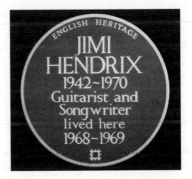

In 2014 the Handel House Trust was awarded a Heritage Lottery Fund grant to restore the Hendrix flat permanently. The flat opened to the public in February 2016.

WOBURN ABBEY

6 JULY 1968, WOBURN, UK

I WAS THERE: TYRONE DALBY

Jimi had just returned from a tour of Spain. I've a feeling Chas
Chandler owned a nightclub there and the group had done some gigs
for him. It was reported that Hendrix had shoved the top end of his
guitar through the low ceiling. Presumably, Chas paid the repairs bill.

Maria (my university girlfriend at Hull) and I always wanted to
see the original Jimi Hendrix Experience, so we went to the Woburn
Abbey Pop Festival. The Experience were top of the bill on Saturday
and went on at the end of the evening. Apparently, the group were
very late getting there. They'd been held up at customs in Spain,
where all their equipment was taken to pieces to see if drugs were
stashed in any of it.

Rick Grech, the bass player with Family and later of Blind Faith,
told me the three members of the Experience were very tired when
they finally got there. All I remember is that I felt they weren't doing
justice to *Are You Experienced* and *Axis: Bold As Love*.

SGT.PEPPERS

15 JULY 1968, PALMA, MAJORCA, SPAIN

I WAS THERE: MONICA BROWN

I was living in Mallorca and knew Michael Jeffreys, his co-
manager at the time, very well. My boyfriend and Michael had a
disco called Sgt. Peppers. The opening night Jimi performed, and
it was spectacular! At the end of his performance Jimi slammed
the guitar into the ceiling and it crumbled and all this white stuff
fell all over him like snow. The crowd went absolutely wild.

When I was in London on a visit we went to see Chas Chandler,
who was married to a Swedish girl at the time, Lotta. Jimi stayed
with them and I saw his bedroom, which was draped in US flags.

He was quite a timid person and used to keep himself to himself. I remember he wore the most beautiful silk shirts, a different one every day and with velvet trousers. Mitch Mitchell was a really nice guy, who adored my dog. Jimi and the band spent quite some time in Mallorca that summer.

Noel Redding remembered that he and Jimi swapped instruments. On 'Wild Thing', Jimi raised his guitar towards the ceiling and smashed it straight through the flimsy material. Jimi left it hanging there.
Deep Purple released their debut album, *Shades Of Deep Purple* in July 1978, including a cover of 'Hey Joe', Hendrix-style.

> I was impressed by Hendrix. Not so much by his playing, as his attitude. He wasn't a great player, but everything else about him was brilliant. Even the way he walked was amazing

Ritchie Blackmore, Deep Purple

On 30 July 1968 the Experience travelled from Los Angeles to Baton Rouge, Louisiana to begin their new American tour. They kicked off the tour with two performances, supported by Soft Machine in the Independence Hall at the Lakeshore Auditorium.

INDEPENDENCE HALL, LAKESHORE AUDITORIUM

30 JULY 1968, BATON ROUGE, LOUISIANA

I WAS THERE: LINDA CHANDLER

I had a roommate who was dating a horn player with John Fred and his Playboy Band. They had a No.1 hit, 'Judy in Disguise'. The band was from Baton Rouge, my hometown. They opened the concert. The horn player, Charlie Spinoza, got tickets for my roommate, myself and my boyfriend. The concert didn't go well, generally, although Hendrix and the Experience were great. Problem was, as Hendrix explained, the record company had made a deal with Sunn equipment, and it was second-rate at best. The sound kept going out. The audience was patient, but the constant interruptions were troublesome. There was also an unpleasant display of racism by a rude ass, who shouted out the 'N' word to Jimi, who like the trouper he was, responded with an angry scowl and extended middle finger.

After the concert, we went backstage to meet Charlie. He told Jimi he had some weed he would be willing to share. An invitation to go up to the suite was issued and we were on cloud nine to have such an opportunity. At that time, the southern states were not tolerant of marijuana and going to jail for possession was not uncommon. Bands touring that region were very careful not to be travelling with it. Our offer was well met!

We took an elevator, knocked and were admitted by Jimi. He and Mitch were in the living room, while Redding was in a bedroom with the door closed. We sat down and were offered beers, which we all took. We smoked and drank and talked, in the way the young do, with no pretensions or expectations. It was a lovely time. Mitch was a bit of a joker, extroverted and humorous. Jimi was quiet in a mystical way. He had no sharp edges, very mellow. My roommate and I remarked the next day that we wished he lived nearby, giving us the chance to sit and chat over tea. We were very impressed with how grounded he was. I don't recall the context in which it came up, but he expressed unhappiness with his vocal ability. We offered our sincere opinion that he was too hard on himself. He was not wrong, though. His vocals were not his strength. Once, Redding came into the room, but he seemed huffy and impatient, and went back to his room without speaking. We suggested maybe we should go, but Jimi said not to worry, Redding was always stand-offish. We picked up our conversation and passed a very memorable evening - a bit of magic I will never forget.

On the day of the 31 July show at the Municipal Auditorium in Shreveport, Jimi Hendrix, drummer Mitch Mitchell and bass guitarist Noel Redding attended a love-in at Congo Square with performances by local bands. Hendrix spoke to the masses from the back of a pickup truck, inviting them to the concert later that night. One eye-witness recalled Jimi arriving in a limo and being handed a Chihuahua, which he proceeded to autograph: 'The dog just laid there with his head down on Jimi Hendrix's fingertips. With his other hand, Jimi took a Marks-a-Lot and wrote on the side of the animal, 'Jimi Hendrix'.

Shreveport's Municipal Auditorium, nationally significant for hosting the Louisiana Hayride radio programme during its heyday from 1948 to 1960 and heralded as the finest example of an Art Deco building in the state, was where a young Elvis Presley got his start and where Hank Williams and Johnny Cash also began their careers.

MUNICIPAL AUDITORIUM

31 JULY 1968, SHREVEPORT, LOUISIANA

I WAS THERE: STEVEN RISER, AGE 15

I was a big Hendrix fan. Just one month before I'd seen my very first concert, also at the Municipal, and that was The Vanilla Fudge. Jimi opened with 'Foxy Lady', after which he said, 'I have to go piss.' He left but of course returned. At some point someone shouted, 'Get the nigger off the stage'. Ugh. Hendrix replied with, 'Thank you, I love you too.'

I WAS THERE: DENISE PRUITT-CHAN, AGE 15

I took my best friend for her birthday using money I'd earned through babysitting. It was 'The City of Churches'. Jimi came on stage with a beer and cigarette, played amazingly but really made the City Fathers mad when he stopped to 'go take a piss' and went offstage. We didn't have concerts for several years after that, although I remember we had John Denver. Yawn! We are still BFFs and both proudly date ourselves by saying we were 'experienced' at 15!

I WAS THERE: JUDY HOLLAND

It was the summer between my sophomore and junior year of high school. I believe it was my second 'real' concert, The Beach Boys being my first. It was a double-date with a really cute boy and I still have my ticket stubs.

I was fairly inexperienced, and it was excitingly different than anything I had seen. He did stop to 'take a piss'. And I really did not understand his great talent until years later. I was very happy my parents allowed me to attend.

I had a new dress (casual, but I was still over-dressed) and new earrings. I went to Pizza Hut after and listened to Otis Redding on the jukebox singing '(Sitting on the) Dock of the Bay'.

I WAS THERE: JOHN BRICE

This was a time of racial turmoil and my city was no exception. My date and I came to hear the music but there were others who came to cause trouble. Most of the audience were standing on the main floor. I don't remember seeing anyone who wasn't white. There may have been one or two in the crowd, but I did not notice one. My date and I were in the balcony. The only other people in the balcony were in two small groups. One group was at the rail near the stage and the other group was up in the last row.

As soon as Jimi appeared on stage, a man with black-rimmed glasses from the group in the last row stood up and, in a loud voice, expressed his wish that Jimi return to Africa. Jimi ignored the heckler and prepared to play his guitar. I was mortified. What must people think of my city? Then I thought about the money I had spent to hear the concert that this guy was trying to disrupt. What kind of person pays to go to a concert that he does not want to hear? At that moment, a man from the group near the rail visited the heckler and politely explained that attendance at the concert was voluntary. Everyone calmed down and Jimi played the first number. The heckler then stood up and made additional crude remarks. It was unexpected. I wondered how anyone who had just listened to some of the most fantastic guitar music I ever heard could heckle him. The man from the group by the rail visited the heckler again and explained what was going to happen to the heckler's nose if he continued his behaviour. The heckler was obviously cowed but not pleased with his situation.

By the end of the next song, I was thoroughly entranced by the music. The heckler started another rant. This time, I tried to ignore the person and enjoy the music. I did not look back at the heckler. Then I heard a strange pop sound. I looked behind me and something caught my eye. It was a pair of black-rimmed glasses spinning high into the air. The heckler had been punched in the nose.

I WAS THERE: TERI GREENE

This was in Shreveport, which was conservative and a little backward, so the crowd was very small. Maybe 40 people? Could it have been 100? Maybe, but I don't think so. But Hendrix didn't water down the show for that reason. He was on, full-hearted and full-blast. He played like he was playing to a sell-out crowd and he and we gave it back and forth to each other. It was a very moving and convincing show, even with only a small crowd to play to.

I WAS THERE: EDDIE OWEN, AGE 15

It was my birthday and I got a very special birthday present. Mom bought me three tickets to the Jimi Hendrix concert, at my request. The venue was the Municipal in downtown Shreveport, LA. It was, and still is, an old historic type of auditorium. I was interested in impressing the ladies, so I invited two of my girlfriends. We loved the music, but I remember being a little disappointed there was no light show. What I remember the most was that the place was packed, completely sold out. The amazing thing was that people from all walks of life were there - black, white, young, old. I even saw people in cowboy hats. It was most impressive to me that here in the Deep South, this most gracious but 'experienced' black dude could bring all these people together. I fell in love with Jimi and his music. The influence he has had on my life cannot be understated. I was crushed when he died, but I'll carry his memory with me until it's time for me to die. And I've lived my life the way I wanted to, waving my freak flag high!

I WAS THERE: STEVE HERGENRADER

It happened to be my birthday and my best friend and two sisters were our dates. My best friend Gordon and I met them on our motorcycle and their parents brought them to the auditorium. I remember we had floor seats and of course it was very loud. One thing I remember about the concert was that I wasn't watching and when I looked up at the stage he was playing the guitar behind his head, and unless you saw him do that you would have thought he was playing normally.

I also remember him burning his guitar using lighter fluid. After the concert we happened to see him get in a limo and we followed him to the Holiday Inn. We saw him on the steps to his room and got him to sign our tickets, which he was nice enough to do. At that time, we realised how small in stature he was. He looked bigger than life on stage. One final note: I married my date Pam and we're still together 42 years later. We were nice guys and gave the signed tickets to our dates; unfortunately, the autographed tickets haven't been found. We talk about finding them to this day.

I WAS THERE: MICHAEL PETREE, AGE 16

I was there with my girlfriend, her brother and his date. We had four seats together on the second row. I was worried that Jimi would perform on the other side of the stage since our tickets were like numbers one to four. But the curtain opened, and he was on our side of the stage, right in front of us. I could see every drop of his sweat. The performance was awesome. He smoked and placed the lit butts in the neck of his guitar while he played the guitar. The auditorium is famous for its acoustics and it showed. He played and rocked the audience, not knowing we were part of something that only someone that was there could appreciate the master of music he was. He finished the gig by slamming speakers and giving the crowd a show. I will never forget that night. He was the man that night.

At the time of Jimi's passing, it was about two months before I got married. I was a student at Louisiana Tech University in Ruston. When I heard the news, I felt a sense of sadness and loss, but also a feeling of gratefulness for all his contributions to music - songs like 'Fire' and 'The Wind Cries Mary' are still my favourites. To me, Jimi was, still is, and probably will always be the greatest guitar player that ever lived on earth.

Tommy in his garden working on his Hendrix riffs

I WAS THERE: TOMMY WILLIAMS, AGE 16

At the time of the concert, I was a guitar player. Ticket prices were a good bit of money for a teenager to spend on a concert. He walked out onto the stage drinking a 16oz Jax beer in a can and placed it on top of one of the Marshall amps. He then took one hand and appeared to turn all his knobs to 10 on the amp. I remember him playing 'Purple Haze', 'Fire', 'Foxy Lady' and 'Red House'. When he played 'Red House', he picked up the Gibson Les Paul. He was extremely confident and had a gentleness to his voice, but when he played and sang it was super-powerful.

He got sounds out of his guitar that nobody had ever heard. It was almost scary. He bumped the amp with his Stratocaster like he was making love. He took the mic. stand and ran it up and down the fretboard for effects, making explosive sounds. He picked the guitar behind his back and with his teeth. At one time, he must have broken a string because he turned the music over to the other two members for solos. He sang out of Altec Voice of Theater PA speakers. I ran down to the edge of the stage within 15ft of him for the rest of the concert. Back then there was no security necessary. I am now 66 years old and I'll never forget it.

I WAS THERE: MARSHALL STEWART, AGE 19

It was a few months before my 20th birthday and I was sitting on the front row of the balcony, just left of centre stage. I had blown off a wedding rehearsal dinner for two friends that night to be there. My wife-to-be (a bridesmaid) was not pleased, but hey, there was no way I was going to miss seeing Jimi live! I'll never

Marshall saw Jimi play left and right-handed

forget seeing Jimi playing left-handed, swinging his guitar around and continuing to play right-handed without ever missing a note! One of my best memories in life.

I WAS THERE: MICHAEL FLANDERS

Not only did I attend the concert, but I also visited him in his hotel room at the Airport Holiday Inn later. The concert drew a small but enthusiastic crowd to a rather run-down venue, yet one with incredible acoustics. When it was restored back to its original glory years later, its acoustic properties were widely noted.

I believe the group that toured with him was the Soft Machine. He destroyed his guitar at the end, which was way out there on the edge for Shreveport in those days.

At that time, there were very few 'heads' in Shreveport and somehow some of us got invited to his room for a party after the concert. My friend Maury and I were out getting truly wasted and got there after it had ended. We woke him up, yet he was very nice. We stood with him just inside his room and had a nice conversation for probably 15 minutes. He was very soft spoken, I recall.

I WAS THERE: ERIKA HULL, AGE 17

People like Elvis, the Everly Brothers and all kinds of country acts have walked those boards. I was raised there. Because my mother worked with a man that put on shows there, and Mom would always get us three kids settled on the front row with our popcorn and coke and as soon as Mom and Dad were gone I'd go backstage. I pretty much grew up backstage at the Municipal Auditorium. And, golly, so many people have played there, from the country people to modern day rock acts. That was kind of like my home away from home.

As a kid, I saw mostly country acts - Merle Haggard and Johnny Horton and Claude King. I loved the Everly Brothers. But there came a time when the Municipal Auditorium needed a lot of repairs and no one was using the Auditorium. And then came Jimi. A month later Vanilla Fudge played, and since then lots of people have - Neil Young,

Jack White, Bob Dylan. Jimi was one of the first rock acts. 'He's coming here?' Boy, I got my ticket right away. I wasn't going to miss that.

I graduated a year early from high school. My friends - sisters Janet and Gloria Hughes – and I were absolutely huge fans. There was no way in hell we would have missed that concert. If I had to crawl on my hands and knees to get there I would have. I wore purple. We were right at the front. Hendrix sent a roadie down and told us where they would be staying and wanted us to join them after the concert. So we did.

I think it was a Holiday Inn motor court. Because there was so much prejudice at that time I don't think they would have been able to get a room in a really nice hotel. We went and hung out in his bedroom and Hendrix was the most delightful man. He had an open suitcase sitting on the floor full of science fiction books, and various things that would get you high – dope, pill bottles, other stuff – but he was so nice, so laidback and just so kind and generous, and had a soft laugh and a sweet smile.

He mostly stayed in his room. When we arrived, there were a few roadies running around and bringing this and that. Then they kind of disappeared. I'm sure they had other rooms, and some of the guys went swimming. I sat with Mitch Mitchell for a little and he was a tiny little guy, but mostly we were with Jimi.

In the wee hours of the morning, everyone got hungry. Our city has grown quite a bit but back then about the only place you could get something to eat in the middle of the night was at a truck stop. We told them, 'You can't come with us. We'll go get it'. Those truckers would have killed them. Mitch insisted on going with us, but we made him stay in the car and I stayed with him while the other girls went in and got food for however many people.

The truck drivers hated blacks. This was the South back then. Jimi stayed at the motel. We never even saw Noel when we got to the motel. He just went into his room. I guess he was a hermit. But Mitch was right in the middle of everything. If he had gone into that truck stop, those big beefy truckers probably would have beaten him within an inch of his life. They hated long hair and if Jimi had gone that would have been even worse. They hated blacks.

I was raised differently. Momma raised me right. Take people for what they are inside instead of how they look outside. But there's no way any of those guys could have gone into that truck stop. I'm ashamed that's how it was back then.

We got back to the motel and I just loved being around Jimi. He was sweet and laidback and would chuckle sometimes about the things we would say. He loved our southern accents.

I was hoping he would do a few strums on an acoustic guitar he had in the room, but he didn't. He mostly just wanted to talk and meet normal people that treated him like a normal person instead of someone famous. We all partied together, got high together, and were with him until dawn, which was when they had to head out to their next place.

I was amazed he wasn't full of himself like some of the other rock star people I've met. He wasn't like that at all. He was the most gentle person. He enjoyed having us there and had such a nice, soft laugh.

The very first music I ever heard of his, it was like, 'Wow, this guy knows his way around a guitar big time'. He did his showy stuff. He did not light his guitar on fire or anything like that, but he did put the guitar over the back of his head and play it and a lot of that kind of stuff.

When he died, I was at home when I heard the news, and it just crippled me. I couldn't believe it. I cried my heart out. I still wish I knew what Eric Burdon has to say about it and be honest about it. And the girl that Jimi was with at the time that he died. I've read so many different things that I don't know what to believe. I was crushed, just totally crushed. I'm still crushed. He was such a lovely person.

I WAS THERE: GARRY HOWARD

I attended with my brother. We were living in Texarkana, Texas. He had just got a great deal on a 35mm camera. Unfortunately, part of the reason it was such a good deal was because it was from the display case. The instruction manual was missing. Consequently, we lucked out on a few of the pictures and managed to get the settings right. Others are a little out of focus and not the optimal exposure setting. A couple of years ago I scanned one of the pictures to use as a background on my computer. A friend saw it and asked if he could put it on his website. Since then I've had several requests for additional pictures from Hendrix fans who found it on his site. I decided to scan the entire set and put them on the web, so collectors can get at them.

The opening act was Soft Machine, undoubtedly the loudest band I've heard in concert, and I've heard quite a few since. When they started playing, my brother broke out in hives, welts all over his chest and stomach. As soon as they stopped playing, it went away. It was a sparse stage setting. No elaborate light-show or sound equipment, just the amps sat on the stage. People were able to just walk up to the front to take pictures. I'm grateful I not only had the opportunity to see Jimi at that stage of his career but to actually look him in the eye.

I WAS THERE: TIM GIVENS

I saw Hendrix that night. I think he stopped playing to go to the bathroom.

On 3 August 1968 Hendrix appeared at the Moody Coliseum, Southern Methodist University, Dallas, Texas. After abandoning a Dylan number because of the poor PA, Hendrix delivered a set of crowd-pleasers, including 'Foxy Lady', 'The Wind Cries Mary', 'Hey Joe', 'Fire', 'Purple Haze' and 'Wild Thing', with some guitar destruction thrown in. He was escorted offstage

Photo on stage by Elaine Bender at the Moody Coliseum, Dallas, Texas

by the police because he'd gone over his time limit and because the police feared a riot. Jimi's sound engineer Abe Jacobs commented, 'Every time we set up, the fire department, police department and mayor's office were saying, 'You can't do this, we don't allow that kind of stuff in our town.' They all thought Hendrix was going to burn the building down.'

MOODY COLISEUM

3 AUGUST 1968, DALLAS, TEXAS

I WAS THERE: KEN HIGGINBOTHAM, AGE 15

My drug-muddled memories have failed me before, but my friend asked me to go with him. His dad was providing transport. Jimi was playing at Southern Methodist University, the same venue we saw The Beatles. We had LSD and when Jimi started playing we were stoned. I had the Experience album and was familiar with his style and music. The actual experience was incredible, designed for our 'high'. A very real/surreal trip would describe it well. I also remember thinking rock'n'roll would change forever. During this performance he shattered his guitar and set it afire.

I saw him again in 1969 at the Texas International Pop Festival in Lewisville. I remember almost nothing about this performance except someone gave me a wild baby rabbit that peed on me. I left soon after for California to join the hippies in San Francisco.

I WAS THERE: ELAINE BENDER

The second time I saw Hendrix was at the Moody Coliseum on the campus of Southern Methodist University in Dallas, Texas. It was a more open setting than the first time, with Jimi on a built-up stage and the audience around him in layers. There were huge Marshall amps stacked high and the volume of the music blew us away. Six months earlier, we were all shocked by Jimi. This time, we were 'experienced' and gladly gave up our eardrums to the screeching guitar!

I WAS THERE: DANNY SMITH, AGE 16

I don't recall too much even though I wasn't 'experienced' at that time. I remember it was a rather unusual crowd consisting of about half Ivy League SMU types and half hippies, or at least hippie wannabees. The Chessmen opened with 'Sunshine of Your Love' and they were great. Then Hendrix came on dressed in his wild garb and proceeded to blow the place away. Toward the end, he started to set his guitar on fire but I think they stopped him because of the fire hazard. Anyway, it was an exciting evening for a 16-year-old and I'm so glad I got to attend.

SAM HOUSTON COLISEUM

4 AUGUST 1968, HOUSTON, TEXAS

I WAS THERE: RICH LAYTON

Billy Gibbon's band The Moving Sidewalks were one of two local openers. They were followed by British art-rock band Soft Machine, who left an indelible impression by performing wearing only something that resembled a diaper. (I hope someone else can confirm that - I assure you no psychedelics were involved on my part). I'd just joined my first band and 'Purple Haze' we just couldn't do justice to by any stretch. Jimi led off with a slow blues that I suspect many of the kids there that night weren't sure what to make of. Truth be told, we were there for the radio hits. It would take me a few more years before I began to appreciate his musical contribution, specifically *Electric Ladyland*, as I'm not a guitar player and generally subscribe to the 'less is more' school of music.

AUDITORIUM THEATRE

10 AUGUST 1968, CHICAGO, ILLINOIS

I WAS THERE: JIMMY GUERRERO

10 August 1968 is a day I will never forget. The father of a bass player friend of mine bought us our first concert tickets. He knew we idolised Jimi after we saw a band play 'Fire'. We had to buy the *Are You Experienced*

album and learn the songs. We were only 14 or 15 and we played them pretty good. That's how I really learned to play guitar. The day of the concert we were dropped off by a friend and walked towards the Chicago Auditorium Theatre. As we passed a parking lot, we saw Muhammad Ali get out of his limo with what I think was his wife. I remember shaking his hand and him being very kind to us kids.

Little Jimmy modelled himself on Hendrix rather than Osmond

We continued to the concert and sat in our seats where we had not a bad view at all. We sat through Soft Machine, waiting impatiently for Jimi. Then the curtain started to rise with a thunderous rumble and you could feel your seat shake and your heart pound. Mine did at least. I knew he would start with the scratch of the guitar and go straight into 'Are You Experienced'. Man oh man, what a beginning. For most of the concert he seemed to play with his eyes closed. He did 'Hear My Train A Comin'', which I believe was the first time anyone heard it, and rammed the Marshalls with his guitar. A friend recorded the show and I took pictures, but they're all lost. What I do have is this memory, something I've cherished ever since.

COL BALLROOM

11 AUGUST 1968, DAVENPORT, IOWA

I WAS THERE: ROGER HOFFMAN, AGE 16

My friend, Terry Hunt, went to see The Who smash their gear with me at the Illinois State Fair two days before Jimi. Terry had a ticket to see the Hendrix show but I was tapped out for cash. Terry was a year older and he knew the people running the light show. We discussed my problem and I went to the grocery store, bought

a bottle of corn oil and went to see
if I could get in. There was a crowd
trying to get tickets at the booth out
front and we passed everyone waiting
in line and went directly to the booth
and told the lady they needed the oil
for the light show and she needed to
let us in. She bought our story and I
was in!

*Thanks to some corn oil Roger slipped easily
into the gig*

It was pretty much standing room
only. I got within ten feet. There were
an estimated 3,500 people there. It
was $5 per ticket and they needed
2,200 people in to break even. Jimi
charged $8,000 to appear and Soft Machine were on $500 but
demanded $1,000. The promoter relented and paid it.

MERRIWEATHER POST PAVILION

16 AUGUST 1968, COLUMBIA, MARYLAND

I WAS THERE: GARY MARKWOOD

The second time I saw him he had lots of amp problems. He wasn't
very happy, and the show wasn't as good as when I saw him at the
Hilton in DC.

I WAS THERE: TIM KANE

He played a duet with a
thunderstorm half way through.
Every time the lightning flashed or
the thunder crashed and rumbled
away, he duplicated it on his guitar.

It was probably the most spectacular thing I've ever witnessed and those of us lucky enough to have witnessed it still recount the story with awe.

CURTIS HIXON HALL

18 AUGUST 1968, TAMPA, FLORIDA

I WAS THERE: ROBERT MARTINEZ

He was incredible. Psychedelic lighting and superlative sound systems made his music even better live. In all his flamboyant glory he dipped, dove, even played guitar with his teeth. In the tradition of showmen like James Brown, Charlie Patton, Elvis and others, he brought the house down. My date and I drove from Orlando, where I was working, just out of college. I had all his albums including his latest, *Electric Ladyland*. One of the best live acts I've ever seen. Three month later, he appeared again in Tampa for a return visit and again we made the trip only to be greatly disappointed. After about five songs, frustrated because of bulbs flashing in his eyes, he stepped back, stopped playing and flicked the audience off. Back then, we said he shot a bird at us. He then threw his guitar down and walked off angry, and never returned. It might have been the beginning of the end. The trappings of fame and incessant adulation was driving him nuts. Also I'm sure he was dosing real heavy by now. In 1970, I saw him at Atlanta Rock Festival as he woke up the crowd at dawn. It was cathartic. Only about three months later he would be dead.

I WAS THERE: CRAIG BURNS, AGE 14

In my most formative character-building years, mine and my friend's parents thought it wise to buy us tickets to see, hear and experience Jimi Hendrix in Tampa. Shortly after my birthday in 1968, James Bray and I found our seats near the front, stage left. Oh, my goodness. I was a fairly naïve person (still am) and was raised in a very rural part of Florida. When Jimi started beating his guitar against the large speakers I really got frightened. I'd never seen anything like this and remember being very uncomfortable with it. I loved his music but when he went crazy on stage, it was unsettling and discordant. To this day, when I hear a Hendrix tune I am transported back in time as a 14-year-old sitting and standing at Curtis Hixon Hall. I appreciate the open-mindedness of my parents, but not so sure, it was parental wisdom to expose me to the 'Experience' at that age. His early death still bothers me.

I WAS THERE: RICKS COCO

His front band both times was Three Dog Night. He was a very exciting performer and did his famous zipper-playing, back then not a common thing to do. That was almost 50 years ago, but I've never forgotten the energy he displayed when he performed. He was truly electric.

I went with my then-boyfriend the first time and as a double-date with my brother, his girlfriend (later his wife) and a friend of theirs the second time. I seem to remember dark leather pants, a purple satin-look shirt and his hair in a big Afro, held back with a headband out of his face. I seem to remember he had funny pointed shoes or boots too. His voice was grand and carried true thoughout the venue. Curtis Hixon has since been demolished but had good acoustics, and he used it well.

THE MOSQUE

20 AUGUST 1968, RICHMOND, VIRGINIA

I WAS THERE: RUDY BOISSEAU

When my friend and I bought our tickets at the box office, we asked if we could have an autographed photo of Jimi, and his road manager was there watching over ticket sales. We told him the picture would be for our two musician friends who had muscular dystrophy. Bobby and Billy Bradley had a band in high school but had gone so far along with their illness that they had to take turns

lying in an iron lung for hours each day. Billy played guitar and loved
to play jazz but had to lay the guitar across his wheelchair and finger
the frets from the top instead of wrapping his left hand around the
neck. Bobby could only tap the snare drum and a cymbal. It was
considered a 'rite of passage' to go to Bobby and Billy's home on
weekends for jam sessions. Jimi's road manager returned with the
signed picture and said Jimi signed it on his hand to make sure we
could see it.

My friend and I were seated about five rows directly in front of
Jimi and I have a picture of him playing his Strat with his teeth.
On the last song they played, Jimi put his guitar on a stand, poured
lighter fluid on it and set it on fire. All the while the guitar howled
away on its own as Jimi walked off. That was quite a show and I'll
never forget it.

VIRGINIA BEACH DOME

21 AUGUST 1968, VIRGINIA BEACH, VIRGINIA

I WAS THERE: ED HAZELWOOD, AGE 17

I was in Seat 1 L 25 and the Wednesday
evening show started at 10pm. It was the late
show. There was an earlier one that night.
Tickets were $4.76 and 24c tax for a $5 total.

I learned about Jimi's music in high
school. 'Foxy Lady' and 'Fire' were the hit
tunes of the day. It was my junior year and
we debated on the school bus if feedback
was really music or not. I argued if it was
repeatable, it was. What did I know? It was
summertime between junior and senior
year and I was working as a swimming
pool lifeguard. A week or so before the
concert, my cousin from Florida was
visiting. We were riding in my car on the

Ed Hazelwood debated the musical merits of feedback with his friends

interstate talking about music and bands when an ad came on the radio announcing The Jimi Hendrix Experience in concert. My cousin instantly said I had to go. 'It will be like nothing you have ever seen.' I bought tickets from the local record store. Then I told my girlfriend Terri we were going.

It was a big deal. We had to cross the river and drive 40 miles to get to Virginia Beach in my old '64 Plymouth Barracuda. Back in the day the Dome was a large venue. These days it's tiny. Soft Machine was the warm-up band. They were OK, a bit discordant. They did not knock my socks off. But Jimi, Noel and Mitch were a mind-blowing experience. The hit songs, 'Purple Haze' and 'Foxy Lady' got an airing. I remember 'Hey Joe' and really loved 'Voodoo Child (Slight Return)'. I'm not sure which song he was playing when he played guitar with his teeth. But, holy crap, it was astonishing. It totally changed my perception of music and bands. In fact I think it changed a lot of my future direction entirely.

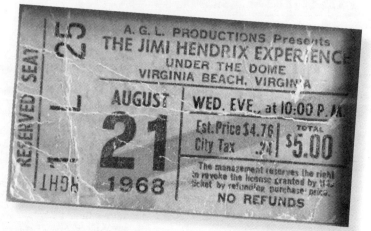

Most notably, at the end of the show Mitch threw his drumsticks out into the audience. They came right at me, slipped through my hands, hit me in the head, bounced and the guy behind me grabbed them. About a year ago on Facebook I encountered the guy that got them. He gave them to his girlfriend and that was the end of that. But I'm so glad I had that 'experience'. Oddly, while I loved it, my girlfriend did not. Too wild for her I guess.

In my senior year drama class, I acted out a performance to 'Have You Even Been Experienced' as part of my exam. I was sent to the principal's office on suspicion of doing drugs.

SINGER BOWL

23 AUGUST 1968, NEW YORK ROCK FESTIVAL, NEW YORK

I WAS THERE: PAUL GILMORE, AGE 16

Tickets were exorbitant for the time, $6. I went with my girl, Lynn Chichester, and a few friends. This was the Experience with Noel Redding and Mitch Mitchell. I can see Jimi in my mind's eye, all white with a red floral pattern running up one side. The music was a blur but I remember being struck at the way his guitar and himself just bended. He was so fluid, you sensed he was born with this appendage that flowed with his every move. I bought a poster and DJ Scott Muni signed it - I was changed.

I had tickets to the Band of Gypsys' New Year's Eve show at the Fillmore in 1969 but went to Martha's Vineyard instead. I was also at Woodstock but didn't make it to the end, when Jimi played. We followed the party.

I WAS THERE: PAUL FAHRENKOPF, AGE 15

I saw Hendrix twice, the first time being at the Singer Bowl in Flushing, Queens in New York on what was the site of the 1964/65 New York World's Fair. It was an outdoor arena, now the Arthur Ashe tennis stadium. The bill was Hendrix, Big Brother and the Holding Company, the Chambers Brothers and Soft Machine. The stage was in the centre of the stadium. I was in a band at the time. I am a bit hazy as to many of the specifics but recall he played a blue Strat and tickets were $6.50.

I lived in New Jersey and was working a summer job. The concert was in the evening. I was going with some friends, one of whom worked in New York and we had to take a bus and subway to get there. We couldn't make it into the city until 6pm or so and the guy that worked in NY got off work at 5pm. When we suggested he meet us in the city at 6pm, he said, 'What am I going to do in New York for an hour? Forget it.' We sold his ticket for face value at the venue. Well, I think there may be a few things one could do in NY for an hour. What an idiot!

The only vivid memory I have of Hendrix is that, after singing the line, 'Excuse me while I kiss the sky', he sort of sang it as 'kiss this guy' and ran over to Noel Redding and either fake-kissed or really kissed him.

On the 25 August 1968 at the Carousel Theater, Framingham, a show was played in the round to two houses of 1,000, with those behind the amps having an obstructed view of the musicians. Jimi apologised for amplifier problems, telling the crowd, 'Once we get this thing going, we're going to play as loud as possible, if not as well as possible.' After the second show, with their driver too stoned to do his job, Jimi took the wheel and drove the band back to New York City, Noel Redding recalling Jimi borrowed his glasses 'in order to be able to see properly. That was the first time I realised he needed glasses but just wouldn't wear them.'

CAROUSEL THEATER

25 AUGUST 1968, FRAMINGHAM, MASSACHUSETTS

I WAS THERE: BOB FALANGA, AGE 16

My father was the promotion man for Warner Brothers and Reprise Records and worked with Jimi whenever he

Bob Falanga ties his shoe-laces ready for another Jimi gig

appeared in the New England area. I got to see him three times. First time was in 1968 in Framingham, Massachusetts at the Carousel with my friend John Narducci. I sat on the stage for that one.

I WAS THERE: BRIAN GARRY, AGE 14

I was one of the lucky ones to see him. He played two shows on that night. I didn't have tickets but sneaked in, like we did for many shows. I was crafty at the time. The first show I made it down to the front row, vacated by someone that rushed on stage. The second show I rushed the stage and was sitting at the base of his microphone. He was sweating on me, which did gross me out a little, but I was amazed at his ability to play the guitar. My claim to fame was that I picked up and gave him his cigarettes when he dropped them. The Carousel was a great venue for bands back in the day.

I WAS THERE: RICHARD ALBERTY

I had just graduated from Woodward Junior High in Southborough, Massachusetts. Life was 13 with summertime blues, swimming at quarries and spinning records. I was an avid Hendrix fan along with most of my schoolmates. I heard from some older sister's friends that Hendrix was playing Framingham, the next town over and about eight miles due east of where I lived. I was so excited, I had to go.

There was no stopping me. But my mother was unhappy with this music. I bugged her to get a ticket for me. She didn't and wouldn't. On the day of the show I was pitching a fit. She told me face-to-face I was to go to

Jimi in full flow. Photo by permission of Richard Alberty

my room and not come out till asked to. I marched toward my bedroom, down the hall and I remember this echoing off the walls in the hall, 'If you sneak out your window to go see that f*cking n*gger, do not come back to this house.' Well, seeing as to how yah put it so nicely....

With no other options, out the window I went with my little hobo sack and walked to the theater. I was dodging cars all awhile and was one of the first to arrive. Mass Pike was just below it. I hung out and watched the joint fill up and went up when there were many folks around, all the while my heart pounding and me wondering if the fuzz was going to take me away.

I went up by the entrance and some older cats pulled up the tent skirt and gestured me in. I went and stood stage right of the round stage-riser and Mitch Mitchell. I can't tell you how excited I was. My first big time show! 'Wild Thing' was the clincher of the songs he played that night. I get goosebumps just thinking about it. I never went back home after that.

I WAS THERE: TOM BRUNEAU

That was a great year for rock'n'roll in Boston. There were venues everywhere and cool shows all the time. It was all good until the drugs and the crime it brings ruined things in the early Seventies. Think about it: The Music Hall, The Orpheum, Boston Garden, The Tea Party, the Psychedelic Supermarket, BU, Commonwealth Armory, Hampton Beach Casino, The Carousel, Tanglewood, The Summer Concert Series on Boston Common, the Summer Concert Series on Harvard Sq. Common, The Harvard Sq. Theater, A Summer Concert Series down the Cape at Truro. I'm pretty sure there were shows at Nantasket, but I never went. Later there was Foxborough and Providence Civic Center. I'm sure I left some out as well. My life was shaped by rock'n'roll!

Hendrix's stage show was amazing in the beginning. At the Carousel, after he tuned up, he asked the audience if they wanted a clean or a dirty show. Needless to say, he gave them what they wanted. But besides the ground-breaking studio creations he turned out, he was truly an original blues guitarist. There's a standard tool box of blues licks and phrasing that everyone starts out with and builds on that with their own variations and phrasing, maybe adding things of their own, and they develop a style their own. But you can still hear the standard stuff.

Hendrix, on the other hand, went through that pretty quick, and developed a unique way to get the same effect of the standard licks, but plays the notes arranged in an atypical blues sequence. Any guitarist who learns some of his lead work learns that. Not every part of what he plays is like that, but there is enough of his own phrasing mixed in to make it truly special. His chord work is also off the chart. 'Little Wing' intro? Genius!

Politics killed Hendrix and drugs and alcohol took its toll on so many others. But for a while, it was glorious.

I WAS THERE: KEITH KRONGARD

I saw him twice. Once was at the Carousel Theater, a tent that was set up and they had plays and live acts. It was seasonal but quite popular in this area. I saw Led Zeppelin there as well. My sister worked there a while and I saw the Dave Brubeck Quartet and met all the members. I was a huge Joe Morello and Paul Desmond fan. As for Jimi, this was the first time I saw him and we snuck under the tent and got in for free. I saw him again at the Boston Garden not long before his passing. He appeared more high than the first time but he was incredible.

I WAS THERE: STAN STANOVICH, AGE 15

I was a drummer. I attended the concert with Dennis Morrisette, a bassist. He drove and Jimmy Witek, a guitarist and my best friend then, and his sister Janice, a keyboardist, came too. Mitch Mitchell was a phenomenal drummer and a favourite of min.!

This was my first time attending a concert by a recording artist.

I only went to the first show. The opener was Eire Apparent, who I believe were from Ireland. Next was Robert Wyatt and Soft Machine. If I remember correctly, Jimi opened with Chuck Berry's 'Johnny B. Goode'. Somehow, I don't recall him doing an encore. The material was primarily off *Are You Experienced*.

All in all, this was an extremely pleasurable and memorable night of music.

I WAS THERE: ED SYMKUS, AGE 18

I saw one other show at the Carousel, about a year before Jimi. My parents took me and my brother to see Liberace. It was an odd venue - a tent with a stage in the middle, set up in the round, so performers could swing around and play to different people surrounding them. This was fairly early in my concert-going days, so it's a little hazy. But I clearly remember Soft Machine opening, and them not getting the best audience response because everyone was there for Jimi, not for their jazzy psychedelia. I recall the Experience being incredibly loud, but don't remember if it was a good sound mix (I rather doubt it). I certainly remember them playing 'Fire', 'Hey Joe' and 'Purple Haze'.

A couple of years later, shortly after Woodstock (alas, I left that show late Sunday night in the midst of the Ten Years After set, due to being cold, wet, and tired, so didn't see Jimi), a friend who was with me in Framingham said Jimi played 'The Star-Spangled Banner' at that show. If he did, it's been erased from my memory.

Local newspaper the *Bridgeport Post* reported that the show at the Kennedy Stadium, Bridgeport, had a crowd of 7,000, less than half the Kennedy's seating capacity, and the lights remained on during the performance, with a heavy police presence because trouble was expected.

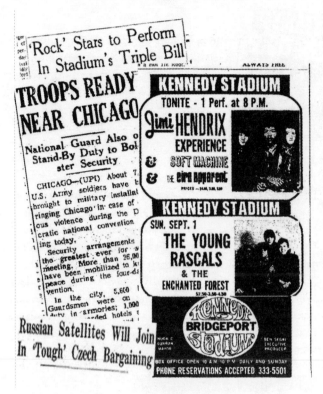

KENNEDY STADIUM

26 AUGUST 1968, BRIDGEPORT, CONNECTICUT

I WAS THERE: NOEL GIBILARO, AGE 17

I'd just graduated high school and was enjoying the summer before starting at the University of Connecticut. I went alone as none of my friends were into Jimi and some were completely unfamiliar with him. I saw some of my fellow high school class-mates, but they were doing their own thing. The stadium wasn't far from my parents' house, so I walked it. It was a warm summer night. I remember lots of kids, especially the women, had hand-sewn batik flowers, butterflies, peace symbols on their denim jeans, vests, jackets, whatever. It was a freak show. Coming

from an all-boys catholic high school, we were starting to let our facial hair grow long.

In those days, we referred to ourselves as freaks, not hippies, a word not yet mainstream. The audience were hippies, with all types of facial hair and hair lengths – a bell-bottom freak show. Hippie chicks were in jeans and granny dresses with long straight hair.

The sound systems in those days were pumped-up PA systems made for just that. So there was really no EQ or mix going on. To hear Jimi best, I got down from the bleachers in the Central High School stadium, named JFK Stadium, and went out to the cinder running track and stood smack dab in front centre, where I could hear speakers on both sides of the stage. I recall he was angered by something someone said and cut his act short.

I WAS THERE: DANIEL MASSEY, AGE 18

I attended with some fellow musicians. We were in an R&B group. We all dug Hendrix. It was an outdoor venue and a rather cool night. Hendrix performed well but was anything but gracious, complaining about the weather and his finger being cold. He even flipped the bird to the audience for some reason.

I WAS THERE: DAN PLATT, AGE 15

Hendrix was my first concert. The guitarist and drummer from our cellar band were with me; suffice it to say we were thrilled just to be there. Since my parents drove my buddies and I to and from Bridgeport, they got a look at what the other concert-goers looked like as they waited for us near the exit. I had to get a haircut the next day but, man, was it ever worth it.

LAGOON OPERA HOUSE

30 AUGUST 1968, SALT LAKE CITY, UTAH

I WAS THERE: CHASE KIMBALL, AGE 14

I was her only grandson, and my grandmother doted on me. That summer she invited me to stay with her in Salt Lake City for my vacation. I jumped at the chance because she always spoiled me and bought me almost anything I wanted. I had nothing to listen to music on, so she bought me a little record player. I had nothing to listen to, so she bought me *Axis: Bold as Love* for my almost non-existent collection of records. It was the second album I ever owned, the first being some teen trash that embarrasses me now, an album by Paul Revere and the Raiders.

As the summer wore on I started seeing advertisements for The Jimi Hendrix Experience at a local amusement park. I begged my

grandmother to let me go, and as with practically everything else, she said yes. That day dawned bright and clear, and she drove us to spend the day at Lagoon playing around on the rides and picnicking until the show that evening.

My grandmother was an extremely charismatic and gregarious woman and wandered the crowds making friends. I found her surrounded by a crowd of hippies towards the end of the day. She was charming them all, making them laugh. They invited me to sit with them at the concert, and I was anxious to be with the 'cool kids' so was very excited. The concert hall had a large floor area for people to sit on, and then well in the back some picnic tables where people could sit normally. My grandmother decided to come to the concert with me, and sat in the back at a table, while I sat on the floor with my new hippie friends.

Soon my new friends were passing a cigarette around, and I asked if it was marijuana. They asked me why I thought so, and I said because it had no filter and they were passing it around. They showed me some Camel cigarettes with no filter, and I said, 'But you're not passing those around'. They asked if I wanted a taste, and all the anti-drug lessons I had been getting in school went straight out the window. I said 'yes' with enthusiasm. I took a hit and asked them what to expect. They said I should start feeling 'physical'. I felt nothing but was too embarrassed to say. Some people around me were taking LSD, but I wasn't nearly brave enough.

At the appointed hour the opening act, The Soft Machine, started up. This was 50 years ago, and I don't remember much. As I recall it was drums, bass, and organ, and I remember the bassist sitting on a little bench rather than standing. I had been to the symphony several times with my father, and even saw pianist Arthur Rubinstein with him, but this was my very first rock concert and I wasn't sure what to expect. They seemed reasonably talented and I remember enjoying them, but very little else. I think they played for about 45 minutes.

Then they rearranged the stage a bit, changed drum sets, and Hendrix and the Experience came out. I was so excited. He opened with 'The Star Spangled Banner' then went into one of his big hits. I can't remember which but perhaps it was *Purple Haze*. I did not own *Are You Experienced* at the time, but had heard most of it on the radio, and was familiar with it. I was very familiar with *Axis: Bold As Love*, and he kept the hits coming. It was very loud, and very hypnotic. I noticed that the wall of (I believe) Marshall amps behind Hendrix mostly had torn covers. Both bands used the same stack of amps, and I wondered at the time if maybe The Soft Machine had blown the covers with their loud playing. Besides performing his hits, I assume he played some things from *Electric Ladyland*, but that was two months before it was released. I do recall he played 'Wild Thing'.

One mildly odd thing I've never read about anywhere; Hendrix had a bald patch in the hair on the left side of his head. Even my grandmother, sitting way in the back, noticed it. She called it alopecia. I've seen countless pictures from all angles, but don't recall ever seeing one where he had a bald patch. Nevertheless, he had one, so obvious that even my grandmother noticed. I would think it was my imagination otherwise.

I wish I could say more about the concert, but I was only 14 and overwhelmed, and it was 50 years ago. I can say I'm proud that the first time I smoked marijuana was at a Hendrix concert, even if I got nothing from it. Also, there are a finite number of people who've been to a Hendrix concert with their grandmothers, so I have that claim to fame too. Even though I have limited memories, it's still one of the highlights of my life, and I'm always ready to brag that I saw Hendrix live, when such bragging seems appropriate.

RED ROCKS AMPHITEATRE

1 SEPTEMBER 1968, DENVER, COLORADO

I WAS THERE: CLARENCE JOHNSEN

Other than the fact that it was a great show with four great acts, three little tidbits still stand out. First, Noel Redding was dressed to the nines in a dark velvet Carnaby Street-style suit, but wearing bright red socks. Jimi made several joking remarks about those socks between tunes and Noel obliged by slightly lifting the hem of his bellbottoms to show them to the crowd.

Second, the Red Rocks amphitheater stage is framed by huge rock formations. Some of the crowd climbed way up high for a better view. Jimi talked to them once or twice from the stage, asking them to please be careful. One time he sort of chuckled and said, 'Of course, you never know. You might just fly!'

Third, I don't remember what Jimi's last tune was but, when he hit the last note, the feedback was intense. With the feedback still droning, he calmly took off his Strat, laid it gently in top of his amp stack and walked off the stage. No pyrotechnics, theatrics or destruction. Just the end of the show.

I WAS THERE: THOMAS NEFF JR

It was a Sunday. I remember because I was making my very first trip to Red Rocks to see a concert. It was cloudy and overcast and I thought rain was imminent. But as we pulled into the parking area the sun popped through. It was around 7pm. It must be said that seeing anyone perform there is a treat, as it's generally considered to be the planet's only acoustically-perfect outdoor amphitheatre. No matter where you sit, the sound's right there. Vanilla Fudge opened and were very good. They closed with their cover of The Supremes 'You Keep me Hangin' On'.

Jimi came on around 8pm. The sun was beginning to set and a sunset up there is a sight to behold. I remember that, after he was introduced, he opened with 'You Got Me Floatin' from *Axis: Bold As Love*, a track I personally loved. Unlike the show at Regis College I saw, he would go on to play songs from the first two albums as well as songs I'd never heard before which I would later learn were from yet-to-be released *Electric Ladyland*. And because he had more material to perform he tended not to over-extend the songs. But the treat for me was hearing him play something I had never heard before, a 12-bar blues track entitled 'Red House', with absolutely smoking hot licks. Even though he was from Seattle and not the Deep South, I remember thinking, hearing that years later, he must have been listening to Buddy Guy. He did that right after sunset. Perfect timing.

Only recently did I discover that, of all the concerts at that venue, going back to 1964 and The Beatles, that's the only concert they have no record of - no pictures, no footage, no nothing.

I WAS THERE: SUSAN SUNSHINE, EARTH POET

He was performing at a big stadium in the foothills at the beginning of the mountains. I didn't have a ticket but really wanted to see him. The people I was with said, 'We're going and we know how to get in for free.' We get there and getting in free meant jumping from one foothill to another. I don't know if anyone's ever died doing that but have really short legs so said, 'I can't do that.' I went up to a man and gave the performance of my life, like Sarah Bernhardt, and said, 'I'm having an asthma attack and lost my ticket. Can you get me in?' They gave me a shot of adrenaline, which I really didn't need and which set me up a little bit, and drove me right into the middle of the theatre. I was in, so I watched the show, which was terrific. Then I couldn't find the people I was with, so hitchhiked back downtown.

Jimi was staying at the Cosmopolitan Hotel, next to the bus station. I'm very much not a groupie type - I was already 27 – so they were all lined up at the hotel and I decided I was going to go to the bus station and get myself a cup of coffee. I walk in and who's sat in the booth but Jimi Hendrix, with two guys from Vanilla Fudge and Noel Redding.

My lip dropped all the way down to my ankles, like, 'Oh my God, I just walked right by Jimi Hendrix'. He looks at me, because it was a booth and the four seats were already taken, and said, 'Pull up a chair and sit with us'. We talked for a while, and then he said, 'Let's go back to the hotel. There's a big party there and you're more than welcome to come up with us.'

We walked back and some security guard tells Jimi he can't bring anybody else up because it's too crowded. Jimi looks at him and doesn't say anything and he looks at me and goes, 'You know, I'm so tired of partying sometimes. Do you live far from here?'

I said, 'No, about a mile and a half. He said, 'I'm gonna call a cab.' He calls the cab and we go to my house on Downing Street. We get to the house and my room-mates were there, Maria and Martha. They were a bit younger than me and from Mexico City, and did the same thing. They dropped their lips down to the floor.

He was so down to earth. He looked at our jewellery and books and records and stuff and wanted to know all the other performers who were our favourites. We had so much fun and he was so humble. We had the greatest time. He spent the night, and in the morning when we got up we all took a cab back to the hotel and had breakfast with him and said goodbye. We didn't get addresses or autographs, it was too personal a moment to try. I didn't feel that celebrity-induced to do that. The only time he acted at all like a star was with the cabs both ways, with a $50 tip.

When I got back to town I wasn't even going to go to the hotel. That's just not me. But there he was in the bus station. And it was one of the most wonderful nights of my life. Of course, we smoked some pot. I did try, unsuccessfully, to get him some LSD. My friend left 10 little purple hazes for me though. 'If he comes back, you'll have enough to give him some.'

I found him to be a very nice person, with a lot of interest in us, me and my roommates. I went back to that house twice, once in 1993 and once in 2003. I walked by the house and sat in the back and these young kids came out and I said, 'I used to live here, and Jimi Hendrix was upstairs.' They walked right by me and looked at me like, 'God, she must have escaped from a mental institution.'

BALBOA STADIUM

3 SEPTEMBER 1968, SAN DIEGO, CALIFORNIA

I WAS THERE: JAMES CHERICO, AGE 18

I was about 100ft from the stage. Jimi came out to tune up and -remembering his past habit of walking off stage mad if the crowd made too much noise - I was hoping this didn't happen because I wanted to hear and watch him perform. But everything went fine and I enjoyed his music that night.

Right after his death, there were rumours about Janis Joplin floating around that she was so into Jimi that she was heartbroken and didn't care for living any longer when he died.

I WAS THERE: LONNIE NAPIER

I was a senior in high school. As a guitar player I was very excited to see him in concert. Nobody sat during the entire concert. The sound was swirling around because of all the bodies around me. He was definitely a showman. Every note he touched on his guitar seemed to sound different to anything I'd heard before. The magic and charisma wrapped the entire arena like a warm blanket.

SWING AUDITORIUM

5 SEPTEMBER 1968, SAN BERNARDINO, CALIFORNIA

I WAS THERE: TIM GERGEN

I saw his first concert in San Bernardino. The second was to end early with tear gas and riot police, but I didn't go to that. It was the late Sixties and I was a hippy with a good job, with hope for equality and justice for all. I was in my early 20s and playing guitar with friends with the wild Fuzz Tone feedback device, emulating Hendrix's famous feedback sounds. When we heard Jimi was coming to Berdoo, well, Jimi was the Second Coming.

We got a group together of two white boys and three Chicanos, all neighbours. We were ramped up for Jimi. I owned a four-track car player that blasted the 'Purple Haze' album while driving to the concert. I remember going into the old Orange Show convention centre that night with our neighbourhood gang. We spotted some security guards and figured where we could light up without getting arrested. Of course, it was a must to get a buzz before and during the Hendrix concert.

Tim was surprised there was zero lighting at the show

For a couple of hours, we were standing and roaming around the Orange show. Surprisingly, there were not many in

attendance. We could get close. Jimi came on. There were no
special effects. It was just like a black and white movie, nothing
like we have today. I was disappointed at first that the Experience
had zero lighting or special effects. Hell, they kept the standard
commercial bright lights on.

I had a room at home dedicated to Jimi and acid rock groups,
with black lights, strobes, pulsing lights - all kinds of lights. But it
was just Jimi and the Experience pounding out these sounds we
came to hear. We were not disappointed. Jimi spat out the sounds
we craved. Hearing him live, seeing the man and hearing his one
of a kind complex but straightforward ripping music created a
special vibe. The crowd all knew this was a moment we would
remember forever. We got to be live with Jimi.

PACIFIC COLISEUM

7 SEPTEMBER 1968, VANCOUVER, CANADA

I WAS THERE: NANCY HEISLER

I'm afraid I don't remember too much. I know we waited a long time for him to come on. There were a few other bands playing before. I remember him lighting his guitar at the end. I believe some of his family were in the audience. His grandmother lived in Vancouver.

I WAS THERE: TERI SHEPHERD, AGE 19

I remember this concert like it was yesterday. Watching Jimi Hendrix perform was mesmerising. I had tickets close to the stage and was blown away by his performance. You could feel the vibe in the building. Because Vancouver is so close to Seattle, Jimi's family were there and he acknowledged them from the stage. I'd seen The Beatles and the Rolling Stones, but Jimi's concert touched my soul. I bought all his albums after that. I'm still a fan. I was very sad when I heard of his death. He was a very talented musician that left us far too soon. As a side-note, my son is a blues guitarist and Jimi Hendrix is his idol.

SPOKANE COLISEUM

8 SEPTEMBER, 1968, SPOKANE, WASHINGTON

I WAS THERE: DEAN CARRIVEAU, AGE 18

I was a recent high school graduate attending my first year at Spokane Community College, later to become Spokane Falls Community College. I also worked part time at a local photography studio, making enough money to keep my old car running and have a little change in my pocket.

I wasn't yet a huge fan. My musical tastes were pretty much mainstream rock, including The Beatles, the Rolling Stones, Beach

Dean remembers Jimi restringing his guitar mid set

Boys, Steppenwolf, soul and R&B artists Aretha Franklin, Otis Redding, etc. In 1968 there was no album-oriented rock station in Spokane and most kids my age listened to KJRB, a popular AM top-40 station where you might hear Jeanie C. Riley, Frank Sinatra, The Kinks, Bobby Goldsboro, 1910 Fruitgum Company, the Stones, the Beatles, and The Monkees within the space of an hour. Nothing too controversial or unconventional, but all the genres were represented, albeit by a rather narrow playlist. I remember spending one summer in the San Francisco Bay Area where Otis Redding and Carla Thomas' 'Tramp' was a huge hit. Returning home to Spokane, none of my friends had heard it. Having said that, I'm happy to say Hendrix's 'All Along the Watchtower' was a huge hit in Spokane and was played on KJRB. My college had a jukebox in the dining area of the students' union building and classmates were constantly selecting 'Watchtower' and another late summer hit, The Beatles 'Hey Jude', that fall.

Some of my friends were creative in the world of art while others were into playing music. They were all miles ahead of me in their appreciation to what was happening to the current music scene. They tried to drag me into the burgeoning psychedelic sound, beyond mainstream, and into album offerings by Cream, Hendrix, Big Brother, Quicksilver Messenger Service, the Doors and many others. I was indeed a late bloomer.

We were fortunate to have an energetic and resourceful program director at KJRB who managed to book a number of high-end concerts in our little Coliseum. Over two years, my friends and I were also treated to Ike and Tina Turner, Eric Burdon and War, and Steppenwolf among others. At that time, Hendrix was still being promoted as a hot British import. Most of those concerts included two or three opening acts and in the case of Hendrix, it was Vanilla Fudge, The Soft Machine, and Eire Apparent. Admission was typically $3 for upper-level concourse, $4 for floor seats, and $5 for floor/front-row seats. Tickets were easy to come by. We usually went to an ancient newspaper/tobacco store downtown, P.M. Jacoy's, for tickets. You could also buy them at the Coliseum box office on the day. It was a different world.

The Coliseum was built in 1954 as a multi-function facility and had 5,400 seats, tiny by today's arena standards. It was affectionately dubbed The Pink Barn or Boone Street Barn. It was used for basketball, indoor rodeos, Broadway road shows, all-city school concerts, the Ice Capades, hockey, and I received my high school diploma at graduation ceremonies there. The acoustics of our beloved barn were not one of the venue's better qualities.

The day before, our group sat in the seats in the upper concourse to the left of the stage marked by a yellow 'us'. These were great $3 seats and we typically sat in this area for most of the shows we attended. I don't remember much about the opening acts other than Vanilla Fudge's rendition of 'You Keep Me Hangin' On', which received heavy rotation on the radio the previous year.

Hendrix finally arrived on stage and stood front and centre in the intersecting beams of two Century carbon arc spotlights, whose operators tracked his every move. There were no adornments to the stage or pyrotechnics whatsoever to distract from Hendrix's raw talent. I don't remember the other musicians other than Mitch Mitchell's extended drum solo during 'Red House.'

Hendrix entertained the crowd with humorous, easy-going banter between numbers as he casually tuned his single guitar. I spoke with a life-long friend who attended as part of our group and he reminded me that at one point Hendrix broke a guitar string. Jimi finished the selection, minus the string, then fished out a new one from somewhere, installed it and tuned the guitar, all while chatting up the crowd. In today's world a 'guitar technician' would rush over to hand the musician a new tuned guitar, pulled from an off-stage rack holding others just like it.

Hendrix's set-list was made up of well-known 'A' tracks and included 'Foxy Lady', 'Little Wing', 'Voodoo Child (Slight Return)', 'Red House', and 'Fire'. He displayed his virtuosity with impossible chords and progressions, blistering, sliding solo picking and performed his famous flash tricks, playing guitar behind his head or plucking strings with teeth and tongue. The crowd applauded appreciatively and politely, laughing at between-number patter at appropriate and sometimes inappropriate times.

I should comment on the behaviour of most Spokane youth at that time. Culturally, we were about 10 years behind the times. Concertgoers in 1968 sat in their seats, applauded politely and laughed at his banter. Cheers, howls, and general hysteria were not the norm and didn't occur here or at others I attended. Steppenwolf played for the Coliseum crowd the following February and John Kay closed his set with 'The Pusher', inviting fans to come on stage. Few did. With his first utterance of 'God damn the pusher man….' County Sheriff's deputies stormed the stage and began unplugging all the equipment. Kay was left singing acapella and vowed to finish the number without his band. With that, a deputy followed Kay's mic. cord and yanked the plug from its PA input. Kay threw the mic. to the floor and walked off. The house lights came up and the crowd of kids filed out of the Coliseum in a calm and orderly fashion as if everything was as it should be.

But six years later, a new batch of local kids rioted at a failed and ill-fated, three-day (little Woodstock) event called the Nor'wester '76 Rock Festival. The festival was held at a speedway just east of town at the state line. The track owner discovered he wasn't going to be paid for the use of his venue and withheld fuel for making campfires and campers/festivalgoers endured a chilly first night. The next day, headliners failed to show up when they heard rumours they too wouldn't be paid. After sitting for hours waiting for acts to show, the promoters announced the festival was closing early. Hundreds of fans rioted, setting fire to semi-tractor trailers, vendor shacks, and anything else that would burn. The angry mob pushed an ice cream truck from the top of the stadium seating over the edge, where it tumbled down the concrete seating risers and ended on the infield on its side, where it was immediately set on fire. What a difference a few years can make.

I wasn't a huge Hendrix fan when I attended that concert. I remember being amused by his colorful outfit, his on-stage persona, being with my closest friends, and enjoying the overall ambience. Truthfully, after so many hours sitting on those narrow wooden Coliseum seats, I was kind of ready for Hendrix to be done.

It's now nearly 50 years since I was privileged to attend that concert. Our beloved Boone Street Barn was razed in 1995 and replaced by a new civic arena with only marginally-improved acoustics. The landmark Hendrix event and the venue that hosted it are now just memories. Someone, however, had the foresight to record the lion's share of the concert, just over 31 minutes. It was probably recorded by one of the spotlight operators in the left and right fly-boxes near the ceiling. It doesn't sound like a patch of what you could hear from the arena's PA system, but I've listened to this amazing recording several times and can't believe how terrific Jimi was. Here is Hendrix live, at the top of his game, playing all my now-favourite Hendrix tracks. I wish now I could be back at the old Pink Barn sitting in that hard, wooden seat, and this is the next best thing.

MEMORIAL COLISEUM

9 SEPTEMBER 1968, PORTLAND, OREGON

I WAS THERE: BERT PAUL, AGE 16

His only concert in Oregon. I went with a high school friend. They cut off the power in the middle of 'Purple Haze'. The concert is written up in two books about Jimi's concerts and both say there was a riot, but that didn't happen. A few people knocked over their chairs. But it wasn't his best concert.

Tickets were $3, $4 and $5. The show was advertised on radio on KPFM. I wish I'd recorded the ad. I had a $4 ticket, so didn't have a very good seat. There were four bands on the bill. Vanilla Fudge, who played before The Jimi Hendrix Experience, were louder than Hendrix. They also cut off the power on Soft Machine, the second band to play. They threw some of their equipment off the stage. The concert ended about 11.45pm when they cut off the

power. Portland is famous for cutting off the power on bands, and that includes The Doors and Eric Clapton.

HOLLYWOOD BOWL

14 SEPTEMBER 1968, LOS ANGELES, CALIFORNIA

I WAS THERE: ALLAN FELDMAN, AGE 13

I won the tickets on KHJ Radio. As a young guitar player, you could only imagine how excited I was. Too young to drive, I convinced my parents to drive me to the Bowl to see the concert. The rest is history. The next month I saw Cream and after that The Doors. I've been going to shows ever since.

I WAS THERE: CARL STONE

I discovered Hendrix at the age of 14 when *Are You Experienced* was released and I was visiting friends in Berkeley who were introducing me to the hippie lifestyle. As this coincided almost exactly with the moment I first smoked marijuana, it's safe to say that while I may not have 'been' experienced, I had quite an experience.

The first live show I saw Jimi perform was at the Shrine Auditorium in Los Angeles. Soft Machine opened and that was also profound. Soon after, my friend Z'EV (then known as Stefan Weiser) and I started a quasi-progressive trio with

Carl discovered Hendrix and marijuana at the age of 14

him on drums, myself on keyboards and Jimmy Stewart on bass.

I saw Jimi a number of times in LA. The time I remember most fondly was when he played the Hollywood Bowl, an outdoor amphitheatre set in the Hollywood Hills. Maybe it was sold out or we were lacking funds to purchase tickets but Z'EV, I and a few others hiked up the back of the Hollywood Hills so we could watch from way up high. We could hear, but the band seemed tiny. I could see Mitch Mitchell's exaggerated drum hits, but we were so far away that the sound was delayed and the image of each strike preceded the sound by what seemed like seconds.

MEMORIAL AUDITORIUM

15 SEPTEMBER 1978, SACRAMENTO, CALIFORNIA

I WAS THERE: JIM WILLIAMS, AGE 17

I saw him four times altogether. First time was at Monterey, where something clinged to my brain and I said, 'I've gotta try and meet that guy in my lifetime if I can.' And one time it happened.

I was in high school. Me and a group of guys drove to Sacramento in my hot rod to see. We were only about three hours away. I got to see him there, see him burn his guitar and everything. That just blew me away and I said, 'Man, this guy is something special.'

I was from a little town called Placerville, California, and

Sacramento was where all the big concerts would go. Whenever anybody came to town that's where we would go. The Memorial Auditorium only seated 3,000 or 4,000 people, so you could get real good seats anywhere. I sat right up in the front balcony. What was cool about this place is that it's a beautiful building and everything, but it's old and you could just leave by the side door and run around back. Whoever played there, the only way for them to get out of that building was that one door at the back. It was up a couple of steps and then they would have to go about 30 yards across the street to get to the limo. That was the only escape. So I figured it out and as soon as the show had finished, I would run out the side door, run around the back and just stand there and wait.

It worked for Eric Clapton and Cream and for Janis Joplin too. But Jimi Hendrix was the main one. I wanted to get up close to him. What was funny was that nobody else figured it out. I was just standing there by myself. It was weird. Luckily, he didn't play an encore. They were really partying hard on stage and I kinda knew they didn't want to give an encore, because they were playing one show after another. My buddy who was with me was afraid to go up there. He stood back by the street and I just waited and did the same routine I did before.

The doors opened and there's a couple of bodyguard types to get him over to the limo. It's Jimi Hendrix, dressed just like you think and you gotta think fast because he's on his way. I was just 17 so boldly said, 'Hey, Jimi - great gig!' He stopped and said, 'Oh thanks, man. What's your name?' I said, 'Jimmy.' He stopped cold, goes 'Jimi? Oh man, we're twins! We're brothers!' The bodyguard guys were going, 'Out of the way', and he looked at them and said, 'It's cool, don't worry. We got time.' They gave me a dirty look, but he just stopped and I had to think fast and went 'Hey, got a cigarette?' I didn't even smoke.

He was kinda shocked, but goes, 'Sure man,' and digs out a cigarette. I said, 'You got a light?' I bummed a cigarette. I said, 'I saw you at Monterey, you know.' He goes, 'Oh really? What did you think of the gig?' I said, 'Man, that was outta sight but I was wondering about the guitar, you know? Did you figure that out or plan it, or how'd you figure it?' He said, 'Well, I knew Townshend and The Who were going to do some off-the-wall thing so I had to do something for 'em to remember me by. Because it was the first time I played and so I had to have that plan.' He goes, 'Sure enough, they destroyed the stage, The Who did. They destroyed everything they owned, and as Pete walked past me, he mumbles, 'Follow that if you can' or something weird. Luckily I had something in my bag that I could pull out.'

I tried not to be too gaga over him, so just wanted to act normal. He said, 'So what do you do around here? What do you do for fun?' I said, 'Go to concerts.' He goes, 'Oh, is that the thing?' I said, 'Yeah. Matter of fact, I talked to Eric Clapton right where you're standing.' And he goes, 'Eric? How's he doing?'

I said, 'He's doing pretty good. I asked Eric what he thought of you and he said you're the greatest. What do you think of Eric's playing?' And he goes, 'I don't worry about that. It's all about the music, you know?'

That was kinda cool. Then I asked some kind of weird question. I said, 'What was it like to open up for The Monkees? People who went to see them were real young.' And he said, 'They booed me off stage.' I said, 'Really?' And he said, 'Yeah. I swore I'd never follow anybody after that if I could help it. Because opening up for anybody like that is a tough deal.'

I guess they didn't know who to match him with when he first came over. But I thought it was pretty interesting that he laughed about that. He was just real cool. He was like the coolest dude in the world. Later on I met Steve McQueen, who was real cool, and I got to know him pretty well. But Jimi Hendrix was the coolest.

Later I thought about it and thought, 'Man, he's just being shipped from here to there and stuck in hotels and this and that.' I felt like he didn't have that much control. When he stopped those guys and said, 'We've got plenty of time,' that was a big deal. He said, 'Walk with me to the limo', which was only 30 yards away.

I wanted to say something else, so I said, 'Hey, you got another cigarette?' He goes, 'Oh, yeah man.' Then he got in the limo and he said, 'Hey Jimmy, it was nice rapping with you.' I said, 'Yeah, it was nice rapping with you.' He said, 'I'll catch you at the next gig,' then got in the limo and off it went.

All in all, it lasted the length of a cigarette, maybe a minute longer, but it seemed like an eternity. And when you're face to face with somebody like that you don't really know what to say. But because I was so young I think I had enough guts to say the stuff I said. I could tell he wanted to talk a lot more. But he knew he couldn't. It was like he just wanted to talk to somebody normal.

What was also cool was that because of my buddy who stood on the other side of the street and watched the whole thing - who said, 'You're crazy' - it got back to my high school on Monday. When I went to school everybody heard about it and I was a king, you know? I must have known how great he was, as young as I was. I must have known, because of wanting to see him so much. I saw a lot of great players and nobody was close to him.

The Jimi Hendrix Experience released their version of Bob Dylan's 'All Along the Watchtower' in the US on 21 September 1968, almost a month prior to the album release on *Electric Ladyland* in October. The single reached No.5 in the UK charts, becoming the first stereo-only single to do so, and No.20 on the Billboard chart, Hendrix's highest-ranking American single. According to engineer

Andy Johns, Jimi had been given a tape of Dylan's recording by publicist Michael Goldstein, who worked for Dylan's manager Albert Grossman. Halfway through the recording session, bass player Noel Redding became dissatisfied with the proceedings and left. Dave Mason (from Traffic), who was playing acoustic guitar on the track, took over on bass.

WINTERLAND BALLROOM

10- 12 OCTOBER 1968, SAN FRANCISCO, CALIFORNIA

I WAS THERE: DEB WONG, AGE 15

I didn't appreciate Hendrix then as much as I would later. I went with a friend who got sick in the middle of his performance, and we had to leave. We were up in the rafters. The smoke got to me, but as I recall, she was smoking hash, which could have been the reason.

Deb's friend smoked too much hash and they left. Deb thought there would be another opportunity to see Jimi

She vomited on the side of the wall, and that's as much as I recall with clarity. The saying is that if you remember it, you weren't there. I remember half of it, anyway.

My friend got the tickets, and I went along for the ride. This is how I got to go to many concerts and events back in the day. We thought Winterland might be a place where we might get to see some cute boys. My friend was upset about how it turned out, but we figured we'd have another chance later. Never did.

Electric Ladyland, the third and final studio album by the Jimi Hendrix Experience, was released by Reprise Records in North America on 16 October 1968 (and Track Records in the UK in October 1968). The double-album was the only record from the band produced by Jimi Hendrix. By mid-November, it had charted at No.1 in the United States, where it spent two weeks at the top. *Electric Ladyland* was the Experience's most commercially successful release and their only No.1 LP. It peaked at No.6 in the UK, where it spent 12 weeks on the chart.

Hendrix expressed displeasure and embarrassment with this 'naked lady' cover, the guitarist wrote to Reprise describing what he wanted for the cover art but was mostly ignored. He expressly asked for a colour photo by Linda Eastman of the group sitting with children on a sculpture from Alice in Wonderland in Central Park.

Three different versions of the Electric Ladyland sleeve

The company instead used a blurred red and yellow photo of his head while performing at Saville Theatre. Track Records used its art department, which produced a cover image by photographer David Montgomery depicting 19 nude women. The cover was banned from display by many record shops as 'pornographic', while others sold it with the gatefold cover turned inside out. The 26 October Bakersfield show was cut short when the venue manager allegedly used the N-word to Jimi and accused Hendrix of assaulting him. The events took place at the end of a tense evening. The show ended in anti-climax when the general manager of the Civic Auditorium cut the power to the stage, feeling the show was getting out of hand. Some concert-goers believed this was a premeditated act on the venue's part.

Ron Raffaelli, invited by Hendrix to photograph the Experience on tour, recalled afterwards that the band was playing its final number when the power was cut. Jimi rushed off stage followed by Raffaelli, who witnessed Hendrix facing off against the venue manager. He had cut the power because he felt the show was getting out of hand. When the manager used the N-word, Raffaelli had to get between him and Hendrix, causing the manager to fall back slightly against a table. Police arrived and the venue manager alleged he was assaulted by Hendrix and Raffaelli. Police escorted Jimi and his entourage, including Hendrix and Raffaelli, in one limousine and Redding and Mitchell in another, to the 99 freeway on ramp.

CIVIC AUDITORIUM

26 OCTOBER 1968, BAKERSFIELD, CALIFORNIA

I WAS THERE: MICHAEL LAFAVE SR, AGE 16

I remember the local cops pulled the plug on him at midnight and he trashed one of his Sunn amps. I think he was a bit loaded during his performance, but it was cool. I sat in the fourth row. What a memory!

I WAS THERE: MARILYN ROBERTSON CASTRO, AGE 15

I just remember being mesmerised with him being so far ahead of everyone else at that time. The show didn't have any elaborate setting like today. It was plain and just the three of them, and they rocked the Civic Auditorium.

I WAS THERE: RICK SCOTT, AGE 13

I was fifth row from the stage and saw him in Bakersfield of all places. I paid $6 for the ticket. Hendrix played with his teeth and at the end of the show tried to play 'Star Spangled Banner', but the rednecks of this conservative town cut off his power, which angered him, and they started arguing.

I WAS THERE: SONNY LACKEY

Seeing Mitch Mitchell nail his drums to the floor was a precursor of things to come. After the obligatory wait, Jimi took a long toke stage right, flicked the roach at the Civic manager and plugged in his Strat to a wall of Sunn amps. He turned his guitar volume control up as he walked to the front of the stage trilling the fretboard and did the splits for the intro to 'Foxy Lady.' It was otherworldly.

I WAS THERE: MITCH GORDON

Hendrix had already become a well-established, larger-than-life cultural icon and an unrivaled musical phenomemon. The anticipation of seeing Jimi Hendrix and the Experience was so great, I hardly remember the opening band. When Jimi and the fellas finally hit the stage it seemed like the audience was almost stunned at first. Everyone was kind of reserved and mesmerised. It was like nobody knew how to act. I don't think the majority of us had ever seen anything or anyone like that. That's one of the reasons it was a life-changing event for me and so many others. This was completely new territory.

At the time I thought the amplifiers had merely failed but apparently it was a premeditated act of aggression resulting in an altercation between Jimi and the powers that be. I've heard varying accounts, some saying they spent the night trying to get him out of jail and others claiming it was all settled backstage with a bribe. Either way, more than a few people have told me they saw Jimi Hendrix (with his girlfriend) in a new Corvette at the Jumbo Burger on Golden State Avenue after the concert, and he was super friendly and personable before driving off into the night.

I WAS THERE: ERIC GRIFFIN, AGE 15

From the moment Jimi cranked up the Experience, the sound coming off the stage was astonishing: immediate, jaw-dropping, proof positive that the immensity of Hendrix's talents had not been overstated.

I WAS THERE: TERRY HUSTON

Hendrix was magical, mesmerising. I'm so grateful I grew up in that era, the music and the movement was unlike after. I mean who even knew you could do that, especially live and in person without the benefit of overdubbing and studio effects? It

opened an entire universe of new possibilities and raised the
bar into the stratosphere. The Strat-o-caster-sphere! The other
amazement, which I don't remember giving too much credence
to at the time, is that he was a black man performing in a
certifiably bigoted, redneck town, playing to an almost exclusively
white teenage audience. Tensions must have been high among
community leaders. It's no wonder some shit came down. I
remember feeling frustrated, ashamed, and embarrassed by the
negative events that unfolded.

MUNICIPAL AUDITORIUM ARENA

1 NOVEMBER 1968, KANSAS CITY, MISSOURI

I WAS THERE: TOM BLAKE

When he walked on stage he was obviously the coolest guy among
10,000 people. Tight purple pants, knee-high white boots with a
scarf tied around one thigh and a choker on his neck. His Fender
was like his dance partner. I remember a massive feedback demo
that we realised after a while was 'The Star Spangled Banner'. It
was a historic 'experience' for sure. In those days the PAs were
not all that great in the cavernous auditorium, but each show
seemed to get better. I saw most of the classic bands in those days,
as we all did. Ticket prices were all under $10, Hendrix might
have been $5.

MY BROTHER WAS THERE: MARIAN LOVE PEARSE DYER

My late brother, Charlie, saw him live in Kansas City. At one
point he broke a guitar string then spent an hour tuning, riffing
and talking to the audience before he got back to the business
of the concert. From what I gathered, he could've stopped then,
called it done and no one in the crowd would've cared.

A staff writer for the *Minneapolis Tribune*, sent to review this show, wrote 'Jimi Hendrix could be best described as a black Elvis Presley. That is to say, he doesn't sing too well, and doesn't play his white guitar too well, but he does have a lot of sex.'

MINNEAPOLIS AUDITORIUM

2 NOVEMBER 1968, MINNEAPOLIS, MINNESOTA

I WAS THERE: ADRIANE HARLEM

I saw him at the Auditorium downtown. I was super close to the stage. I threw my love beads to him!

I WAS THERE: JOHN SIEFF, AGE 17

My older brother had given me a copy of *Are You Experienced* as a Christmas gift in 1967. We both became diehard fans. When the Experience came to the Minnesota Auditorium a year later, I was 17 and my brother had just turned 21. Of course we got tickets. Cat Mother and the All Night Newsboys were under Jimi's wing and opened. He produced their album.

You could hear the amps sizzling behind the curtain. The audience was ready and the opening licks of 'Fire' sounded as the curtain slowly rose. Jimi had a white Strat that night and my brother rushed the stage like a groupie. A friend of ours and I were soon standing on our steel folding chairs, jumping up and down. The set was 'Fire', 'Are You Experienced', 'Voodoo Child (Slight Return)', 'Red House', 'Foxy Lady', 'Little Wing', 'Spanish Castle Magic', 'Sunshine of Your Love', 'Star Spangled Banner' and 'Purple Haze'. There was no encore. Jimi kept apologising for being new in town and staying with a pretty tame set. He promised to return and let it rip. 'Red House' really knocked me out that night.

KIEL AUDITORIUM

3 NOVEMBER 1968, ST LOUIS, MICHIGAN

I WAS THERE: DOUG STOVERINK

I have seen many of the top rock groups that came through St Louis, including Hendrix, Ten Years After (five times) and Wishbone Ash. Jimi played 'Voodoo Child (Slight Return) but not 'All Along The Watchtower'. He only played for a little over 45 minutes.

I WAS THERE: BRENDA NIEDERHOFFER

We sat in the third row. I remember him playing his guitar with his teeth and then behind his back. He gave an amazing performance and at the end smashed his guitar on the stage floor. What an experience for a young teenage girl.

CINCINNATI GARDENS

15 NOVEMBER 1968, CINCINNATI, OHIO

I WAS THERE: CRAIG KOEFLER, AGE 21

Back in those days you could reserve tickets and pick them up at the 'will call booth' or buy them at the gate. I'm fairly certain we did 'will call' because the Gardens was a real small venue and we got to choose seat location. I went with a roommate, Stewart. I discovered Hendrix from hearing his music on radio station WEBN. I also had his first two albums and *Electric Ladyland* had just been released in the US the month before.

Craig remembers the cops being out in force

I recall a fairly-pronounced police presence, which was common, for they found concerts an easy mark for busting people for drug use.

The venue was small and designed for

hockey, basketball and small trade shows. The acoustics were terrible, with everything being concrete and steel. The stage was at one end of the hockey rink floor and was elevated about five feet. The floor seating was metal folding chairs and ours were in the second-row centre aisle, great for seeing the band. There was no exotic lighting that I recall.

I can't recall exactly the playlist, but they opened with 'Are You Experienced'. The show seemed to fly by and unlike many of today's concerts the crowd remained seated and focused on the music. The final song ended with Hendrix on his knees a mere 12ft in front of us, igniting his guitar with Ronson lighter fluid while it was reverbating, finally grabbing it by the neck and smashing it to the stage floor.

I WAS THERE: TIM NEWTON UMINA, AGE 21

I was a music nut. I loved Ray Charles and was into the blues at an early age. I got to a lot of concerts and had friends that were musicians that were in a blues band and had his first album, *Are You Experienced.*

I was a fine arts student working on a Bachelor of Fine Arts at a local state college. Art students, or 'heads' as some referred to us, liked to share new music. For a long time, AM radio was all grew up with, listening to the top rock singles. AM is a signal that is more of a straight line and gets easily interfered with. FM on the other hand bounces and can broadcast further.

I graduated high school in 1965. One of my friends was a big blues addict, old and pure blues such as Bobby 'Blue' Bland, BB King, Albert King, Freddy King, Little Willie John, Little Milton and Big Mama Thornton. He told me about an AM station, WLAC out of Nashville, Tennessee. We had to drive to the top of a cemetery in Dayton, Ohio and wait until late evening for the signal to make it that far.

In 1967, WEBN FM started in Cincinnati, Ohio. Cincy is 45 miles south of Dayton, where I was, and in 1967 WEBN, which started as a classical and jazz station, switched its format to pioneer album-oriented rock. So you were no longer tied to singles.

They were playing all the newest American and British albums such as Pentangle, Cream, Zombies, The Byrds, Loving Spoonful, T Rex, The Who and so on. Exposure became exponential with the advent of FM, which basically killed AM for youth. In fact, it was at that time that cars started having FM.

At Cincinatti Gardens, I got to see him set his guitar on fire, play it behind his back and pluck it with his teeth, then at the very end take his Stratocaster and beat those speakers right off the back of the stage.

I WAS THERE: BRUCE GINN, AGE 16

He played Cincinnati Gardens with Cat Mother and The All Night Newsboys. That was my very first rock concert, no drugs or booze, and I was absolutely blown away!

I WAS THERE: BOB GILKER

I saw him again later that year after I graduated from high school. I believe that venue was the Ludlow Garage, Cincinnati's version of the Fillmore, but I was pretty high that night. I do remember Jimi's playing was phenomenal and not as gimmicky.

I WAS THERE: EVERETT L MCINTOSH

I lived in Cincinnati when I first saw them. The best at that time was at Cincinnati Gardens, where many types of sports, circus, live bands were featured. It's since been torn down with much larger facilities built. It was the first time I'd seen someone rich enough to destroy their instrument on stage. I can't remember a warm-up, but Jimi and the band were great. Linda Meinking and I went and sat on the right side of the stage in the regular seats. I was shocked how young his band looked. Towards the final songs he began lowering himself onto his knees and rocking back. Then he took the lighter fluid cans we used to fill our cigarette lighter and pumped it on his guitar. He took his lighter and began to light it. It didn't start very quickly. After a minute, it began to flame up and burn. Everybody was yelling and crazy for him. He then stood up and began smashing it on the stage until it broke. He did a lot of bows for a tall lanky guy, then held his arm up with a fist and walked off. It was over and everybody seemed exhausted.

I was able to see him in Hawaii and he died soon after that. It was another great performance with all his songs, at least from his first two albums. Just before he had hit it big, we saw

Everett witnessed Jimi burning and smashing his guitar

him at the Ludlow Garage when it was only 50c a ticket, a venue for bands developing their act. Some friends went to Woodstock and saw Jimi, but I couldn't. I'd been drafted and went into the Marines.

I remember the bell-bottoms, platform shoes, button-front trousers, rock'n'roll silk shirt, sweater vest and long hair. We saw Jimi a second time at Cincinnati Gardens and that was my first experience with acid. It seemed the town became flooded with small purple barrel pills a couple of months before they played. It was somewhat unsettling, but the band was so good, playing his recent songs. The crowd went wild when they played 'Purple Haze'.

BOSTON GARDEN

16 NOVEMBER 1968, BOSTON, MASSACHUSETTS

I WAS THERE: RICHARD BUTZE, AGE 16

I spent a lot of time in the Harvard Square record stores. At that point I was buying the stuff I heard there, including The Doors, Grateful Dead, Quicksilver, The Yardbirds, and that's how I discovered Jimi's music. This was my first concert. The place was packed, and I remember lots of bikers. It was very loud but a great show. He set his guitar on fire and played 'All Along The Watchtower'. I remember I was taken away by the sound three musicians could make. This was the beginning of a long life enjoying music.

His death was a sad loss, as were the losses of Duane Allman, Janis Joplin and Jerry Garcia.

I WAS THERE: ED SYMKUS

After seeing him in Framingham that year, I also saw Jimi play the Boston Garden in November. The McCoys opened, but that part of the show has completely vanished into the ether of my mind. I don't have the clearest memories of the show, but remember him playing faster and crazier than he did just a couple of months earlier, and I could hear the guitar much better this time. I made a mental note of that when he played 'Fire', which I believe was the opener. That was also likely the first time I heard 'Voodoo Child'. Noel Redding was far too low in the mix that night.

I WAS THERE: DICK MOHRE

I saw Jimi twice at the Boston Garden. The first time he was with the Experience and Mitch Mitchell and Noel Redding were awesome! 'Fire', 'Purple Haze' and 'Stone Free' rocked the house. The Garden was a great place to see a concert because the balconies hung out and over the lower seats, so you were close to Jimi and the band. I'm a guitar player and couldn't wait to hear and see him in person. I saw him again a few years later at the Garden playing with Buddy Miles and the Band of Gypsies. I still play his music today live on my guitar and I am so glad I can tell my kids, now in their late-30s and 40s that I saw the greatest of all. Clapton is great with his riffs, but Jimi was friggin' incredible. Listen to him now and his overlays and tracks are unbelievable. He disappointed a lot of people in Boston because his show was very short. The crowd felt shafted. But the bandana, bell-bottoms and that Afro was something I'll take to my grave. Bending strings, lighting the axe on fire and playing like no one ever before him, he will always be the greatest in my mind.

WOOLSEY HALL

17 NOVEMBER 1968, NEW HAVEN, CONNECTICUT

I WAS THERE: DIONISIO CARDONA

The second time I saw him was almost identical to the first, except it was in New Haven, Connecticut. Me and a different friend tried doing the same thing I did in Hartford. We did manage to get in, but when we went in Jimi and his band were on stage soundchecking. We immediately went on stage and approached him, asking for an autograph. He said, 'Hey, what are you guys doing? I'm rehearsing for tonight!' Noel Redding and Mitch Mitchell stopped playing and just stood there watching while Jimi gave me an autograph on en envelope that had Iron Butterfly tickets in it. I remember Noel and Mitch were really skinny. We left and hung around town until showtime. Many years later I took the autograph to work to show some co- workers that I had met Jimi, and I eventually lost it. The autograph said, 'Stay groovy, Jimi.'

He was a funny guy and would crack a joke before songs. At one show he mentioned Cream and was going to play 'Sunshine of Your Love' but announced it as 'Sunshine of Your Superman', with a nod to Donovan's song. The crowd roared with laughter. But he was all business on stage.

I was aboard a ship in the Mediterranean Sea as a US Marine, listening to Armed Forces radio when they announced his death. Man, was I bummed out.

I WAS THERE: ANTHONY PEDEVILLANO, AGE 17

I was a junior in a small Connecticut high school, and loved Hendrix. My Latin teacher had two tickets to Woolsey Hall on the Yale University campus and asked if I'd like to go. In those days, the climate was very different, and attitudes were much more open and relaxed, so I jumped at the chance.

Our seats were in the first row of the balcony and turned out to be the best in light of the lousy acoustics of the building and the volume of the music. The opening acts were different, yet the mood was so positive that the energy carried the night. Once Hendrix finally came on, I was enthralled with the selection of his hits and most notably amazed at 'The Star Spangled Banner', an absolute ode to the turbulent times of the Sixties in which we lived.

Although this could never occur in today's overly-paranoid, suspicious climate, I treasure that experience as a natural extension of my high school education that informed my choice to also become a high school teacher. Now retired after 37 years, I sometimes wonder about my old Latin teacher and her wonderful ability to connect with students in a way that touched them forever.

Going to see Jimi with his Latin teacher inspired Anthony to become a teacher

I WAS THERE: BRIAN EBIN PARKER WOLFE

I was at the early show. I remember: (1) It was cold. Our seats were very close to the stage (maybe third row); (2) I went with a blonde girl whose name is lost to time. She wore a wool sweater that was very itchy; (3) We wondered if Jimi would smash and/or burn his guitar (he didn't do either); (4) There were two support bands, Cat Mother and the All Night Newsboys and Terry Reid; (5) I became a true believer in Terry Reid from the first note. I left the show thinking more about Terry than Jimi. To this day I'm not sure who had the greatest influence over me as a musician; (6) It was a very long time before Jimi came out. The story I heard over the years was he didn't know there was an early show. I kept wishing they would let Terry do another set; (7) Jimi came out on stage and said he was going to make it up to us for the wait and play 'Foxy Lady' like never before. He played the first few notes and the hall fell into complete darkness. It seemed the band blew some sort of main fuse. They had to run a power line from another building to get lights and complete power to continue the show;

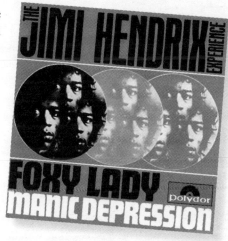

(8) Jimi told a joke, something like, 'What's green and hangs from the trees in Africa? Elephant snot'; (9) He said he was going to play the next song real loud (not the second song, but the intro to the song was referred to as 'the next song'). He turned up and played an insane version of 'Red House'. It was so loud I thought my ears would bleed; (10) Looking back, I've had the great honour of seeing many of the guitarists who have influenced not only my playing, but also

my world view. I learned from Jimi you can never underestimate
the power in your left hand, Fuzz and Wah can create magic
in the right combination and most of all, nothing in music is as
important as a beautiful melody.

'I'm the one that's going to have to die when it's time for me to
die, so let me live my life the way I want to, sing on brother, play
on drummer'.

I WAS THERE: HARRY TRAMONTANIS

There were two shows scheduled, and I went with my younger cousin
and some friends to the earlier show, since my cousin was a bit young …
unfortunately for us.

Also on the bill were Cat Mother and the All Night Newsboys plus
Terry Reid. Cat Mother was produced by Hendrix and recorded in his
newly-built Electric Lady Studios. There may have been one or two local
bands too.

The bands started playing, and quite a long time seeing as there was
a second show. The MC finally said we're running a little late and Jimi's
on his way from Boston. I remember us saying, "Yeah, via Mars!"

After a long wait Jimi took the stage and whipped right into an
energetic version of 'Fire' when pop … the sound goes. Apparently,
Woolsey Hall was wired for DC and the amps were AC and a lot more
of a load than the converters had ever faced. We had to wait until they
handled that. In the meantime, Mitch Mitchell did a lengthy drum solo.

Finally, the power situation remedied, he finished 'Fire' and went on
to do maybe half a dozen hits. As I recall, 'Foxy Lady', 'Hey Joe', 'The
Wind Cries Mary', and of course 'Purple Haze'.

He was dressed in typical Hendrix cool and played great. Lots of wah-
wah, playing behind his back and with his teeth, humping the speakers
with his Strat, etc. He used the white Strat until he broke a string, then
switched to a black Strat.

The show was short but went almost until nine, which was
problematic because the late show was supposed to start at 8.30. From
what people told me the second show was much longer, and he did a lot

of nuggets he didn't do for us, like 'Sgt.Pepper' and 'Voodoo Child'.

While we had some limitations, it was still a great 'experience', one I hoped I'd get to repeat many times in the future. Alas, the fates were fickle. But I was able to go right up to the stage and take some pictures with my pos. fixed-lens Kodak Instamatic.

CURTIS HIXON HALL

23 NOVEMBER 1968, TAMPA, FLORIDA

I WAS THERE: SCOTT PETERSON, AGE 14

I saw him three times, twice in Tampa at the Curtis Hixon Convention Center. The second time he played four or five songs, got angered by all the photos being taken, gave them the finger and walked off. Then he showed up at a jam on a Sunday after the show. Very cool, free, he sat in with some locals.

I WAS THERE: MICHAEL PETRUZZI, AGE 16

Second time I saw him was kind of strange. I didn't have a car. My girlfriend's dad drove us. We had both ate some LSD. The show was great until some ass yelled out for 'Purple Haze' or one of his earlier tunes. From what I remember, Jimi wanted to play some of *Electric Ladyland*. He was tired of playing the same songs. I'm not sure if it was the same ass who yelled the 'N' word when Jimi played there before, but Jimi shot a bird and walked off in what may have been the second or third song. That really sucked. I had to call my girlfriend's dad to come get us early. All I can say it was a long ride home.

I WAS THERE: GARY GRADICK

I saw Jimi when I was just a pre-teen in Tampa, Florida. The most distinguishing thing I remember was that the show ended early, Jimi tossing down his guitar and exiting the stage in frustration. At the time, gunpowder flashes for cameras were often used to illuminate performers at concerts. As a performer each time a flash goes off you're temporary blinded for a few seconds. This is why Jimi ended the show early. Several times he informed the crowd the blinding flashes were affecting his playing. Sadly for all attending, nothing changed, the flashes kept happening. I'm guessing that about half-way through his scheduled appearance time he made his exit. Of course, the crowd was disappointed at him, but I think they were more disappointed at the lack of courtesy by those with the flashes. He never returned to this area.

I WAS THERE: DENNY JOHNSON

I saw him twice at Curtis Hixon Convention Center in '68. Second time, he got upset that the crowd wouldn't stop yelling 'Watchtower'. He gave the audience a finger and walked off stage. I remember the newspaper criticised him for not being at his best during the two concerts I saw. I played guitar at the time and loved seeing him. He had a wall of Marshall amps behind him. The only other band I saw that I remember being as loud as him was Vanilla Fudge.

Denny heard reports that Jimi was hanging out in Florida

I lived in St. Petersburg, Florida. Treasure Island used to have dances with a live band on Wednesday nights during the summer. I wasn't there, but several of my high school friends told me Jimi wandered in about a month or so before he passed away. They said his hair was cut short. Not everyone recognised him. Over the next week or so, there were reports of him being spotted at other locations around St. Pete.

MIAMI CONVENTION CENTER

24 NOVEMBER 1968, MIAMI, FLORIDA

I WAS THERE: ROBERT STEVENSON

I was a student at the University of
Miami. I sat about thirty rows up on
the side, nearly even with the stage.
What struck me, besides feeling I
was sitting on the front cowcatcher
of a runaway locomotive barrelling
through the Alps, was that during
a guitar solo - with wild echo and
reverberation swirling around
sideways and backwards - he walked
over and took off the guitar, placed
it on a guitar stand, then picked up
a different guitar and started playing
again. The sound of his solo was
never interrupted.

*Robert witnessed Jimi switching
guitars without interrupting his solo*

RHODE ISLAND AUDITORIUM

27 NOVEMBER 1968, PROVIDENCE, RHODE ISLAND

I WAS THERE: PAM COSTELLO, AGE 14

It was at the Cranston Auditorium. Someone set fire to a wooden
railing. When we got outside there were many fire trucks and
ambulances there.

I WAS THERE: RICK SANTOS, AGE 14

The opening act was a band called Cat Mother (and the All Night Newsboys). I think Jimi was the producer of their first record. My brother took me. We were up near the front and before Jimi came on he took me around backstage. We were leaning on the rail near the aisle when Jimi walked in. I could have reached over and took the hat right off his head. That's how close we were.

I WAS THERE: GARY NILSSON

I saw Jimi twice in the Sixties at the old Rhode Island Auditorium. The thing I remember most, aside from him playing lengthy sets and sounding great both times, is that a couple of fans accidentally set a seat on fire. While mayhem broke out as the fire was put out, Jimi never broke stride and never missed a note. I always thought that was remarkable.

With 13,000 tickets sold for a full house, Jimi nearly missed the show at Cobo Arena on 30 November 1968, having apparently, in the words of Noel Redding, 'freaked out'.

At 5pm, Jimi was still in New York and due on stage in Detroit less than four hours later. When the Detroit promoter rang to check on his whereabouts, anxious that Jimi wasn't at his Detroit hotel with Mitch and Noel, Jimi's management told him, 'You don't have to do this for money. You have to do this because you are Jimi Hendrix and you have over 10,000 people in that hall waiting to see you. You owe it to them.' Jimi finally agreed to fly to Detroit and his management rang an aviation company and blagged a Lear jet, pretending it was required for Frank Sinatra ('Hold on, sir, I don't know'. 'There are no ifs, ands or buts about it. If you're going to say no, you tell it to Mr. Sinatra. Because I'm not.') Hendrix arrived in the nick of time. Redding remembered the show as 'a good one: probably played well out of sheer relief.'

COBO ARENA

30 NOVEMBER 1968, DETROIT, MICHIGAN

I WAS THERE: ARTHUR LITTSEY, AGE 18

My first rock'n'roll concert, and it was a wild and crazy experience. I turned 18 a month prior and was totally amazed by the size and look of the crowd. It was overwhelming.

He started with 'Spanish Castle Magic' and from that point on he took me, my brother and a couple of friends on an unbelievable journey. After covering 'Sunshine of Your Love', he announced he had a slight cold but when he came back in the future he'd put on a much better show. I don't know what he was talking about, because he was fantastic.

The thing I liked most was it was without fanfare. I read somewhere that Jimi preferred to just stand there and play his guitar - he wasn't really into all the moves he became famous for. He would test the audience and if they were into the jumping around, playing behind his back and with his teeth stuff, he would give them that, but he gave a better show and put more of himself into it when he could just stand there and play. If my memory is as good as I believe it is, he stood pretty stationary that night and played his head off.

The one thing I remember most was when he played 'Voodoo Chile (Slight Return)' at the end of the night and hit a note that was so loud it was incredible. He was using what I now know was his Uni-Vibe, a rotating speaker effect, and it felt like it was going through me, around me, under me and above me all at once. I wasn't high. The feeling I got was totally from the sound of the guitar. I felt then as I do now - it was the loudest guitar note I've ever heard, and I've heard a lot of loud guitarists.

The second concert, in May 1969, was even better. As he promised in November, Jimi came out strong. I believe the first song was 'Fire' and that set the tone. This night he did it all, including all the moves he was famous for. If there was a letdown it was that he didn't do 'All Along The Watchtower', which everybody wanted to hear him play. As a student of guitar, I was interested in how he would pull off the solos from that song in particular, but it was not to be. Regardless, it was another fantastic show by a great artist. I had great seats for both shows, main floor 15 rows back in November and only 11 rows back in May, right in front of him.

I WAS THERE: ROGER DELISO, AGE 14

My older brother Dave introduced me to the world of Sixties psychedelic and British Invasion music, which of course included Jimi Hendrix. Dave was 17 when he brought home the *Are You Experienced* album. He'd already been playing drums a few years and I started guitar lessons later that year. In 1968 I joined my first band, and the other guitar player, his girlfriend and the drummer were the people I went with that evening. Cobo Arena, with 12,000 seats, was home to the Detroit Pistons and was a typical open court floor with seats rising up on all sides. My recollection is that we sat on the floor on wooden folding chairs.

Cat Mother and the All Night Newsboys were the openers and I remember thinking they were good but of course I was anxious for Jimi to come out. When the stage was reset for Jimi, his Marshall stacks were clearly visible, the grille cloth was ripped to shreds, and I remember wondering how it happened. Also, I remember he had an entire rack of guitars, all Stratocasters — each a different colour — and one white Gibson SG Custom, which he used to play 'Red House'. I also remember being impressed by Noel Redding's wall of Sunn speaker cabinets, laid sideways to form a sort of U-shape, rising up left and right, and in the middle was a stack of Sunn amplifiers, one on top of the other.

There was pandemonium when he was finally announced and there was the thrill of seeing him walk out. I remember him talking a good bit and tuning before starting and have a vague recollection of him saying he'd been on the road for years and was tired. 'Fire' was the first song and I was glued to Mitch Mitchell because of those wonderful drum-fills. I'll never forget as the song progressed and Jimi's solo was about to start, watching him jump around and click on his pedals on the floor, trying to get them all turned on. When he finally did, his solo came through loud and clear.

'Spanish Castle Magic' was next, a big favourite from my favorite Hendrix album, and it was so cool seeing him actually play it live!

The most memorable moments came with the next song, 'I Don't Live Today', which with the maturity of later years I came to realise is about serious Native American issues. There's a part three-quarters through the original where Jimi depresses the vibrato bar, the device that loosens the string tension, making a sort of 'falling down into a spinning vortex' sound, and where he explores unique psychedelic audio effects. That night, at the moment he began depressing the vibrator bar, the lights for the entire arena went completely black! It was the most incredible effect of the walls being sucked in and being plunged into that psychedelic state. Then at the very moment he eventually began to release the downward pressure on the vibrato bar and raise the guitar strings back up to tension, all the lights in the arena were brought back up. It was a truly mind-bending, incredible effect to have pulled off 50 years ago!

Beyond that the other song that remains in my mind is 'Red House', how unique it was to see him use the Gibson guitar, how long the song was and how great his playing was. As for as all the Stratocasters, I clearly remember his guitar tech came out after every single song and handed him a different Strat for the next song; again, each one of them being a different colour.

In 2001, I was living in Seattle and my brother Dave came to visit. Knowing how much he loved Jimi, I surprised him with a special treat and with great difficulty found out where Hendrix is buried, in a fairly near suburb of Seattle. As we were driving South out of Seattle, excited to be sharing this with my brother, I started a conversation about the time we saw Jimi at Cobo Arena and how lucky we were and what a thrill it was.

In a matter-of-fact kind of way, my brother replied, 'I never saw Hendrix'. I said, 'What are you talking about? Of course you did, we saw him at Cobo!' He repeated that he never saw him, and that I went with Johnny, the other guitar player in the band I was in. I practically started screaming and got very upset. I'm surprised I didn't have an accident and I started shouting, 'You mean all these years I thought you and I had that special experience together and now you're telling me we don't?' I finally calmed down and slowly started remembering he was right. My brother died in 2005 and I cherish his memory and all the great music of our generation that he introduced me to and the bands we actually did see together. I went on to become a pro musician because of him. Love and miss you, bro.

1969 The band appeared on live UK TV show Happening For Lulu on 4 January 1969. The plan was for The Jimi Hendrix Experience to open their set with 'Voodoo Child (Slight Return)', then play 'Hey Joe', Lulu joining Jimi onstage at the end to sing the final bars with him before segueing into her regular show-closer.

Noel Redding describes the scene that day as 'so straight' and the band decided to have a smoke before performing. Things did not go to plan when the band dropped their hash down the dressing room hand-basin, having to enlist the help of a BBC maintenance man to retrieve it. By the time they were due to appear, the band were in good spirits. They tore through 'Voodoo Child'. The director cut away to Lulu introducing 'Hey Joe', which the band began and then abandoned halfway through, Hendrix signalling to the others to stop playing. 'We'd like to stop playing this rubbish,' he said, 'and dedicate a song to The Cream. Regardless of what kind of group they may be in. We dedicate this to Eric Clapton, Ginger Baker and Jack Bruce.' The Experience then launched into an instrumental 'Sunshine of your Love', playing past the point where Lulu might have joined them and ignoring the hysterical director pointing at his watch, silently screaming at them to stop. Allegedly the BBC banned Hendrix from appearing after that, but Redding remembered, 'The result is one of the most widely-used bits of film we ever did. Certainly, it's the most relaxed.'

In a 2015 interview, Lulu acknowledged, 'I will always get asked about that TV performance with Jimi. I'll always be connected to him through that moment.'

I WAS WATCHING: PAUL JOHNSTON

I was a little too young to see Jimi Hendrix live but remember watching him on the *Happening for Lulu* show in 1969, where he was playing 'Hey Joe' on live TV and stopped it after the first verse to play 'Sunshine of Your Love', which he dedicated to Cream.

I WAS THERE: ALAN GRAVES

I remember the *Lulu* show, when he was supposed to play 'Hey Joe' and started playing the Cream thing, 'Sunshine of Your Love'. He wasn't following the script. He was good at that. I think he just thought, 'That's a good riff, let's do that'. That was how he seemed to be. Impulsive.

REVOLUTION

SPRING 1969, LONDON, UK

I WAS THERE: DANIEL GRIMINGER

I was living in London with my aunt, Mary Arnold. She was his agent, booked shows for him and the head of Capable Management, a booking agency for Tom Jones, Humperdinck, The Walker Brothers, Petula Clark - many artists. They came to the flat in Marble Arch and hung out. I met Jimi and went to a couple of parties with him. We went to a trendy club in London, Revolution. A lot of showbiz people went there. Crazy times! I had my first encounter with cannabis thanks to Jimi. He was a great guy. He made a lot of fun of me because of my accent. I came from Argentina and wasn't too fluent in English.

Jimi performed a series of Scandinavian, German and French dates during January 1969 before two iconic shows at the Royal Albert Hall, six days apart.

ROYAL ALBERT HALL

24 FEBRUARY 1969, LONDON, UK

I WAS THERE: DANEK MARCUS PIECHOWIAK

I moved to London about nine months before and a couple of students I was with at art school in north Devon were then in the art school at St Martin's. They organised tickets to see Hendrix.

Danek saw the last of Jimi's iconic shows at the Royal Albert Hall

It would have been his last big concert at the Albert Hall, a very intimate venue.

He divided the gig into two halves, and there might have been a break – I can't quite remember. In the first half he played very much what you'd expect – his hits. He did all the tricks, playing behind his back, using his teeth, setting light to his guitar, bashing it around, rubbing himself up against his guitar, and did all the stuff that he'd released as singles or on his albums. I think he thought, 'I have to give the people what they expect, what they've seen on television.'

In the second half he totally changed his style and gave us what he wanted to give us. He went right into being the real artist he really was as a blues player, playing blues, gospel. He had so many different styles, but was basically a very good blues, jazz and soul performer, anything within those genres. He must have played an hour or more, one song after another, sometimes on his own, sometimes with his drummer and bass player, and played his heart out. You could see that the man was a real genius.

I saw him at another concert a few months before but realised then what a truly amazing man he was. I knew I was seeing something very special. I went to see the Stones in Hyde Park in 1969 and that was the same – another of those moments. And that evening seeing Jimi was one of them. He could talk through his guitar. I'd never seen anybody do that before and haven't seen anybody do it since.

I WAS THERE: TONY DERRINGTON

Support was Fat Mattress. Jimi was playing in a different way to the gigs I'd previously seen. My main memory is 'Room Full of Mirrors', members of Traffic joining him. It was a slower version featuring Chris Wood on flute. The set was longer (at the Saville there were generally three to four acts and the second show started two hours after the first). Definitely the best of the three gigs from my point of view.

I WAS THERE: NIG GREENAWAY

It was my first hearing of 'Foxy Lady' that really turned me onto Jimi Hendrix. I'd heard and enjoyed the early UK singles but my first listening to *Are You Experienced* really blew my mind! 'Red House' was another standout and I had to buy the album for myself. *Axis: Bold as Love* followed and then *Electric Ladyland*. I'd heard some tracks beforehand on Radio Allouis. Goodness knows how we ever discovered that, but they'd play one track each evening, surrounded by a lot of French chatter that (despite my French GCE lessons) I couldn't understand.

Then my mate Frank and I heard Jimi was playing the Royal Albert Hall and sent off a postal order (15/- or 75p today) with a request for seats. We received our postal order back and a letter saying the gig was sold out but an extra one was planned, and did we want seats? Off went the postal order again and we found ourselves in a second-tier box. Perhaps tickets didn't sell so well - we had the box to ourselves.

The gig started with Van Der Graaf Generator, who I remember enjoying, then Fat Mattress, Noel Redding's band, who I can't remember very well. And then Jimi and the Experience took the stage. He'd named the band well - the experience will never leave me. Somehow, Jimi didn't seem to so much play as channel the music through himself. I can't remember the order of the songs, but he included favourites like 'Foxy Lady', 'Red House', 'Voodoo Chile' and 'Little Wing' as well as new numbers, including 'Room Full of Mirrors', 'Bleeding Heart' and an instrumental 'Sunshine of your Love', as we heard on the *Lulu Show*.

Jimi seemed completely at ease and to have time for his friends sat around the edge of the stage, including a young boy. How many artists of his standing would make time for a youngster like that?

The band came back for an encore that included 'Purple Haze' and 'Wild Thing', culminating with him 'making love' to his amps with his Strat before smashing it. I love guitars and hate the thought of destroying them, but it ended the show on a high and made it clear the show was over!

The gig was filmed and parts of it have appeared online. I understand the rights to this are an issue but would love it to have an official release. Hopefully Experience Hendrix are working on a 50th anniversary release.

I WAS THERE: LINDA WALKER

I was at Hendrix's last concert at the Royal Albert Hall. He was just terrific, as he always was. I remember the show not just because it was Jimi but because I was pregnant with my son. I had to sit at the end of a row for ease of access to the loo. We've always said it was the vibes that night which led to my son playing lead guitar.

Taste, led by guitarist Rory Gallagher, released their eponymous debut LP on 1 April 1969. Arguably the most traditionally blues-oriented album of this burgeoning new generation, *Taste* was nevertheless infused with the restless energy that was supercharging blues as the decade closed. Hendrix himself was

Rory Gallagher

evidently impressed because, when asked how it felt to be the greatest guitarist in the world, he's said to have replied, 'I don't know, go ask Rory Gallagher.'

❝Before Hendrix, Jeff Beck had distorted his guitar and so had Keith Richards, and there was distortion on the early '50s blues records. They didn't use it as a technique but had small amplifiers turned up very loud and it became part and parcel of the Chicago blues sound. Hendrix trimmed it and made it into an art form❞

Rory Gallagher

DORTON ARENA

11 APRIL 1969, RALEIGH, NORTH CAROLINA

I WAS THERE: STEVEN BURGESS

They were backed by Fat Mattress, including Noel Redding. He was someone to behold. No one had ever seen a guitarist like him before. It was a great show, though he really had a limited style. I remember him playing our national anthem. I saw him in March and by the summer he'd played at Woodstock. I feel truly lucky to have had the opportunity to see him. Not many had the chance. I had pictures of the show, with Jimi playing the guitar with his teeth and behind his back, but they were stolen in the early Seventies.

I WAS THERE: JOHN CRAFT, AGE 18

I was fortunate to see Jimi Hendrix live at four different venues. The first was in Raleigh. I remember going with a girl from high school. Kathy and I were able to get a ride to NC State University. We met with a friend that then walked over to the Dorton Arena. Noel Redding's band, Fat Mattress, were opening. Redding performed some songs, then left the stage. Later, Jimi Hendrix, Mitch Mitchell, and Noel Redding came out on stage. Hendrix plugged in and started tuning then started playing 'Fire'. He was wearing a black outfit.

I WAS THERE: ED TOMOLONIUS

I saw Hendrix twice. The first time was at Dorton Arena, the main building on the North Carolina State Fairgrounds, which despite its ultra-modern appearance, is best suited for livestock exhibitions and has terrible acoustics for live music. I was a high school senior, had played in garage and soul bands since 1967, and was familiar with the Experience's first US album. My main recollections are that, despite the poor acoustics

Ed doesn't think Jimi invented shoegazing

and inadequate PA system, the band sounded great. The songs and arrangements were sparse, which benefitted from the echoey qualities of the hall. Noel Redding's Fat Mattress opened, probably used more as a soundcheck (much to Noel's chagrin) for the main event. Fat

Mattress were not that good, or memorable. The bands used Sunn amplifiers as Marshalls weren't generally available in the US at the time. I've read that the band's Marshalls were shipped over from England and hadn't arrived. My strongest memory is Jimi's stage presence and constant movement. He would seemingly disappear from one spot on the stage and reappear instantly on another spot. He was definitely not a 'shoe gazer'.

The second time I saw him was at the second Atlanta International Pop Festival, with Billy Cox on bass. This performance is well documented, so I won't bore you with personal details about the heat, traffic jams, and the cost of bagged ice.

THE SPECTRUM

12 APRIL 1969, PHILADELPHIA, PENNSYLVANIA

I WAS THERE: CLYDE CROASDALE

After seeing him at the Factory in 1968, I saw Jimi a year later at the Spectrum in Philadelphia, a 20,000-seat arena. He was much less flamboyant. He seemed to be concentrating on the music. I remember 'Red House' in particular. The other thing I remember was the opening act, Noel's Fat Mattress. They were just okay.

I WAS THERE: STAN DENSKI, AGE 15

The Spectrum was an 18,000-seat basketball multi-purpose arena. My memories of the show are almost a half-century old. It was the Experience, with Mitch and Noel. That band would break up about a month or two later and the first version of Band of Gypsys would form. Noel Redding's band Fat Mattress opened. They all played on a circular stage in the centre of the floor that

Stan was astounded by Jimi's version of 'Red House'

slowly revolved throughout the night, so part of the time I remember our view was the back of the amp stacks. I do remember feeling lucky, fortunate I had the opportunity to see Jimi play. That blend of charisma and talent was unique. Ticket prices ranged from $3.50 to $6.50, and 14,489 was the official attendance.

He opened with 'Fire', but the most vivid memory I have is of second song, 'Red House'. I'd never seen anyone use volume in such a way that they could play guitar with just the left-hand hammering notes on the fretboard. There was a moment where he dropped his right hand and continued to play. I remember being astounded by that.

I WAS THERE: TOM SHEEHY

The first thing of significance on this, the third time I saw the Experience, was the size of the place, an arena built for basketball and hockey which held 17,000 for concerts, and since its opening in 1967 produced all concerts in the round. This meant the stage was in the centre of the venue and was placed on top of a circular platform which turned around in circles as the act performed.

This was not a problem for me, because unlike the other venues I saw Hendrix at, I could leave my assigned seat, go up to the stage and shoot photography, as I did that night. Opening was Noel Redding's band Fat Mattress. There were rumours that Redding might be leaving to pursue his new band full-time. The Fat Mattress set wasn't memorable in the least, for the debut album had yet to be released and the material played from it was somewhat weak. Plus, like the other thousands of kids in the building that evening, I wanted to see Mr. Redding playing with Jimi Hendrix, not his new mates.

After the intermission, the lights went down and, as that crowd of thousands made a tremendous roar, I could see Jimi climb up to the stage with his white Stratocaster; it was the entrance afforded a superstar, which that musician clearly had become. Jimi was wearing an orange ruffled shirt with a vest and blue headband. Also of immediate note were the two kick-drums; each had a name across them; one read Mitch, the other Mitchell.

Jimi opened with 'Fire' and the audience exploded with approval, probably because although this was an extremely large venue, that trio of musicians were still able to create that thunderously-loud Hendrix sound they generated in the smaller venues they played in Philadelphia previously. Next up was 'Red House', a much needed slow-down in pace after such a torrid opening. Even the stage looked red as the spotlights seemed to use red gels. That was followed by 'Foxy Lady' then 'I Don't Live Today', both played with exquisite feedback.

'Star Spangled Banner' was a stunner, the man playing the American national anthem having served his country in the military and now in search of peace and an end to war. 'Purple Haze' and 'Voodoo Child' closed that momentous show. Walking out of The Spectrum, I was in awe of what I had witnessed for the third time. Little did I know that by the end of the year, The Jimi Hendrix Experience would be no more.

ELLIS AUDITORIUM

FRIDAY APRIL 18, 1969, MEMPHIS, TENNESSEE

I WAS THERE: GENTRY JONES

My first ever concert. I'd been living in Seoul, South Korea for the previous year and a half because my father was a US military officer stationed there. I had a seat on the aisle and the show was late starting. When I looked back up the aisle, there was Jimi running down with a guitar case in his hand.

The opening act was Fat Mattress - the bassist's band. They weren't that great. Then Jimi came on and I simply passed into another dimension. I was forever transformed. I learned to play many of his tunes and earned a reputation because of that.

Jimi's appearances at the Sam Huston Coliseum, Houston for one of the evening's two shows was delayed and he didn't appear immediately after the band was introduced. When he did, he told the crowd, 'OK baby, give us about a couple of seconds to tune up' followed by, 'We would like to dedicate this first song to people like the cops'. In front of a crowd of 10,000, he performed a set including 'Star Spangled Banner'. The band over-ran an 11pm curfew and there were bad vibes backstage with the cops, clearly not enamoured of Jimi's earlier dedicating a song to them, wanting to stop him mid-tune. One crew member wondered 'if we were going to get out of there'.

SAM HOUSTON COLISEUM

19 APRIL 1969, HOUSTON, TEXAS

I WAS THERE: RANDY ORCHID

Chicago Transit Authority and Fat Mattress opened the show. To be honest, I expected to be completely blown away by Jimi and, in fact, I just was not. Although I have memories of being there, I do not

remember anything about Jimi's
set. I just remember thinking
he seemed a little subdued or
perhaps burned out. Years later,
my wife and I would stand beside
his grave in Renton, Washington.
That was very memorable.

I was a junior in high school in
a redneck town. A guy I knew,
but not too well, invited me. I
was over the moon. We left and I
picked up a beenie weed. It was
like we had a kill of hash.

Randy Orchid and wife at Jimi's grave

The venue wasn't packed. Noel Redding's band, Fat Mattress,
opened. It was lack-lustre and I was freaking out for the headliner,
Sir Hendrix. I can't tell you what the set-list was but, my God, this
cat was so much larger than life and rewrote the word 'cool'. He
was awesome and a master of not only his axe but the crowd too,
commanding their attention. I remember 'Foxy Lady', 'Manic
Depression', 'Watchtower', 'Axis: Bold as Love' and many more. He
was so fucking cool and breaking new ground with every song. And
Mitch Mitchell blew me away. He pushed Hendrix into uncharted
territory, especially when he blew into 'Hey Joe'.

MEMORIAL AUDITORIUM

20 APRIL 1969, DALLAS, TEXAS

I WAS THERE: GENAR BEARD, 16

I had a guitar and had managed to learn the chords and vocals for
'Gloria' by Van Morrison. The Beatles were still a huge part of my
music life. Then a friend happened by on a Sunday and said, 'Hey, let's

go to Dallas.' I asked, 'So what's in Dallas?' He replied, 'Some guitarist named Jimi Hendrix is doing a show and I hear he's pretty good.'

Our seats were on the very back at the top. I remember them introducing Noel Redding and his group Fat Mattress. I remember they were OK but not memorable until I found out the other group Noel was in. I can remember thinking after the concert what a dumbass he must be to step outside the Experience's circle.

I was stunned. Hendrix delivered utter musical magic. Totally free and abstract, not bound by the confines of symbols on paper or the expectations of what it should be but what it could be. And he delivered it so smooth in the coolest laid-back style. During his last number he rammed his guitar into the amps and shouted, 'Tear it up, Mitch.' Mitch trashed the hell out of his drum set and Noel joined the mayhem. Smoke was coming out of the back of the amps and I wondered if it was because Jimi was smashing them with his guitar or because they were unable to process music of his magnitude.

He walked off stage, their instruments reduced to rubble. The amps hummed with a low groan as if to take a last breath. The audience sat motionless and for several seconds didn't make a sound. When it soaked in what we had witnessed, the audience erupted with a thunderous cheer that lasted a long while. And when our real-world senses were restored, we figured out there wasn't going to be an encore.

I looked at my friend and said, 'Damn, did you see that?' I wanted to tell someone but didn't have the words to describe it. I couldn't compare it to anything. I knew I'd witnessed a legend whose mastery of music would become the zenith of guitar players to pursue for decades to come. When I got home I put my guitar under the bed.

I WAS THERE: ANGUS WYNNE

The next date I saw him was again at Dallas. They tended to repeat the dates a lot when they were successful. Chicago Transit Authority opened the show and that was a stunner. They were an amazingly powerful band, nothing like the kind of stuff they do today, Terry Kath being the band-leader, main singer and guitarist.

Jimi came out after that and tore the place up. This was an afternoon show and after seeing it I went AWOL. I was in the Texas Air National Guard by that time, on a weekend manoeuvre, and just said, 'To hell with that. I'm going out there to see him, no matter what happens.'

I WAS THERE: KENNY LUCAS, AGE 17

Hendrix was king of the hill. I saw him three times - in Dallas, in Fort Worth and then at Atlanta Pop 2. All great shows. That first was probably the best. He was still doing all the crowd-pleasers, playing with his teeth, behind his back and stuff. At the end, they destroyed the equipment, from Jimi's Strat to Noel's bass and the coup de grâce, Mitch Mitchell kicking the shit out of his drum-kit. His drums were nailed to the stage, so this took a little effort. When they were done ripping it up, Hendrix lit a joint and passed it to Noel. Noel walked over to the mic, and said, 'Happy Mother's Day. All you girls who want to be mothers come to our hotel room.' My eyes were bugging out of my head.

THE FORUM

26 APRIL 1969, LOS ANGELES, CALIFORNIA

I WAS THERE: DOUG PAULIN

I was only a freshman in high school. An older friend and neighbour, later the drummer for Survivor of 'Eye of the Tiger' fame, took me along. My memories are hazy. I know Cat Mother and the All Night Newsboys opened the show, then Chicago Transit Authority, who killed it, and then Jimi. Noel Redding was not with him that night. It was a low-key show. Jimi was not very animated and as I recall did not play many of his hits or smash up anything like we had hoped for. In fact, he hardly spoke, just focused on playing. Kurt Russell and Kam Nelson sat a few behind us and we didn't have the best seats.

I WAS THERE: ELLEN BERMAN, AGE 15

As a 15-year old teenager, I had a big black and white poster of Jimi on my bedroom wall. He was always staring at me with his low-cut open shirt. He was *so* incredibly sexy. His three albums were constantly playing on my stereo.

The Experience were set to play the Forum, the largest LA in-door venue at that time. Capacity was 17,500 and I couldn't wait. My seats were good, raised up off to the front side of the big stage, and tickets cost $5.50.

The opening act was Cat Mother and the All Night Newsboys. There was great excitement and electricity in the air. Finally, Jimi walked on wearing eclectic colourful clothing. My black and white poster had now come to life in living technicolor.

With his very first guitar riffs of the psychedelic instrumental song 'Tax Free', I was enthralled. His playing looked effortless but I knew it was really complicated. I watched him feel the music – it became a total extension of his whole being.

Eileen Berman took this live shot at the LA Forum

I was totally mesmerised. He was pure m*agic*. Jimi took me along to another world - his world. He was creating sounds out of his white Fender Stratocaster that I had never heard before from any other great player. His distinctive style was spellbinding. Jimi's intentional use of guitar feedback was so very innovative and dynamic as he incorporated it into his songs. Even when he played with his back turned to the audience, one could still feel his power. I had never seen a musician play his guitar behind his head. Then with his teeth. Amazing. His unique voice was so ultra-cool over his phenomenal playing. One song after another, Jimi was the Master blowing my mind. With Mitch and Noel, the trio was a powerful force. The total performance was *truly* a remarkable experience, just like the band name.

Jimi was the greatest guitarist I've ever seen play. And, yes, also the sexiest.

I WAS THERE: JON LEE, AGE 15

I grew up in Los Alamitos, Orange County, just south of Los Angeles County. It was very conservative and still is. I first heard 'Purple Haze' on the hippest underground FM station, KPCC, in what must have been 1967. It blew my mind. I thought it sounded like some outer space sci-fi music. Jimi's voice seemed so dark, so big, so soulful. The riffs of that song just felt gigantic, the coolest thing I'd heard. I loved it. I became friends with Craig. He had the *Are You Experienced* album, and I just fell in love with it all, but especially 'Foxy Lady', 'Manic Depression', 'Fire' and of course 'Are You Experienced'. It sounded like something from the future. It just seemed otherworldly, magical, and for me incomprehensible. Craig also played guitar and started teaching me parts of all those songs on my sister's cheap Sears Silvertone guitar.

Eileen Berman thought jimi was pure magic

I was too young to drive so asked my sister to buy the Hendrix album for me when she happened to be going to the

record store. She came back with *Axis: Bold As Love*. I liked a lot of
the songs but liked *Are You Experienced* better. It was more distorted
and heavy, what my 15-year-old mind craved. Craig taught me a
couple of those songs, like 'Little Wing' and 'Axis Bold As Love'.
Then I heard Hendrix was going to play LA Forum, with Chicago
opening for him. We got tickets, and Craig and his brother and I
went. Craig brought a tape recorder and taped the whole thing.
This is the concert that was part of a four-disc CD that came out
around 1991. I still listen to it.

On about the second or third song, 'Foxy Lady', which Jimi
introduced as 'here's something for the teenyboppers', I rushed
the stage and sat on the floor about 10 feet away from Jimi for the
rest of the concert. I remember thinking that the guitar seemed
like part of his body. He handled it so effortlessly, so fluidly.
He did all the tricks, played behind his head, behind his back,
between his legs (like he was masturbating the guitar neck) and
also with his teeth. I also saw when he played a lead, he would
mouth the notes like he was singing the lead. And by the way, it
was really loud!

He was sweating a lot too. So here I am in this crush of people
at the foot of stage, and there are uniformed police as security
on the stage, and Jimi would tell the audience to be cool, and not
cause the police to stop the concert. Then he steps back from the
mic, and with his guitar only, lets out a 'Fuck you, mother-fucker!'
using his wah-wah pedal to form the words, while looking directly
at one of the policemen, then makes the guitar laugh using
groaning feedback, as he bounces up and down to the screeching
'ha ha ha' sounds he's making with the guitar. That's on the LA
Forum CD at the beginning of the last song, 'Voodoo Child', but
the laughing part isn't. *Electric Ladyland* had come out about a
month before, and Jimi kept playing the opening riff to 'Voodoo
Child' between songs, like he was tuning up with it or something.
He did 'Tthe Star Spangled Banner', which I realised now was
such a brilliant re-invention of that piece for a new generation.
He closed the show with 'Voodoo Child (Slight Return)' during

the middle of which he went into 'Sunshine of Your Love' by
Cream. To my young inexperienced ears, it seemed like I was
hearing two guitars when he did the lead and the rhythm at the
same time. He didn't sing the lyrics but played the vocal part
with his guitar. When it was over, I remember Noel Redding
banging his bass into his amp, like they were going to smash their
instruments, but the road-crew came out and started tearing down
the set before he could go any further. I found a white guitar-pick
that Jimi dropped. I'm not sure what I did with that. One funny
thing I remember was there was a foil hotdog wrapper on the
floor next to me and this girl picked it up like it was a precious
religious icon, looking at it, saying, 'He stepped on this' as if in a
trance. She walked away holding it like a valuable piece of art.

Jimi was wearing a purple handmade long-sleeve shirt and
white bell-bottoms and his hair was cut shorter than what I'd seen
in pictures. I also noticed that the amplifiers and their shoes seem
scuffed up and worn out, dirty even, like an old tired carnival
coming through town. But I loved seeing Jimi and still think of
it as a seminal moment in my life. I saw him as an exceptional,
creative artist.

I felt like I wanted to live in the world he conjured with his music
and lyrics. I didn't become a musician, but Jimi's music inspired me
to become a visual artist. I could see his music. I eventually got into
computer-animated graphics and became an graphic animation
director, I've worked for many for the major TV networks, ABC,
NBC, CBS and FOX. In the mid-'80s I directed a couple of rock
videos because I really wanted to visually create music. But I didn't
like the record business and realised music was very personal and
I couldn't create something good to music I didn't like. So I stuck
with animating network logos and promotion graphics for TV
shows. I just retired after 37 years in the motion graphics industry,
the last 20 years running the promo animation department at CBS
Television. Jimi's inspiring genius led me to finding my career and
I'm forever grateful.

COLISEUM

27 APRIL 1969, OAKLAND, CALIFORNIA

I WAS THERE: JIM FRENCH

In 1969 I was a senior in high school and played a little guitar. We were Cream fans and thought Clapton was God. Then along comes *Are You Experienced*, and our Clapton loyalty was out the window. I found out the Experience was coming to the Oakland Coliseum, so had to get tickets. Because it was a big deal, I invited the prettiest girl in school and she went with me, and another high school couple came along too. The eight-page program was published by the Electric Church Productions, and I still have it, along with some very early bootleg recordings of Jimi. My main memory of the concert is that Jimi came out onstage by himself, messed around with his mountain of Marshall amps, and just started jamming feverishly. Then, after about 20 minutes, Noel and Mitch came out and the jam morphed into 'Come On', which has great lyrics, and of course screaming guitar like I had never heard.

Jim found God. Then he found Hendrix

Jimi was late for the show Larry witnessed

COBO ARENA

2 MAY 1969, DETROIT, MICHIGAN

I WAS THERE: LARRY MALINOWSKI, AGE 15

It was my first big arena show. He was late and only played about 45 minutes. When he did 'The Star Spangled Banner' - and this was before he did it at Woodstock - we didn't know what he was playing until halfway through when we noticed a spotlight on the American flag.

After landing at Toronto International Airport on 3 May 1969, customs agents detained Hendrix after finding a small amount of what they suspected to be heroin and hashish in his luggage.

A mobile lab was set up to determine what had been found, and at 1.30pm Metro police detective Harry Midgley arrested Jimi for illegal possession of narcotics. After being booked, finger-printed and photographed, he was released on $10,000 bail and required to return on 5 May for an arraignment hearing.

At a preliminary hearing on 19 June, Judge Robert Taylor set a date for 8 December, at which Hendrix would stand trial for two counts of illegal possession of narcotics, facing as many as 20 years in prison. While there was no question as to whether the drugs were in Hendrix's luggage, for the Crown to prove possession they had to show he knew they were there. In his cross-examination of Canadian customs officials, defence attorney John O'Driscoll raised doubts about whether the narcotics belonged to Hendrix, who had no drug paraphernalia in his luggage or needle tracks on his arms. After a trial that lasted three days, the jury deliberated for eight hours before returning a not guilty verdict, acquitting Hendrix of both charges.

MAPLE LEAF GARDENS

3 MAY 1969, TORONTO, CANADA

I WAS THERE: LINDA BILOROSEK, AGE 16

It was my very first major concert. On his way to the concert Jimi was busted at Toronto airport for possession of narcotics and it was really big news.

I had a cheap ticket for the Grey section, high up in the Gardens, but a friend and I sneaked down to the Red section, in the front row, very close to the stage, from where we watched the entire show. You could do that in those days. The concert was amazing. I was blown away. Jimi played 'Hey Joe' twice.

I WAS THERE: PHIL CIGLEN, AGE 18

It was my 18th birthday and also the day of a major charity walkathon in Toronto called *Miles For Millions*, and the day Hendrix was busted at the airport for allegedly 'illegally possessing narcotics'. I completed the walkathon then walked up from City Hall towards the Gardens, mostly on Mutual Street, which was mainly deserted, smoking a joint

Jimi came to life for 'Foxy Lady' at the show Phil witnessed

along the way. When I got to my seat, on the side to the right of the stage, about halfway back in the arena and about a third to half the way up from the floor, Cat Mother and the All Night Newsboys were into their opening act, about which I remember very little.

I think I knew about the bust at the time, and he referred to it obliquely. What I remember very clearly is that he seemed kind of detached for the first part of the concert. He played well but didn't seem to be fully involved, which is not surprising under the circumstances. However, when he got to 'Foxy Lady' he walked up to his wall of amps and got the feedback going and then seemed transformed. From that point on it felt like he was all there. That was very exciting.

From an audio point of view, two things struck me: the incredibly deep and powerful bass sound from Redding's huge Sunn amps and the slap-back echo from the sound bouncing off the rear wall of the arena, which added to the trippy vibe. As an occasional bass player, I always tried to emulate that bass sound, and as a guitarist Hendrix's tone and touch have certainly influenced my playing.

That remains one of my most memorable concerts.

SYRACUSE WAR MEMORIAL AUDITORIUM

4 MAY 1969, SYRACUSE, NEW YORK

I WAS THERE: ANNA CARLSON, AGE 18

I went with an old boyfriend. The concert was held at a venue now known as the Oncenter. The venue was only about half to three-quarters full, with everyone crammed up to the stage as close as they could. I thought that was odd, but he was so underground that the mainstream never caught on to him, at least not at that time. I can't recall the playlist but 'Purple Haze' was part of it. Besides his larger than life presence, it was the volume that left the biggest impression. And the fact that at least two techs or roadies were climbing all over the amplifiers throughout the entire show, making adjustments and repairs.

I WAS THERE: DAWN CARROLL

My best friend Babs and I had heard so much about this upcoming concert. We got tickets and my parents dropped us off into a milieu of swarming bodies. The building had no security save a half-dozen retired city workers in ushers' uniforms. There were people climbing the walls to be let into the second-floor bathroom windows and the atmosphere was charged with the promise of Jimi's electric experience.

Once inside my first impression was the smell of smoke. At first, it was cigarettes but as we waded into the crowd, marijuana was everywhere. We were freshmen in high school and this was our first 'real' concert. Every place we looked was a new experience - really 'dangerous' looking dudes, and chicks in outrageous outfits with feathers and fishnets. We weren't holding, but we were offered many free tokes by a free-spirited crowd. I don't remember too much about what we were wearing except for bell-bottoms, long straight hair and headbands.

As we made our way to our seats we bumped into our science teacher. She was legit and looked like the rest of the crowd. We exchanged nods and moved on. Our seats were on the mezzanine, but front-row, near the stage. We sat in a great crowd of kids a little older than us and had to squeeze together to make room for the extra people who sneaked in, but no one cared. We couldn't wait for the concert to start.

There was no opener, as was often the case in the Sixties. The stage lit up and a local DJ came on stage to briefly introduce He who needed no introduction. The DJ asked if we were ready for The Jimi Hendrix Experience. The crowd roared and the stage lit up in red.

Jimi opened with 'The Star Spangled Banner', 'Crosstown Traffic', 'Voodoo Child', 'Foxy Lady' and the one everybody was waiting for, 'Hey Joe'. Jimi hunched over his guitar and played it with his teeth. We were blown away. The auditorium was so thick with smoke that we couldn't see the people on the mezzanine across the room. It was loud, crowded and hot, but no one cared as Jimi's loud, electric and colourful performance commanded our complete attention. The only pause was to hit the joint and pass it on. Being my first real concert, Jimi set the stage for my future experiences.

MEMORIAL COLISEUM

7 MAY 1969, TUSCALOOSA, ALABAMA

I WAS THERE: AL CANNON

I saw Hendrix when I was 14 or 15 at the University of Alabama, nearly 50 years ago. My most vivid memory is of him doing the 'Star Spangled Banner' with his teeth and with the guitar behind his back.

CHARLOTTE COLISEUM

9 MAY 1969, CHARLOTTE, NORTH CAROLINA

I WAS THERE: BOB GUERRIN

I left for college in the Deep - for me at least - South in Charlotte, North Carolina. We only got the chance to see a few concerts until May 1969 when Hendrix was playing the Coliseum and Chicago Transit Authority opened. CRA were amazing but Jimi was on

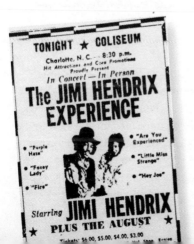

Bob had grown his hair and was taking lots of drugs

another level. I sat in amazement that night. I seem to recall the arena was not sold out. I could be wrong. We had all grown our hair very long and were taking all sorts of drugs. In the middle of my sophomore year I found out the small Catholic college I was attending wanted to kick us all out for drugs and other assorted things. So at Christmas time I came home for good.

I WAS THERE: JAN CIVIL, AGE 12

I was turning 13 on 28 May, so my mother went with me. I don't remember buying the tickets, it wasn't my money. Hendrix wasn't doing a lot of schtick by this time. He played long guitar solos on every song. So obviously it was not like most things. It was fairly loud but wasn't extreme - it wasn't like a Who show of that time. Oddly, my mother was not put off but said she thought it was good. I was quite enraptured. I was a drummer and was taking lessons at the time. The next Saturday my drum teacher, who also attended, asked which drummer I liked best. Chicago Transit Authority was the opening act, so it was a case of Mitch Mitchell vs Danny Seraphine. I liked Mitchell better and he was impressed by Seraphine. I would in all probability have the same opinion if I saw that show again today. I was working on the drum part to 'Fire' and my teacher had me deconstruct it and write it out on a drum stave. Then I started trying to pick out Hendrix's leads off 'Are You Experienced'. In fact, I switched to guitar before too long, and that was why.

Two years earlier, the Jimi Hendrix Experience performed as support to The Monkees at the Civic Center, Charleston. Back in Charleston as headliners on 10 May 1969, they performed in a venue that was barely half-full. Reviewers described it as the 'end of the beginning', Jimi telling an interviewer before the show 'we're not actually breaking up. We'll play some special events together now and then, but we're bored with the Experience. We've got to do some of our own things.'

Mitch Mitchell told the same interviewer, 'We're not really breaking up. We never really formed. We have just been meeting our mutual needs.'

FAIRGROUNDS COLISEUM

11 MAY 1969, INDIANAPOLIS, INDIANA

I WAS THERE: DAVID BAILEY

I saw Jimi with Chicago as a warm-up back at the State Fairgrounds Coliseum. What I remember most was how impressed I was with Terry Kath of Chicago, who I'd never heard of before that day. It was loud and the mix was a mess but it's an experience I'll never forget. I don't remember details. I was probably stoned!

I WAS THERE: TERRY JOHNSON

I saw Jimi at the State Fair Coliseum. The show was incredible. I sat and watched him do things on guitar that simply can't be done. But he did them. Unbelievable.

Larry remembers hippiedom reaching Indianapolis

I WAS THERE: LARRY BATTSON

It was the first concert I ever went to. It was at the Coliseum at the State Fairgrounds. The Beatles played there in September 1964.

It was on a Sunday and I remember, going to the show, how colourful everyone was. It was hippie days, tie-dye and all that. Hippiedom reached Indianapolis. It may have taken a little longer to reach than it did the West Coast or New York. We may have been six months behind the time. But it got there. And I'm sure there were people from all over the country that came to that show. I bought a poster. It was pretty exciting. I remember the tickets were three, four and five dollars.

It would seat around 12,000. It was an acoustic nightmare for concerts. When I went to concerts after that, you always prayed that the band had the sound down for the Coliseum. One of the best concerts I saw there was Jethro Tull, premiering *Thick as a Brick*. They didn't try to blast you out of your seats. That's the reason they pulled it off so well. Dr John used to say of Jimi, 'Why does he have to play so goddamn loud?'

He had a new look. He had short hair with a bandana or scarf tied around his head and dressed entirely in pink. He had no problem with masculinity, that's for sure. When he came out, he said, 'Just pretend you're in another place.' People got excited just listening to him tuning up, playing licks.

It was a short show. He only played 40 minutes. For the opening number he played 'Come On', which he rarely performed. The last number was 'Voodoo Child'.

He was not happy with the police. He gave the finger and everybody in the audience thought it was about us but apparently the police had been harassing people in the front row and Jimi didn't like it too much.

I read afterwards they weren't happy with the concert because there were no alcohol sales in Indiana on Sundays, so they couldn't buy booze. But Noel Redding played the whole concert with a half-gallon of Jack Daniels on the stage, which he'd take a couple of sips on every once in a while.

The opening act was the Chicago Transit Authority, which no one had heard of, and they were really good. Hendrix was great but we were surprised it was over so quickly. But The Beatles only played 25 to 30 minutes.

CIVIC CENTER

16 MAY 1969, BALTIMORE, MARYLAND

I WAS THERE: GARY MARKWOOD

The third time I saw Jimi was in Baltimore. Like the second time, he had problems and only played eight songs. He seemed miserable. So, foolishly, I didn't go the next year when he played Baltimore again. Billy Cox was on bass and played a longer set. My friends said he was really on. I loved him and the music he made. I still buy whatever comes out from the estate.

I WAS THERE: JANICE FLINCHBAUGH, AGE 16

I was a skinny little 16-year-old able to get my way up to the front of the stage with my arms folded, leaning on the stage. He was only 10ft from me. He was wearing orange bell-bottoms and his signature scarf. I was in heaven. His fingers were so long, they wrapped around the guitar. Back then, it was just the bands, no fancy stage gimmicks. What a wonderful time for true music-lovers. It will always be in my top-10 highlights of my life. I saw tons of the top bands over several decades. My granddaughters love to tell their friends that their grandmother saw Hendrix live. And almost 50 years later, I'm still talking (gloating) about it.

Gloating granny Janice likes to tell the youngsters she saw Jimi in concert

RHODE ISLAND AUDITORIUM

17 MAY 1969, PROVIDENCE, RHODE ISLAND

I WAS THERE: TIMOTHY MILHOMME

It was a life-influencing event. Because of stadium seating I was able to make it to the stage and, worming my way through, was noticed by a couple that saw this kid in the crowd. I was invited to stand with them on their front-row chairs. My ears rang for three days. Van Halen in 1984 was the second concert where that happened. The only other person I know or met in my life that saw Hendrix was at that show. We are still friends today. He also attended Woodstock in '69 and invited me to go, but my mother wouldn't let me. There hasn't been a guitar player that has made the instrument as important to any type of music as him. Of course, there are many unbelievable guitar players, but I wonder how my life would have been different without Hendrix.

I WAS THERE: DAVID SHERMAN, AGE 15

I was a budding guitarist and discovered Jimi Hendrix in either seventh or eighth grade. He was my musical god, and still is. Seeing Hendrix with Mitch Mitchell and Noel Redding and the Buddy Miles Express with original guitarist Jim McCarty was my first concert experience. All this and heaven too, for a ticket that cost a small fortune at $5.50. Too much time has passed for me to remember specifics, but he played many of his tunes of the day. I was mesmerised by Mitch Mitchell's drumming on an extended opening to 'I Don't Live Today'. Periodically, Jimi asked the crowd if he was playing too loud.

SEATTLE CENTER COLISEUM

23 MAY 1969, SEATTLE, WASHINGTON

I WAS THERE: HOWIE WAHLEN

I had heard some Jimi Hendrix Experience on Seattle radio ('Hey Joe', 'Purple Haze'), but finally took the deep pocket plunge for the *Axis: Bold As Love* album. The opening track, 'Exp', had me wowed from the get-go. Sci-fi on record? How can this be? It blew my little teenage mind. Guitar that enabled me to travel to unknown places in the universe. That album is still amazing to this day.

Fast forward a couple of years. I was nearing the finish of my first year in high school. Hendrix was about to make another hometown appearance and I wanted, needed to get experienced. I had an ad from the *Seattle Post Intelligencer* stapled to my bedroom wall for at least a month. Still not old enough to drive, but savvy in the ways of the Seattle transit system, I pooled my paper route money for two tickets. One for me and one for my high school sweetheart and future first wife, Elaine Briggs.

Our seats weren't the best, but we were there. We were kind of up in the bleachers on one side. We could see the whole venue and the stage well from our vantage point. The summer days are long in the northwest and I remember still seeing light from outside shining in as the show began.

Noel Redding's new band, Fat Mattress, was up first. I wasn't familiar with them. It was good enough that I purchased the album in the months after the show, but I can't say it had staying power - I don't own the LP anymore.

Then the main event, Jimi Hendrix. I wasn't as prepared as I thought I was. The 'live' Hendrix is a totally different animal than the 'studio' Hendrix. Live Hendrix is more about the showmanship than the intricacy of the studio Hendrix. It took a few songs for me to get it. Remember, all we had for visuals were TV and movies in those days. It wasn't on demand with a touch of a button. He had no live albums out.

He opened with a favourite cover song, 'Come On (Part 1)' off the *Electric Ladyland* album following a long jam on 'Hear My Train A Comin''. By the next song, 'Foxy Lady', we were on our feet. The next long jam, 'Red House', was new for me. I wouldn't hear it again until the *Smash Hits* album that fall. I seem to remember Jimi trying to calm the crowd a bit and the house lights being turned on before 'Red House'. I think there were a bunch of people out of their seats and crowding the aisle and the stage. It wasn't an open or festival seating show and the powers that be didn't like blocked aisles. 'I Don't Live Today', 'Fire' and 'Purple Haze' followed after everyone went back to their seats. He ended a seemingly short set with the magical 'Voodoo Child (Slight Return)'.

So many years have passed that it's hard to remember the finer details. I don't remember him talking a whole lot. Looking back, Jimi gave the hometown crowd a greatest-hits show from the last two years. I'm certainly glad I got the chance to see him. I have more than a few younger friends who only wish they could have seen Hendrix. He came through Seattle one more time in July '70. I decided not to go, thinking there would be more opportunities when he had more new material. Boy, was I wrong. Damn!

I WAS THERE: DOUG SCHENKER

I was out visiting my cousin in Seattle, Washington at the end of summer vacation before going back to college when he and I went to see Jimi Hendrix. The opening acts were Eire Apparent (who Jimi was producing) and Vanilla Fudge and I think maybe Fat Mattress, Noel Redding's group, may also have performed. What I remember most was that Jimi Hendrix was in Seattle, his hometown, and had received something from his high school, Garfield High. He namechecked many, if not all, of Seattle's high schools that day. His performance was incredible.

I WAS THERE: WARREN DOGEAGLE

I saw Jimi at two separate concerts in the late Sixties. These were a year apart and at the Seattle Center Coliseum, now known as the Key Arena. One concert had a traditional stage at one end of the arena. The next year the stage was elevated, centred and slowly revolved. A friend, Bobby (aka BJ), and I went to the later concert. I don't remember who I was with at the first one. I may have gone alone. When 'Voodoo Child' was played, the sound and vibrations made one feel the Coliseum was a large ship experiencing lift off! As we left, BJ said, 'Man, I didn't want that to ever end!' I couldn't have said it better.

SPORTS ARENA

24 MAY 1969, SAN DIEGO, CALIFORNIA

I WAS THERE: LONNIE NAPIER

I went to see Jimi at San Diego Sports Arena. I was a high school senior. As a guitar player I was very excited to see him in concert. I remember nobody sat the entire concert. The sound was swirling around because of all the bodies around me. He was definitely a showman and every note he touched on his guitar seemed to sound different than anything I'd heard before. The magic and charisma wrapped the entire arena like a warm blanket.

SANTA CLARA COUNTY FAIRGROUNDS POP FESTIVAL

25 MAY 1969, SAN JOSE, CALIFORNIA

I WAS THERE: BOBBY ASEA, AGE 16

The Northern California Folk Rock Festival took place at the Santa Clara County Fairgrounds. It was a three-day festival that featured many great acts, including Led Zeppelin, Chuck Berry, Eric Burdon, Taj Mahal, Muddy Waters, Spirit, Jefferson Airplane, Chambers Brothers and Santana. On day three, the final day headliner was Jimi Hendrix. He'd performed in Monterey and San Francisco in previous years but it was difficult for me to go and see him as I didn't have a driver's license and to find a lift to the city, an hour's drive, wasn't easy. Fortunately for me this concert was in my hometown, and I had friends who were older that drove us to the show.

I remember that most of the venue was general admission, which meant you were on your feet the whole day along with a ton of other concertgoers. There was some seating directly across from the stage set back a distance, and somehow my friends and I scored seats in that section. It certainly was worth it, because it was a long day and Jimi Hendrix was the final act.

Bobby saw Jimi on a bill also featuring Zeppelin and the Airplane

We're talking almost 49 years ago and there's only so much that really stuck to my memory, but I remember it was thrilling to see

him live. When he hit the stage it was like true rock'n'roll royalty right before my eyes. Like the rest of the people who followed the scene in the late Sixties, I was blown away when he released *Are You Experienced*. Little did I realise at the time that what he offered the world with his talent and fashion would and could never be surpassed. In my world, he is the ultimate rock guitarist.

I WAS THERE: JIM FRENCH

My second Hendrix concert was at the Santa Clara Folk Rock
Festival in San Jose. As we were standing in line to buy tickets, the
promoter came out front and said he needed some folks to guard
the back fence right next to stage. I instantly signed up and got in
for free. The opening act was the Doc Watson Family, and they were
wonderful, but we came to see the man. Before it was time for Jimi
to come on, there he was standing backstage, complaining that the
band wasn't being paid enough and he might not play. As I recall,
they were paying $24,000 and he wanted more. I said 'Hi' and told
him I was looking forward to seeing him play. I thought it was too
cheesy to ask for his autograph. A flood of others were doing just
that. I later regretted that decision, but that's life. Other than the
music, my abiding memory was of him walking on stage and telling
the crowd it was close to Mother's Day, and he would gladly oblige
any young ladies who wanted to be mothers after the show.

We might be old, but living in the Bay Area in the Sixties we got to
see a lot of great bands.

Attended by an estimated 200,000 fans, The Jimi Hendrix
Experience were the headline attraction at Newport Pop Festival. Jimi
played with the Experience on the Friday and reappeared on Sunday
evening to jam with Buddy Miles, Eric Burdon and Mother Earth.

NEWPORT POP FESTIVAL

20- 22 JUNE 1969, DEVONSHIRE DOWNS, CALIFORNIA

I WAS THERE: THOMAS HERIOT

I remember seeing Jimi the opening night at Devonshire Downs and
he played like shit. The good news was he came out Sunday morning
and killed it with an all-star band. All in all, I saw Hendrix seven or
eight times throughout the LA region, from the Forum to the Swing
Auditorium in San Bernardino, from the Experience to Band of
Gypsies. Except for the DD show, he was always excellent.

I WAS THERE: CATHY ANDERSON KILPATRICK, AGE 19

We were waiting for him to come on stage, which seemed to take forever. Then an announcer came on and said until we calmed down, Jimi wouldn't come on. So guess what? We calmed down. What a show, him with that white jumpsuit and psychedelic headband and sash around his waist. I was not disappointed. I love his music to this day. I am not a violent person at all, but I love 'Hey Joe'. Who would have thought it?

Cathy loves Jimi's music still

MILE HIGH STADIUM

29 JUNE 1969, DENVER, COLORADO

I WAS THERE: SALLY MOSER, AGE 17

This was a particularly memorable concert for many reasons. People were sneaking over fences to get in, so a large part of the crowd were tear-gassed by cops, including me!

I was 17 and in high school in Lincoln, Nebraska. I heard Jimi Hendrix was going to play at a three-day music festival in Denver and convinced my friend to jump in my 1964 Valiant and we drove there. We rented a cheap hotel near the stadium. She lied to her parents, told them we were going to a friend's cabin, thinking we shouldn't tell them about the festival. It was largely overshadowed by Woodstock two months later, which ended up being the next time Jimi would play. Attendance was estimated at 60,000.

Part of the line-up was Frank Zappa, Joe Cocker, Johnny Winter, Creedence Clearwater Revival and Three Dog Night. It was to be the last time the Experience played together. Noel Redding, Jimi's bass player, quit right after that performance. They had a problem with crowd control and on the second day there were gate-crashers tearing down fences and riots. Police decided to use tear gas to disperse the crowd. The gas wafted into the stadium and chaos ensued. People were running down onto the field, panicking and screaming. They said over the speaker to protect your head and eyes and take a wet cloth to your face. The day of the Hendrix performance they decided to give the rest of the tickets away for free. But when they ran out of tickets they had the same problem of gate-crashing and decided to use tear gas again. In the final few minutes of Jimi's last set he played 'Star Spangled Banner'. It was very symbolic as it felt as if we had been in a war zone while in the midst of all of this great music. We were in awe to see what Jimi did with his guitar. It was a moment in history I feel fortunate to have been a part of. To say I left the concert 'experienced' would truly be an understatement!

I WAS THERE: CARSON WILDER, AGE 24

I'd just got out of the army and was playing with the Wind River Blues Band. I was a drummer and liked Mitch Mitchell. I don't remember much about the concert. We listened to Zephyr and then, when Hendrix started playing, the kids were storming the gate, so we got tear-gassed. We were probably tripping too. Beyond that I can't remember much, just the tear-gas and the stoned crowd freaking out.

> ❝Clapton's blues style was very sophisticated and charming. Very 'on the money'. Hendrix comes over. [His playing] wasn't ugly, but it was more ballsy. A little out of tune, but it was full of passion. I think it's his passion that I love most of all❞

Peter Frampton

On 15 August 1969, the first day of the Woodstock Music and Arts Fair was held on Max Yasgur's 600-acre farm in Bethel, New York, about 80 miles north of NYC. Attended by over 400,000 people, Woodstock Festival provided one of the most pivotal moments in popular music history.

Those behind Woodstock were Michael Lang (who organised the largest festival on the East Coast at the time, the Miami Pop Festival), John Roberts, Joel Rosenman, and Artie Kornfeld. It was Roberts and Rosenman who had the finances.

Roberts and Rosenman placed an advertisement in the *New York Times* and the *Wall Street Journal* under the name of Challenge International Ltd, reading: 'Young men with unlimited capital looking for interesting, legitimate investment opportunities and business propositions'. Lang and Kornfeld answered and the four men got together to discuss a retreat-like recording studio in Woodstock, that evolving into an outdoor music and arts festival.

All they needed were acts to attract the crowds. They approached various with little success until Creedence Clearwater Revival signed a contract, agreeing to play for $10,000. Once the news was out that CCR had confirmed, others followed: Joe Cocker, Crosby, Stills, Nash & Young (their second live show), Santana, The

Who, Grateful Dead, Janis Joplin, The Band, Santana, Canned Heat, and Joan Baez.

The Doors considered appearing but declined, as did The Byrds and Jeff Beck. Joni Mitchell, originally booked to perform, canceled at the last minute on the advice of her manager after seeing the traffic chaos on the TV news. She didn't want to miss a scheduled appearance on The Dick Cavett TV Show the same weekend. Joni did write a song about the event, capturing a moment in time perfectly. Although the festival was in his backyard, Bob Dylan decided to 'get out of town', instead signing up for the Isle Of Wight Festival, held two weeks later.

Technical problems and poor weather prevented Jimi from taking to the stage until 9am on the Monday. The Experience having split, Jimi's backing band was Gypsy Sun and Rainbows.

WOODSTOCK

18 AUGUST 1969, WOODSTOCK, NEW YORK

I WAS THERE: DONALD SZTABNIK

The Woodstock Music and Arts Fair. That was the name on the posters with the iconic guitar and dove illustration. By the time we got to Woodstock we were half a million strong, as Joni Mitchell sweetly memorialised later on. There were so many bands spread out over that special weekend just weeks after the moon landing. Times actually were a-changing. Being at Woodstock was exhausting – non-stop music, heat, cold, dry, scorching sun, no food, freezing rain and wind, mud, mud, and more mud.

By the time Jimi got to the stage it was Monday morning and the huge crowd was thinning out. We'd been there since the previous Thursday with very little food or water. I was so exhausted that I couldn't make the trek back to the viewing area in front of the stage. I was caked in mud, hungry and so fatigued that I listened to Jimi from the comfort of my tent. Remember, we all thought the song would last forever. No one could foresee the unforeseeable or know the unknowable. Jimi was suddenly gone and never forgotten.

When I hear 'Purple Haze', 'Hey Joe' or any of Jimi's legacy I flash back to the Summer of '69 in a split-second. But the song that really makes me stop and listen is Jimi's cover of Dylan's 'All Along The Watchtower', which sends chills down my spine. Jimi playing Dylan, who we were searching for back in Greenwich Village all those years ago...

I WAS THERE: STEVE BOISVERT

I'd just got back from Vietnam. I went with a few Hells Angels. I was riding with a motorcycle gang called the Slum Lords out of New Haven, Connecticut. I awoke to Jimi playing 'The Star Bangled Banner' on his guitar. It was unbelievable.

I WAS THERE: CJ KOERNER, AGE 21

I was a year out of nursing school, living in Pittsburgh, Pennsylvania. My friend, Mary Ellen (Mic, RIP), along with others headed to Wildwood, New Jersey to spend the summer at the beach. Mic and I lined up jobs as graduate nurses at a nearby hospital. We packed into my 1968 yellow MG Midget and hit the road. We found an apartment in a house near the beach and began that summer of '69. While walking the boardwalk one night, we saw a poster for a concert called Woodstock. It seemed as if it would be a good time if we could get a ride to NY, if the hospital would give us the time off - which they didn't, so we picked up our pay-checks and didn't go back.

The salt air and lack of maintenance left my MG unavailable, so we started talking with two guys also checking out the concert poster. Turns out they too were from Pittsburgh. We agreed to pay for the gas if we could get a ride with them. I packed a small suitcase with a change of clothes and toiletries, thinking we would be sleeping at a motel near the venue. I had a fringed, beaded, suede bag I carried a few personal items in such as driver's licence, contact lenses and a harmonica I loved but could not play. In the bag was the only picture I had of my father, who passed away a few years prior.

We made our way to NY before the masses arrived, Mic and me eventually walking beside the car, slowly driving to a wooded parking area close to the fenced-in concert area. We left our belongings in the car and made our way to the entrance, but by this time the fences were torn down and we entered without the need for tickets.

The first evening was spent down front-centre, waiting for the musicians to come on stage. As the musicians played, the crowd grew and time passed, we eventually walked around to try to buy something to eat and use the port-a-potties. The music played and could be heard no matter where we were on the farmland. It was unlike anything we expected. We watched helicopters overhead, not realising the roads were blocked and the choppers were bringing the musicians to the farm. And it rained, so much rain that we walked back to the car and climbed in, trying to stay dry for a bit.

After the deluge, there was mud and more mud. And the food was pretty much gone. Others shared what they had, especially those who prepared to camp in advance. And the music played. The announcements came and went - warnings about which acid not to drop, or where to meet up if you were lost from your friends.

And Hendrix, on stage. The concert coming to an end.

Mic and I got separated from the guys that drove us to the concert. In fact, when we returned to the parking spot, the car was gone. Mic and I hitched rides from NY back to Wildwood, returning only with what we had on our backs. The looks we got waiting to find a ride, wearing the same clothes we had arrived in four days earlier. But what an Experience!

Eventually, after returning to my apartment in Pittsburgh, I received an envelope containing my driver's licence, my contact lenses and the picture of my father. The guys who drove us had given my suede bag to someone 'backstage' before they left, hoping we would hear an announcement of my name being read from my driver's licence.

I WAS THERE: LINDAKAY BOWMAN, AGE 17

I remember the music being so awesome and that it was very rainy. We had traps and sat close to the stage. We were too young to drink and too scared our parents would find out where we were. No cell-phones back then. We had a Beetle van and at least six of us, including what would be my hubby, were sharing. He was on leave from the Navy and a friend of my uncle, who was only seven years older than me and also in the Navy. Janis was loud, but Jimi just rocked. Dressed in Sixties clothes as we all were, bell-bottoms all muddy, some of us just stripped off and put on bathing suits and long dresses over them. And wore sandals. It seems the more the crowd yelled, the more Jimi played. Drugs were all around us and we were among the very few not doing them. Just breathing the air was enough to get high. I am sure all the musicians were high. They played till they dropped. The music was all night long.

I WAS THERE: MATTY MATARAZZO, AGE 21

What I mainly remember was his performance of the national anthem on his guitar. It had everyone in the audience mesmerised, including me.

I WAS THERE: JEFFREY STAPLETON

I grew up in the late Sixties and early Seventies. Age-wise, I was around 20 when the music scene really changed big time in America. The Beatles were just starting out and really started the music change here. So many new groups from both England and America followed suit, too many to list. I was a working hippie at the time. It was all about sex, drugs and rock'n'roll and I gladly participated in all of them.

I saw Jimmy a couple of times, once at a very small club in Boston called the Boston Tea Party. Jethro Tull, Santana, The Animals, The Allman Brothers, The Cream, and countless others played there. My routine was to hit this place with friends after dropping some LSD and enjoy the bands.

I was lucky enough to attend Woodstock and saw Jimi there. That was a last-minute thing. A bunch of us drove up from Boston without tickets. They only sold something like 18,000 tickets and 400,000 people showed up, but that's a whole other story.

It was this short period of radical social change in America. It spilled over into the late Sixties with the Civil Rights movement, the opposition to the Vietnam War, feminism and the start of the birth control pill, which really gave women the freedom to do as they liked. Also, abortion became legal. Just about everything was changing from our parents' values. Up until then the position was that the Government had the people's best interests at heart and could do no wrong. The new generation took the position that really the Government was there to serve big business on a global level.

Jimi was a special musician, one of a kind. No one has filled his shoes since his untimely death from a heroin overdose. Casual usage of heroin at the time was not that uncommon. Today, we know a lot more about drugs and their short and long-term effects than we did back then. Drug use, even hard drugs, were pretty mainstream at the time. For me, the thing other than his music that separated him from everybody else was that he seemed to have this seamless connection between his brain and ear that got transposed to his guitar. He was a natural and his talent appeared to be more genetic than a learned ability. His music really felt like it was not scripted but rather improvisational.

Jimi always came across as someone who had a lot of humility. Some people may have a hard time seeing that because at times he would do attention-getting stunts such as burning his guitar at the Monterey Festival. But Jimi had this raw talent, sometimes primitive in nature, that people connected with. His guitar abilities were such that it seemed as though he was just making it up as he played. He was not heavily rehearsed like, for instance, the Rolling Stones. It seemed effortless for him.

I WAS THERE: JIM WILLIAMS, AGE 19

I was in the navy. We were in Virginia Beach, Virginia. My ship was going to head off to Vietnam and it was all over everywhere about Woodstock being about to happen. So me and another guy went AWOL, jumped ship and hitchhiked up to Woodstock. Nowadays nobody would pick you up if you hitchhiked, but back then you got a lot of rides. The hippies would give anybody rides. Most of them were broke, but they would give me dried fruit or whatever they had, a lot of free love and a lot of, 'Hey man, take a hit off this joint.' And because I was AWOL they were on my side - totally. 'Man, we'll take care of you.' It was neat.

Jim chose Woodstock over a trip to Vietnam

Janis, I liked a lot and got to see her a couple of times. But at Woodstock, she was so wasted her actual performance really wasn't that good. Jimi was the headliner and he played last on everything. He got paid more than everybody else too, I heard. Everybody was so exhausted they just started leaving, because they were freaking out about how they were going to get home, because the roads were all blocked. When Jimi played, it was the last day and so many people had left you could get right up close. I just kept waiting for him at the end. Man, if you had made it the whole three days you were exhausted. I was exhausted. I dropped a bunch of acid. Everything was free. We didn't have a dime. We were AWOL and we ate free, we got free pot and free LSD and everything. It was like a three-day party.

It seemed like it was 700,000 people strong when it was really going, when The Who played. There were 69 bands. At the end, for the people who got to see it, it was like, 'God, what a performance!' It was like, 'Nobody's here.' I'm looking around and, 'Where is everybody?'

Being at Woodstock turned out to be a massive big deal. At the time it was just, 'Man, what a massive concert this turned out to be.' Later, it was the greatest concert in history because of all the bands that were there. And Jimi was beautiful, he looked really cool. He was polished. He was great.

After Woodstock I finally got back home and lost a bunch of weight and then went and snuck into my girlfriend's bedroom. Her ma found out I was there and called the FBI. That morning, they kicked the door in. I'm stark naked and these great big dudes jerk me out of bed. I'm down to about 175 pounds so I'm light, I'd lost a lot of weight, and these two guys are 6ft 6, 285 lb. They jerked me out of bed and dragged me out to the front yard and handcuffed me, naked. I said, 'Jesus Christ, can I get some pants?' Then they realise I'm not some killer, like the girlfriend's mother said, and so they said, 'Okay' and ook me back to the bedroom and I got to put clothes on. Then they took me to the Treasure Island naval base in San Francisco on Bay Bridge.

I got thrown into what's called restricted barracks and waited for my court-martial. They threw me in the brig for 30 days. The Vietnam War was going on. But the kicker was that it was the East Coast that I went AWOL from, so that saved my ass. Because normally they send you back to your ship and you're screwed. Well, my ship had gone over to 'Nam, so they said, 'OK, you're going to do your 30 days and you're going to stay here in California.' And I said, 'Great!' As soon as they let me go, I found a lawyer in San Francisco helping people get out of the service legally, and he said, 'Give me $500 and I can get you out.' He told me what to do.

I borrowed $500 off my dad and went AWOL again, then turned myself in and went back to the brig. When I got out the second time they said, 'We've got a shrink' and the lawyer said, 'Here's what you say. Act like you're gonna lose it and then tell them you're gonna kill somebody if they give you any more orders.' I got out on a passive-aggressive thing, like I couldn't control my anger. It cost me five bills but I got out after doing a year and a couple of months, so they couldn't draft me again. Because they were drafting people back then. And that's why I joined in the first place, so I wouldn't go to 'Nam in the front-line.

I would have been stuck. Our ship was going to be nine months on the ocean, right outside of Vietnam, launching and recovering jets. It was a big decision to go AWOL. But it all worked out. I didn't get killed, anyway.

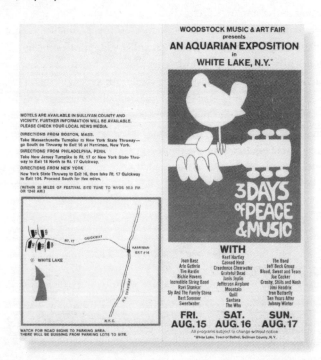

The day I got out of the brig, I got out of the navy and got a general discharge that turned honourable six months later, if you put in for it, with all the benefits and everything. I did seven months of what's called 'good time' and the other five months 'bad time', in the brig or AWOL. So when I got out, my opinion was that I didn't get drafted and I got to see Jimi Hendrix at Woodstock!

I WAS THERE: DEAN THOMSON

I was one of the lucky few that went to Woodstock and saw the whole event. Nine of us drove down from Verdun, Quebec in a friend's Ford Econoline van. Just the road trip down was an adventure. When Hendrix came out and started playing on the Monday morning, we were helping pick up garbage on the hill. There was garbage everywhere. It was like a mini-dump. We weren't paying too much attention to the set. We were tired, hungry and dirty.

The day before we ate US army rations - orange tang, rolled oats and raisins and spiced cake with industrial tea. Or coffee. I don't know what it was, but it was free, warm and contained caffeine. We were pretty close to the stage for the whole concert, so we saw or at least heard most of it. I thought him playing 'The Star Spangled Banner' was kinda funny. I was hoping for a more serious set of his LP material, but it didn't really happen. I think they made a huge mistake by scheduling him as the finale. In my opinion he should have hit the stage Saturday night/Sunday morning, like the Airplane and The Who.

I WAS THERE: ANGUS WYNNE

The next time I saw him was actually at Woodstock. I produced a
show here in Dallas on Labor Day weekend '69 called the Texas
International Pop Festival and it fell between the Atlanta Pop Festival
and Woodstock. It was about two weeks after Woodstock and there
was so much that we didn't know about putting festivals on - we were
just a bunch of kids. We didn't know until about 40 days before this
festival that we were going to even do it. We had to hustle up a place
to have it, which was hard to do because we wanted a place that
was outdoors and around some woods and lakes where people could
camp out. We had 30 major acts in three days, 10 acts a day. In fact,
11 acts, because we had this little band no one had ever heard of
to open the show every day on some plywood down in front of the
stage. At the time they were called Grand Funk Railroad.

We didn't know what was going to happen at Woodstock and
only had the experience of some of our partners who had been in
on the Atlanta Festival to go by, so we caught a ride on a plane that
was going up there. It was stunning to say the least. We rented a
car, but pretty much stopped on the highway, which turned into a
big parking lot about six miles from the place and walked down. We
wound up coming up to the side of this big bowl where all the people
were, walked over the rim and looked down into this thing and just
gasped at the amount of people down there. We looked to one side
and saw a big roll of metal fencing that had never gone up, so they'd
never even had security. The only people with tickets were those with
advance tickets, which apparently wasn't a lot. Otherwise it was a
free festival from the beginning.

We left right after Hendrix, but we were there for the whole three
days. We had backstage passes that allowed us to go anywhere we
wanted. I spent most of the time on the stage or on the walkway,
about halfway down it or in the artists' hospitality area in the back,
which was very lavish. There were helicopters going in and out of
there and it was quite a spectacle. I saw Jimi's set and I thought it
was lacklustre. It wasn't how I had seen him at the start of his career

as the Experience. He'd been through the mill and probably wasn't making a whole lot of money off that. He never saw a dime of any of the money he made on the road. That was all taken in by the gangsters that owned his management contract. Apparently, the mob were central to his dates and they just worked him to death on the road. He never saw any record money at all.

I WAS THERE: ROBERT ROWLAND

The last day of Woodstock, I was playing that weekend up in that general area with my band, so couldn't go Friday, Saturday. But when we were finished on Sunday morning me and one of the other fellows up there went and we stayed the day. A lot of people had left by that time because of the rain. And Hendrix went on super late. It was daybreak when he went on.

MIDTOWN MANHATTAN

SEPTEMBER 1969, NEW YORK, NEW YORK

I WAS THERE: JIMY BLEU

While a student at Performing Arts High School in Manhattan (as immortalised in the movie and TV series *Fame*), I was an active member of Hendrix's official fan club at Warner-Reprise records during my sophomore to senior years, between late 1968 and 1971. A few of us from the fan club were responsible for having Jimi speak informally at our school for a small assembly thanks to our jazz band teacher, because Jimi was not a popular candidate for speaking there, according to the other conservative faculty, who were used to the jazz and classical masters lecturing there.

Performing Arts was then located at West 46 Street and Times Square, Manny's Music Store was and still is at West 48 Street and the Record Plant was then at West 44 Street. Buddy Miles was dating a woman whose younger sister attended Performing Arts, so on their way to Manny's, Greenwich Village, the Record Plant or to

Harlem, he and Jimi would occasionally pull up in front of the high
school in a few of the Corvettes he had at one or other times, or in
Buddy's Mustang, and just hang out in front of the school, sitting
on the steps. R&B star Jimmy Castor was also with them a few
times. It was one day in late 1969 while Jimi was in Manny's that
we talked him into coming to the high school to give an impromptu
'lecture'. This period was during the brief time he was documented
doing public speaking lectures.

The fan club was also on the outskirts of his entourage whenever
he was on the East Coast and sometimes Mid-West from early 1969
until his death in September 1970. The vice president of the club
was also a student there and we prided ourselves as having the most
extensive 'Hendrix watch' at that time, just as his British fan club
had their fine 'Hendrix watch'. We knew nearly his every move -
when he was out of town, in town, whose house he was partying at
and which studio he was at, and even getting kicked out of studio
sessions by his appointed 'bodyguard' Velvert Turner. We also got
into concerts of his in the Tri-State area free by just flashing the fan
club button at the door and got kicked out of his manager's office
by his secretary.

Although Jimi never knew my name personally, there were
about five or six times when we from the fan club were alone with
him. One of those times, he was speaking about a college devoted
specifically to jazz music that he was taking a correspondence
course with thanks to his friends, guitarist Larry Coryell and
Quincy Jones. He told the three of us out of the group who were
going to Performing Arts that we should try out for the college. So
he's actually responsible for me taking the test for Berklee College
of Music and I was the only one of those three who passed the test
for that college.

There were numerous instances of Jimi describing his music as
a 'religion' or saying his aim was to 'awaken sleeping people'. If
ever there was a 'musician as magician' who felt his calling was
roaming the planet spreading a message of love, peace and self-
empowerment through music, it was Jimi Hendrix. That's why

I've devoted the past 48 years of my life to presenting the most
meticulous and authentic Hendrix show ever.

A full US tour, scheduled to commence on 18 September 1969 in
Boston, was cancelled. Jimi had to pay $25,000 in reimbursements
and expenses to promoters Concerts West.

RECORD PLANT

7 NOVEMBER 1969, NEW YORK, NEW YORK

I WAS THERE: LESLIE WEST (GUITARIST, MOUNTAIN)

When we were recording *Mountain Climbing* in the Record Plant, Jimi
was recording Band Of Gypsys in the next door studio (working on
'Izabella' and 'Room Full of Mirrors'). He came in and listened to
Never In My Life and looked at me and said, 'Nice riff, man.' He
gave me a compliment. That was all I needed to hear.

FILLMORE EAST

31 DECEMBER 1969, NEW YORK, NEW YORK

I WAS THERE: ROBERT ROWLAND

This was one of the few times I paid for a ticket. In those days
tickets were only $3 or $4 anyhow, but I used to go to the Fillmore
almost every week and give the guy a buck. You'd think you were
getting away with it, but it was only $2 or $3 to get in for three acts.
At Forest Hills Tennis Stadium, when I went to see him with The
Monkees, you would give the guy at the door a dollar and he'd sneak
you in and pocket the money.

The Band of Gypsies were playing New Year's Eve and the line
was around the block for the Fillmore. Standing on the corner were
seven or eight black dudes singing and panhandling, people throwing
money in their cases and stuff, singing acapella. When we went inside
we realised it was the opening act, The Voices of East Harlem. There

was a lot of diversity then. There was a little scene where groups like the Edwin Hawkins Singers could get a hit record. The Voices of East Harlem were like that, a group of 12 or 13 people.

I WAS THERE: WILLY PUIG

The combination of Jimi, the Fillmore East on New Year's Eve and the Band of Gypsies show can only be described in one word – magic! He had started to play this new music with the Band of Gypsies and I wasn't sure what to think. It was certainly different from his earlier releases. But a couple of minutes in, I was hooked. He still played more familiar stuff later like 'Stone Free', 'I Don't Live Today' and 'Crosstown Traffic'. More often than not at the Fillmore East there was a show going on in the crowd too. The instant you walked in the lobby, you were stoned from the clouds of illicit smoke, among other things. The things that went on were weirder than you can imagine. But I'm lucky I was alive in those times to experience them.

I WAS THERE: JOSEPH TOMASELLO

The last time I saw him was with the Band of Gypsies at the Fillmore East. What I remember most is that after the show people came out and said how much it sucked. I was saying that he really blew me away. Buddy Miles is a great drummer. It was a great band.

I WAS THERE: JOHN FRIEL, AGE 14

I saw the Band of Gypsys perform on New Year's Eve at the Fillmore East. I've been to well over 150 concerts in my life and this is in the top three. I was sitting in the 'cheap' seats in the balcony at less than $5. I get to relive the concert anytime I want by listening to the *Band of Gypsys* album, which was recorded live at the show.

> ❝I grew up going to Fillmore East, seeing Jimi Hendrix, Led Zeppelin, Humble Pie. Jimi Hendrix was like somebody from another planet. God bless Stevie Ray Vaughan, but there wouldn't be an SRV without a Hendrix ❞

Paul Stanley, KISS

1970

FELT FORUM

28 JANUARY 1970, NEW YORK, NEW YORK

I WAS THERE: RONNIE D'ADDARIO

I saw him with Buddy Miles on drums at the Felt Forum in NYC. He barely played for half an hour before he walked off. He kept telling the audience to stop the cameras flashing. They didn't, he got pissed and said, 'Oh man, these cameras' and walked off. Everyone was really angry, including me, and that was it. We went home. I don't remember what he played.

Reprise Records released 'Stepping Stone' as a single on 8 April 1970. Recorded early in 1970 with the short-lived Band of Gypsys line-up of Hendrix, Billy Cox and Buddy Miles, the song first appeared in part when Jimi performed at Woodstock Festival with an interim band, sometimes referred to as Gypsy, Sun and Rainbows. Hendrix incorporated the song's rhythm into the long rendition of 'Voodoo Child (Slight Return).

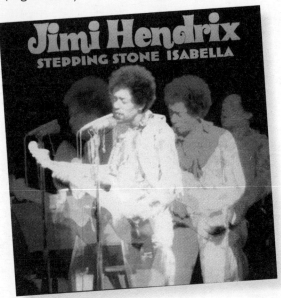

THE FORUM

25 APRIL 1970, LOS ANGELES, CALIFORNIA

Jimi is back in the US. His band, now a trio with Billy Cox on bass and Mitch Mitchell on drums, has been rebranded Cry of Love.

I WAS THERE: RANDY ELMORE

I saw him three times, at the Newport Pop Festival in 1969, the Forum in 1970 and at the Swing Auditorium in San Bernardino. The Forum was best. I was able to get down to the front, six feet away from him, he looked at me, and we made eye contact. I was blown away. I remember it like it was yesterday. He was an amazing guitar player.

I WAS THERE: MARC SILVERSTEIN, AGE 16

When Jimi came onto the scene, I was 13. Rock music was exploding, with so many good bands as the hippie psychedelic movement peaked. When *Are You Experienced* was released, it changed my life. I was blown away by the lyrics and especially Jimi's guitar style. No other guitarist played or looked like Jimi. *Axis* and then *Electric Ladyland* were all so amazing. Every song was good. I hoped it would never end. His interview on *The Dick Cavett Show* gave us a glimpse of his humility and the kindness he had for the world.

Marc stuffed tissues in his ears as the music was so loud

I remember visiting my insurance salesman brother in San Francisco. He asked if I would like to look at the 'weirdos' in the Haight/Ashbury district. When we drove through that area, there were freaks everywhere. There was a band playing on a flatbed truck with topless girls painted in psychedelic colours dancing as they slowly drove past. Hippies and flower children jammed the street. All I wanted to do was get out of the car and join them.

In those days, civil unrest was growing in our society as the Vietnam war was raging and anti-Vietnam and anti-draft protests empowered the youth to be defiant of 'The Establishment' and 'The Man'. Assassinations, the Black Panther Movement, nuclear threat drop-drills in class as well as teacher strikes were the norm. The police had no tolerance for long-haired hippies and made it clear we weren't welcome anywhere.

In 1970, I was 16 and went with some friends to the Forum in Los Angeles to see Jimi. While entering the Forum, we were met with police checking everyone out, pulling people out of line and searching them. Paranoia abounded. We made it to our seats where the other kids around us were excited with anticipation. Joints were passed around. Some kids got pulled from their seats by police. More paranoia.

On stage was a wall of Marshall amps. This added to the excitement of what was to come. Jimi was late, the crowd growing anxious. The Purple boxset has a track recorded at the Forum, 'I Don't Live Today'. You can hear and feel the crowd's unrest on that track. Police blue hats could be seen across the lower front part of the stage,

I don't remember the exact set-list but remember 'Foxy Lady' and 'Purple Haze' and a lot of extended versions of familiar songs as well as a few unfamiliar. I also remember it was loud. I stuffed tissue in my ears anticipating the volume, but the volume and frequencies Jimi created were excruciating. I left the concert with ears ringing, absolutely spent.

My previous concert experiences were of bands recreating their songs flawlessly onstage. Jimi went with the moment, in jam-session mode, creating new twists to a known song or an extended solo leading into a different song. Playing behind his back and with his teeth was something I had not seen before. He made it all look so easy. My impression was that it was both amazing and disappointing. It's not until years later that I appreciated live music and the musician's interpretation presented on stage. In retrospect, I realise just how fortunate I was to see Jimi in his element. The live concert recordings of Jimi are all very familiar to me and any video of a live performance brings me back.

Today, any guitarist onstage going into a short Jimi riff always brings a smile to my face and, once again, brings me back.

I WAS THERE: DENNIS WATTS, AGE 18

I saw Hendrix at the Forum in LA in April '70. Pacific Gas and
Electric and Buddy Miles Express opened. This was the first concert
I went to that had a video screen, which was constantly in close-
up on Hendrix. It was the first
concert with Mitch and Billy as
his trio partners. The Forum was
two-thirds full at best. Hendrix
made everyone stand for 'The
Star Spangled Banner' ('Stand
up for once in your lives'). He
also dismissed everyone to go get
popcorn and candy while they
jammed on some less familiar
material such as 'New Rising
Sun' and some instrumentals.
Other than that, he seemed in
a good mood, and had his usual
bag of jokes, 'Girl in the yellow
underwear', 'Yours truly on public
saxophone', 'Excuse me while
I kiss this guy'. There was zero
merchandise on sale. How times

*Seeing Jimi was Dennis's 18th birthday
present to himself*

have changed. The crowd was very reserved - no rushing the stage,
just a lot of pot-smoking. I'd just celebrated my 18th birthday and
this was my birthday present to myself. I couldn't even find anyone to
go with so I went alone, high on mescaline. Yikes!

I WAS THERE: MIKE HICKS

I saw him at the LA Forum and left halfway through an indulgent
version of 'Room Full of Mirrors'. For all his undisputed brilliance,
Hendrix was an erratic performer. The '68 show at the Hollywood
Bowl was quite brilliant, '69 at the Forum was okay, but a year
later I was getting bored. And I had high school the next day and

thought I would catch him on a better night next time. I was and remain a fan of his recordings, but his concerts could be erratic and his playing unfocused.

STATE FAIRGROUNDS

26 APRIL 1970, SACRAMENTO, CALIFORNIA

I WAS THERE: JIM WILLIAMS

I saw him at Cal Expo, where they have the California State Fair. They had a huge outdoor concert and a giant grandstand where they have horse races. They filled this huge grandstand, so it was just the stage on the ground facing the grandstand, and it was full of people. That arena was so sold out they had a line that wrapped for two miles around the whole thing. While that was full and he was playing, the people in that line were outside listening, because it was all outdoors. It was a free concert. That was the last time I saw him and I didn't get to speak to him. He died five months later. That devastated me - it was just a kick in the gut.

The first time I saw him it was a mind-blowing, experimental kind of thing, and by the time Woodstock happened everything was just put together. The Sacramento concert could be considered one of his best because it was towards the end of his career and he really had his shit together then. He was much more polished than in the other two performances. He was just super-professional.

MILWAUKEE AUDITORIUM

1 MAY 1970, MILWAUKEE, WISCONSIN

I WAS THERE: DICK THURNER, AGE 19

I barely knew who Jimi Hendrix was, and had never been to any live concert of any kind. My older sister asked me to go with her. The Milwaukee Auditorium at the time was an older concert venue,

rather small by today's standards. It was a Friday, the concert
started at 8pm, my ticket was for Row 5, seat 12, and cost $4.50. I
still have the stub.

Apparently, the opening act was a group called Oz, although
I remember nothing of their performance. I only remember
Hendrix. The backdrop for the stage was a massive dark red
curtain that seemed to hang floor to ceiling. When the lights were
all on, that entire end of the Auditorium glowed a bright, lurid
red, as if the band was standing in front of the gates of hell. I'll
never forget that.
Hendrix had something reflective all over his guitar, like sequins.
When the spotlights were on him, these reflected the light in
bright little beams that flashed all around the audience and the
auditorium walls and ceiling as he played. It was almost as if the
sound of his music had become a thing of material substance that
you could see flying off his guitar.

At various points in the concert he played the guitar behind his
back and with his teeth. I'd never seen anything like that and had
never imagined such a thing possible. I also remember the crowd
went crazy as soon as he came out on stage, and the excitement
never let up. By the end everyone in the place was on their feet
and had surged forward to the foot of the stage.

Many of the young women in the crowd by then were up on
the shoulders of their dates, the entire crowd surging around in a
frenzy. I'd never been in a concert situation like that before and
was equally frightened and thrilled at finding myself in the middle
of that wild crowd.

Over the years, whenever I've told people about seeing Hendrix
live, I always say this concert changed my life. I truly believe I
walked out of that place a different person from when I walked
in. Over the next 10 years I went to every major-act concert I
could, in Milwaukee, Madison and Chicago, hoping to duplicate
that first experience.

DANE COUNTY COLISEUM

2 MAY 1970, MADISON, WISCONSIN

I WAS THERE: TOM BAUKNECHT, AGE 18

I was at that show with my older brother, a sophomore at University of Wisconsin. I was a Northern Wisconsin high school student who took his little 14-year-old sister to her first rock concert. Everything about it seemed a little unreal and, being an unworldly bumpkin, Madison seemed like Paris, France. The Coliseum seemed cavernous and raucous and everyone seemed impatient, waiting for the lights to go out.

When they finally did, the undercard band was Savage Grace, a Detroit area band in the mould of MC5. The only noteworthy thing was they had the nerve to play 'All Along the Watchtower' as their encore. I should add that, moments after the show started, my sister and I got our first smell of pot. Contact high to follow. The wait was worth it when Jimi hit the stage. He was mesmerising and you couldn't take your eyes off the stage. He seemed engaged and energetic, not always the case when some artists play in the Midwest.

I can't remember the playlist but remember him holding the guitar between his legs and playing on one foot. He also played the guitar behind his head and even played using his teeth. It was somewhat a defining moment - my musical taste changed overnight. I shit-canned my Three Dog Night and Simon and Garfunkel records as soon as I got home. No more 'Joy to the World' for me. I had witnessed real rock.

I WAS THERE: RICHARD LEINBERGER, AGE 18

It was my first big-time concert. What a one to start with. I played guitar in a band with some friends from high school. At that time FM radio was just starting to be popular. I listened to WIBA-FM. They had a program called *Radio Free Madison* that ran from 7pm to midnight. They played what we called underground music, music from albums. That was where we first heard about most bands. We got to hear longer cuts that would never have been played on AM radio. They announced that Jimi would be playing at Dane County Coliseum. I heard it and told my friends in the band. We thought it would be fun to go. We sent in our money for the tickets in the mail. I know there were at least three of us. I was 18, the other two 16 or 17. I'm not sure if there was a fourth person. The radio ad had been playing for a while. I think the tickets cost somewhere in the $5 to $10 range.

The tickets came and we went along. We lived in Darlington, Wisconsin, about 60 miles from Madison. I drove us in my parents' car. We got to the Coliseum and showed our tickets to the usher. It was a reserved seating concert. I'm not sure how many people the Coliseum held, but I would guess around 10,000. We watched the other ushers showing people to their seats and they all seemed to head towards the back. The usher looked at our tickets and started toward the front. He kept walking and we ended up in the sixth row, right in the centre of the stage. They were fantastic tickets. I've never had such good seats since.

There were two opening acts. The first was a band called Savage Grace, I think from Michigan, and we thought they were pretty good. The second was a popular Madison band, I think called Tayles. We didn't think they were as good. They played one long song, something about robbing a train.

We noticed a kind of sweet smell in the place. Of course, marijuana. We were rather naïve smalltown kids. I don't think any of us had ever had any before. I never did, only second-hand. People were passing joints around from time to time. I think we all declined.

The MC came on after the other bands were finished and said Jimi was backstage and rather nervous and told us to give him a big welcome. He came on and of course got a great ovation. The other members of the band were Mitch Mitchell and Billy Cox. Mitch had a beard and wore a tank-top. I don't recall what Billy was wearing. I don't remember what Jimi was wearing, but I think it was his usual stage clothes. The first number they did was 'Fire'. They also did 'The Star Spangled Banner' and 'Purple Haze'. We didn't have money to buy every album, so I'm sure there were songs I'd never heard. They might have done 'Machine Gun'.

Jimi was very nice and asked more than once if the band was too loud. Once during a break between songs, a man from the audience stood up and yelled out, 'What can we give you?' and Jimi replied, 'A joint!' which got a big laugh. This was of course way before the big video screens, but we didn't need them. We had a great view. I don't think Jimi did encores. I think he might have left with his guitar feeding back, but can't say for sure. We were hugely impressed and for our first big concert couldn't have had a better time.

We returned home to our town with its population of about 2,300 later that night. We had a lot of stories to tell our friends.

I WAS THERE: JONATHAN LITTLE

The Factory was a small night-club whereas the Coliseum was a sports venue that could seat nearly 10,000. The majority of the audience was seeing Jimi for the first time live. Playing guitar behind his back was an audience-pleaser and I'm quite sure at the end of the show he doused his guitar with lighter fluid and set it on fire. We'd never seen that before.

I WAS THERE: DEBORAH VAUGHAN, AGE 19

This was the first big concert I'd been to since The Monkees in Chicago, a very different experience. This was the beginning of a great summer of music, with two three-day rock festivals at Kickapoo Creek in Heyworth, Illinois and Galena, Iowa, A Beautiful Day concert at the Aragon in Chicago, Jethro Tull at Whitewater, Wisconsin (listed as Lake Geneva), Iron Butterfly at the Illinois State Fair and Cheap Trick and Alice Cooper.

My boyfriend's brother worked with Ken Adamany, one of Madison, Wisconsin's largest promoters (who also managed Cheap Trick) and he had six tickets, eighth-row centre. We were living in Bloomington, Illinois. I was just home from my first year at Western Illinois University where I demonstrated against the Vietnam War more than attending classes and they dutifully flunked me out. I didn't care, there were more important things at the time. My boyfriend had been drafted the fall before, his birthday came up number one in the lottery. He was home from basic training but due to report back soon. We were aggressively free at that moment.

We drove four hours up to Madison and stayed with his brother and his wife and the other couple attending. Madison was running full-tilt boogie, with a lot going on. We decided to prepare appropriately for the concert with mood adjustment to better appreciate the music. This consisted of marijuana, possibly some other chemicals, and something we hadn't tried yet, marijuana brownies. The concert was at the Coliseum, a short drive, we thought we were timing our ingestion perfectly. However, I overshot the mark considerably as we didn't realise the time delay or body high on edibles.

The concert was loud. Very, very loud. I couldn't believe it was only three people playing. We were close enough to see Jimi sweat. There were no lights, dancers or big production, just amplifiers and musicians and Jimi Hendrix a few feet away, creating a forcefield of music. It was assigned seating so there were folding chairs for us to sit on. However, I remember we stood for almost the whole concert, a challenge for me due to overshooting the mark.

At one point someone near us asked Jimi if he needed anything. He said, 'A joint', and lots were immediately thrown up on the stage. One close to him was lit and burning. He had been busted in Toronto a year before for possession. Jimi pinched his fingers together and started to reach down to pick one up but then said, 'No, can't do that'. My future brother-in-law had some juicy details from the contract with Adamany involving women and chemical support. However, I decline to tell it here. Not my story to tell.

I WAS THERE: GARY STEUCK

A couple of the guys I went to the 1968 Factory concert with were
my roommates in 1970 and they went to the show. I was significantly
short of funds, we had a great stereo that played all the time and
I was more into Dylan by then. But Hendrix's albums were in
the rotation. Their appraisal of the show was 'OK' and the most
experienced and astute was very saddened because he said at one
point Hendrix asked, 'Is this too loud?' or words to that effect, and
that it was obvious he was doing heroin or something similar by that
comment and the music. Jimi was dead in four months. My friend
was correct.

I WAS THERE: JAY SMITH, AGE 10

I heard he was coming to town. I hounded my mother and father
unmercifully to let me go. I hounded them for weeks. My mother
finally relented because it was going to be on a Saturday night and
not a school night. My father purchased four tickets - one for me, one
for my brother, one for the neighbour kid, and one for himself. It was
my first concert. When we arrived at the Coliseum, the kids all took
their seats and my father stood at the opening to the concourse. He
stood up there with the Dane County Sheriff. He was drinking beer.
When we arrived everyone was throwing beach balls and frisbees. We
were up on the second concourse, so could see it all. They dimmed
the lights for the opening act and for the first time I saw someone
smoking marijuana. We really didn't know what it was. They made
the attempt to pass it to us and we shook our heads – 'No'. Then the
opening act came out. I believe it was a band called Oz. It kept us
quite entertained.

The crowd was starting to get crazy and loud, chanting his name.
I didn't know until later that night that the Sheriff and police were
getting very nervous, because Sly and the Family Stone were to play
the night before but Sly stayed at a local strip-club getting drunk
all night and didn't make it to his own concert until midnight. He
played one song and left the stage. The crowd got irate and ended

up tearing the place apart. So the police were nervous that would happen again.

The lights started to dim. Someone from the audience yelled, 'Jimi, what can we give you?' Hendrix said, 'A joint.' In the blink of an eye the whole floor of the stage was covered in joints, completely white. He reached down to grab one and someone backstage motioned for him not to. Then he started his set. I sat mesmerised for an hour. I don't remember how long the concert lasted. I know I felt the tap on my shoulder saying it was time to go. We had to step over someone lying in the middle of the aisle with a pack of Marlboros on his forehead, yelling, 'Go Jimmy go'.

The reason we had left before the concert had finished was because of our age. At the end these shows would get a bit out of hand. On the way home, my father asked us not to tell our mother about the marijuana. A minute after we stepped into our house we told her about the marijuana. She rolled her eyes and said, 'That will be the last one of those you go to.' Since that time, I have been to many different concerts for a variety of artists. My father, still alive and 80 years old, would probably give you a completely different story of this concert.

I WAS THERE: CATON ROBERTS, 16

Early in the show, after the entire crowd had left their seats and stormed the stage to get the closest, most intimate view possible -a Seventies version of a mosh-pit - somebody a handful of rows into the crowd hollered out to Jimi, 'What can we give you?' and he answered, 'A joint.' The place was filled with the sweetness of swirling smoke. The instantaneous crowd response was that about 30 joints flew threw the air and landed on the stage. I was tripping on acid so it was pretty amazing to see the trails, if you get what I mean. But there were cops all over the place and he didn't pick any up. It was pretty funny.

I drove my 1964 Plymouth Valiant there. I had a little trouble finding my car after.

I WAS THERE: PAT NOLES

It was the night after Sly Stone came on stage two hours late and
was so wasted he announced after two songs he couldn't remember
the lyrics. It caused a riot. As a result, people were rather on edge
about Jimi's show. There was no need. He came on clear-headed
and played a great set. At one point, he said with a smile he 'could
really use a joint'. So it began raining joints on stage. He picked one
up, looked in the general direction of the cops offstage and said,
'I thought it was a cigarette, I swear to God'. He never lit it but
promptly launched into the next piece. I remember him announcing,
'Thank you for three great years.' It turned out to be prophetic. He
was gone three months later.

I WAS THERE: JOHN A GRIDE

This concert was memorable for many reasons. It was the first
I ever saw, the first time I ever smelled marijuana, the biggest
crowd I'd ever been in - the Coliseum was packed with about
10,000 people – and it was Hendrix! At 80 minutes, Hendrix's
performance was short by today's standards. And there was no
staging at all, just Hendrix, drummer Mitch Mitchell and bassist
Billy Cox up there playing. It's always fun telling people Hendrix
was my first concert.

It took place at the end of my freshman year of high school. A
couple of friends and I wanted to go, and somehow I convinced
Dad to give us a ride there and back. The Coliseum is a half-hour
from DeForest, so this was a big chunk out of Dad's Saturday night.
Well, I screwed up. Having no experience with concerts, I told him
the show would be over at 10.30pm, and that's when he should
drive back to the Coliseum and pick us up. The concert didn't end
until midnight. When we got back to the car there was Dad, having
been sat there for 90 minutes waiting. He was royally pissed off. I
can't say I blame him. The two hours he had planned to devote to
this errand had expanded to almost four. No wonder he was pissed!

As it happens, this is the last thing I remember doing with Dad. He died seven weeks later. He must have been really pissed off.

I WAS THERE: TOM HEIBER-COBB

We felt and still feel so fortunate we got to see this legend and master. My impressions were that he was burned out from all that time on the road, but he was still fantastic to see and so very skilled. I remember a blistering version of 'All Along the Watchtower' played by the support band, Savage Grace, and it was my first exposure to a whole shit-load of pot being smoked.

I WAS THERE: JAMES COBB, AGE 18

Both my brother and I were there. I was 18, Tommy 16. My sister bought the tickets. She had a friend who worked at the Coliseum box office, and just assumed we would want to go. An older brother gave me *Are You Experienced* a few years before for a Christmas present. The tickets were fifth-row centre, reserved seating.

Jimi would put his cigarette in the strings at the top of his guitar. He was just one cool dude on stage.

I WAS THERE: HT NELSON, AGE 16

He was amazing, but the thing I remember most about the entire show was the band who opened, Savage Grace. Not only were they very good, but they played 'All Along the Watchtower' so well that Hendrix didn't play it. I was impressed, or rather surprised. I recorded part of the concert on cassette. I'm not sure I have it any longer. I'll have to look in my old box of tapes.

I WAS THERE: CARL WELKE, AGE 17

What I do remember is that the house-lights were down and in the darkness we heard, 'I'd like to dedicate this song to all the men fighting in LA, New York, Chicago and - oh yeah – Vietnam!'

Then 'chunk-a-chuck-a chunka-' - the opening salvo from 'Machine Gun' and a single spot on the man himself. Freaking fantastic! My ears rang for two days!

I WAS THERE: WILLIAM HUTCHISON

It was a Saturday and the weather was a little cooler than average, about 50 degrees F. My friend Harold drove his parents' Dodge Dart, as he'd just got his licence. His girlfriend, Sherri, was also with us. We were sophomores at Madison's Lafollette High School, soaking up the music of artists like Hendrix, The Doors, Creedence, The Allman Brothers, Blind Faith, and the Stones. But we knew Hendrix was in a world of his own.

Some officials, be it the promoter or the fire marshal, announced that everyone on the floor would have to move back from the stage and open up the aisles. It didn't apply to us, as we were seated in the second concourse level, straight out from the stage. Every couple of minutes there would be a threat or plea made to the crowd, to back away from the stage. I remember them saying, 'Jimi doesn't want anyone to get hurt, so please move back.' We could tell it would be a while so the three of us went out to the inside hallway that circled the coliseum. Harold and Sherri were busy smooching, so I decided to take a little walk and have a cigarette. The hallway is curved and it wasn't long before I was alone. As I walked by a door marked 'Authorized Personnel Only', it opened and a black guy walked out. He was dressed in bright, flowing clothes, bell-bottoms and a colourful headband on his Afro. He looked left and right, then headed down the hallway in the opposite direction. I did a double-take and by the time I turned back to follow, he was gone. Up close, he was smaller than I expected. But it was without a doubt Jimi!

I WAS THERE: CHARLES CARPENTER, AGE 14

I went with a buddy, Ron Bard, a classmate at Sherman Junior High School. We were about to graduate from ninth grade and move up to big bad East Senior High. To be charitable, Ron and I were on the quiet, bookish side (I had lots of 'complexion problems') and were not at all the cool kids. I think we were the only Sherman kids to attend.

Madison at that time was a hotbed of protest against the Vietnam War, and related incursions into Laos and Cambodia. We would regularly smell tear gas blowing across Lake Mendota from the UW campus. Jimi Hendrix certainly fitted into the spirit of the times and Madison's hippy vibe.

I remember my Mom drove us out to the Coliseum and dropped us off. In a simpler time, it was easy to drive right up to the front door. She made sure we had a dime to call her from a payphone after the concert, and we jumped out of the old brown Chevy station wagon and into the Coliseum.

The Coliseum was the newest and biggest venue in town. We watched the UW hockey team play there for many years.

As for the concert, many thoughts and adjectives come to mind. The rendition of 'The Star-Spangled Banner' was especially thrilling and seemed to build on difficult times in the United States. I don't know if Jimi broke his guitar after one song, or if I've recreated that. Ron and I were greatly entertained by the smell of marijuana in the air, although we were very much on the straight and narrow.

After the show we pulled out the dime, called Mom and were whisked back home. It's always been a point of pride to tell my three kids I was there. I'm not sure they were sufficiently impressed, but it's a wonderful memory.

On 8 May 1970, Jimi performed two shows at the University of Oklahoma sporting an armband with a black K on it in memory of the four students shot dead by the National Guard at Kent State University four days earlier. 3,500 attended the first show and 5,500 the second.

OU FIELD HOUSE

8 MAY 1970, NORMAN, OKLAHOMA

I WAS THERE: RANDELL CHAPMAN, AGE 13

Hendrix was on his Band of Gypsys tour when I saw him at the OU Field House in Norman, since demolished. My brother was in college there and obtained tickets for myself and a classmate. He dropped us off and we went without parental supervision, unthinkable these days. Our tickets were on the very back row, just before the exterior windows, but we never saw those seats.

There were campus police guarding the doors that led to the floor seats. They were barely holding back the press of college students trying to get in. We ducked under them and they couldn't grab us without losing control of the crowd.

There was not a single empty seat on the floor. As we strode down the aisle, I became unsure of where we were going to end up. We got to the first row without finding an open seat. In those days, the front row ended several yards from the stage, so there was a huge gap of empty floor between the front row and the stage. Band of Gypsies were already playing. Their support band was Bloodrock, whose big hit was 'D.O.A.', a song about a victim of a fatal auto accident. They used Kustom amps, known for their tuck-and-roll upholstery. The amps had been moved to the side of the stage to make room for Hendrix's Marshall stacks.

When we got to the stage, my buddy noticed a gap between two of the Kustom amps large enough for us to squeeze into. That gap was

Randell and his brother had back row seats but ended up on stage

the first part of a maze that snaked through the side stage. As we felt our way through, the light and sound faded almost completely out, then became louder and brighter until we emerged at the side of the stage, only a few steps away from Billy Cox, the bass player for Cry of Love.

We stayed hidden until the song they were playing, 'Machine Gun', had ended. We asked if we could stay, and Mr Cox told us we could sit on that tuck and roll upholstery! We spent the rest of the show watching Jimi play the guitar behind his back, play with his teeth, and be the most amazing live artist I've ever seen. We screamed at him to pose for a pic, and he finally did. With his guitar held vertical, he went down on one knee, mouth wide open in a rock scream, just for us. My buddy snapped a pic with his Kodak Instamatic. It was absolutely over the top.

School started the following Monday, and my friend told everyone the story. I was walking from band practice to math class when three ninth graders pinned me to the wall and asked if the story was true. When I told them it was, they told me, 'You guys are both a couple of fucking liars!'

My friend showed up the next week with the pic, a glorious 2' x 3' testimony to our proximity to the Rock God. I was making the same walk from band to math class when the same dudes pinned me to the wall and said, 'Well, I guess you fuckers weren't lying after all.' I walked the rest of the way to math class on a cloud.

The Cry of Love tour ran from 25 April to 6 September 6, 1970, and saw Jimi playing 41 dates in the United States and Europe. The tour turned out to be the last on which Hendrix performed before his death in September, and featured many songs he was working on for double album *First Rays of the New Rising Sun*. Though the band did not feature original bassist Noel Redding, the trio of Hendrix, Mitch Mitchell (drums) and Billy Cox (bass) was often billed as 'The Jimi Hendrix Experience'.

WILL ROGERS AUDITORIUM

9 MAY 1970, FORT WORTH, TEXAS

I WAS THERE: RAY DUKE, AGE 15

I heard 'Foxy Lady' first on our Fort Worth AM radio as a 'Pick of the Week' in mid '67. It blew my mind as I had never heard guitar or a sound like that before. I immediately went out and bought the 45 with 'Hey Joe' on the B-side, which to me was just as amazing. I played that single even after it was so worn out that the surface noise was as loud as the music. It cracked but was still playable. My older sister heard the single and went out and bought me *Are You Experienced* the day it came out. 1967 was a great year for music but for this Beatles fan, Hendrix was the real thing.

The Jimi Hendrix Experience had been through Dallas Fort Worth a couple of times since '68 and I missed them every time. I was determined I wouldn't miss them this time. I had a steady girlfriend who wanted to go with me, plus she had a car! I bought the $5 tickets at the Will Rogers Auditorium box office.

On the night I was excited that we had pretty good seats. Bloodrock were the opener, our homegrown Fort Worth rock band starting to break out after their first album. We were excited to see them and they sounded good, but we were there for Jimi.

When Jimi came on, I was a little surprised to see Billy Cox as I'd heard Noel was back in the fold, but it was all good. Mitch was there. The crowd was electric, they started with 'Fire' and we were off. It was loud and glorious. I watched the band through binoculars. Mitch and Billy looked happy, both watching Jimi for cues. Jimi looked intense, only occasionally smiling. My best friend from school smuggled in his tiny reel-to-reel recorder and taped the show, which from where he was sounded horrible but was a lovely reminder of a good time in my life.

On our way home the brakes went on my girlfriend's car and we rear-ended someone.

I WAS THERE: RICK WARD, AGE 13

It was my birthday and I went by myself. I don't remember how I got my ticket. It was a full house and the music was loud. I saw Three Dog Night, Elton John, The Who, Sly and the Family Stone, and two or three more in the same place back in the day.

Everyone in the crowd was smoking a joint. I was sat close to the stairs going in the underground. Three men came out from the tunnel before the show started and stopped to talk. They were concerned that Jimi would not show up because he was late and concerned they would lose millions on this concert. Will Rogers holds 5,500 people and he had a bad record for not showing up. But he did, and all was well.

TEMPLE UNIVERSITY

16 MAY 1970, PHILADELPHIA, PENNSYLVANIA

I WAS THERE JIM CURCIO, AGE 16

I saw him at Temple University Stadium, which no longer exists. He was sharing the ticket with The Grateful Dead, Steve Miller Band and - I think - Cactus. I remember him playing his guitar and the sound was awesome, like it was from another planet. But I also remember I thought his skin looked like it was yellow, probably from drug abuse.

WAIKIKI SHELL

31 MAY 1970, HONOLULU, HAWAII

I WAS THERE: BRYANT SERONIO

He had concerts scheduled for the Friday and Saturday nights, and my tickets were for Saturday. For Friday I heard he came out on stage, strummed his guitar and then walked off. This almost caused a riot, so the Shell offered everyone with a ticket the option to come on Saturday, and then he gave a free concert at the Shell on the Sunday as well. His concert on the Saturday met all my expectations. I wasn't too high to not enjoy every second. I wish he never left us and, throughout the years after, I found a little Jimi in Robin Trower.

ROBERTS MUNICIPAL STADIUM

10 JUNE 1970, EVANSVILLE, INDIANA

I WAS THERE: CLIFF PAYNE, AGE 16

It was an unforgettable evening. I remember our mother told us Jimi Hendrix was going to be in town and saying, 'I'm going to buy you tickets because you'll remember this concert for the rest of your life.' She was exactly right. The tickets cost $2.98. That was pretty cheap. You'd spend more than that on parking on a concert in 2018.

I was born in Harlem but grew up in the Midwest. It was his last tour. He was going through a major re-evaluation of himself musically and that was obvious at the concert. People were calling him 'the wild man of guitar' and he'd come to not like that.

At school I played violin in the orchestra, so I played in that stadium many times before I saw Hendrix and it never even occurred to me that night that I had performed in that place myself.

This was back in the day when everything was open seating. The stadium probably seated 10 to 15,000. The doors were all locked and the crowd was building up outside. It was shaped like a bowl. They opened the doors and a stream of people ran down the steps, seeing who could get to the stage first. My brother Don and I made it to very close to the stage, maybe 10ft away. We'd just seen James Brown there and a slew of other concerts.

One of the main things I remember is that he wasn't jumping about the stage. He basically just stood in one spot and played, and got a lot of flak for that. I remember reading a review a day or so later and they were calling him, 'The former King of rock'. I just went, 'Wait a minute, just because the guy was not jumping up and down and doing all kinds of things.' The only physical thing I remember him doing was that he had this one thing where he put the guitar between his legs and he'd squat.

But if they were expecting to see the Jimi Hendrix from the Monterey Pop Festival - that was not the Hendrix in terms of his antics. But in terms of his presence? My goodness, his presence and the power of his guitar. People say you could always identify BB King by one note he played and that note was always so powerful. And Hendrix was like that. One note just went right through you. It was very powerful.

The whole aura of the concert for me was that he wanted to be taken seriously as a musician. Not as a wild man doing crazy things with guitar. That's what I distinctly remember. He was tuning up briefly and one of the first things he said when he came out on stage, he was talking about the sound and said, 'We want to play for your hearts, not for your ears.'

The band had Billy Cox on bass and Mitch Mitchell on drums and I remember he was having equipment problems, because he played 'Machine Gun' and tried to get that Fillmore East New Year's Eve version, where the solo starts with this long note that sustains seemingly forever. He tried to get it and couldn't get it to sustain.

I remember when he started playing 'The Star Spangled Banner' I could still hear people on the outside of the stadium banging on the doors, trying to get in. There was probably only a dozen, but it seemed like there was 100 people. My mother told me that when the concert was over she saw all the folks still trying to get in. They didn't have tickets but wanted in anyway.

I found out about his death on Walter Cronkite. They cut in and Walter said, 'Rock musician Jimi Hendrix was found dead today'. I remember being totally stunned, so stunned that I made a makeshift black armband that I wore to my high school the next day. I remember I got complaints that I did that – 'Oh, Jimi Hendrix was a drug dealer' and 'What are you doing wearing that black armband?'

I was very impressed with Mitch Mitchell. I'd never seen a rock drummer play drums like that. It was like a combination of jazz and rock and I never once saw his face. They had long hair just flying everywhere and he had his head down the entire night, playing like his life depended on it. Which kind of makes sense, because at that time the powers that be were trying to work out a deal with Miles Davis and Hendrix to do something together musically. One of the influences Hendrix had on Miles was that after hearing Hendrix he decided he had to have that kind of a guitar player in his band, playing a Stratocaster to get that sound. I saw Miles Davis in 1984 and sure enough, he had that Hendrix vibe in all his bands of the last 10 years of his life.

When Hendrix died, the only celebrity other than Mitch Mitchell and Noel Redding who were there was Miles Davis. And Miles writes extensively about that funeral and how embarrassing it was - the preacher kept mispronouncing Hendrix's name and … no one ever thinks they're going to die suddenly aged 27.

I had a band called Brothers and Friend. It was a high school power trio based on the music of Jimi Hendrix, largely from the *Band of Gypsys* album. We played everything on that album, and some things that weren't.

Right after that Hendrix concert I asked my Mom if she would buy me a Fender Stratocaster, and she did. I've seen many guitarists in my time. Rock and jazz guitarists. I stood about four feet in front of Richie Blackmore. I still have some wonderful 110 photos, which look as if they were taken yesterday from that concert. But the Hendrix concert is the one that stands out.

I WAS THERE: DON PAYNE, AGE 15

My brother and I played in a rock band. Our mother bought him a Stratocaster and he played and dressed like Jimi and used to play with his teeth. And we listened to everything Jimi Hendrix did. We heard he was coming to Evansville and we had to be there. It was three weeks after my 15th birthday.

I remember the tickets were $5.55. We were in the second row. We thought it was going to be the Band of Gypsys playing with him, but it was a combination of the Band of Gypsys and the Experience, because Billy Cox was on bass and Mitch Mitchell was on drums. I was hoping it was going to be Buddy Miles.

It was a really big deal. He had the big stack of Marshall amps. He had four or five Stratocasters and when a string broke they just brought him another Stratocaster. He played very well. He was kind of subdued, but the band sounded good. He played 'Foxy Lady' and 'The Star Spangled Banner', and when he played that everybody stood on their seats. It was the last song he played.

Don and brother Cliff were huge Hendrix fans

My brother and I started listening to rock music and particularly to Jimi Hendrix and were so taken with what he was doing that Cliff decided to play guitar and, being the dutiful younger brother, I said, 'Well, I'll learn how to play bass.' His models were the two Jimmys – Jimi Hendrix and Jimmy Page. A lot of what he learned he learnt from Jimi's first album in this country, *Are You Experienced*.

We didn't hear any other guitar player doing anything he did. There were no black musicians playing rock music at that time. When Hendrix came along some African-Americans thought he was trying to be white, playing rock music. But the type of rock music he did was totally different from anybody else, so he influenced us.

We listened religiously, hours on hours, and I remember Cliff practising six to eight hours a day just to try and imitate him. Then we put together a group called Brothers and Friend. We were living at that time in southern Indiana and were part of a group that toured around that area throughout high school for about four years. We toured in southern Indiana, southern Illinois and northern Kentucky for several years. We played everywhere. We did all kinds of different things. We did Hendrix and Black Sabbath, which was kind of unusual because most African-American bands did soul music – The Temptations, things like that. But we did rock. And there weren't too many black groups that did Jethro Tull. We were very unusual but were also very popular.

Jimi influenced me as a bass player. When Jimi played the Stratocaster left-handed, he played it upside down. That's what I did to my bass. To this day, I still play bass left-handed with the strings upside down. Some of the things Hendrix could do we thought he could do because of the way the strings were arranged, upside down on his guitar.

I was driving in a car when I heard he had passed. We were just in shock. 'He's not 30 yet!' Then when they told us how he died, it was like, 'Are you kidding me?'

We heard a rumour that he was going to get together with Emerson, Lake and Palmer, which would have been great because we were also ELP fans. He was so innovative in his 20s. What would he have been like in his 30s and 40s? His stuff sounds as fresh today as it did when he hit the scene in 1967. Here we are 50 years later and still nobody is able to duplicate what he did.

I WAS THERE: ROBERT B WALKER, AGE 16

My first encounter with Jimi Hendrix was through a high school friend who, like I, was not into top-40 music, but he shared with me his copy of the *Axis: Bold as Love* album.

On my 16th birthday, I was given the *Smash Hits* album. Later I acquired the *Are You Experienced* album, leading me to get *Electric Ladyland*.

I bought two tickets and took my girlfriend Karen, who still remembers the concert and the seat row, for the concert, paying top price: $5.50 each, Orchestra, Section A, Row 11, Seats 1 and 2 (our seats were 11 rows from the stage).

The concert might have been a so-so performance, especially according to Hendrix's standards, but who cares? Jimi Hendrix was in Evansville!

The whole audience endured the opening act (I don't remember who they were) but when Hendrix came out, the electricity was jolting every seat and everyone was standing up, applauding and screaming. Jimi simply laughed and said his opening greeting, 'How ya'll doing, boys and girls?' and off he went into his first song.

There were technical problems that night: with the spotlights, problems with his amp and with the electrical power to his stage equipment. He bowed out of the spotlight while he and his roadies tried to tinker with his amp, but a spotlight followed him while he needed some privacy and he became angry. He gave a scowl at the light and flipped the bird at the spotlight operator. The light went out and Mitch and Billy carried the several musical measures while Jimi got his sound right again.

It was an epiphany, especially in Evansville, Indiana. That concert was –and is — *the* concert of my life, just because he was, and is, the ex-nihilo guitarist, ever.

CIVIC CENTER

13 JUNE 1970, BALTIMORE, MARYLAND

I WAS THERE: ERIC DYE, AGE 14

I was two months shy of my 15th birthday. I explained to my dad that I just had to see Hendrix and he kindly drove a carload of kids from metro DC to Baltimore and sat next to me in the balcony with a bird's eye view of the stage. I'm a drummer so I could see what hero Mitch Mitchell was doing. They closed with 'Voodoo Child (Slight Return)'. Wow!

My friends and I were precocious young ones and were tripping on Orange Sunshine acid. It was an early voyage for me, but it seemed the right way to see Jimi. In retrospect, it was kinda reckless, but at the moment it was fantastic and perfect. I don't know if my dad was aware or not, though our pupils would certainly have been as large as saucers.

As we walked to the car after the show, I set a quick pace with my dad. Behind us a young lady was looking skyward and repeatedly saying 'the moon, the moon!' as another friend tried to get her to keep walking toward the car.

I later spoke with Billy Cox after one of the 'Experience Hendrix' shows, and he said he remembered the Baltimore show.

I WAS THERE: MARV EGOLF

I first met Jimi Hendrix late one Sunday night in May 1967, in the living room of my mother and stepfather's apartment, across from the couch that passed for my bed. School was next morning, but each Sunday night after my parents retired for the evening. WCAO, the AM top-40 radio station, featured the 'Kirby Scott Underground Hour', a programme that featured 'underground' music from 11pm until midnight. Sandwiched in their playlist of top-40, pop and prevailing soul music (Motown, Stax, Philly, James Brown, etc.) was this hourly slice of explosive new music each week.

In the darkness, I would sidle over to the wooden console 'entertainment centre' - a turntable, AM-FM radio and reel-to-reel tape recorder combo unit - where I would place an ear to one of the speakers, the volume turned down low to avoid detection by my parents, both channels panned to that one speaker to listen to some incredible, unimaginable music. Early in the programme, Kirby ran three or four songs in sequence without commercial interruption. The last song in the sequence started low, quietly and rose to an amazing crescendo, introducing me to 'Foxy Lady' and an entirely new dimension of sound and story and life. Later in the show, he started a sequence with 'Purple Haze'.

Transformation! That night, my life changed in every way. I was fortified and emboldened. I was ready. And three years later I got to see Jimi at Baltimore Civic Center.

BOSTON GARDEN

27 JUNE 1970, BOSTON, MASSACHUSETTS

I WAS THERE: BOB FALANGA

The third time I saw Jimi was at the Boston Garden, three months before Jimi passed. I was with John Narducci and our girlfriends. The opening acts were Cactus and Illusion. My father was with Jimi whenever he appeared in the New England area. At the

Boston Garden my father told me Jimi was really a nice guy but there were a lot of drugs involved.

The Second Atlanta International Pop Festival took place from 3-5 July 1970, held in a soya bean field adjacent to the Middle Georgia Raceway. Tickets for the festival were priced $14 but like Woodstock, it became a free event when the promoters threw open the gates after large crowds outside began chanting 'Free, free, free. Music belongs to the people.' The line-up included The Allman Brothers Band, Mountain, Johnny Winter, Spirit, B.B. King, Mott the Hoople, Ten Years After, Procol Harum, and Grand Funk Railroad.

Jimi performed at around midnight on 4 July to the largest US audience of his career, presenting his unique rendition of the 'Star-Spangled Banner' to accompany the celebratory fireworks display.

ATLANTA INTERNATIONAL POP FESTIVAL

4 JULY 1970, BYRON, GEORGIA

I WAS THERE: CAROLE BECKER PARKER

I still have the original festival programme. That festival had the
biggest influence on my life. I was in college and went with friends.
I'd been listening to Jimi at least a couple of years, but seeing him in
person … well, there are words to describe it. His death devastated
me. No one could copy him. He was truly one of a kind. Even the
shows about him don't do him justice. I feel lucky just getting to see
him in person - something I will never forget.

I WAS THERE: JACK BORNSTEIN

The Allman Brothers were the host band. I crashed on a blanket
after a long hot day in the middle of a soybean field and a buddy
woke me to tell me Jimi had hit the stage. The feeling was surreal, a
year after Woodstock. Jimi, not Eric, was God.

I WAS THERE: LIZZIE BOWMAN

Interior Georgia in July is a blistering place to be. But there we were
by the tens and tens of thousands. Tents and bodies sheltering in the
pecan groves through the day, waiting for the night shade and to dive
back into the body electric of our peers seeking the holy baptism
of our religion. Hot as biscuits. Hot as firecrackers. It was July 4th
weekend, 1970. That Saturday night, the holiest of the holy would
walk out on a stage under the gaze of the assembled and, goddamn,
were we ever assembled! The glorious wave of tribe, of burning young
desires and dreams - both audience and the bands who played before
us - met their raison d'etre, the explosion of Jimi, after laying the fire
all weekend with the chooglin', unfolding glory of the build- up bands.

The Allmans never sounded so authentic to me as when they blazed in the July heat of their Georgia, just a moonlight mile down the road from Capricorn Studios and the Macon farm.

Forgive me if my timeline is hazy in regard to the exact set. To this day, it exists in my head as more a mythical communion I was able to swim in. Some very psychedelic waters, to be sure, but still yet waters I swam in from recordings and the burgeoning world of 'underground' FM radio. A little more strut, a little more digging into their best groove possible, but still Jimi's recognizable stuff. Until the night split open with the shrieking, bent, tortured howls of 'The Star Spangled Banner'. It raged and awed.

In that moment, that perfect moment, Jimi told us everything could be reimagined and what was old and staid could be reborn as protest fit for our fire. It was the thread that held us together that night. And always would so. Baptised in a blaze of Mr Jimi that night under the fireworks.

Paul Cutrell in cut off shorts at Atlanta Pop

I WAS THERE: PHIL CUTRELL

I did not see him live but I heard him. I was in our tent having sex with a girl when he came on stage. I had to make a decision to come or go. I decided to stay. He sounded good though. I am also on a still pic in the Hendrix film of that performance. I'm the one with the cut-off shorts, no shirt and black hair with mutton chops.

I WAS THERE: CHANDLER ALBRECHT EDMUNDS, AGE 18

I saw him twice, once at Virginia Beach Dome and again at the 1970 Atlanta Pop Festival. I went with friends. We travelled from VA to GA in a VW Beetle. He was amazing. He played 'The Spangled Banner' amidst a display of fireworks. The Allman Brothers Band also played and there was speculation as to whether Duane Allman met Jimi at that festival. Gregg Allman, in his book, said of Jimi at Atlanta Pop II something like, 'I thought he could have played better'. I thought Jimi was awesome, but I guess when your brother is Duane Allman you're pretty critical.

I WAS THERE: GEORGE IRVING

In 1968, while in the Air Force stationed at Clark Air Force Base in the Philippines, I had two nights of some kind of a fever. I sweated so bad that I had to find a bunk that wasn't being used. On the third night I'm laying there listening to Armed Forces Radio. This song came on that I had heard before, but not by this band. The song was 'Hey Joe'. As it played I could feel the fever flow out of my body. I was dumbfounded at the feeling that had just happened to me. It took me a couple of days to find out who the hell this Jimi Hendrix was.

George heard 'Hey Joe' on Armed Forces Radio

Fast forward to 1970. I'm stationed

at Langley Air Force Base in Virginia. I just got back from a 90-day TDY (temporary duty) at Mildenhall in England and was told that a party was going to happen the following weekend. I go with some friends and meet a few others. I started to talk about a festival that was going to happen in Atlanta the next weekend. By the end of the party, a guy called Ruben Norman came up to me and asked if I was thinking about going. At that time, I hadn't really thought about it. Then, talking to Ruben for about a half-hour, we decided we would hitchhike from Hampton, Virginia to Atlanta that next weekend. The next Friday midday, four of us met to start out. Before we got a mile down Mercury Boulevard in Hampton, two of the guys said maybe this wasn't a good thing and dropped out. So it was just Ruben and me on our way.

I'm not sure how many rides it took to get to Atlanta, but we got there early in the morning. By then you could see cars with signs saying 'going to the festival' so it was easy to get a ride to the site in Byron, Georgia. We missed the bands on Friday night but bands started to play from around noon on the Saturday, the 4th of July.

Jimi came on stage going on midnight or so and started to play with fireworks going off in the background. I was thinking back a few years to when I first heard him while in the Philippines and how the fever flowed out of my body, while not knowing who he was. This whole thing was so magical to me.

On Monday morning, after seeing Richie Havens sing 'Here Comes the Sun' while the sun was coming up, we started walking out of the concert site and my friend Ruben saw a guy he knew from Hampton. We found out he was on his way back to Virginia and had a van with plenty of room for us, so we made it back home that day.

A few weeks later, my squadron went to Rhine-Main Air Force Base in Frankfurt for a 90-day TDY. One day I'm walking past a newspaper stand and see Jimi's picture on the front page of the *Stars and Stripes*. Of course, I stopped to look at what the story was, and I was heartbroken to see Jimi had passed. I'm still heartbroken to this day.

I WAS THERE: BOB GILKER, AGE 19

I went with three friends and we drove there in my Simca, a tiny French car. The car itself was a piece of shit, but got over 50 miles to the gallon and the seats inside folded down to make a bed, handy for a poor 19-year-old. Gasoline was about 25c per gallon and only cost us about $8 for the trip. Unfortunately, the car had a tendency to overheat unless the heater was turned on full force, so we were driving through 100 degrees weather with the heater on full blast. The festival had an incredible line-up of musicians, and Hendrix was scheduled for midnight on July 4th. He ended coming on later than that and I was pretty high by then. It was an amazing show and the highlight was 'The Star Spangled Banner', as he'd done at Woodstock the previous summer, backed by what was billed as the largest fireworks show ever in the South.

I WAS THERE: MATTHEW E JAMES, AGE 23

I was a college graduate from Fort Valley State College. A few friends and I were camping in nearby woods for two days, warmed up by The Allman Brothers and others. It was a great experience with an integrated group of young people, black and white and peaceful. Seeing him live was an experience I will never forget. His singing and playing was phenomenal. I was already a fan and that performance made him one of the greatest players ever.

Matthew had The Allman Brothers as his Atlanta warm-up act

I WAS THERE: TIM KANE

After seeing him in 1968 I saw him again at the Atlanta Pop Festival a couple of years later, a few months before he died. He stood motionless on the stage and seemed quite a different person. Thanks to the 'atmosphere' of those times, my memories are somewhat clouded.

I WAS THERE: MICHAEL PIERCE, AGE 18

I saw Jimi Hendrix in 1970 and it changed my life. I grew up in Macon, Georgia. Johnny Jenkins was an old blues guitar player from Macon and he played his guitar left-handed and upside down. The story goes that when Jimi was about 13 his grandma lived there and he came to Macon and met Johnny, who was a big inspiration to Jimi. Little Richard is from Macon too, and Jimi played with Richard.

In high school we were listening to all that soul stuff. In '68, when Jimi released that first Experience album, one of my neighbour friends had that record and that's all I needed to take me over the edge. So Jimi was my hero then and in '69 Duane Allman was discovered and he moved to Macon and then Duane just filled all my pores.

When they had the first Atlanta festival in '69, my Momma wouldn't let me go. But in '70, I had graduated from high school. There were some hippies older than me working with the health department and they were hanging out with all these young kids and getting them on the right path, and they set up the OD tents out there at the festival. I was asked if I wanted to go out there and work the tents. And so I did.

I was like, 'What the hell is going on here?', because everybody was tripping. Everybody was on acid. I asked this guy I was working with, 'What's the deal here?' And he said, 'You see that purple tent down there? Go ask that guy down there what the deal is.'

I went down to that purple tent and there was a guy down there that had this purple haze. That was my first experience of acid. I went back on up to the OD tent and just took a bed. Then at some point towards the evening the guys running this OD tent came over and said, 'Michael, come on, you gotta go with us'. I got up off that cot and we went outside and there were 500,000 people there. So the five of us held hands going out through the crowd to make it to the backstage area. We had backstage passes and went around to the back of the stage and they put us right down in front of the stage. Jimi was about 15ft away. I was, 'Wow!' He had that fringe thing going on and it blew my mind. That moment right there, seeing Jimi, just took me onto the other side.

I went over and helped unload the helicopter when they brought Richie Havens in. I ran into Richie some years ago in Athens, Georgia and said, 'You know, I've met you before'. He said, 'Oh really? Where?' I said, 'The Atlanta Pop Festival.' And he went, 'Oh man, that was a good one.'

When I got home from the Atlanta Pop Festival my Mom knew I'd been out, staying up all hours. She's 92 years old now. I've told her all the stories and she says, 'You're crazy.'

I WAS THERE: JAYNE KELL

He put in a great performance and played 'Star Spangled Banner' while people were skinny-dipping in the fountain! I was angry as hell when he died. I took it personally, because I loved his music and felt cheated I wouldn't get to see where it would go. I was and remain a true Jimi fan.

Jayne saw people skinny-dipping as Jimi played 'The Star Spangled Banner'

THE SECOND ANNUAL
ATLANTA INTERNATIONAL
POP FESTIVAL
JULY 3-4-5

X: THE DAY I WAS THERE

I WAS THERE: JOHN NEWSOME

It was really hot and dry and attended by well over 100,000 people. Like so many others, I dropped LSD, better to 'experience' the event. An hour or two after I 'dosed' I lay shivering - from fever, reaction to the drug or just plain fear as he began to play. I began thinking of President Nixon's hatred of all the dirty, long-haired, anti-war 'peaceniks' and realised how vulnerable we were, gathered together, and how easily we could be annihilated by Nixon's death planes. I was expecting to have bombs raining down on our heads. I was truly terrified. Fortunately the moment passed, and I eventually came back to some grasp of reality and hung on, feeling his music course through me and him shining like a diamond on that stage.

I WAS THERE: MICHAEL PETRUZZI

In 1969 and 1970 I went to the Atlanta Pop Festivals. The '69 show was a blur. But the '70 show was great. Being in Georgia, fireworks were everywhere. We were ducking the fireworks. There were Roman candle duels. I remember meeting a girl on the way from the campground to the stage area. She had a medics' shirt on. We started chatting and ending up in the middle of the crowd, standing on a VW Beetle. We jumped up and down during Jimi's performance and then I remembered we were on top of some person's car. What was a VW doing in the middle of the crowd? I want to apologise to the owner of that VW.

I WAS THERE: ED TOMOLONIUS

At the second Atlanta Pop Festival, a bag of candy bars represented the only food I had left after consuming the ham sandwiches my mother packed for me to take along. It was extremely hot that day, even for central Georgia in July, and I remember that local yokels were selling bagged ice for $5 to $10.

I WAS THERE: RODNEY RIVERS, AGE 19

He seemed to me to be a deep down beautiful individual who got caught up in a world which did not give back to him what he was willing to give; and it seems apparent to me that he did not know to what source he could find true happiness. Like an addict ever chasing the elusive dragon which provided temporary relief and a deceptive source of satisfaction, he could never again find 'the feeling' from his earlier experimentations. Thus, his constant experimentation and searching led him to the complete dead-end which concluded his time on Earth. It's sad that he, like so many others of our time, were constantly searching for that spiritual high which would never produce or fulfil their expectations.

MIAMI JAI ALAI FRONTON

5 JULY 1970, MIAMI, FLORIDA

I WAS THERE: JOHN MASCARO

I remember climbing on the stage, with others, and being perhaps less than 15ft away from Jimi. At one point he looked directly at me.

RANDALL'S ISLAND

17 JULY 1970, NEW YORK, NEW YORK

I WAS THERE: BOB GUERRIN

 The last time I saw Jimi live was at the New York Pop Festival, which was originally a three-day show but some asshole radicals

demanded money and other things from the producers so it was
reduced to one day. However, Jethro Tull, Grand Funk Railroad and
Hendrix played. That day we all dropped some incredibly potent
mescaline and were very fucked up. Hendrix was great but the
atmosphere at the concert was very tense. There were 30,000 people
there and it was a hot sunny day.

I believe he only played one more concert in America. By
then I was heavily immersed in The Grateful Dead and took my
girlfriend (now my wife of 43 years) to her first Dead show. It was
18 September 1970, the day Jimi died. It was so weird, as they
remembered Jimi that night.

SPORTS ARENA

25 JULY 1970, SAN DIEGO, CALIFORNIA

I WAS THERE: TOM ARENDT, AGE 19

I was finishing high school and working full-time at the local TV
station in Alexandria, Minnesota so missed Jimi's show in Madison,
Wisconsin. But me and two other guys made a 4,000-mile round-
trip by motorcycle from Alexandria to San Diego, where my older
brother was a US naval petty officer on shore duty at a San Diego
base school called BE&E (Basic Electricity and Electronics. We were
crashing his place and he, his wife and their four young children were
making it seem like we were family.

The trip lasted 40 days and it was memorable, with the Hendrix
concert being just one of the highlights. We stayed in Denver, Colorado
for five to seven days, including July 4th, and stayed with my brother and
family in San Diego for 10 days, leaving just after the Hendrix concert.
The rest of the time was spent on the road and never staying overnight
in a hotel. We slept in cow pastures, next to Native American tents in the
Grand Canyon, in the middle of a salt flat in Utah and even one night
- for protection - in a Colorado jail cell. Even in those early days, for
someone from rural Minnesota, Jimi Hendrix was a big deal. I just didn't
realize at the time how good he was and how short his life would be.

Now, 47 years does a lot to dull the memory, but my older brother purchased three tickets at the Navy exchange, one for each of the motorcycle dudes camping in his Navy-provided apartment living room. The three of us went to a clothing store and each purchased a special shirt for the night, since our travelling clothes weren't what we thought was appropriate for a concert. It was the very first I would attend and I was very excited by the opportunity. I can't remember what my friends picked out, but I went off the deep end, selecting a white lace shirt. Yup, an all-white lace, long-sleeve shirt, one of those late Sixties fashion mistakes. I don't know what happened to that shirt and have no idea if I even put it in my bags for the trip home.

My brother probably drove us there and picked us up later. I've asked him but he says his memory is even foggier than mine - he had a drinking problem at the time, one I was oblivious to. I remember very little of the actual concert except that the crowd was huge and we sat on the ground floor in the arena, midway back from the stage. The music was great but not being tall I saw very little of Jimi. Not long after he started playing, the proverbial joint was offered to the three of us and we partook of that offer. We weren't traveling with pot because we were so broke and were concerned the cops would hassle three guys on motorcycles. I can't say we got especially stoned, but I believe there was a good buzz from the few tokes we took. That's about all I recall, expect the status that comes from being able to let friends know through the years that I saw Jimi Hendrix in concert less than two months before his untimely death. Which is almost as good as relating that about three years later I would myself be in the Navy and had the opportunity to see Led Zeppelin twice in a week, once in San Diego and once in LA.

I WAS THERE: ANTONIO CASTRO, AGE 17

His old Army bass player friend played that night. Mitch Mitchell was on drums. Cat Mother and The All Night Newsboys were the opening act. I remember being very bored by that band. There was seating on the arena floor. During the break, I noticed people walking up to the edge of the stage. I decided to go down and check out the stage equipment. Hendrix played out of three Marshall stacks. I believe his army buddy played out of three Marshall stacks as well. Mitch had these huge monitors to the left and right of him. They looked like they were five feet tall.

I WAS THERE: BEA GREEN

It was July of 1970 and I was visiting my great aunt in San Ysidro, California when I read in the San Diego newspaper that Jimi Hendrix would be playing. I called my friend Carolina asking if she would like to go see him. Since she had a vehicle, it was imperative that she go. Her having agreed, I went into Chula Vista and bought the tickets. We got there while the opening acts were playing so I really don't remember much about them. We went in, found our seats and from somewhere behind us a voice announced, 'Jimi Hendrix'. The packed stadium erupted in screaming, clapping and general hysteria.

Of course, the massive amounts of weed being smoked may have contributed to the level of elation we reached. He played a song and then, after it was finished, proceeded to tune his guitar. He said he had to take care of our ears. Well that got a huge rise out of the audience. He was doing a really fine job of it prior to tuning it. When he spoke to the audience it was as if he were speaking to you alone.

He took us on a rollercoaster ride of unbelievable riffs that only Hendrix could play with those very long fingers of his. In my experience of concert-going, it was a premiere concert. The only other band to achieve that height was Led Zeppelin who I also saw in San Diego.

I WAS THERE: BARBARA SCHETTINI-BURTON

I saw Jimi a month before he died, in San Diego. We met a group of Navy guys who got us tickets. He was absolutely incredible. He played his guitar like no one I've ever seen before. If my memory serves me correctly he walked out with a joint in his hand!

The state-of-the-art Electric Lady Studios in New York, opened with a party on 26 August 1970, the night before Jimi was due to fly back to England to play the Isle of Wight festival.

Hendrix retreated to the steps outside the studio, where he met young singer-songwriter Patti Smith. 'Out came Jimi and sat next to me. And he was so full of ideas; the different sounds he was going to create in this studio, wider landscapes, experiments with musicians and new soundscapes. All he had to do was get back to England, play the festival and get back to work...'

EAST AFTON FARM

26 – 31 AUGUST 1970, ISLE OF WIGHT FESTIVAL, ISLE OF WIGHT, UK

The Isle of Wight Festival was held between 26 and 30 August 1970 at Afton Down, near the village of Freshwater on the west of the Isle of Wight. Attendance was estimated at up to 700,000 people. Preceding festivals in 1968 and 1969 had built up a good reputation, with the 1969 festival securing Bob Dylan's first appearance since his 1966 motorcycle accident and subsequent disappearance from live performance.

The Jimi Hendrix Experience were given top billing to close Sunday's proceedings. Other acts included The Doors, The Who, Joni Mitchell, Free, Miles Davis, Chicago, Ten Years After, Sly and the Family Stone, and Emerson Lake and Palmer. It was to be Jimi's last scheduled UK live performance.

An electrician working backstage on the night recounts a nervous Jimi asking how the crowd were just moments before he went on: 'There's over 500,000, they've all come to see you.' Jimi: 'How does 'God Save The Queen' go?'

I WAS THERE: CHARLES EVEREST

I lived quite close and I'd already built up quite a good reputation with the BBC, where I'd won an international TV award for work I did with them, and apparently the organisers knew about me. They wanted me to vet applications from television, radio, and media companies from all over the world, which I did as a voluntary arrangement and, as a result they asked if there was something they could do for me. I said I'd like to be able to photograph the performances from the stage as I didn't want to be down in the press area, and they agreed. That's how I became involved in photographing all the artists (or most of them). In some cases I shot them backstage, or just listening to and watching other performers. I got very little sleep, maybe an hour or so a day. (I used) just 35mm mostly, I did have a Hasselblad which I used very occasionally. I had three or four cameras each set up for different uses, I had one for black and white but didn't shoot very many black and white pictures.

I slept wherever I could …. anywhere on the site. I was present for the duration of the festival. Jim Morrison was one who controlled everything concerning his performance. We only had one conversation and it was quite a friendly one. He wanted the lights to be really low but he did allow a little bit of extra lighting, which enabled me to take one really good picture. I did take others but only with the (low) lighting he'd specified; it was quite difficult.

I took over one hundred photos of Jimi performing and there

were times when I felt he seemed quite weary. I think it was tiredness more than anything. One of the things we talked about was when I said to him, 'I don't really want to shoot any of the antics you do, whatsoever' and he said to me, 'That's the hardest part of my life, doing what I need to do to attract attention and to keep it going.'

He told me he was going to Denmark for a break and just a few weeks later he was dead. I'd like to say I had a lot more to do with him, but I was so busy with everything else. All these years later I feel I was privileged in some way to be there.

I WAS THERE: ALAN EGFORD

With the festival five minutes by bike up the road, I found plenty of employment erecting fences, siting waste bins, heaving stuff from here to there, acting as a gofer for anyone and everyone.

Come the event I struck gold. Someone I knew well was one of the main electricians - he'd go on to festival fame as photographer Chris Weston. He got me a job as security on the backstage press area. With transient staff being what they were, especially with a rock festival happening 20ft above you, I quickly 'graduated' to I/C backstage press security, being the only one mostly there. This quickly morphed into checking all the passes at one of the backstage entrances. Journos to the left and round to the front please, roadies straight through please. I had a clear view straight through the stage, about 10ft from whoever happened to be left-hand side of a band. A good spot to share with Pete Townsend and Paul Kossoff among the many.

So to the early hours of Monday 31st August. By then it was impossible to predict within around two hours what time any act would actually play. The whole backstage area had become increasingly busy by six on Sunday evening and the press arena was jammed. Hendrix was in town!

A quick side-note: since being declared a free festival, the Hell's Angels had taken over security. Again I'd 'lucked out', and the 20 stone monster who replaced me - Stomp, from the Gravesend

Chapter - decided he 'liked' me so I could stay, but I had to behave as he 'didn't do drugs.' What were the chances of that on the Isle of Wight in those heady days?

What he did do were vast quantities of bitter, cheese sandwiches and Woodbines, all of which suited me fine and which he produced at no cost for both of us from somewhere for 48 hours straight.

So, Hendrix was in town and it was a fascinating experience from close up. Most real stars aren't egos on legs and Hendrix, Mitch Mitchell and Billy Cox had been up on stage for minutes before most people took in that reality. Hendrix was kind and gentle to all around him, a feat in itself given the technical issues surrounding him. An understatement - there were problems getting any of the clarity a guitarist like Jimi both needed and deserved, and security announcements intermittently blared from his speakers.

'Excuse us while we tune up,' was his opening. Flowing orange kaftan and matching flares, shimmering and sparkling. A couple of chords and he hit that wah wah pedal. Only one man in the world sounded like that, and we were sold! Everyone! It really is Hendrix, here, with us on our little island and the world watching!

'Stand up and sing for your brothers and your country,' he said, followed by, 'It might make this sound better,' almost under his breath, as if accusing the audience, whose sort of 'We want, we want, give us free' attitude he didn't seem impressed with. 'God Save the Queen' - great choice and great soundcheck. Then a two-minute 'Sgt. Pepper's' - more soundchecking.

Then we were off. Somehow on that early morning the stage stood still for 90 minutes. Mitchell was exhausted, dripping wet. Billy Cox was about as emotional as super solid bass players ever get. And Hendrix? You had to watch him as well as listen. He bent every sinew of his body on occasions as his fingers dug in to reach notes. He felt and breathed every finger-slide and squeeze of the pedals. He lived the show. I'd never seen Jimi Hendrix live before, but now knew you had to live it with him. Just being

Hendrix took you to that place, you became a part of what he was doing and knew you'd become a part of him too. He gave everything to feel his music out to you.

I was thrilled next day. Finally, after years of band-watching, I had THE ONE who I'd see at every opportunity.

I WAS THERE: KARL BRUDELL

I sat at the front of the stage during the Jimi Hendrix performance. I leaned back on the amplifiers on the right side of the stage, close to Billy Cox, and was there for the second half of the performance. Later I moved, with assistance, to the back of the stage during Joan Baez's and Leonard Cohen's performance.

At the time I was in a biker group, which had contacts with more well-known gangs, so I looked the part. Apart from the last night, my group of eight sat on the hill, where we had ample tents (including a scout tent) and comfortable surroundings. Some of us decided to go down into the arena and my 'garb' allowed me to quickly move through the crowds. Unfortunately, I got separated from my friends and only came to a halt at the VIP fence. I stared at the security people, who looked away, so I decided to hop over the fence and see how close I could get. On the right side a chair was abutting the stage and a line of photographers were taking turns standing on it. I ignored the queue and when one photographer came down I challenged the next in line. He immediately yielded. I stood there for a long time and eventually was asked to let the next person up.

I hesitated for a moment, then thought, 'Let's go all the way!' I struggled to haul myself onto the stage and was helped up by the photographers, who were glad to see me go. Although there were many people alongside and behind the band, few came to the front where I was propped up. I stayed there for the rest of the performance. I must have slumped at some stage and recall two guys helping me around to the back of the stage. I thought they were going to throw me out, but instead they put me down behind some backstage equipment. I don't recall being asked to leave, but towards the end of Leonard Cohen's performance I left and made my way back to the hill and relayed my little story to my friends.

I WAS THERE: ALEX BIELAK, AGE 16

Much to the concern of my parents, two friends and I went to the Isle of Wight for the festival. We were 16 or so and it was a wonderful adventure. I don't think I saw our tent from the time we pitched it till we left.

The music saturated us. Literally. The bands were for the most part incredible. We had a pact that if one of us was asleep for a good band the others would wake him up. That way I got to at least see The Doors, for a while, until I fell asleep again. But it was impossible to sleep through bands like ELP, who gave an electrifying concert in the middle of the night.

By the end, as the Woodstock headliners were coming on, we were exhausted. In the middle of Hendrix's set we realised that if we hoped to get off the island in any reasonable time we had to leave ... then. So we upped and left not long after he began. We did get to witness what felt like a butchering of 'God Save the Queen', and other songs too by the supremely-talented Jimi, but by then we couldn't take any more. So, yes, we walked on Hendrix, and departed before Baez, Cohen and Richie Havens if I recall rightly. I think about that concert often. It was transformative in so many ways.

I WAS THERE: HOWARD GARDNER, AGE 15

I had been a fan since seeing him do 'Hey Joe' on *Ready Steady Go!* in 1966. I had just started work. I wasn't going to the Isle of Wight festival because I couldn't get time off work (I was nearly sacked), but the friend I went with bought the ticket. Thankfully it was one of the warmest weekends of the year, because all we had was a sleeping bag and no tent. From arriving on the island, the atmosphere was electric, so many people making their way to the site. Each day you had to queue to get into the arena and even though some bands didn't stop playing until the early hours, everyone had to exit the arena and then queue up to get back in.

On a morning we would go to a farmhouse selling the most delicious homemade soup, then walk into the village to buy food. We would go for a beer in one of the local pubs, spending time with a big gang of Hell's Angels before heading back to the arena. Most of the acts were fantastic, even Tiny Tim once he started doing Jerry Lee Lewis and old rock'n'roll songs. The only disappointment was The Doors - Jim Morrison had no idea what planet he was on.

Waiting for Jimi to come on stage that Sunday was the longest day I've ever known. I was like a child on Christmas Eve. Some commentators and journalists say it wasn't his best performance, but in that huge crowd the sound didn't appear that bad. When he did 'Voodoo Child (Slight Return)' the sound seemed to hang in the air. To this day I've never heard a sound like it. I've since seen the DVD of the concert and can tell he had sound problems at the beginning, but those problems went when he started to play 'Red House'.

The five days I spent at the Isle of Wight Festival are among the best five days of my life.

I WAS THERE: JERRY CAHILL

I stayed awake for three days, with occasional cat-naps. It was fucking great. I fell asleep on Sunday evening but was awoken really late by someone saying, 'Hey, Jimi's on!' I sat up long enough to see him coming on and then fell back asleep before waking up again to hear the guitar break in 'All Along The Watchtower' for just long enough to think 'Ah, that's how he did it'. I then fell back asleep. Afterwards, I thought 'Oh well, I'll see him again, but in more comfortable circumstances'. My eternal regret. I've become known as the bloke who slept through Hendrix!

I WAS THERE: NOLA GOULD

My husband was a member of Newport Round Table, and we were helping on their refreshment stall during the weekend of the 1970 festival. As we were folk music fans, we were very keen to see Joan Baez, so went into the arena at the time she was scheduled to perform. However, the organisation was chaotic, and the acts were running several hours late. We found a spot to sit, next to a group of Aussies in sleeping bags. I'm afraid I can't recall much about Hendrix's performance, but what happened afterwards has always stuck in our memories. A head peeped out from a sleeping bag and an Australian accent was heard to ask, 'Is Jimi Hendrix coming on yet?' 'Aw, mate, yer just missed him!' was his friend's reply. 'Yer mean, I travelled halfway round the world to see Jimi Hendrix, and yer didn't wake me! Aw, man!' No doubt he was even more gutted a few weeks later, when he knew he would never have another opportunity to see his idol. As for myself, I was very grateful for the delays, which made us stay up half the night waiting for Joan Baez. Not only did we get to see Jimi Hendrix, but also Leonard Cohen, who made a huge impression on me and has been my favourite singer ever since.

I WAS THERE: MICK GREEN, AGE 17

I first heard Hendrix on the shitty little transistor radio my parents gave me for passing my 11-plus exam. I was 13 and it was just before Christmas in 1966. It could have been Luxembourg or some pirate station. It was like it was the music I had been waiting for, 'Hey Joe' by The Jimi Hendrix Experience. I loved lots of the music at the time, The Beatles, Stones, Kinks … but this Hendrix fellow blew me away. The voice, the guitar, the whole thing was just so direct and powerful. I went out and bought it with my money from my paper-round and played the single to death. The flip, 'Stone Free', was just as good. I remember it was on the Polydor label.

In spring '67, Hendrix brought out 'Purple Haze' and it totally blew my tiny 14-year old mind. I live in Grimsby, a bit of a backwater, but Hendrix played gigs very near in '67. He played Hull and Lincoln, just an hour away by bus or train. I'd look in the dear old *NME* for the dates and I wanted to go but my parents would never let me; too young, school and all that.

My pal Rob and I got our tickets from Gough and Davy Music in Victoria Street, Grimsby. They cost three quid and we hitched it there, an experience on its own. It was fabulous hitting the site. I seem to remember they stamped your wrist with a decal or transfer. I'd never seen such a sea of bodies. You had the feeling of being part of something very important. We saw great sets by Free, The Who, Jethro Tull, John Sebastian. The Doors were very subdued, Ten Years After were disappointing, The Moody Blues boring. Then it was Hendrix.

I think the expectation was way high when he hit the stage in those early hours. I was about 60 yards from the stage, so the view wasn't that clear. I just remember being so excited to see and hear the man. The sound was not great. He seemed to be struggling to grab hold of the music at times. The interference with security walkie-talkies didn't help. He was, however, wonderful on 'Red House' and 'Machine Gun'. 'Foxy Lady' was brutal. He seemed to drift in and out of the gig, with moments of brilliance and then indifference and torpor. 'All Along the Watchtower' was quite brilliant considering he was trying to do justice to a layered masterpiece laid down in studios. Mitch was great but overplaying sometimes to fill in the gaps when some songs started to drag.

In hindsight and regarding what happened later, Hendrix was totally drained and exhausted by the pressures and the lifestyle, but we as an audience were unaware of that. It wasn't until I saw the DVD years later that I realised how drained and exhausted he looked. We just thought he would go out there and be as great as he could be. It was great to see and hear him, but how I wish I could have seen The Jimi Hendrix Experience on a club date in late '66 or early '67.

I remember the morning when Rob and I were tramping off the site past the Release tents, provided for people having bad times with drugs. The wind was up, it was chilly, and Richie Havens was still on stage belting it out. Even as a happy 17-year-old with a contented life, I thought something important had just slowly died and passed.

I WAS THERE: GORDON CHIVERTON

I saw him play, but it was all a bit of a let-down. He tried his riffs and to be honest there were some good bits, but it wasn't his best. I only had a half- hour walk into Freshwater and then into a nice bed.

I WAS THERE: PAUL DAVIS, AGE 17

I was born on the island and was just coming up to 18 when I went with about 25 mates to Acton Down. I'd been to the previous IOW Festivals at Godshill and Wotton. This experience was totally different due to the numbers. It was larger than Woodstock and three days of non-stop music. I remember sitting on the slope with my mates at the left side of the stage. It was early morning and the crowd were getting a buzz for hours before he came on stage, the smell of dope wafting around everywhere. His actual performance was good, but he was obviously stoned and the group not together musically, wrong notes hidden by feedback. However, whether it was the size of the crowd or their drug-fuelled euphoria, he carried it off. I wasn't disappointed. But the performer who impressed me most was Richie Havens, who came on at about six in the morning.

I WAS THERE: MICHAEL GREEN

I rode a Lambretta but was more of a Scooterist than a Mod. I preferred my long navy blue civil defence great coat to a parka. I sang in a local band, Dream Machine, that played mostly progressive or underground covers, but I wasn't a hippy. I paid to go to the first, missed the second, and worked (though not musically) at the third.

The first festival had its RCA 'Lite' Show and John Peel in a distinctly-hippy phase. My 25/- (£1.25) ticket for the event, number

Michael Green (left) and Paul Hunter of Dream Machine

8822, proceeds in aid of the Isle of Wight Indoor Swimming Pool Association, bore the autograph 'Peace John Peel' and a hurried drawing of a flower. Despite other big-name bands such as The Move, Tyrannosaurus Rex and Fairport Convention being there, my most vivid memory from that occasion is of Arthur Brown. I walked through the field towards the stage as he sang the exciting 'Fire', and I wondered if the distant acoustics were playing tricks or if he was indeed singing flat.

The second festival I did not attend because of teenage romance problems. I got as far as the entrance and with other matters on my mind, gave it a miss.

The third Festival was to be my 'clever' Festival. I would work in a hut selling food and drink, and between 8pm to 8am shifts would catch the acts for nothing. This worked well for a couple of shifts, but I got so tired, and being unable to sleep leaning up against the perimeter fence, I went home. My Lambretta LI 150 Mk I somehow got me home and I slept right through until it was time to go back to work again. As I rode up through Wootton High Street, I noticed a motorcycle combination behind me and no matter how much I slowed down to let it pass, it wouldn't. As we sailed down Lushington Hill, there was an almighty smash of breaking glass on my crash helmet. I just managed to stop myself going straight through a hedge. I would like to think these three leather-clad yobs with German helmets and swastikas would not have used a beer bottle in such a way had I been without a helmet. As yet it was not a legal requirement to wear a crash-hat and I often rode without one.

At first I was totally shocked, then incredibly angry. I telephoned

Newport Police Station from a kiosk and then went there. After determining that I had virtually no chance of the bikers being caught with the great numbers of people on the Island for the Festival (some estimates think 600,000), I carried on to work. Arriving at the festival site I was immediately stopped by a policeman who, having his 'wires crossed', somehow thought I had stolen my own scooter. I was not pleased.

Inside food hut 'I', the sound of Emerson, Lake and Palmer's cannon-fire surprised us. I had just discovered a sealed but empty Coca-Cola can to go with my sealed but empty Lyon's (apple and blackcurrant) individual fruit pie box. As the night wore on, now and again the hut shook rather dramatically. Some over-excited, possibly French students, people from Devastation Hill as it became known, were trying to knock down the perimeter fence of which we were a part. A panicked lady appeared from one of the other food huts, gave us her takings and told us she was off home at the earliest opportunity.

Trade was brisk, as the aroma of hot snacks wafted its way towards the dense crowds of people in their tents, gathered round bonfires or walking ankle deep in litter; the people a multi-national mix of real hippies and weekend hippies who would hang up their long wigs, cow-bells and cola ring-pull headbands on Monday.

By about three in the morning, even the smell of hot food couldn't get people out of their sleeping bags and tents. Quite frankly we were bored. To create a little interest, I decided to make use of my starting pistol. I suppose I could have got lynched for my lack of consideration, but most people woke up dazed and confused and a few even hungry. It's a pity we didn't get commission on sales.

Whilst not working, I got to sit about six rows from the front when Jimi Hendrix did his set. Although I was a great fan I was somehow disappointed with him live. The events of the next few weeks would show he had big problems on his mind; so perhaps he can be forgiven for not giving the best performance of his career. Of the ones I saw, the best live performances were by Jethro Tull and The Who. Brilliant.

I WAS THERE: DAVE LONGMAN

Jimi Hendrix was our rock god. As a group of students, Neil, Tim and I knew every album, every song, every band he ever played with. We avidly sought articles in *Melody Maker, NME, Rolling Stone* and magazines no one would ever admit to openly reading. *Woodstock The Movie* was released in May 1970 and we visited the Grand Cinema on four consecutive nights simply to watch that magical moment

as 'The Star Spangled Banner' melded into 'Purple Haze'. When we knew he was to headline the Isle of Wight Festival we knew there could be no other place on earth to be than East Afton Down.

For four days we sat through one of the greatest under-cards ever assembled - Joni Mitchell, The Doors, Jethro Tull, The Who, and the cream of late Sixties rock music came and went as we sat and waited for the greatest of them all. Sunday night turned into Monday morning as we fought fatigue, hunger and a burning bladder waiting for The Man.

Dave fought hunger and a bursting bladder in the wait to see Jimi at the Isle of Wight

Then, 'A bit more volume on this one, Charlie. We're gonna need it.' There he was. The man we had waited for - had dreamed of seeing in the flesh, standing there like a psychedelic vision in orange. And then surrealistically he began playing not 'Star Spangled Banner' but 'God Save The Queen' and then 'Sgt. Pepper' instead of 'Purple Haze'. We were transfixed. The sound was not the best, his playing was not the best, but he was there and that was enough. More than enough. As the set progressed the playing became more confident. We each awaited out favourite songs and were not to be disappointed. The sublime 'Red House', 'Hey Joe', 'Purple Haze' and then finally the riffing chords announcing 'Voodoo Chile' – for me the absolute moment of the set and the whole festival.

We were blown away. We had no taste for more music after that performance, so gathered our possessions, paused to watch the drama as the main stage caught fire, then headed for the ferry back to the mainland. We dissected the set, the playing, the lighting and vowed that we would take in as many dates on his next British tour as we could afford.

Just 18 days later we sat shell-shocked in Neil's bedroom. We sat up all night and played every album Jimi had ever made and a few bootlegs as well. We were lost in a sea of emotion. The greatest guitarist the world had ever seen would tour no more.

I WAS THERE: STEVE HOMEWOOD, AGE 18

My most vivid memory is of Jimi coming on very late, about 2.30 in the morning. My future father-in-law, who I met for the first tine about 30 years later, was postman on the island and recalls delivering a telegram to Jimi. Unfortunately, he did not keep the receipt Jimi signed for the message!

I WAS THERE: EDDI LAUMANNS, AGE 18

I went from Germany to London with a friend, where we split up. I made it for five days to the Isle of Wight, where I teamed up with four lads from Slough. I went back to London with them by bus, then back to Germany, hitchhiking. Not a lot of memories left after five days with little sleep, too much pot and almost no food. I cannot even say what songs Jimi played. The sound was poor as we went almost back to the

Eddi can't remember what songs Jimi played

entrance in order to leave the site immediately after his appearance.
I came home after losing quite some weight, where my Mom asked
if I had been to Biafra rather than the UK. I had my brother's
Voigtländer camera with me on the island but left it at the British
Rail left luggage office in the ferry port, because I was afraid I would
lose it at the festival site. My brother would have gone berserk as I
had no money to buy him another. As a result, I do not have a single
pic of my own from the festival. That year I was running about like a
copy of Keef Hartley. Fringed jacket, cowboy hat, high-laced boots.
I'm 99% certain I was wearing the same clothes during the festival.

I WAS THERE: RITA LOCK, AGE 16

I had never been to a festival before, and my word it was a
shock. The crowd was enormous and like an awful lot of people I
didn't have a ticket. Nobody was worried about that - I just got on
a bus and went. I made my way through the huge crowds to find a
place on the hill, and remember nude men dancing in a huge mud
puddle. I'd never seen a nude man before. It was quite a shock. It was
obvious they were stoned – a feature of the whole festival. Over the
weekend there was so many fantastic bands and I was a Who fan,
so it was brilliant. But Jimi Hendrix - I will never forget him playing
'God Save the Queen'. It was beautiful, haunting and I know I felt
immensely proud. As I recall, his set wasn't that long and he missed
out some of his chart hits. But it was unforgettable.

I WAS THERE: MENNO VAN DUINEN

I was there living for a week or so on Desolation Row. It was weird,
freaky, trippy and nice all together. I met my holiday friend Don there.
On the last night I was very tired. Don woke me up when Jimi started.
I heard a few songs and fell asleep again. When I woke up there was
daylight and Richie Havens had started to play, the final act.

I WAS THERE: JOAN COBERN

Jimi arrived on the stage to a rapturous response from the crowd. The set was brilliant and all the old favourites were played. After speaking to the crowd he then addressed the guys up on the hill, saying, 'Hi to all those guys pissing and fucking against the wall!' I was a bit shocked as the latter word was very rarely used in the Sixties and Seventies. The response from the crowd was to laugh and cheer.

Later that evening I was queuing to get the bus back to board the ferry. Joan Baez was on stage. I noticed a large car, possibly a red and white Cadillac, a few yards away, and inside was the great man sat between two young women. I was a bit awestruck and regret not stopping the car and asking Jimi to sign my programme!

I WAS THERE: JEANETTE LONGMIRE, AGE 18

I got together with four other girls from London. My cousin Alan was also there, working with the electronics on stage, but I camped with the girls. The atmosphere was fantastic and unforgettable. I loved Jimi Hendrix. He was the highlight of the festival for me. I've never heard anybody else say it, so perhaps they didn't believe their eyes, but not long after Jimi's performance, late at night, he wandered through the crowds. He was a couple of yards from me. I went to a couple of other festivals that year but none like the 1970 Isle of Wight Festival. It really was the last great event. I don't think I slept the whole weekend.

I WAS THERE: GEOFF MITCHAM

They had him in a caravan at the back of the stage, and when he came out to walk up the ramp there were so many cameras and press around him. You couldn't get close. I did follow him up the ramp though and stood at the back of the stage behind the amps, so never got to see him properly. There were so many people at the side of the stage already. I was hoping to get on the film, but no such luck.

I WAS THERE: MIKE MURTAGH, AGE 17

It proved to be an important and pivotal year in my life for all sorts of reasons. I went to one of the local grammar schools and was I think a fairly capable student but had, and still have, a bit of a rebellious streak, and that spilled over into my musical tastes. It's almost impossible to convey now the excitement of those times in just about every sphere of life but, for my 17-year-old self, it had already centred for a few years in the music that was emerging. In October 1966, my life changed irrevocably one Thursday evening with a performance of 'I Feel Free' by Cream on *Top of the Pops*. I'd never seen or heard anything quite so thrilling.

Mike Murtagh (in shades) had enough of festivals after the Isle of Wight

I'd never been to a festival before. Some of my schoolmates saw Dylan at the Isle of Wight the previous year but the 1970 event was promising to eclipse it in every way. I went to three festivals that year, also getting to the Hollywood Festival and Bath Festival. By the time I staggered out after seeing Leonard Cohen at 4am at the end, I'd absolutely had enough of festivals and have never attended another. When I got back to Swansea, guess what was showing in the cinema? *Woodstock*! It honestly took me a good 30 years before I could bear to watch it!

One of the misconceptions I find quite fascinating when you mention hippies and music to people is this idea of everyone doing floaty weird dancing. The few who indulged themselves in this way were regarded by the vast majority of progressive music followers as beneath contempt and highly embarrassing. Dancing was not part of the culture. It detracted from the chamber music-type aspirations we had for appreciating the superior musical standards of our chosen musicians. Indeed, these dancers were known pejoratively as 'idiot dancers' and almost universally scorned. We allowed ourselves to indulge in what became known as 'headbanging' in time to the music, but that was about it.

I went to the Isle of Wight with Les Williams and Bruce Curtis. We went by train to Southampton, then over to Cowes where we caught a bus to Newport and then by bus to East Afton Farm. We had to change trains in Cardiff and took the opportunity to wander around Cardiff Market. We had heard you could get a significant 'buzz' from eating Morning Glory flower seeds. We had no idea about dosage, so bought a few packets and started munching one or two at first and, when there was no observable effect, the entire contents. Big mistake. By the time we got to Southampton, I felt about as co-ordinated as a baby and must have represented a pitiful sight as I climbed the gangway, gingerly feeling my way, one hesitant step after another. The effects had thankfully disappeared by the time we got to the Festival.

My friends and I were setting up our shelter, stretching a plastic sheet from the top of the fence to the ground when someone wandered past asking if any of us were artists. I was doing A-level art so volunteered and found myself with a nice little job prior to the festival as a sign-writer for the souvenir marquee (matches and toilet tissue, candles, t-shirts, etc.). Nice little earner. I could afford to eat from the food concessions around the site, a definite bonus. You can see the dark blob of my 'Matches & Toilet Tissues' sign hanging on the roof of the marquee in one of the aerial photos.

One of the bonuses of working in the marquee was that we were able to sleep there in much greater comfort. It was noisy and very busy all the time, though, especially when one American was doing his trumpet practice. Eventually, we were ousted by the security dogs who arrived in the marquee on Wednesday, but the two-day free portion of the festival was set to start and were spending 24 hours a day in the open, the weather outstanding.

There was a lot of dope available. Most seemed to be centred in what became known as 'Desolation Row', a bunch of early arrivals sheltered in their tents in a hedgerow on the eastern side. I was never one for taking chemicals and, as a working-class boy, was never sufficiently wealthy to be able to afford to be a hippy. They were pretty exclusively middle and upper-class kids who indulged themselves in 'The Life'. I managed the occasional joint when I could afford it, but nothing else. I was glad of that at Bath, which had a horrendous 'bad acid' problem.

I remember the toilets vividly. You see them in Murray Lerner's documentary - three-sided cubicles, no doors and back-to-back in rows. Square plastic seats were supported by a couple of wooden beams, perched over huge pits. The gents were surrounded by a trench serving as a pissoir. Pretty grim. People would only go at night initially. This had its dangers, the arc lighting so strong that it was difficult to see at ground level in some shaded areas and it was easy to miss your footing near The Pit of Ordure. One friend was wearing a sort of Gandalf cloak and attempted a number

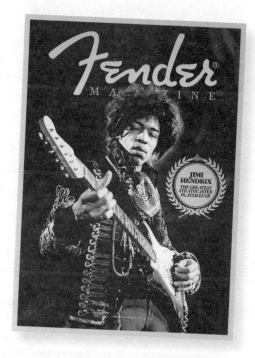

two, but the seat slipped off the supporting beams and he followed it into The Pit. We managed to catch him by the cloak before he went all the way.

By the end of the week, nobody cared much and we just went as necessary. On the last day, I decided to go for a last number two before the evening and Jimi's gig. By then, it was difficult to find a seat that wasn't wet with something and I was surprised to find a totally dry seat near the entrance. I settled on the seat, listening to Sly Stone, only a little nagging voice wondering why this seat had been unused. Once I finished, it suddenly dawned on me. My back was facing the entrance and the cubicle had no back panel, so all those streaming in and out had a superb uninterrupted view of me wiping my fundament. Oh, dear.

I only really went to the Isle of Wight to see Miles and Jimi who, as it turns out, had been collaborating musically, Jimi even doing so with Gil Evans and John McLaughlin.

The two-day lead up to the main festival was entertaining, populated as it was with lesser bands of the time. Some were better than a few headliners - Groundhogs, for instance - and it really helped pass the time. Not to say that there weren't problems. Kris Kristofferson's band turned up one night and ended up getting totally eviscerated onstage. I've never experienced anything like it. Nobody knew anything about them but word was that they were a sort of sub-Johnny Cash act. They were definitely not to the taste of the majority and the crowd turned on them. They couldn't even hear what was being played and it just seemed to gather momentum until you had half-a-million voices baying for blood. If you watch Murray Lerner's movie, you get the full flavour of it.

By the time The Who appeared, there was a tendency to get blasé about the plethora of top-quality, legendary bands. You had to weigh up whether you wanted to sleep or eat or see some classic band. I reached that point with The Who. They were always regarded as an OK but definitely second-order band in the progressive music pantheon. Then came *Tommy* and their gig at Woodstock and suddenly their star was in the ascendant. Well, not for me. I needed sleep and sloped off outside the arena (I could still hear them, of course), lay in my sleeping bag beside a van and tried to doze off. Not for long though. The van caught fire and some were going frantic trying to clear the area before it blew. Most, however, like me, were too bloody shattered or stoned to move and so we accepted our likely fate until the arrival of the fire brigade. Apparently, it was one of The Who's greatest performances.

Free were a lovely little gig on a bright Saturday afternoon. A month later, I found myself carrying their gear into a gig at Swansea University. I hung around stage doors a lot and asked the roadies if I could help with the gear if I couldn't afford a ticket or a gig was sold out. I met the guys after we'd set up their kit and they gave me a lift home.

Miles Davis was everything I expected. I didn't understand it but its appeal was so visceral and these guys were obviously very accomplished musicians.

By Sunday, I'd had nine hours' sleep in four days. All my efforts were geared towards seeing Jimi later in the day. It was all people could talk about.

It seems quite clear now, from his crowd announcements and general demeanour, that Jimi was unhappy, probably in many respects but especially with the material he was playing. He said he wasn't really that keen on the old stuff but he'd better play it - it was what was expected of him. For 'Machine Gun', he prefaced the song with a dedication that included 'the soldiers in Vietnam'. I don't think a lot of fans appreciated Jimi supported the war, if only because as an ex-paratrooper in the 101st Airborne, he identified closely with the plight of the ordinary soldier in that conflict. 'All Along the Watchtower' was notable for me. For me, he didn't disappoint, but I think others might have found him a bit lacklustre that night. But given the time of night and his generally bad mood, I don't suppose that would be too surprising.

Then the most bloody awful thing happened! I slept through a portion of Jimi, all of Joan Baez, and Lenny 'Chuckles' Cohen was coming onstage! It was now about 4am. I was shattered, I'd been in a field for a week, I was hungry and filthy, I was at the end of the third such gruelling event I'd attended in three months and I'd really had enough. I wanted to go home. Having Leonard Cohen droning away at me on top of this made me feel like opening a vein.

I WAS THERE: RUSTY SHIRLEY, AGE 21

I turned 21 in March, so this trip over from the US was my coming of age extravaganza. My buddy was 22. The festival occurred at the end of a long summer that I spent living out of a small bag strapped on the back of a used BSA. We were tired and probably malnourished. I arrived with a small cut on my finger that had become infected. As the festival progressed it only worsened. There was a first-aid tent visible from the stage area but there was always a long queue, so I suffered in silence until when Jimi hit the stage. Then the queue disappeared and so, after a couple of tunes from Jimi, I chose to leave to have my infected finger lanced, disinfected and dressed - with no numbing agent. I don't remember crying but remember vocalising my displeasure loudly.

I hurried back for the remainder of his set. The truck we lived in was set between Hendrix and The Who, so I was stoked to see him. The Who were on site for the entire festival but Jimi waited until the last minute. The crowd backstage was mammoth when he arrived. I was always a huge fan and was not disappointed. I was mesmerised and my vantage point was pure bliss. The whole experience was like I was living someone else's life, and that someone else was one lucky son of a bitch.

We flew home to the States four days after and I spent the whole while spouting off about the Isle of Wight to anybody I could get to listen when word of Jimi's death stunned me to the core. Then Janis, then Morrison… a combination of gut punches. JFK, RFK and MLK, Vietnam and now this. It was very hard to assimilate all of it. The sparkle of the era was gone.

I WAS THERE: TONY SMITH, AGE 17

I'd seen Blind Faith in June '69 and the Stones in Hyde Park the following month and was at the Bath festival in June 1970, which I thought was better than the Isle of Wight, musically-speaking. I was not keen to go, in a van with a friend and two girlfriends driven by one of their dads, just because of Hendrix. It was more for the experience of a large festival. I didn't have tickets so was pleased when the Notting Hill people and French 'anarchists' (that didn't last long - they're mostly centre-right politicians in France now) fresh from May '68 breached the walls. I remember Jeff Dexter, MC-ing the event, popping his head over the wall to say, 'Hey everyone, please cool it' and then the wall being pushed over seconds after! Hendrix's set was a bit of a shambles and for years I wondered if I really heard him play 'God Save the Queen' or imagined it. I was obviously touched and sad when learning of his death two weeks later.

I WAS THERE: RICK SUTHERLAND

In 1970, hitchhiking in England, I was picked up by a bunch of hippies in a 1961 40hp VW bus. They told me they were going to the Isle of Wight Festival and Hendrix was there, but were going first to Piccadilly Circus, London, to watch the movie *Woodstock*. We were

Rick watched Jimi from the top of Desolation Hill

stunned by his 'Star Spangled Banner' rendition, from where we then went to Nottingham to visit a friend who was friends with local pub musicians who entertained us with their beer and dry humour. We hung there for a couple days and then headed over.

As the van had a four-foot roll-back canvas roof, I was able to play my harmonica as we journeyed south at 50mph. With six of us aboard it took a while. There was a long line at the ferry. After crossing to the island, we all set up our tents.

They've made a movie of this 1970 festival. It had a stellar line-up that often played all night long. At the front of the stage, I watched Sly and the Family Stone sing 'Stand'. There were many disputes as to who was in charge and whether people should have to pay to get in. Dutch radicals tore down the fence and a lot of money was not collected for the musicians. 600,000 ferry tickets were sold.

The first day, the wind was blowing and the sound from a distance waffled in and out. On the third day, our bunch walked to the top of Desolation Hill as Hendrix was just about to go on and we settled in for a great show. We were a quarter-mile from the stage as the crow flies and again the wind waffled the sound in and out a bit. But we were all quite mesmerised by his performance. What a genius musician!

I WAS THERE: JAAP VAN DER GALIEN, AGE 20

I read about the festival in Dutch music magazine, *Hitweek*. I was blown away by the line-up, talked about it with a colleague. We were both 20, worked at a post office and shared a common interest in music. I ordered two tickets at £3 each and borrowed a one-person tent.

We arrived in Portsmouth late at night and had to wait more than four hours before we could get on the boat to the island. We arrived at the camp-site in the middle of the night and discovered a one-person tent really was much too small, so the next day we bought another in Freshwater. A big surprise: we

Jaap got five days of music for the price of three

bought tickets for a three-day festival, but when we arrived there were five days of music!

There's been written a lot of all the mess that happened, but I never noticed anything of all the trouble except that, on the day of the 'riots', we went shopping for some food and weren't allowed to return by car as the police had closed every road with cones. The only thing I could do was put some cones in the back of the car and cross a small ditch to get back to the site with the car.

The night Jimi played, I was sleeping in my tent because I was just bloody tired. But I was woken by the music, left the tent and attended the Jimi Hendrix gig just from behind the fence. It was an unbelievable experience.

When I heard of his passing a few weeks later, I was in shock: I couldn't believe it but at the same time I felt so lucky I witnessed his last great gig.

I WAS THERE: ALAN WATTERS

I hitchhiked there from Scotland on my own and just outside London got a lift down to Portsmouth in Roger Daltrey's Rolls Royce. One of their management team, possibly the road manager, was driving and he told me lots of stuff about The Who that people wouldn't generally know - like how he took every new guitar for Pete Townsend apart and then bolted it back together again so when Pete smashed it up on stage they could salvage some bits and put them back together.

When Jimi Hendrix started playing I was zonked out up on the hill and the sound of his guitar woke me up. I was pretty stoned and didn't quite know where I was. All I could remember was 'floating' towards the music and ending up just a few feet from the stage. The stage was quite high above me and I was just staring up at Jimi, my mouth gaping. I remember telling everyone afterwards that Jimi's guitar was talking to me. I was convinced it was screaming out words, and in sentences I could understand. Well, I was stoned I suppose.

I WAS THERE: HELEN WOOD, AGE 15

I had gone almost three days with barely any food and by the end of the last day I couldn't keep awake. I have memories of the festival per se but precious few of Jimi's performance as I fell into a deep sleep around 10 minutes after he started.

I WAS THERE: NEIL MOORES, AGE 16

My friend Pete and I hitched there with a tent from Warrington, Cheshire. It took us two days of travelling, including a night camping in a field in the vicinity of Wolverhampton and later hitching a ride on the back of an open lorry carrying bales of hay in the Bath area.

My memories of the festival are fairly sharp, given I was 16 and my friend 15 at the time. Perhaps my most vivid memory is of the mildly primitive conditions (toilets); the corrugated iron sheeting and shanty town feeling we got from the construction of food outlets and other structures; the earth beneath our feet and wandering through crowded spaces. We accessed the main arena to begin with, using our tickets, but our experience was such that we were aware of trouble spots and unrest. I think this was due to the issue of the festival becoming a free event. I seem to remember being very aware of this - it was a diversion from the entertainment. For this reason, and also to enable to us to find a better vantage point, we moved up the hill. By Sunday we were well up above the main site.

The advantages to us were less disturbance and better visibility, though because the stage was more distant, picking up details was more difficult. In sleeping bags we lay under a partially-cloudy, partially-starry night sky, with a line of low tree scrub, variously sculpted by wind and weather, providing a form of shelter for us.

Hendrix's set was, I recall, a bit 'stop-start'. The whole atmosphere that night was a mish-mash of lights and sounds, I remember it eventually petering out and dying down as we were simultaneously overtaken by sleep. I don't think it was one of Hendrix's best performances. If I can explain that more clearly, I'd say he sounded in his playing and speaking between numbers a touch sardonic. Maybe that was a portent of things to come.

I WAS THERE: ROB ELLIS, AGE 16

Am I the only person who was neither drunk nor stoned in the Sixties and still can't remember? I remember how damn cold it was on that hill. We had tickets for Chicago a couple of days earlier but left the arena because the sound and view were better from the hill. I remember a friend's discomfort as we watched Family though. I lived in Northwood on the Isle of Wight. Looking back, I had no idea what I was witnessing. We travelled out in my friend's Reliant Robin van, equipped with a mattress in the back in case he got lucky.

I WAS THERE: DAVID WANSTALL, AGE 16

I lived at East Afton with my mum and stepfather. I actually lived opposite 2 Tollgate Cottages and the festival was across the road. I believe I'm able to say without fear of contradiction that Hendrix, The Doors and The Who played in my backyard.

I was very fond of Jimi and a lot of the bands who played there, waited up until the early hours and actually watched him. He was a little worse for wear. I can't remember exactly what he played but I remember thinking, 'Brilliant, I've actually seen him.'

I was quite close to the stage. I could see him quite well. One of my heroes at the time was just there playing and it was lovely. I can see him now, looking up at the stage he was just fucking – wow!

I WAS THERE: PAUL WAVELL

I was at Afton for Jimi Hendrix in 1970, selling firewood to the punters. I made £400 and bought my first speedboat on the proceeds.

STORA SCENEN, GRÖNA LUN

31 AUGUST 1970, STOCKHOLM, SWEDEN

I WAS THERE: YVONNE BROD, AGE 16

I was very young, but I saw Jimi three times. At this show, the manager of the place was a very old man and when the gig was over, he pulled out the plug on Jimi's guitar. Jimi just laughed and stopped playing.

DEUTSCHLANDHALLE

4 SEPTEMBER 1970, BERLIN, WEST GERMANY

I WAS THERE: EVA-MARIA KÜHNE-WEHRMANN, AGE 19

I grew up in West Berlin and we had a strong subculture. All the groups came here, and we went to all the concerts. There was also a TV show, *Beat-Club*, where pop culture was transmitted, and I

remember an argument with my Mom when Jimi was on. I am honoured to say I saw Jimi here in Berlin. The Deutschlandhalle has been torn down, but not all the precious memories. Jimi was the highlight of a really great 'Super Concert', although he was very serious. Two weeks later he was gone. I was very sorry to learn of his death, of course, but glad that I had the honour to have seen him. I think I heard the news at home. I still can't believe he had to go so early. Too early. But the drugs were

Eva-Maria saw one of Jimi's last performances

everywhere then, so it wasn't such a surprise after all. I still miss him. He's my brother.

In what would prove to be Jimi's last live scheduled appearance, he took to the stage 24 hours later than planned due to bad weather at a festival in Fenmarn on 6 September 1970, backed by Mitch Mitchell on drums and Billy Cox on bass.

OPEN AIR LOVE AND PEACE FESTIVAL

6 SEPTEMBER 1970, FEHMARN, GERMANY

I WAS THERE: ALEXANDER MITCHELL, AGE 17

I became a big Hendrix fan at the age of 16. At 17 I went to the Isle of Wight Festival and saw Jimi perform there. After the festival finished I went on holiday with Mum and Dad to Krefeld in Germany. On arriving, my cousin said he had tickets for a nightclub in Hamburg that weekend and we got to see Jimi in a crowd of about 500 people. I even got to speak to the guy - my five minutes of fame. I shouted out, 'Hey Jimi, you were great at the Isle of Wight.' He replied, 'Thanks man. It was a great festival.'

I WAS THERE: HARRY HARRIS

I should have gone to the Isle of Wight but went to Fehmarn instead, a typical nerdy thing to do. Plus, a mate was visiting a friend near Kiel. It's not the best place in the world for a festival, in the Baltic, but it was on his tour and apparently, he had to do it. He played most of his repertoire. It rained. The atmosphere was rather awkward and heavy, bikers fighting anarchists, although I didn't see it. After that, he played a couple of gigs in London, then he passed. Barbiturates mixed with wine was a popular way of getting smashed, but it took away many souls that didn't know any better, including mates of mine.

I WAS THERE: PETE FORBES, AGE 19

Having played as warm-up band to the Rolling Stones in March 1964 at Blackburn, my next public performance was in early September 1970, when I managed to top the bill after Jimi's last performance, as it turned out.

I'd started on my first hitching trip in Europe. A friend dropped me off in Hamburg, and within hours I'd made a new pal, Henrik, a saxophone player from Bavaria and fellow hitcher. He told me about the first ever German rock concert to be held on the island of Fehmarn by the Baltic sea, sponsored by Beate Uhse, an infamous sex shop moguless of the Sixties.

We bought tickets then spent an extraordinary time tag-hitching together round Denmark and north Germany for three weeks, until we got to Fehmarn and the festival next to the beach. Having found a convivial corner of an enormous ex-army communal bell-tent, courtesy of Beate, in came the first of many wild German heads, with lush Teutonic hair down below his waist and a timely offer of, 'Anyone need marijuana, speed, cocaine, heroin, chocolate?' The chocolate was popular, especially second time around. My subsequent blur of festival virgin experience took in all the bands and more. 'I'm on the road again', roared Bear from Canned Heat at some point, and so was I.

Saturday night and Jimi was about to play, but then a wind-storm blew in from the Baltic, torrential rain streaming horizontal into the stage. 'Jimi cried off as he didn't want to get electrocuted' went the rumour, but luckily for us Sly and the Family Stone did. They blasted out 'Dance to the Music' and strutted their stuff for over two hours as we churned up and danced in the first and finest festival foot-deep ground gloop you could imagine, and saved our lives for another day.

Which was Sunday, a gloriously warm and sunny morning when a rumour went round that Jimi had stayed over and was going to do his set at 11 am, so we all charged down to the stage. Sure enough he was there, at last. He was the man, and we all had a sublime peak experience. Could it get better?

Sometime after Jimi signed off, for good as it turned out, smoke began to emerge from behind the stage. Soon a rumour went round that the management had run out of cash when the Hell's Angels festival security posse failed to get paid and the organisers had fled the site, with their management caravan ablaze. Myself and a few thousand others were left to our own devices with a fully-equipped festival stage, which I wandered right up to.

'Hey man, you play guitar?' gestured an impromptu impresario, calling me on stage when I shouted 'Yes'. 'This is the people's festival now. Let's have a people's band.' Just a few hours after Jimi had finished his last ever performance, I had joined the people's jam band to headline the Fehmarn after-party ... and we played on.

To have heard and seen one of the world's greatest black and mixed-race musicians and performers blowing away the cream of Germany's post-war hip youth with me, a white English boy, in the middle of them all only getting love and peace from everyone, was a profoundly liberating, revolutionary and transcendent experience. My Dad had been fighting their Dads less than 30 years before. Jimi just tore up history, and we all joined in.

When Jimi died, two weeks after the Fehmarn concert, he was 27. When I die, I'll also be 27, as I have been most of my life. It is, and was, a good time to peak.

A planned show in Rotterdam on 13 September 1970 was cancelled because Billy Cox was ill. An on-stage spot at Ronnie Scott's Jazz Club in London's Soho on 15 September with Eric Burdon and War was shelved when Jimi arrived too stoned to play. He did play with Burdon the following night though, performing two songs. It was his last public performance.

From Ronnie Scott's, Hendrix went on to a party with a German woman, Monika Dannemann, and back to her rooms at the Samarkand Hotel in Lansdowne Crescent. Jimi had apparently been drinking, taken amphetamines and some of Danneman's Vesparax sleeping pills, not knowing their strength. He vomited during an ensuing deep sleep, insufficiently conscious to throw up. Danneman panicked and telephoned Eric Burdon, the one-time Animals lead singer, who urged her to call an ambulance. The greatest guitarist of all time was dead on arrival at St Mary Abbot's Hospital, aged 27.

CENTRAL LONDON

18 SEPTEMBER 1970, LONDON, UK

I WASN'T THERE: CHARLES TODD

I worked in Fulham as an ambulanceman and often paired up with an 'old timer', who had transported Jimi to hospital. He was conveyed, unconscious, in a chair, with his head unsupported, and apparently died from asphyxiation consequent upon vomiting.

I WASN'T THERE: JIM WILLIAMS

He might have said, 'If that ever happens, wake me up with cold water or call Eric Burdon or call some friend, but don't call the cops.' Who knows what he told her, and perhaps it scared her. She supposedly called Eric Burdon and he said, 'Call 999. Call Emergency Services.' I heard they kept him upright in a chair rather than laying him down, so he could throw up, and strapped him in the chair so when he did it wouldn't come out and went right back down into his lungs. I also heard he snorted some powdered LSD, which has got to be stronger still. It's very sad.

I WAS THERE: WENDY GREENE

On the day Hendrix died I was working at Liberty/UA Records and rumours were going around. I phoned my friend who worked for his record company and she said, 'We're not making any statement.' I put the phone down and said, 'It's true.'

I WAS THERE: ROD HARROD

Eddie Kramer likes to call himself producer, but there was only ever one producer of Jimi Hendrix and that wasn't Eddie. It was Chas Chandler. The minute Chas left him is when Jimi was overdoing the drugs and overdoing everything else and spending six months to record one track. Chas kept him in line. Jimi respected Chas. There was talk of them getting back together again, but Chas would not go to America and get involved in the whole Electric Ladyland drug scene. Time was booked at Olympic Studios in Barnes and the tapes were sent for from Kramer, who tried to resist bringing over what Jimi had worked on to date. Then the whole thing went belly up with Jimi's death.

Chas was the one person that could have saved Jimi.

I WAS THERE: JIM LEA

We were going through our skinhead stage at the time. Chas (Chandler, who also managed Slade) called us down to London, and we couldn't work out why. It took us around five hours to get there. Eventually, after lots of small talk, he told us Jimi had rung him and asked him to manage him again. And I said, 'Well, I think it's fantastic'. Jimi Hendrix was my hero, you see, and I thought I'd get to play with him. I wouldn't have left the band but would have loved to have played with him. I played bass like he played guitar. I wasn't bothered about other bass players.

Unfortunately, little did we know that while Chas was having that conversation with the band, saying, 'Would you be upset if I managed Hendrix as well?' Hendrix was already dead. But the last time I spoke to Chas, he said, 'Y'know, Jim, when you're in the studio and you're playing guitar, your confidence and the way you play is like Hendrix. You're very much like him in a lot of ways. Why didn't you become a guitar player? How did you end up on the bass?' I just said I didn't want to be noticed. I ended up playing bass like Jimi played, so I got noticed anyway, but not by the general public, because I wanted to still be able to walk the streets.

I WASN'T THERE: JIM VANNER

After Jimi died, I was lucky enough to purchase his car, a red Chevrolet Monte Carlo with personalised number JYM1. I still have that plate.

THE STARS ARE OUT TONIGHT

It's impossible to compile a book of Jimi Hendrix memories and not ponder the question, 'Where would his music and career have gone had he not died so young?' These are some of the thoughts of contributors who saw him live on the subject of his passing.

JIM WILLIAMS

When I saw him at Cal Expo in 1970, I thought, 'Oh yeah, I'll be able to see him again, no problem'. He played at Sacramento State and I didn't even go. I was going to Santa Cruz and said, 'Should I cancel my Santa Cruz trip? Oh no, not to worry.' But then he died. I was lucky I got to see him when I did. There's no telling what he would have gone on to do.

He'd been going for months, one after another. I've heard stories that there were bags of cash that his manager, not Chas but the other guy (Mike Jeffery) had, and it was just a money machine. I can imagine a lot of that money just disappeared. They've made millions and millions of dollars and you wonder who's getting the money. I know they took care of his dad.

In his career I don't think he got to enjoy the spoils of victory, the money that he made. I think they just cranked him up and had him performing like a robot.

Eric (Clapton) got to enjoy his. I give him a lot of credit for quitting drugs, which supposedly saved his life.

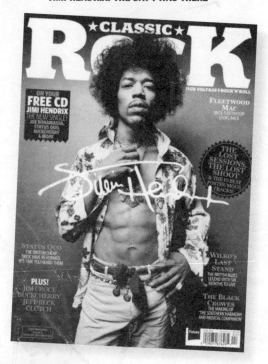

JOE BONAMASSA

I don't think there's any music that you hear on the radio today that would be possible without Jimi Hendrix

JOE SATRIANI

He was the deepest blues player. He played the saddest stuff and he played the funniest. He played the most outside stuff, but it was really from the gut. He strayed from the traditional blues playing, yet he always seemed to incorporate the moans and the cries into a phrasing that was completely blues

SLASH

I think the attraction with Jimi was just that he had this uninhibited, fluid guitar style that basically screamed. It had this over-the-top sound to it that just kind of drew me in

STEVIE RAY VAUGHAN

I loved Jimi a lot. He was so much more than just a blues guitarist. He could do anything

FREDDIE MERCURY

Jimi Hendrix is very important. He's my idol. He sort of epitomises, from his presentation on stage, the whole works of a rock star. There's no way you can compare him. You either have the magic or you don't. There's no way you can work up to it. There's nobody who can take his place

KEITH RICHARDS

Everybody else just screwed it up and thought wailing away is the answer. But it ain't; you've got to be a Jimi to do that, you've got to be one of the special cats.

PAUL McCARTNEY

He was very self-effacing about his music but then when he picked up that guitar he was just a monster.

KURT COBAIN

They're claiming that [the grunge bands] finally put Seattle on the map, but, like, what map? I mean, we had Jimi Hendrix. Heck, what more do we want?

> **I've been imitated so well I've heard people copy my mistakes**
>
> Jimi Hendrix

ACKNOWLEDGEMENTS

I should like to thank my many contributors for sharing their Jimi Hendrix memories with me. Without their stories, there would be no book. I'd also like to thank those local and regional newspapers in the UK and US that kindly printed my original appeal for Hendrix fans to come forward with their memories.

In particular I'd like to thank: Ellen Berman, for putting me in touch with various West Coast contributors; David J Coyle, for posting my appeal for Jimi Hendrix fans to contact me on his Central Ohio's Rock & Roll Scrapbook Facebook page; John A Grinde for allowing me to quote from his book *Your First Concert was Hendrix?*; Neil Everest, Steve Elphick and Jimpress, for permission to use extracts from an interview with Charles Everest about photographing Jimi at the Isle of Wight Festival; my cousin Chris Green, for his story of Jimi's almost-but-not-quite visit to Rushden; Rod Harrod, whose book, *Jimi Hendrix – 50 Years On; The Truth*, covers Jimi's first appearances in the UK in more detail; Steve Kitchen for permission to quote from an interview from his BBC Radio Gloucestershire show about Jimi's appearance at the Blue Moon Club in Cheltenham; Bill Lueders, of *Isthmus* in Madison, Wisconsin; Stephen Mayer of Bakersfield.com for permission to quote from his article about Jimi's appearance at Bakersfield's Civic Auditorium in October 1968; Karen Schneider, who writes for the *Sun Journal* in Lewiston, Maine; Ken Voss, of the Jimi Hendrix Information Management Institute; Lynn Wehr and *Columbus Monthly Magazine*, for Lynn's memories of Jimi's appearance in Columbus, Ohio in March 1968; Alan White, for permission to use an extract from his book, *Rock Around the Block*; Roger White of *Big City Rhythm & Blues* magazine, for his memories of seeing Jimi at the Fifth Dimension in Ann Arbor, Michigan; Helen Wood, for directing me to the Facebook group 1970 Festival Veterans.

Researching a book, one is inevitably drawn to the Internet to cross-check facts and both crosstowntorrents.org and jimihendrix.com were invaluable resources. But most of all I'd recommend the sadly out of print *Jimi Hendrix Concert Files* by Tony Brown, published by Omnibus, which helped me enormously when I was trying to verify dates.

I'd also like to thank Neil Cossar at This Day In Music for his unstinting enthusiasm, Malcolm Wyatt for his proofreading skills and donating his story of Jim Lea remembering Jimi, both Stan (RIP) and Sid for dragging me away from the keyboard every once in a while to get some fresh air, and Kate Sullivan for everything.

ABOUT THE AUTHOR

Richard Houghton lives in Manchester with his fiancée Kate. His The Day I Was There series encompasses books on The Beatles, The Rolling Stones, The Who, Pink Floyd and Jimi Hendrix which are published by This Day in Music Books, as are his books on The Wedding Present (Sometimes These Words Just Don't Have To Be Said, co written with David Gedge) and Orchestral Manoeuvres in the Dark (Pretending To See The Future, co written with the band). Richard is presently working on The Day I Was There books on Led Zeppelin, Prince, Black Sabbath, The Faces and Neil Young. When he's not writing or walking his pomapoo Sid, Richard can usually be found watching Manchester City or hoping for an upturn in the fortunes of Northampton Town.

If you have a gig memory you'd like to share with Richard, drop him a line at iwasatthatgig@gmail.com

THIS DAY
IN MUSIC .com

*If you like music history then visit
This Day in Music.com*

Music facts, trivia, classic
albums, for 365 days of the year.

And you can see which song was
number one on the day you were born.

More from This Day
in Music Books

Fans, friends and colleagues tell their stories of seeing, knowing and working with Bob Dylan from his hometown of Hibbing right through to finding Jesus - with first-hand accounts of seeing him live from the smallest of venues to festivals and arenas, this book reveals a contemporary view of the younger Dylan.

More from This Day in Music Books

During his six-decade career, he has played with all the greats. His career sky-rocketed when Crosby, Stills & Nash played only their second gig together at Woodstock in 1969. Stephen Stills is the only person to have been inducted twice in one night into The Rock and Roll Hall of Fame.

More from This Day in Music Books

This book features over 250 accounts from fans that have witnessed a Bruce Springsteen live show. From late Sixties concerts in New Jersey right through to his marathon shows from recent times, fans from the USA, UK, Australia and Europe share fascinating anecdotes, stories, photographs and memorabilia that have never been published before and tell us about their experiences of seeing one of the world's greatest live acts.

JIMI HENDRIX QUITS ONKEE TOUR

'Mickey Mouse has replaced me'

HENDRIX EXPERIENCE

RNING OF THE MIDNIGHT LAMP

Fender
MAGAZINE

JIMI HENDRIX
THE GREATEST
STRATOCASTER
PLAYER EVER

KFJZ & CONCERTS WEST PRESENT
JIMI HENDRIX
FT. WORTH WILL ROGERS COLISEUM · SAT., MAY 9 AT 8 P.
TICKETS: $3, $4, $5, $6

UNDER THE DOME
VIRGINIA BEACH, VIRGINIA

WED. EVE at 9:30 P.M.

Est. Price $4.28
City Tax .21 | TOTAL $4.50

The management reserves the right
to revoke the license granted by this
ticket by refunding purchase price.

NO REFUNDS

WED. EVE
APRIL
3
1968

Jimi Hendrix
STEPPING STONE ISABELLA

NILS LOFGREN
PHOTO: BRAD CHESIVOIR

HEY JOE
JIMI HENDRIX EXPERIENCE

THE JIMI HENDRIX EXPERIENCE
PURPLE HAZE
51st ANNIVERSARY

The Jimi Hendrix Experience

ROBERTS MUNICIPAL STADIUM
EVANSVILLE, INDIANA

ADMIT ONE — NO REFUND

Orchestra Seat $5.50

Evening at 8:00 P.M.

WEDNESDAY
JUNE
10

Orchestra Seat $5.50   ROW   SEAT
SEC.   A   11   2

OPEN AIR
LOVE+PEACE
INSEL FEHMARN
GERMANY
with
Hendrix Exp
other top groups

OPEN AIR
POP FESTIVAL

OSTSEEINSEL
FEHMARN
tral für Mitteleuropa
Skandinavien

5. 6.
September

JIMI HENDRIX EXPERIENCE

FOXY LADY
MANIC DEPRE

READY STEADY GO